CRIMINAL
JUSTICE

CRIMINAL JUSTICE

By

STEVE UGLOW,
Senior Lecturer in Law,
Kent Law School at the
University of Kent

LONDON
SWEET & MAXWELL
1995

Published by
Sweet & Maxwell Limited of
South Quay Plaza,
183 Marsh Wall,
London E14 9FT

Typeset by Mendip Communications Ltd, Frome, Somerset
Printed in England by Clays Ltd, St Ives plc

A CIP catalogue record
for this book is available
from the British Library

ISBN 0 421 505109

No natural forests were destroyed to make this product:
only farmed timber was used and re-planted

For Jenny

Preface

This book has grown out of my experience of teaching in law schools for 20 years. Although a teacher of criminal law, the day-to-day reality and, for me, the fascination lies in the interstices of enforcement: the processes which precede the accused's appearance in court, the problems of establishing facts at the trial or the operation of the penal system. Doctrinal niceties of appellate decisions had less appeal. Perhaps I share that relative lack of interest with some members of the House of Lords whose lack of concern with principle and with coherence in criminal jurisprudence should give cause for concern, especially in decisions such as *Brown*. No doubt criminal appeals may be seen as of marginal importance when compared with other weightier matters competing for their attention. But in any society one of the acid tests of "fairness" rests is the manner in which we deal with those embroiled in the criminal justice system. Getting the substantive criminal law and procedure right should be regarded as a basic requirement.

For students, substantive law should always be placed in its context. At one level this can be simply a procedural context, for example ensuring knowledge of the powers of arrest or the rules for drafting indictments. But more importantly (and to the students' dismay) it is necessary to grapple with the historical and cultural aspects of "justice". Equally important is knowledge of how the police, prosecutors and prisons operate and an understanding of how governmental policies affect these. This book is the result of seeking to teach criminal law in context.

There is a singular lack of texts covering "Criminal Justice A–Z" although there are many excellent books on the subject of the police or prisons. I now know why that vacuum exists. The sheer breadth of the subject is daunting and the changes, particularly at this time, constant. It was a serious mistake to stop smoking during the writing of this book. I have sought to do "justice" (whatever that might be) to all aspects of the criminal process, not simply from the legal perspective but from the standpoint of the system's history, its ethical basis and the social policy issues involved. It was an ambitious remit and I know that I have failed to give proper attention to several areas—for example, women, ethnic minorities and victims all deserve more systematic attention than I have been able to give them.

Twenty years ago the writing of such a book would have been much more difficult because of the relative dearth of material. Students of criminal justice owe a debt to those whose pioneering research has created a wealth of material to draw upon—I must acknowledge Andrew Ashworth, John Baldwin, Tony Bottoms, Pat Carlen, Doreen McBarnett, Mike McConville, Rob Reiner as well as the work of the Home Office Research Unit. As a result of this work, the institutions of criminal justice are more open. Public and political debate has no excuse for not being properly informed.

The last five years has seen possibly unprecedented turbulence throughout the criminal justice system and successive Home Secretaries, notably Michael Howard, have alienated professionals in almost every part of the service—the repercussions from the reorganisation of the police resulting from the Sheehy Report will scarcely die away before the report on the "core" functions of policing will emerge in 1995 with the prospect of the privatisation of some police tasks; sentencing policy which was radically changed (for the better!) in 1991 was turned on its head in 1993 with the abolition of unit fines and the prospect of still more crowded jails; the effect of Woolf on the Prison Service with improved conditions and regimes in our prisons has been nullified by unnecessary restrictions on home leave and temporary release, kneecapping many resettlement programmes; ironically the prisons themselves have had major security scares and the staff are demoralised by creeping privatisation; civil liberty lawyers are dismayed by a cavalier overturning (against Royal Commission advice) of a right to silence which goes back centuries, let alone by the widening of the criminal law by the criminalisation of squatters, partygoers, hunt protestors and travellers; probation officers and social workers are outraged at the creation of prisons (secure training units) for 12 year old children.

History will no doubt acknowledge the Home Secretary's contribution. Closer to home, I would like to thank Peter Amey and Chris Hale, colleagues in the UKC Police Research Group for their willingness to talk about policing issues, to Deborah Cheney and the members of Canterbury Prison's Board of Visitors for concentrating my mind on prison issues and to Dick Whitfield, for his enthusiasm in organising the UCK/Kent Probation criminal justice seminar programme which has provided many insights into the practical realities. My colleagues at Kent Law School have been a fertile seed bed for many years and I have received particular help from Liz Cable and Freda Vincent.

Much of this was written over the summer of 1994 and revised over the following Christmas—my family saw very little of me and I owe them much for their understanding, not least to Jenny whose encouragement has never wavered but she understands "obsessive writing syndrome" better than most.

Despite the passage of the Police and Magistrates' Courts Act 1994 and the Criminal Justice and Public Order Act 1994, I have endeavoured to state the law as it is on January 1st 1995.

Steve Uglow
April 1995

Contents

Table of Cases

Table of Statutes

Table of Statutory Instruments

Frequently Used Acronyms

ACPO—Association of Chief Police Officers
ADP—Average Daily Population
BCS—British Crime Survey
BCU—Base Command Unit
BOV—Board of Visitors
CCP—Code for Crown Prosecutors
CNA—Certified Normal Accommodation
CPS—Crown Prosecution Service
CRO—Criminal Record Office
CSO—Community Service Order
DPP—Director of Public Prosecutions
ENM—Ecole Nationale de la Magistrature
HMCIP—Her Majesty's Chief Inspector of Prisons
HMI(C)—Her Majesty's Inspectorate (of Constabulary)
JP—Justice of the Peace
LPA—Local Police Authority
LRC—Local Review Committee
MCC—Magistrates' Courts Committee
NCIS—National Crime Intelligence Service
PACE—Police and Criminal Evidence Act 1984
PCA—Police Complaints Authority
PICA—Public Interest Case Assessment Schemes
PII—Public Interest Immunity
PSR—Pre-Sentence Report
RCCP—Royal Commission on Criminal Procedure
RCS—Regional Crime Squad
SIR—Social Inquiry Report
TIC—Offences Taken Into Consideration
YOI—Young Offenders' Institution

A System of Criminal Justice?

1.1 INTRODUCTION

This book aims to explore the criminal process in its procedural and legal aspects and to analyse its dynamic qualities in its day-to-day operations and its social significance. Criminal justice is a complex process with many dimensions. This chapter intends not simply to outline the basic structure but to introduce some ethical, political, constitutional and economic arguments that affect criminal justice policy-making.

The building bricks of criminal justice are:

(a) a structure of procedural and substantive criminal law—that structure proscribes particular actions and provides a legitimate basis for the state to prosecute and punish individuals for the commission of an offence. This chapter explores both the development of this procedural structure and the boundaries of substantive criminal law, in particular why we should treat certain behaviour as worthy of punishment.

(b) the investigation of complaints of crime—although initiated by the public, investigation and pre-trial procedure is dominated by the police forces.

(c) the prosecution of offenders—this is undertaken by the Crown Prosecution Service with adjudication through the magistrates' and Crown Courts and appeal.

(d) the sentencing of those found guilty or who have pleaded guilty—the court has power to impose penalties ranging from the financial to community-based to custodial sanctions.

(e) a penal system which enforces those sentences—the mechanisms range from probation services to prisons.

The network of criminal justice agencies is fully occupied. In 1983:

- 3,247,000[1] notifiable[2] offences were recorded by the police.

[1] *Criminal Statistics 1993* Cm. 2680, Table 2.2, p. 38—the nature of crime figures is discussed more fully in Chap. 3.
[2] This includes most indictable offences and offences triable either way, as well as certain summary offences such as assault and unauthorised taking of a motor vehicle.

- that represented 6,546 offences for every 100,000 people.
- excluding summary motoring offences, 1,099,300 were cautioned by the police or found guilty by the courts. 1,317 people in every 100,000 were cautioned or convicted for indictable offences.[3]
- 78,200 were sentenced to immediate custody, 1 for every 42 recorded offences.[4]

In 1993:

- 5,526,000 notifiable offences were recorded by the police.
- that represented 10,777 offences for every 100,000 people.
- excluding summary motoring offences, 1,072,000 were cautioned by the police or found guilty by the courts. 1,153 people in every 100,000 were cautioned or convicted for indictable offences.
- 58,400 were sentenced to immediate custody, 1 for every 95 recorded offences.

During this period:

- 94 per cent of offences were against property.
- the clear-up rate for all offences has declined in that period from 37 per cent to 25 per cent with only 17 per cent of offences in London being solved as opposed to 50 per cent in Dyfed-Powys.[5]
- the actual number of offences being cleared up rose from 1,143,300 to 1,328,200,[6] a rise from 9.4 to 10.9 offences cleared up per officer.

Although statistics are produced to tell us what the producer wishes us to know, and criminal statistics are notoriously unreliable, recorded crime has been rising inexorably in the post-war era. Today we report, record and deal with much more crime than ever before. The overwhelming bulk of this increase is property crime since the spiralling prosperity of the past 40 years has resulted in a huge amount of high value, easily moveable, personal possessions in cars, shops and houses. Inter-personal violence has not increased to the same degree.[7] When compared to other countries, we appear to be a rather dishonest but relatively peaceful society.[8]

If we use the statistics as a moral barometer of the state of the nation, have we become less honest? We might argue complacently that the recorded figures merely reflect the increase in opportunities for crime. Alternatively, we might see a shift in moral standards as the individualism and materialism of the free market have changed aspirations, and as structural unemployment has opened up a gulf between cultural goals and realistic opportunities of achieving those goals. Have we become more violent? In 1870s London there were over 200 offences against the person per 100,000 of the population.[9] In

---

[3] *Criminal Statistics 1993, op. cit.,* Table 5.11 and 5.24, pp. 113 and 122.
[4] *Criminal Statistics 1993, op. cit.,* Table 7.15, p. 173.
[5] *Criminal Statistics 1993, op. cit.,* Table 2.11, p. 46.
[6] *Criminal Statistics 1993 op. cit.,* Table 2.8, p. 43.
[7] There were 400 incidents initially recorded as homicides in 1952 and 675 in 1993.
[8] Mayhew P., "Findings from the International Crime Survey" *Research Findings* No. 8 (Home Office Research and Statistics Dept. April 1994).
[9] Gurr T., Grabosky P. and Hula R., *The Politics of Crime and Conflict* (1977), p. 128.

1993, there were 574 offences of violence.[10] Given the unreliability of the Victorian data, this is a modest rise. Although there is considerable fear[11] of violence, and well-merited concern about sexual and physical abuse of women and children and racially motivated assaults, there is insufficient evidence to suggest that we are a less orderly or more violent society than previously.[12]

Our late capitalist society may (or may not) have produced more crime than other social forms but it certainly has produced an explosion in the number, size and functions of criminal justice agencies. This raises further questions. Do more police produce more crime? If you build more prisons, do you create more prisoners?[13] There is a chicken and egg problem here—what comes first, the increase in reported crime or in the activity of criminal justice agencies? In the 1990s we deal more formally with behaviour which previously might have been the subject of informal resolution. Agencies, especially the police, make the public more aware of crime and people then respond by involving the police more. More agencies contribute to that involvement—educational and social services and also insurance companies and private security firms. The criminal justice net is thrown ever wider, both in terms of the behaviour of which we take official cognisance and of the people who come within the purview of the agencies. The net has become so wide that, as we shall see, it has placed the courts and penal system under great strain.

Any discussion of the criminal justice system starts with assumptions that "crime is crime", that it is immoral and intolerable behaviour and that something has to be done. Crime is seen as a clearly separable category of behaviour which, allied with statistical analysis, leads to the assumption that "crime" is a defined and quantifiable given, behaviour which can be objectively measured. Furthermore, once discovered, it can only be approached in a one-dimensional, punitive fashion which is reflected in the language of confrontation ("war against crime", "battle on the streets"), too often employed by journalists, politicians and judges using a simplistic set of moral prescriptions. It is a language through which most of us acquire our second-hand knowledge about crime, and leads to the belief that a crime must be investigated, prosecuted and punished. Policies advocating alternative means of dealing with disruptive and deviant behaviour are inevitably marginalised.

Perhaps with the decline of organised religion, we need a place for society to demonstrate such moral certainties and ethical boundaries. But we should not forget that deviant behaviour has played its part in most people's biographies. Almost everyone has committed offences for which they could be imprisoned and most of us by luck or accident avoid involvement in the

---

[10] *Criminal Statistics 1993, op. cit.*, Table 2.3, p. 38—the 1870s figure will very significantly understate the true amount and the rise will be much less. The difference in the rates of property offences is much more dramatic—burglary in London rises from under 10 in the 1870s (Gurr, *et al., op. cit.*, p. 122) to 2,671 in 1993.

[11] Hale C., *Fear of Crime* (Metropolitan Police Working Party on Fear of Crime 1994) for a modern review of the literature.

[12] Pearson G., *Hooligan* (1983).

[13] Michael Zander has pointed out that in the 1970s those American states that built most prisons increased their prison population significantly whereas those that built least decreased theirs. *New Society*, December 13, 1979.

criminal justice system. There is an infinite variety of motives and meanings that we attach to that behaviour and we justify and explain our actions to ourselves, rarely labelling ourselves as "criminals". Individually and socially we approach such conduct through a range of interpretative and therapeutic mechanisms. The court and penal system is the crudest of all of these and this is reserved, sometimes for those who pose a high risk of danger to the community, but more often for those who are persistent, inadequate, disturbed or addicted nuisances. Should we punish such people or do we need different policies and responses? Dealing with the illiterate, the alcoholic, the drug addict or the mentally disturbed through a penal system is of dubious morality.

This argument will continue as will the search for the ethical principles which should underpin reforms within the system. But it is unlikely, to say the very least, that the criminal justice system will be fundamentally overhauled. First, it is scarcely a practical possibility, especially given social beliefs. Secondly, no political party stands to gain capital from such a programme and thirdly, we should also recognise that criminal justice is big business: the value of property taken in 1992 in recorded offences of burglary was £1 billion and in other cases of theft £2.4 billion.[14] As well as the defendants and their dependents, large numbers of professionals are involved in the criminal justice system—there are over 130,000 police personnel, several thousand lawyers, judges and other court employees, there are social services and probation officers, prison officers and ancillary staff, the insurance industry, security systems and private security firms, crime journalists, civil servants, dozens of different victim and offender charities and policy pressure groups, (let alone the academic criminologists).

Marx, slightly tongue-in-cheek, suggested that crime and the criminal contribute economically and in other ways:

> "The criminal produces an impression now moral, now tragic, and renders a 'service' by arousing the moral and aesthetic sentiments of the public. He produces not only textbooks on criminal law, the criminal law itself, and thus legislators but also art, literature, novels and the tragic drama ... The criminal interrupts the monotony and security of bourgeois life. Thus he protects it from stagnation and brings forth that restless tension, that mobility of spirit without which the stimulus of competition would itself become blunted ... Crime takes off the labour market a portion of the excess population, diminishes competition among workers, and to a certain extent stops wages from falling below the minimum while the war against crime absorbs another part of the same population ... The influence of the criminal upon the development of the productive forces can be shown in detail. Would the locksmith's trade have attained its present perfection if there had been no thieves?[14a]
> ..."

There is a serious point here—crime is seen in terms of right and wrong, in terms of moral absolutes and as underpinning an ethical system. By pointing out crime's contribution to the economic life of the country, Marx also hints at the relative nature of crime—two decades ago, insider dealing was seen as

---

[14] *Criminal Statistics 1993, op. cit.*, Tables 2.18 and 2.20, pp. 53 and 55. This figure for theft includes over £1.7 billion as the value of cars stolen or otherwise taken.
[14a] Marx K., *Theories of Surplus Value* (1969), Vol. 1, pp. 387–388.

clever use of the system by sharp manipulators whereas today the same behaviour is morally reprehensible and severely punished. The boundaries of permissible and impermissible economic activity have moved.

Criminal law and criminal justice have important symbolic functions as well as instrumental ones—while their goal of protecting individuals from violence and exploitation is obvious (though their efficacy is far from unquestionable), the part played in regulating the economy[15] or in establishing ethical frontiers is less clear. Furthermore, the criminal justice system has an important symbolic role in regulating our political life. Any country that lacks a written constitution requires constitutional arrangements, the relationships between citizen and state, to be visibly demonstrated. The key adjectives, "liberal" and "democratic", in relation to the state, only have meaning if the overwhelming power of the state in dealing with individuals is visibly demonstrated to be restricted by the rule of law: that police investigations are limited in their legal powers of detention and interrogation and in their use of force; that convicted prisoners can rely on proportionality of punishment and on humane treatment. State and citizen are both bound by law which itself rests on ethical notions which might be summarised as "fair dealing".

1.2 A SYSTEM GOING WRONG

The early 1990s has seen the criminal justice system come under unprecedented public scrutiny and criticism. There are two main causes for this attention:

(a) Following the release of the Guildford Four in October 1989, the Court of Appeal has quashed convictions in a number of highly publicised cases. Miscarriages of justice are not new—throughout its history, the criminal justice system has seen its fair share of disasters. At least Adolf Beck survived his imprisonment for fraud in 1907, having been wrongly identified by several victims. On release he was imprisoned a further time, again through misidentification. Timothy Evans, however, was executed in 1950 for murders committed by John Christie[16] and in 1962 James Hanratty was hanged for the A6 killing of Michael Gregsten.[17]

Since 1989, the trickle of wrongful convictions has become a flood with convictions quashed in cases such as the Birmingham Six,[18] Stefan Kiszko, Broadwater Farm, Judith Ward,[19] the Cardiff Three,[19a] let alone those attributable to the activities of the West Midlands Serious Crime Squad.[20] Civil liberty organisations and TV programmes such as the BBC's "Rough Justice" have identified dozens of further cases where there is cause for doubting the propriety of the convictions.

---

[15] Hall J., *Theft, Law and Society* (2nd ed., 1952) explores this idea in relation to the history of property offences.
[16] Kennedy L., *Ten Rillington Place* (1961).
[17] Foot P., *Who Killed Hanratty?* (1971).
[18] Mullin C., *Error of Judgment* (1989).
[19] (1993) 96 Cr.App.R. 1.
[19a] *Paris* [1994] Crim.L.R. 361.
[20] Kaye T., *Unsafe and Unsatisfactory* (1991).

Inevitably the public have become aware that there are serious flaws in the criminal justice system.[21]

Analysis of such miscarriages[22] has revealed no single cause but shows that different elements of the system itself have at times been at fault: poor investigative procedures or oppressive interrogation by the police; failure to disclose evidence by the prosecution; the trial court's failure to assess properly the weight of evidence; the unwillingness of the Appeal Court and the Home Office to admit that things had gone wrong. Even worse has been the way that these implied a culture unwilling to see its function as the uncovering of the truth and more concerned with results—arrests and convictions; a culture moreover that refused to deal with defendants with openness and fairness and that regarded recognition of such injustices as undermining the criminal process system. That culture shows little signs of change—the key recommendation of the Royal Commission on Criminal Justice which reported in 1993[23] was the introduction of an independent body to investigate miscarriage cases to replace the woefully inadequate Court of Appeal. This recommendation was supported by Sir John May's report into the case of the Guildford Four. Legislation to implement this has still to be introduced.

Awareness of the flaws of the investigation, prosecution and appeal system in dealing with defendants fairly have been paralleled by a recognition that prisons are also failing to deal with inmates humanely. In the early 1990s there were many disturbances, the most serious being at Strangeways Prison in Manchester; this started on April 1, 1990 and continued until April 25 with loss of life, injuries and enormous property damage. It led directly to the Woolf Report[24] with its plethora of proposals and recommendations for the improvement of the physical conditions, the regimes and the management of the prison system, proposals which have been consistently reinforced by the reports of Her Majesty's Chief Inspector of Prisons, Judge Stephen Tumim, a twentieth century John Howard. These reports have led to some important changes in the prison service, not least in the disciplinary system.

(b) The second reason for the current public scrutiny of criminal justice has been its ineffectiveness in dealing with crime. This is a complex issue with criticisms, sometimes contradictory, emanating from several fronts:

  (i) crime levels have risen consistently since the 1950s with sharp rises in the early 1990s. Significantly, fear about crime has also risen,[25-26] both in general as well as in specific categories (drug-related, the use of firearms, juvenile offences).

---

[21] We are not alone. Langlois D., *Les Dossiers Noirs de la Justice Francais (Editions du Seuil 1974)*; Begue B., *La Mauvaise Reputation (Politis October 10, 1991).*
[22] Sir John May has produced two reports into the Guildford bombings, the first into the ancillary Maguire convictions and the second (in July 1994) into the Guildford Four convictions. See Chris Mullin's comments in *The Guardian*, July 1, 1994, p. 24.
[23] *Royal Commission on Criminal Justice, Report*, Cm. 2263 (1993).
[24] *Report of an Inquiry into Prison Disturbances April 1990*, Cm. 1456 (1991).
[25-26] Hale C., (1994), *op. cit.*

(ii) different groups have attacked police enforcement policies, either for failure to police, for example, domestic violence, sexual assaults or racial attacks, or for over-policing in industrial disputes or in inner city areas.

(iii) the Crown Prosecution Service (CPS) have come under criticism for decisions to discontinue certain prosecutions and, less publicly, for the level of acquittals in contested cases in Crown Court.[27-28]

(iv) the courts have also been criticised especially when sentencing has been regarded as too lenient or for occasions when confessions have been excluded from evidence and the defendant has been acquitted.

(v) the growth of victim support groups has increased awareness of the poor treatment that victims receive at all stages of the process[29]: the initial interview by the police (especially of sexual assault victims); the failure by the CPS to keep the victim in touch with the course of proceedings; the witness's treatment while testifying especially where cross-examination involves allegations of lying; the lack of legal advice and representation leading to lack of awareness of compensation orders or the criminal injuries compensation scheme; the lack of any requirements for the court to take into account "victim-impact" statements in sentencing.

While the "miscarriage of justice" cases have highlighted the need for protection for the accused, these other factors have led to greater awareness of the needs of the community and of individual victims. Between such divergent positions, public and political debate tends to polarise, with the liberal wing advocating the protection (and increase) of the rights of defendants, and more conservative thinkers advocating policies espousing greater police powers and higher tariff punishments in the belief that this will reduce crime levels in the interests of the community and the victim.

How can these opposing positions be reconciled? The police,[30] prosecution service, courts and prisons[31] have all been the object of government reports, inquiries and unceasing legislation,[32] but scrutiny and analysis of the process as a whole has been non-existent. Although there have been two recent Royal Commissions, the first reporting in 1981[33] and the second in 1993,[34] neither considered the manner in which we *structure* criminal justice: yet the critical flaw is the lack of overall structure. Comparison with other public services, such as education or health, is illuminating—they are characterised by

---

[27-28] For further discussion, see *infra*, para. 4.9.

[29] Shapland J., *et al.*, *Victims in the Criminal Justice System* (1985); Morgan J. and Zedner L., *Child Victims* (1992).

[30] *Inquiry Into Police Responsibilities and Rewards*, Cm. 2280 (Sheehy Report (1993)); White Paper: *Police Reform*, Cm. 2281 (1993).

[31] *Report of the Inquiry into the United Kingdom Prison Services* (HMSO 1979), Cmnd. 7673 (May Report); *Report of an Inquiry into Prison Disturbances April 1990, op. cit.*

[32] There have been five Criminal Justice Acts in the last eight years.

[33] Royal Commission on Criminal Procedure, Cmnd. 8092 (1981).

[34] Royal Commission on Criminal Justice, *op. cit.*

unifying purposes and principles, a clear organisational structure, identifiable lines of management and recognised and effective means of accountability, normally ending with ministerial responsibility to Parliament. Although such a description may be seen as a rose-tinted view of our education or health systems, it is basically accurate. It is not possible to identify any of these characteristics within the English criminal process which is simply a historical accident.

In criminal justice, the possibilities for a unified approach are more limited than those in other public services. In education, for instance, although certain aspects may be controversial (for example, the details of the national curriculum), there is a broad consensus about the overall aims of the teaching profession. A coherent system should have consistent principles, objectives and mechanisms of accountability. It may be that the demands we make of our criminal justice agencies are too varied to permit this. At present, although individual agencies have objectives and performance indicators, the values and principles underlying and affecting the work of the different agencies are often irreconcilable—for example, the police associate themselves with "uncovering the truth" and "putting villains away" so that identification with victims can weigh more heavily than the means by which that is achieved[35]; the lawyers and the court assume the legal values of "due process" which are inevitably more technical and whose abstract rationales rarely appeal to the everyday concrete experience of the police[36]; probation officers and social workers, especially in the juvenile sphere, are most concerned with the development of the individual, "the best interests of the child", often seeing the police and court experience as an irrelevance, if not a hindrance, to the substantive objective of the reform of the defendant.

Furthermore, while individual agencies may have clear objectives and principles and are accountable in various ways, most of these agencies operate autonomously. The extraordinary facet of criminal justice is that there is no overarching ministry of justice with responsibility to Parliament for the whole structure. Different ministers of the Crown, such as the Lord Chancellor (for the magistracy), the Home Secretary (for the police, prisons and probation service) and the Attorney-General (for the Crown Prosecution Service) assume responsibilities for different parts of the system. Certain agencies, especially the police and the courts, avoid even this direct constitutional accountability. Such a structure invariably affects the extent of mutual co-operation and shared coherence of policy objectives.

1.3 REMOTE ORIGINS—REPARATION TO RETRIBUTION

The disarray of the system is largely due to its historical development. Criminal justice is about state interference with people's behaviour. The concept of crime is used to justify our collective interference with and control of the actions of others, seeking that justification in such ideas as preventing

---

[35] The quasi-judicial role which police interrogations take on under the PACE Codes of Practice fits uneasily into police culture.
[36] The police even dub the Crown Prosecution Service (CPS), their natural allies, the "Criminal Protection Society" for discontinuing prosecutions which the police wish to pursue.

harm or exploitation as well as to the objectives of deterring or reforming "criminals".

But where does this concept emerge from? There is a great temptation to read our history from earlier and simpler societies to modern times in terms of a straightforward progression—as society becomes less "barbaric", more "civilised", we act collectively to protect the individual members from harm and to preserve the overall interests of the group. The vulnerability of individuals leads us to act co-operatively in self-defence and to develop shared norms of behaviour which reinforce social cohesion. While these are important factors, suggesting a "natural evolution" for criminal justice, the system's history shows a more complex relationship between criminal justice, social order and the state.

In Anglo-Saxon England, the existence of normative codes did not inevitably involve the infliction of state punishment. State involvement in investigation or in the infliction of punishment was rare. Social structure was centred on the kinship group, as land settlement and the development of agriculture had led to significant autonomy for the family. The role of the king was very limited. But this was not some rural idyll—England in the tenth and eleventh centuries was certainly a place where people were easily provoked to anger, and violence was a common feature of life.[37] Legal sanctions could be equally bloody—outlawry, slavery or even summary execution for the thief caught in the act. Underpinning all these was the system of private, not state, retaliation known as the "feud" by which a family would wage war upon another in redress of grievances.

For the Anglo-Saxons, wrongs were wrongs and were not to be differentiated by whether they were litigated in the magistrates' court or the county court. In other words, there was little distinction between modern categories of crime and tort. Additionally, wrongs were at base private matters between the individuals or families involved and could always be paid for—in livestock, armour, money or, if necessary, in blood through the feud.[38] Each person had a set of rights according to status and these were protected by money penalties (*wer, bot, wite*). In addition there was collective responsibility of the kin group for the wrongs of its individual members, with the ability to provide collective resources for compensation. Sophisticated ideas of individual responsibility and state punishment were for the future.

Public involvement through the king was minimal, the kingdom was self-governing, and what government there was was local government. Routine disciplining of the population was not the king's affair—he intervened only when his interest (usually matters concerning his purse or his authority) was aroused. The legislation (decrees) of the Anglo-Saxon kings[39] bears this out; none assert any overriding public interest in the wrongs themselves, although the king may be concerned about the destructive effects of the feud on social order. When conducted between powerful kin groups, feuding could threaten the political consensus and the fragile basis of

---

[37] Gurr T., "Historical Trends in Violent Crime" (1981) Vol. III, *Crime and Justice: An Annual Review of Research* 295–353.

[38] Goebel J., *Felony and Misdemeanour* (1976), pp. 15–16.

[39] Aethelbert in early 7th century Kent; Ine in 7th century Wessex; Alfred in 9th century Wessex; Cnut in 11th century England—described in Plucknett T., *Edward I and the Criminal Law* (1960), Chaps. 1 and 2.

kingship, so the laws sought to restrict the right to self-help and insisted that compensation must be demanded and refused before resort to the feud. Yet the general legal framework for maiming or homicide was "How much?", and the legislation laid down detailed tariffs of payment for particular wrongs, not merely to the victim but to the kin, the lord, the owner of the land where the act took place as well as the king.

Such a system, based on compensation, seems to contradict theorists such as Durkheim who suggest that penal law moves from the repressive to the restitutive.[40] In fact, the movement from the eighth century to the eighteenth century suggests an opposite movement, away from the private and compensatory towards a public and ever more brutal form of criminal law. The initial change is prompted in the eleventh and twelfth centuries by the imposition of feudal political and economic structures and by the changing face of kingship that accompanies these. The role of the Anglo-Saxon king was quite limited, a leader in time of war but with little machinery of government or power. He was *primus inter pares* and possession of royal blood was only one factor in his ascendancy to the throne, to be placed alongside others such as nomination by the late king and acceptance by the aristocracy.[41] Gradually, however, the Anglo-Norman kings became much more territorial leaders through the imposition of the system of feudal land tenure, the strengthening of the system of primogeniture and the increasing sense of the king's divinity—the coronation ceremony, first emerging in the ninth century, cast God's protection upon his anointed.[42]

The strengthening of the monarchy, increasing stability and centralisation, initially made little difference to the systems of social control which remained local (either community courts or franchised ones in the hands of the major landholders) and private (the compensatory principle still applied). For William I and also in the *Leges Henrici Primi*, passed by Henry I on his accession, the old restitutive principles still applied in full force. Under the Anglo-Norman dynasty, even the killing of a Norman soldier could be excused by the community paying the "murdrum fine". This continues until the reign of Henry II (1154–1189) when the first legal "textbook", known by the name of its author as Glanvil, no longer uses the language of restitution of *wer, wite or bot* but talks the language of "felony".[43]

It is at this point that an embryonic criminal justice system emerges,[44] with its key components of itinerant royal justices and juries of presentment. These developments do not come about in response to a "crime" problem or to protect the individual rights of the victim but evolved as a result of the political and social conditions of the time, in particular the changing form of the machinery of state. At the point of Henry II's accession, the "state" in England is weak—an economy based on feudalism is invariably decentralised and destabilising unless there is some form of strong central control. Under

[40] Durkheim E., *The Division of Labour in Society* (1984); Maine H., *Ancient Law* (1915); Sheleff L., "From Restitutive to Repressive Law" (1975) *Archiv. Europ. Sociol.*, Vol. XVI 16.
[41] Loyn H. R., *The Governance of Anglo-Saxon England* (1984).
[42] Barlow F., "The Holy Crown" in Barlow F. (ed.), *The Norman Conquest and Beyond* (1983), p. 3.
[43] The essence of felony was personal, namely the breach of the homage vow between lord and man which was the core of the feudal relationship. It was not the substance of the act but the breach of loyalty that mattered.
[44] Jeffery C. R., "Crime in Early English Society" (1957) 47 *Journal of Criminology, Criminal Law and Police Science* 647.

feudalism, the landowning "lords" were able to accumulate the surplus product from the land with little to hinder them. However there was vast scope for conflict as to rights over land and over such appropriation. In the twelfth century, the "anarchy" of Stephen's reign saw a struggle between Matilda and Stephen over the succession, with private baronial wars and massacres of the peasantry: the legitimacy and the power of central authority was at a low ebb.

Henry II was faced with the aftermath of this civil war. In addition not only was he the Duke of Normandy but marriage and succession in Aquitaine and Maine meant that his realm stretched from Scotland to the Pyrenees. This compelled the building of an administrative structure that relied upon delegation to local officials (sheriffs) but also reliable channels of communication and decision-making (itinerant justices and an extension of the use of juries). The criminal justice system emerges, it is suggested, as a by-product of measures introduced by a king who saw the need to develop stable and more centralised structures to maintain his own authority and the overall political and economic system. In the process he created "... a royal state unrivalled in its authority and efficacy throughout Western Europe".[45]

Such centralism was shown in Henry's pragmatic response to rights over land since unlawful entries and evictions of previous decades had caused chaos. In 1164 he arrogated jurisdiction over land possession through a set of emergency courts known as the "possessory assizes" which superseded the delay and technicalities of the old procedure.[46] He also expanded the jurisdiction of the royal courts in Westminster, and thus began the process of downgrading the communal courts of the county and the hundred as well as the seigniorial courts belonging to the lord of the manor. He also attacked the jurisdiction of the Church through the Assize of Clarendon in 1166. A further initiative was the institution of a system of itinerant royal justices travelling throughout the realm on "eyre". These justices could call together juries of landholders in any locality who would "present" to the justices any information that they had about royal interests. This included any felonies that had been committed, since the king had a pecuniary interest in the conviction of felons as all the felon's property was regarded as forfeit to the Crown. Thus, for the first time the king is taking the initiative in gathering information about, and prosecuting wrongs.

These changes signal the end of the compensatory system since the king also stiffened punishments, and the right to inflict punishment slowly came to be monopolised by the Crown. The old concept of felony or breach of homage was *botleas*, un-atonable except through physical punishment, mutilation or death. But felony had been a private affair between lord and man—whereas through the twelfth and thirteenth centuries, the pleadings of *vi et armis* and *contra pacem regis* gave it a different flavour as a matter between king and subject. Composition between victim and wrongdoer thus became more difficult: victims of theft who entered into agreements with the thief could be prosecuted themselves. Change was slow—through the thirteenth and fourteenth century, private prosecutions for homicide or rape (known as appeals of felony) continued to be discontinued by agreement on

---

[45] Anderson P., *Lineages of the Absolutist State* (1979), p. 113.
[46] Simpson A. W. B., *A History of Land Law* (2nd ed., 1986).

the compensation to be paid.[47] But hangings were the province of the king and a symbol of royal authority—local lords were fined for infringing the royal rights. There is little evidence however of excessive executions or other physical punishments. Barbarous punishments are the hallmark of the sixteenth century and beyond.[48]

Angevin reforms were directed as much at the nobility as at the lower classes. Henry had no real interest in the peasantry although there was an immediate interest in the doings of the aristocracy and a desire for "legitimate" techniques to control them. Although there is little evidence of criminal prosecutions of the nobility *per se*, "justice" was an important symbolic representation of the king's power and authority (especially when embodied in a hanging). The nobles who exercised jurisdiction did so as delegates,[49] no longer possessing power as of right but as subordinates to the monarch.

Despite the reforms, the vast majority of cases would be before local and seigniorial courts.[50] Social discipline must still have rested firmly in the manor,

> "... the manorial system arises at the end of the Old English period mainly in consequence of the subjection of a labouring population of free descent to a military and capitalistic class".[51]

Even in front of royal justices, local juries made up their minds on their own knowledge of the facts—with 40–50 cases in front of the court each day, Medieval justice was still local and, though rubber-stamped by the royal imprimatur, far from the system of routine state control to which the population in the twentieth century is so accustomed.

1.4 FROM SAVAGERY TO CELLS

Henry's reforms produced a genuine, but embryonic, criminal law, although the consolidation of feudalism through centralised royal power was far from over. Other monarchs (especially Edward I in the last quarter of the thirteenth century)[52] sought to develop the system, but it was the Tudors who achieved the absolutist feudal state[53] and, hand-in-hand with this new authoritarianism, went an expansion of criminal justice. This expansion was in two directions, against the aristocracy on one hand and against the new poor on the other. In the early sixteenth century, the Crown was in direct conflict with the nobility over such issues as the maintenance of private armies. The ordinary mechanisms of criminal law were failing to control such subjects and Henry VII and Henry VIII developed new courts such as Star

---

[47] Given J., *Society and Homicide* (1977), p. 100.
[48] This is borne out by Chambliss' study of the Vagrancy Acts in the 14th century which, though penal in form, were operated leniently compared to their enforcement two centuries later— Chambliss W., "The Law of Vagrancy" Chambliss W. (ed.), *Crime and the Legal Process* (1969) 51; *infra*, para. 8.2.
[49] Sutherland D. W., *Quo Warranto Proceedings* (1963).
[50] Though justices of the peace were known from 1195, their duties only expanded in the 14th century: Moir E., *The Justice of the Peace* (1969).
[51] Vinogradoff P., *The Growth of the Manor* (1911), p. 235.
[52] Plucknett, *op. cit.*
[53] Anderson, *op. cit.*

Chamber, outside the common law system, as well as special courts for other purposes: High Commission, the Councils of the North and of the Marches.[54]

The focus of attention, however, now swings away from the aristocracy towards the large pool of surplus labour created through economic policies such as the enclosure movement and the dissolution of the monastries. The penal law became increasingly repressive, with severe punishments, more power to justices of the peace as well as the development of the Poor Law and new laws against the able bodied poor.[55] No longer tied to particular localities and with the increasing size of the towns, this army of unemployed began to pose a public order problem. The criminal law takes on a modern tinge as the mechanism for class domination of a social and economic underclass.

In 1554, in Mary's reign, came legislation which enabled justices of the peace to play a more active role in investigating and prosecuting offences.[56] When these statutes are linked to the stiffening of the Vagrancy Acts in 1571 and the consolidation of the Poor Law in 1597, we can see the beginnings of the more active use of the machinery of justice as social control.

This is certainly the impression gained by considering the eighteenth-century criminal justice system—gone is the link with the personal authority of the monarch. There has been a major transformation of the nature of the state and in the powers of Parliament, while at the same time the economic base is in transition with the growth of trade, the development of industrial and agricultural capitalism. There are demographic changes as more and more people are forced off the land through enclosures. The old patterns of social authority are breaking down—no longer does the land-tie relationship permeate all levels of society, and the traditional authority structures of rural England can no longer be depended upon.

There are changes in property relationships and in property itself—the old rights of common are disappearing[57] as property becomes private. Equally, the reciprocity of social relationships diminishes. For John Locke at the end of the seventeenth century, the chief ends of government were the maintenance of civil peace and the security of person and of property. "Such a theory, diluted by self-interest and prejudice, might provide the propertied classes with a sanction for the most bloody code penalising offenders against property ..."[58] The "new property" is protected through the criminal law with a mass of legislation, all ultimately dependent upon the death penalty. By the turn of the eighteenth century there were well over 200 offences punishable by death.

In the eighteenth century, the criminal justice system was no longer directly representative of the authority of the monarch but of the interests of the dominant classes. The old feudal relationships of subordination and deference, ideas of personal loyalty, local ties and custom and a sense of social place had been fatally weakened by social and economic change as gradually the factory, wage labour and the contract of employment were to take over in

---

[54] This is a process that might be compared to the creation of the Diplock Courts in Northern Ireland in the 1970s—Diplock Commission: Report (1972), Cmnd. 5185.
[55] For further discussion on the history of punishment, see para. 8.2.
[56] Langbein J., *Prosecuting Crime in the Renaissance* (1974).
[57] Thompson E. P., *Whigs and Hunters* (1975).
[58] Thompson E. P., *The Making of the English Working Class* (1968), p. 87.

place of the reciprocal and all-pervasive nature of rural life. During this period of transition, Douglas Hay[59] has argued that the propertied classes mobilised and enforced the criminal law, through which they sought to maintain and reinforce the new property interests while masking the reality of the social world through the majesty of the law and through the process of pardons and mercy.

As the pace of this change quickened in the early nineteenth century, government recognised that the law needed to intervene between the capitalist and labour—the subjective and discretionary justice of earlier eras would aggravate the more overt tension between the classes. Law (and criminal law) needed to be presented as a neutral force in this conflict. In the nineteenth century criminal justice took the shape that we recognise today. The laws themselves were reformed—larceny, for example, had become very complex as new forms of property and of theft had emerged in the eighteenth century[60] but it had also become quite personal with statutes protecting the property of specific companies: these were repealed when the law was generalised in 1816. Theoretically the law protected everyone, property owners and the dispossessed alike.

Victorian social policy, linked with political reforms, was very interventionist in many areas such as public hygiene, schools and welfare. This approach also showed itself in criminal justice, although there was a more ideological impact as concepts of criminal justice underpinned the "rule of law" which was so important in the incorporation of all classes into the parliamentary, democratic state. The most visible sign of the "rule of law" was the "New Police", starting in 1829 with the creation of the Metropolitan force but with forces all across the country by 1856. The police were the embodiment of the values of the rule of law—neutrality, equality, universality. Reform affected all areas: the repeal of many of the capital punishment statutes in the early nineteenth century removed much of the brutality of the old law, reflecting the utilitarian principle that punishment had to be proportionate to the offence; the new penitentiaries that were completed in the 1840s[61-62] were designed for the reform of the offender through work, the Bible and solitary confinement in individual cells; more formal trial procedures and rules of evidence also took root at this time.

One obvious finding from this brief survey is that the criminal justice system has never been planned as a "system" and to refer to it as one is simply a convenience. A second conclusion is that its origins are not to be found in the objectives of crime reduction or of protecting victims but in the political exigencies of medieval England. This focus must not be lost since criminal justice has to be understood, at least in part, as a means of maintaining and reinforcing state authority and its evolution has as much to do with politics and economics as law or morals. The form that the criminal justice system takes necessarily changes as the form of the state changes. In protecting the state, the criminal justice system necessarily protects the interests of those individuals and classes that dominate and form the state—the personal monarch, landholders, industry or finance capital.

[59] Hay D., "Property, Authority and the Criminal Law" in Hay D. (ed.), *Albion's Fatal Tree* (1975).
[60] Hall, *op. cit.*
[61-62] Ignatieff M., *A Just Measure of Pain* (1978).

Marxist scholars would accept such a focus, emphasising that "core" substantive and procedural values are not absolute or universal but are shaped by economic and social determinants. The "values" are relative and also ideological, in the sense that they disguise and legitimate class interests. Criminal law certainly is open to the charge that its definitions only proscribe particular categories of dishonesty, violence and exploitation while permitting others. However, criminal justice is not simply a system of disguising the interests of power. It is inevitably linked with moral discourse and part of its origins can be traced to the role of the church courts in enforcing moral standards in medieval England. Codes of conduct and the manner in which we deal with criminals reflect important values about cultural identity and constitutional relationships.[63] The criminal justice system is one place where moral codes and notions of "due process" are made concrete by definition and enforcement. This is not just a legal exercise but also a cultural one—the way in which we deal with dishonesty, violence and exploitation and with the perpetrators of such acts, expresses certain ideas about how we should relate to each other and certain values which provide us with reasons for social cohesion and identity.

However, as soon as we mention "values", issues became subjective and complex. Moral values are debated and negotiated within each society, shaped by the history and the present. Penal sanctions are justified by social beliefs that certain conduct is wrong. This implies that there are no universal standards of right and wrong, that these are relative to each society and that we are not able to criticise another society's standards. But seeing penal law in terms of cultural relativism has serious limits—the fatwah pronounced by Iranian Islamic courts on the novelist, Salman Rushdie, may be understandable as a reaction from a deeply religious culture but such understanding should not debar us from criticism of such decisions: expression of ideas should never be a criminal offence; conviction should only take place after trial with proper opportunities for representation, for confronting witnesses and for producing counter evidence; and punishment must always be proportional and the minimum necessary for the offence.

1.5 CRIMINALISING BEHAVIOUR

Having looked at the evolution of the system, the Rushdie example immediately illustrates the next problem which is about the substance of penal laws—what behaviour is so serious that collective intervention is required? The argument here is that the boundaries of the criminal law should be as narrow as possible, involving conduct where there is a positive harm to another person and where there is an identifiable public interest in imposing penal sanctions. Those who have checked the index of a criminal law textbook will realise that the awesome breadth of the current substantive law does not reflect these principles. That breadth encompasses not only physical violence and property offences but also a plethora of public order offences (now increased by the 1994 legislation), moral offences where it is often difficult to discern a "victim" in the traditional sense (possession of drugs, prostitution, kerb-crawling or the behaviour of consenting sado-

---

[63] Dostoevsky said that if you wanted to know about a society, you should look at the state of its prisons.

masochists in *Brown*[64]), offences which are created for the protection of the state and a vast array of regulatory crimes, from traffic to factories to pubs (the regulation of public enterprises of all kinds). This entire area of some 7,000 offences is defined as "crime".

Once a complaint from the public has been received, the critical issue for the police is whether this amounts to a crime? The whole idea of the criminal law rests on the idea of offences—people cannot be arrested, charged, prosecuted or punished without legal authority. What gives this legal authority and defines an offence? This is straightforward—an offence must either be created by statute or by the operation of the doctrine of precedent in case law. Although the majority of offences are statutory, a number of significant ones are still common law offences, including murder, manslaughter and rape. Often these have been affected by statutory amendment (the Homicide Act 1957 introduces various defences to murder or section 142 of the Criminal Justice and Public Order Act 1994 which affects rape) but the core definition is still to be found in the common law itself. This definition from statute or caselaw will give us the basic elements of an offence which the prosecution must prove to obtain a conviction. Without such specific legal authority, the police cannot proceed.

This is the basic principle of legality for criminal lawyers—the Latin tag is *nulla poena sine lege*. This principle is designed to fetter the power of public officials—if certain formal steps to create law must be followed, officials cannot exercise arbitrary powers. Such powers are the hallmarks of totalitarian societies where immense control is placed in the hands of state officials over what constitutes crime,[65] as well as over the manner of enforcement.

Ashworth[66] stresses that there are central characteristics of this principle, in particular the principles of non-retroactivity, maximum certainty and strict construction:

(a) although statutes are unlikely to be expressed retrospectively, the English common law, because of its reliance on judicial interpretation and law-making, necessarily involves amendments to the law which infringe the principle of legality.[67] It is shown at its worst in *Shaw*[68] where the accused published a reference book to London prostitutes, only to be convicted of a conspiracy to corrupt public morals. In *Shaw* Simonds said:

> "... I entertain no doubt that there remains in the courts of law a residual power to enforce the supreme and fundamental purpose of the law, to conserve not only the safety and order but also the moral welfare of the State and that it is their duty to guard it against attacks which may be the more insidious because they are novel and unprepared for."

---

[64] [1993] 2 All E.R. 75.
[65] An example would be the Nazi legislation that proscribed "anything which is deserving of punishment according to the fundamental idea of a penal law AND the sound perception of the people".
[66] Ashworth A., *Principles of Criminal Law* (1991), Chaps. 2 and 3.
[67] Smith A.T.H., "Judicial Lawmaking in the Criminal Law" (1984) 100 L.Q.R. 46.
[68] [1962] A.C. 220.

Although the courts disclaim their lawmaking role, this re-emerged in *R v. R*[69] where the defendant was convicted of raping his wife. The House of Lords upheld the conviction—could this be seen as creating a new offence or at least denying the defendant the benefit of a defence that had existed for centuries?[70]

(b) the idea of certainty itself reflects the principle of non-retroactivity but it also means that penal laws should be accessible and specific, with only the minimum necessary scope for discretion. General terms such as "reasonableness" and "dishonesty" are difficult to avoid. However there are certain offences, such as conspiracy to defraud,[71] which are so inherently vague that the outer limits are barely discernible.

(c) there is a principle of statutory interpretation that requires penal statutes to be interpreted narrowly and in favour of the liberty of the defendant.[72] This principle is rarely mentioned, let alone invoked by the appeal courts. One example would be the extension of the law of theft by the House of Lords in *Gomez*,[73] an obvious case of obtaining property by deception[74] but which had been charged as theft. Their Lordships chose the broader of the possible interpretations of the term "appropriation" under the Theft Act 1968 s.3, reducing the offence to one where the key element of the offence is the "dishonesty" of the accused and obliterating any sensible distinction between theft and deception. Although the accused was patently dishonest in this case and to that extent deserved to be convicted, there is a further principle that offences should be properly demarcated and labelled and that people are entitled to rely on this.[75]

A criminal offence can be created in conformity to such principles but substantively it might still be argued that the conduct it proscribes is not the business of the criminal law. A crime involves conduct prosecuted by the state which results in a court punishing the individual. This requires a vast network of criminal justice agencies, following complex procedures at no little cost to the public: the involvement of the state suggests that there has to be a definable public interest as criminal justice should not be a way of pursuing purely private affairs. But even where there is a discernible public interest, penal approaches should be kept to a minimum if that interest can be protected by other means.

1.5.1 *The Case of Heroin*

The difficulty of identifying the boundaries of penal law can be seen with the misuse of drugs. Cannabis users are (sometimes) imprisoned whereas

---

[69] [1992] 1 A.C. 599.
[70] Giles M., "Judicial Law-Making" [1992] Crim.L.R. 407.
[71] *Scott v. MPC* [1975] A.C. 819.
[72] Jeffries J. C., "Legality, Vagueness and the Construction of Penal Statutes" (1985) 71 Virginia L.R. 189.
[73] [1993] 1 All E.R. 1—another example would be *Charles* (1976) 63 Cr.App.R. 252—for discussion, see Smith A., *op. cit.*
[74] Theft Act 1968, s. 15.
[75] Ashworth, *op. cit.*, p. 71.

smokers are (frequently) hospitalised. This contrast arouses controversy but there is much less disagreement about the criminalisation of narcotics, possession of which is generally agreed to be "criminal". However, during the 1960s, Britain had an enlightened attitude towards narcotic addicts who were treated by ordinary doctors able to prescribe heroin for their patients. As a result, the addict got a pure drug and clean needles at low cost, proper advice and assistance. The cost of this was over-prescribing by some doctors which led to a "grey" market in the drug—this was sale by patient/addicts. It was a medical/therapeutic model of dealing with a social problem.

But the various moral panics about the hedonistic use of drugs by young people in the 1960s led to the Misuse of Drugs Act 1971, introducing a more punitive approach. Treatment and prescribing were taken away from GPs and treatment centres were established, often using methadone as a substitute for heroin but addicts avoided these. Quite quickly a black market in narcotics was established.[76] As a result the cost soared, the product was adulterated, the addicts used poorly sterilised needles, stole to finance the habit, failed to eat. Deaths occurred from overdoses (since addicts no longer knew the purity of the drug), from malnutrition, from blood poisoning and diseases such as hepatitis B and, more recently, AIDS which are contracted through sharing dirty syringes. The average daily prison population of drug offenders has risen from 781 in 1981 to 3,150 in 1992.[77] Such figures underestimate the numbers of drug-users in prisons since the cost to the addict of supporting the habit has also led to a vast increase in drug-related property offences. It could be argued that the consequences of dealing with the problem of drug abuse through the penal model were worse than the problem of over-prescription created by the medical model.

It is difficult to distinguish the addictive nature, the health-threatening qualities and the distressing social consequences, of heroin abuse from alcoholism or smoking. But public opinion would certainly find intravenous narcotic use both repellent and "wrong" in the sense that people should not act in that way.[78] Hence the criminalisation of heroin poses no difficulty for a traditional model of criminal justice that sees the law as representing the moral judgments of the majority of the community. This model considers that "immorality" is a necessary condition of any act to be criminalised—only conduct generally and without significant dissent considered "immoral" should be penalised.[79]

One problem for such a model is that of discovering whether something is immoral—the criteria can be based either on some absolute idea of good and evil to be found in an acknowledged and authoritative text such as the Bible or Quran. Alternatively, some commentators give it a more secular and democratic meaning so that what people consider immoral can only emerge through demonstration, referendum or through the editorials of national newspapers. Even assuming that this difficulty can be overcome, and while it

[76] The number of offences of trafficking in controlled drugs recorded by the police in 1983 was 4,994. In 1992 it was 14,840. (*Criminal Statistics 1993*, *op. cit.*, Table 2.23, p. 58.)
[77] *Prison Statistics 1992* Cm. 2581, Table 1(b), p. 16—350 of these are simply convictions for possession as opposed to those imprisoned for importation and dealing.
[78] It is interesting to consider how "knowledge" of this kind is constructed through social processes—Berger P. and Luckman R., *Social Construction of Reality* (1971).
[79] Packer H., *The Limits of the Criminal Sanction* (1968), p. 262.

can be argued that the criminal justice system gains its legitimacy from the fact of an action's "immorality", is the labelling of conduct as "immoral" sufficient to justify its criminalisation.

1.5.2. *Immorality, Crime and the Sado-Masochist*

The example of the imposition of the fatwah on Salman Rushdie illustrates this—both religious text and popular feeling in Islamic countries would treat the publication of the *Satanic Verses* as immoral and thus justify the sentence. Heroin use in this country fulfils the latter condition—the majority certainly regard it as an evil. But is this enough? In other words, is immorality not just a necessary condition but also a sufficient one? Most commentators would argue that behaviour must not only be immoral but must have some other quality before it can be criminalised—classic liberal commentators such as Mill[80] in the nineteenth century, or Hart,[81] would argue that immorality *per se* is necessary but not sufficient and that we must also search for an objective harm to others. Against that, Devlin[82] argues that public morality is a vital ingredient for society, the cement between the bricks, and that the state has the right to safeguard its existence. Devlin uses that position to argue that the practice of homosexuality is injurious to society which thus has the right to limit or eradicate it.

In *Brown*,[83] the House of Lords were considering whether a person might consent to physical assaults on their person which caused actual, but not necessarily serious, bodily harm. The context was the practices of a group of homosexual sado-masochists. In legal terms, there were two issues—the first of these was the question whether a person could consent to any level of physical injury at all? There was authority going back to Fitzjames Stephen[84] to suggest that the line should be drawn so that you could not consent to being maimed or killed but could to lesser forms of harm. (The rationale suggested was that the able-bodied male had to be prepared to serve king and country, a discernible public interest). More recently the Court of Appeal has gone further to hold that it was not in the public interest for people to cause each other actual bodily harm.[85] This involved a brawl outside a pub—there was a limiting factor that might have been used since such brawls can easily lead to public disorder but the court rejected this approach and held that consent was irrelevant regardless of whether the incident was in public or in private. In *Brown* the House of Lords agreed that while people could injure themselves, they could not consent to an assault by another causing any visible physical harm. The only exceptions to this (the second issue) was where the assault had social utility such as competitive sports or surgery, including cosmetic surgery, and also, bizarrely, tattooing.

Liberal commentators would argue that a core idea of liberal society must be ownership of your own body, expressed in the "right to physical

---

[80] Mill J. S., *On Liberty* (2nd ed., 1859).
[81] Hart H. L. A., *Law, Liberty and Morality* (1963).
[82] Devlin P., *The Enforcement of Morals* (1965).
[83] [1993] 2 All E.R. 75.
[84] Stephen J.F., *A General View of the Criminal Law* (2nd ed., 1890).
[85] *Attorney-General's Reference No. 1 of 1980* [1981] Q.B. 715 following prize-fighting cases such as *Coney* [1882] 8 Q.B.D. 534.

integrity", that nobody else has a right to interfere with your body. If you choose to have your ears pierced, your torso tattooed, circumcision or even suicide, it is a voluntary choice that must be respected if individuals are to be treated as autonomous rational beings with self-determination. Limits on that right in the name of "public interest" become very difficult to justify—if my right hand offends me and I chop it off, I surely cannot be prosecuted for causing myself GBH. If I hire a surgeon to do the chopping, how can he be blamed?

The justification must be sought in paternalism and in discussing drug abuse, Lord Templeman states, "... the criminal law restrains a practice which is regarded as dangerous and injurious to individuals ..."[86] and later refers to the dangers of contracting HIV and AIDS. The need to protect the young is also mentioned as the appellants "... were responsible in part for the corruption of a youth "K" ... It is some comfort at least to be told ... that "K" has now it seems settled into a normal heterosexual relationship."[87] But this also shows a Devlinesque moralism. If such practices were allowed and extended, this would be "harmful to society generally" which Lord Templeman later expands on; "Society is entitled and bound to protect itself against a cult of violence. Pleasure derived from the infliction of pain is an evil thing. Cruelty is uncivilised."[88] Such words can be compared with those of Lord Simonds in *Shaw*[89] quoted above. Lord Simonds sought to justify the creation of an offence not previously known to law. But his words can equally be applied here to the restriction of the defence of consent. The "moral welfare" of the state is being pursued by penalising homosexual behaviour,[90] the expression of which is barely tolerated and then only within the narrow ambit of the 1967 legislation.

For Devlin, legislating for morality is justified on the grounds that such action is necessary to preserve society from disintegration. The laws possess a symbolic importance in reaffirming certain cherished values in society. The importance of the economic, reproductive, socialisation and protective functions of the family is affirmed by motivating people to form families, adhere to them and accept their discipline. Prostitution, adultery, homosexuality are discouraged as posing a threat to the stability of family relationships providing attachments that compete for the "man's" loyalty, affection and resources.

The weaknesses of Devlin's theory are a loose use of the concept of morality and also the lack of specificity about the nature of the "injury" that society allegedly suffers—in *Knuller*,[91] the House of Lords was faced with a "conspiracy to outrage public decency", upholding the existence of such an offence when it was "destructive of the very fabric of society". Since the case involved publishing adverts from homosexuals seeking like-minded partners, it is difficult to understand the factual basis for upholding the convictions.

---

[86] *supra*, at 82f.
[87] *supra*, at 83a–b.
[88] *supra*, at 84g.
[89] *op. cit.*
[90] The House of Lords give considerable attention to the Wolfenden Report (*Report of the Committee on Homosexual Offences and Prostitution* Cmnd. 257) and the Sexual Law Reform Act 1967. What relevance do those texts have to the issue of consent? Had this been a heterosexual gathering, would they have been mentioned?
[91] [1973] A.C. 435.

Indeed Hart has pointed out that empirically this traditional model suffers from the difficulty that no society can be demonstrated to have collapsed as a result, for example, of liberalising its sexual codes.

Devlin talks of "deep disgust", an attitude mirrored by the Lordships in *Brown*, more an emotive reaction based on ignorance, fear and superstition rather than rational judgment which would demand clear identification of the social threat. Ultimately it is a position that lacks limiting conditions—it is only too easy to discover "harms" from which society must protect itself, as opposed to protecting the individual. Again it is useful to consider *Brown* in this context—in essence this was a private affair[92] and if there is consent to the practices, where lies the "harm" when the "victim" refuses to see himself as such? Can there be a public interest in criminalising people's voluntary actions in relation to their own bodies?

1.5.3 *Autonomy and Public Welfare*

Neither Devlin's moralism nor its diluted version in the paternalism of *Brown* fit with the more liberal tradition of Mill and Hart which points instead to the idea of "harm to others". Society is entitled to intervene and to punish to prevent objective harm to others, if only for the reason that, without such collective protection, individuals would not be motivated to remain in society. This tradition argues that we are not entitled to use social power to impose a set of moral standards where breach of the standards causes no injury to another nor should we use our collective might to dictate a person's behaviour because it is felt that it is not in someone's best interests to act in a particular manner. This "harm principle" rests on the idea of autonomous choices and this requires that a person has the capacity to make those choices. However, the element of capacity to choose permits the protection of juveniles or of the mentally handicapped even under this theory since it can be argued that young people should be limited in their ability to drink, engage in sex or bet until they are of an age when they can appreciate the consequences of such behaviour.

The criterion of "objective harm" limits the scope of criminal law but still has inherent problems. The feminist would argue that the publisher of pornography degrades women as a class and renders them more likely victims of sexual attack. The moralist would say that such publications "deprave and corrupt" their readers.[93] Is there sufficient "harm" to justify criminal sanctions here or does the liberal, having identified harm to others as justification for intervention, limit that by specifying that there must be a direct damage rather than indirect harm? The word "harm" is wide and not inherently self-limiting, for example, to physical or property damage. But as soon as we accept emotional trauma,[94] what is the barrier to accepting "offending sensibilities" through pornography or blasphemy as potentially criminal harms? Additionally the word "harm" does not limit itself to direct

---

[92] Though Lord Templeman adverted to Art. 8, European Convention on Human Rights which talks of "... the right to respect for his private and family life ..." and suggests that these activities were not exercises of such rights.

[93] Obscene Publications Act 1959, s. 1.

[94] *e.g.* a hoax telephone caller to the parents of a kidnapped baby has been charged with causing "grievous bodily harm".

injury—it can logically encompass indirect consequences. Thus it has been suggested that penal sanctions to enforce the wearing of crash helmets or seat belts are justifiable since young children "model" themselves on adult behaviour and are thus being put at greater risks.

When we consider crimes by corporations, who suffers directly when a board of directors act illegally to block the takeover of their company by another organisation? Yet the community response is often a desire to see the prosecution of senior management and the labelling of their actions as criminal. If we allege that there is a stronger public interest in such cases (that large corporations must be effectively regulated) and that as a result, there is less need to show direct harm, are we falling back into the logic of legal moralism?

The "offence principle" often concentrates on the idea of harm at the expense of that elusive element of "public interest". The shopkeeper is obviously harmed by shoplifting but would be equally harmed were there to be an intentional breach of contract by one of the shop's suppliers. Yet, in one case, the police can be called while in the latter, the shopkeeper is limited to a county court action for breach of contract. Perhaps the reason for this is to be found in the origins of larceny. The public interest in larceny was the threat to public order—the medieval indictment would contain the allegations that it was "with force and arms" and "against the king's peace". Although those allegations rapidly became fictional, in modern times the threat of a breach of the peace following a unilateral taking of property, especially by a stranger, can still be seen as a public interest justifying penal intervention. That threat is considerably diminished in the context of ongoing contractual relations.[95]

This criterion of "public interest" is addressed by Lacey[96] with her principle of "welfare". In this approach, criminal justice is the imposition of standards of behaviour on individuals and those must reflect the values, needs and interests which a society decrees as fundamental to its proper functioning. It is this principle and not individual autonomy that Lacey sees as the predominant criterion in criminalising conduct. However it is a principle that skirts with moralism, especially where "morality" and "welfare" are both identified by the will of the majority. But Lacey sees "welfare" as bringing in creative tension with "autonomy". As Ashworth rather optimistically puts it, "The adjustment between welfare and autonomy is a matter for reasoned debate within each society."[97]

1.5.4 *The Politics of Legislating Morality*

The core of a criminal justice system is the criminal law, which identifies the behaviour defined as crime. Not only do we lack a code of Penal Law but as the previous discussion has shown, there is no consensus over what principles should govern the proper boundaries. The continuous tinkering with the criminal law by Parliament often reveals political expediency to be at the root of the process. There is a steady and insidious expansion, creating new offences without attention to underlying principles, as to what should

---

[95] But see *Gomez* [1993] 1 All E.R. 1 which ignores this principle and concentrates solely on the dishonesty of the accused—another example of the "legal moralism".
[96] Lacey N., *State Punishment* (1988).
[97] Ashworth, *op. cit.*, p. 26.

constitute a crime and, when social issues such as drug use, abortion, homelessness and squatting, raves and travellers are approached[98] through the medium of the penal law, it might be argued that penal law has expanded beyond its proper boundaries.

There is a fundamental problem about the nature of politics in a democracy. Drawing the line between the acceptable and the unacceptable is difficult, especially where there is wide diversity of moral and cultural beliefs and attitudes. But the legislature eschews any scientific or principled approach and political considerations dominate, often concealed under the rhetoric of the overall public interest, but lying behind this are real issues about economic and social interests and social authority, let alone votes.

Where the laws seem unrelated to the economic, the campaigns to get such legislation on the books can, in Howard Becker's terms, be seen as a "moral enterprise" with the campaigner as a "moral entrepreneur".

> "Rules are not made automatically. Even though a practice may be harmful in an objective sense to the group in which it occurs, the harm needs to be discovered and pointed out. People must be made to feel that something ought to be done about it. Someone must call the public's attention to these matters, supply the push necessary to get things done and direct such energies as are aroused in the proper direction to get a rule created."[99]

Such campaigns are often symbolic crusades on a broader level—Gusfield suggests that for those who affirm a strong moral position, the power to legislate documents their status in society. In his study of the prohibition laws in the USA,[1] he suggests that drinking was a focus of conflicts between Protestant and Catholic, rural and urban, native and immigrant, middle class and lower class in American society. Legal affirmation was thus important for what it symbolised—even if the law was broken, it was clear whose law it was.[2] It is not enough in talking about crime to state simply that it deals with immoral or evil behaviour. Even the most fundamental crimes such as violence or homicide are tolerated in certain situations. But the vast bulk of offences become crimes for very different reasons—it becomes important to recognise who is doing the defining and for what reasons.

1.6 DEFINING THROUGH ENFORCEMENT

The theoretical boundaries of crime are delineated by the text of penal statutes. The practical boundaries are measured by the day-to-day enforcement through the police and the courts which can produce a different image as to what is socially acceptable or unacceptable and can distort social perception of what is seen as "real" crime. An illustration is the area of physical violence where the laws present a clearly delineated hierarchy of offences, ranging from murder, manslaughter, through serious physical harm (grievous bodily harm), unlawful wounding to lesser physical harm (actual bodily harm) and common assault.[3] The parameters of the law are drawn in a

---

[98] Criminal Justice and Public Order Act 1994, Part V.
[99] Becker H., *Outsiders* (1963).
[1] Gusfield J. R., *Symbolic Crusade* (1966).
[2] Generally, see Schur E. M., *The Politics of Deviance* (1980) Chap. 3.
[3] For an overview, see Ashworth, *op. cit.*, Chaps. 7 and 8.

precise and objective fashion,[4] carefully scaling the offences to the degree of injury caused. Is this all that is needed to be known about the violence which society finds acceptable or unacceptable?

To concentrate on simply the text of the law would inevitably be misleading—in practice, the enforcement by police, prosecutors and courts defines the limits. Boxing, even in an unlicensed bout, will not be defined by the courts as assault and battery. Change the context to outside a public house and the courts will convict.[5] Change the victim to a wife and the police become unwilling to prosecute what is still termed a "domestic" and unworthy of overlong police intervention. Such practice reflects public perceptions of "real" crime but also affects those perceptions.

Underlying the enforcement of these laws is a complex moral debate, resting upon the ethical basis that we all possess a "right to physical integrity" and requiring elucidation as to when that right can be infringed. This discussion surfaces in many forms—the doctor with the terminally ill patient or the severely deformed new born baby, the soldier on checkpoint duty in Northern Ireland shooting an unarmed joyrider believing him to be a terrorist, the police officer using excessive force to restrain a suspect. All of these might frame a dramatic individual instance of what is acceptable violence. The law presents us with different coded messages—the doctor still does not have a clear-cut defence to murder even when the motive is to relieve unbearable suffering[6]; whereas the soldier is regarded as justified, even though not fired at, if he believed mistakenly that he was acting in self-defence.[7] Both felt compelled to act as they did but the law regards only one as "justifiable force".

There is a still wider frame of reference. One function of the criminal justice system is to protect us from physical injuries and yet the major causes of death and disablement are rarely prosecuted. Reiman[8] and Box[9] give the illustrations of the tobacco industry[10] and factories and workplaces[11]: many thousands of avoidable deaths and injuries are either regarded as accidents (traffic),[12] as not criminal (lung cancer through smoking)[13] or not real crime (occupational deaths).[14]

In its enforcement if not in theory, the criminal law acts as a "distorting mirror", portraying criminal violence as individual acts of brutality usually by a stranger. We accept almost nonchalantly the corporate violence of the factory or of retailing dangerous substances. Equally we accept the violence

---

[4] There is a little poetic licence in this statement as lawyers rely on an ancient and outmoded statute, the Offences Against the Person Act 1861.
[5] *Attorney-General's Reference No. 6 of 1980* [1981] Q.B. 715.
[6] See the discussions in the case of the patient in a "persistent vegetative state". *Airedale NHS Trust v. Bland* [1993] 1 All E.R. 821.
[7] *Attorney-General for N. Ireland's Reference* (No. 1 of 1975) [1977] A.C. 105.
[8] Reiman J., *The Rich Get Richer and the Poor Get Prison* (1984).
[9] Box S., *Power, Crime and Mystification* (1983).
[10] Deaths attributable to smoking are in the order of 100,000 a year.
[11] Bergman D., *Deaths at Work: Accidents or Corporate Crime* (1991)—there are significant numbers of avoidable deaths through breaches of the health and safety regulations in the workplace.
[12] Causing death by dangerous driving is still less likely to attract a prison sentence than burglary.
[13] An innovative prosecutor might see it as grievous bodily harm, administering a noxious substance or even a conspiracy to corrupt public health!
[14] Often dealt with, if at all, by prosecutions for infringements of the Health and Safety Regulations.

of the school or the family as outside the criminal justice system. The "right to physical integrity" for women and children is a fragile one since the home can be a very dangerous place. In 1993, in 389 (65 per cent) of 606 homicides,[15] the murder suspect was part of the family or a friend. Possibly 20 per cent of all assaults are domestic in character.[16] This violence is widely spread through all sectors of the community. Yet it can go unreported by the victim; if reported, it can be unrecorded by the police; even if recorded, it is often not prosecuted. It is still not perceived as "real" crime and thereby conceals an underlying reality of male aggression towards women. In its enforcement, if not in its definition, the criminal law incorporates a gender bias. Rather than being the neutral factor suggested by the simple text of the law, the enforcement process changes our definitions, in this case providing one which underpins patriarchal social relations.

The employee, the consumer, the wife and women generally are subjected to a range of physical threats against which the criminal law offers either no protection or very partial safeguards. Criminal law's definition of its own subject matter is eroded and distorted by structural factors—economic, gender, race.

1.7 CRIMINAL JUSTICE AND CONSTITUTIONALISM

Public expression of concern about crime rates and miscarriages of justice often shows how the criminal justice system operates as the barometer of the moral economy, providing a pivot around which we discuss moral issues; there is an expository or denunciatory aspect, as the system lays down the limits of acceptable and unacceptable behaviour. But alongside this moral discourse, the system has a constitutional significance: its operations provide the acid test of fairness within society and of the relationship between individuals and the state. This is crucial where a state has no document to lay down the principles on which the society is constituted, the rights of citizenship and the limits of state power. In the absence of a written constitution, these rights and principles need to be represented by other means. "Injustice", it appears, has a symbolic status of its own:

> "The importance of a fair trial is advanced as much by its failure as by its success. Any violation of the symbol of a ceremonial trial arouses people who would be left unmoved by ordinary non-ceremonial injustice. Harmless anarchists may be shot by the police. Liberals will be sorry and forget . But let them be treated unfairly by the court and before dissatisfaction has died away, the prejudice and phobia which created the atmosphere of the trial will receive a public analysis and examination which otherwise it would not get."[17]

As long ago as 1962, Arnold was suggesting that the trial has great symbolic force, not merely representing the rule of law, but metaphorically embodying moral and rational government. It is a thesis that can be applied to the criminal justice system as a whole. Liberal democracy has at its root the categorical opposition of the individual against the state. The system of

---

[15] *Criminal Statistics 1993, op. cit.*, Table 4.4, p. 79.
[16] Edwards S., *Policing Domestic Violence* (1989); Wells C., "Domestic Violence and Self Defence" (1990) New L.J. 127.
[17] Arnold T., *Symbols of Government* (1962), Chap. VI.

justice incorporates many of the ideas and values that we hold about that opposition, especially in regard to the rights of the individual opposed to the state and the balance between authoritarian and libertarian forms of government. Criminal justice is an area where this balance is constantly and dramatically demonstrated and where the rights of the individual should be seen at their most inviolable. The investigation, prosecution and punishment of crime are points at which there is not merely intervention by state agencies—such intervention can also be seen with other public services—but that intervention has an intensely coercive quality. The enforceable detention of an individual by the state has constitutional significance as it lays down the borderline between state power and the liberty of the citizen. This is done in a formal and dramatised fashion, whether in the police station or in the trial.

The process is not merely concerned with fairness between the parties—it is the embodiment of the idea of the "rule of law" itself in that law is a body of doctrine that not only controls the individual but also the state. The niceties of due process highlight that separation of the law from the social and political world. Hay makes this point in regard to the eighteenth century:

> "The punctilious attention to forms, the dispassionate and legalistic exchanges between counsel and judge, argued that those using and administering the law submitted to its rules . . . It became a power with its own claims, higher than those of prosecutor, lawyer or even the judge himself. To these too, of course, the law was The Law. The fact that they (the judges/lawyers) reified it . . . heightened the illusion. Its very inefficiency, its absurd formalism, was part of its strength as an ideology."[18]

1.8 CONCLUSION

Throughout this discussion of development and the boundaries of the criminal justice system, it has been argued that the criminal justice system has always fulfilled purposes other than the straightforward. The system has always had a metaphorical quality, which nowadays implies certain underlying principles. The concrete demonstration of those principles through the criminal justice system is expository of constitutional relationships. But this argument sits uneasily alongside the approach that would configure the system around the requirements of "crime control",[19] stressing the instrumental, rather than symbolic purposes, in particular the reduction of crime:

> "The failure of law enforcement to bring criminal conduct under tight control is viewed as leading to the breakdown of public order and thence to the disappearance of an important condition of human freedom. If laws go unenforced, which is to say, if it is perceived that there is a high percentage of failure to apprehend and convict in the criminal process, a general disregard for legal controls tends to develop."[20]

People are entitled to security in their lives and protection from those harms from which individuals find it difficult to protect themselves. Failure to provide this may well bring the law into disrepute. Yet so does the

---

[18] Hay, *op. cit.*
[19] Packer H. L., "Two Models of the Criminal Process" 113 U.Pa.L.Rev. (1964), p. 1.
[20] *supra*, p. 9.

imprisonment of the innocent. "Crime control" and "due process" should not be alternative models of the criminal process. The problem is simply stated: can we ensure that there is effective machinery of enforcement to meet the legitimate concerns of the public while at the same time ensuring that there is no derogation from principles of fairness.

CHAPTER TWO

The Police—Organisation and Control

2.1 STRUCTURE AND FUNCTIONS

The police forces are the gatekeepers of the criminal justice system. Under statute (notably the Police Act 1964),[1] local government is obliged to maintain police forces. In England and Wales there are currently 43[2] separate forces—two of these are in London (the Metropolitan and the City forces),[3] others are based on either major conurbations (Merseyside, Greater Manchester, West Midlands), single counties (Kent, Cheshire, Gwent) or on groups of counties (Thames Valley, Dyfed-Powys, Devon and Cornwall). These forces vary in size—the largest is the Metropolitan police with an establishment of 28,240 in 1992 whereas Gwent's establishment in that year was 1,010. In 1992, the total force comprised 126,941 officers[4] with another

---

[1] As amended by the Police and Magistrates' Courts Act 1994.
[2] For a list, see Her Majesty's Inspectorate of Constabulary: *Annual Report 1992* HCP 1992–93/679 Appendix. The Government has plans to amalgamate existing forces—see White Paper: *Police Reform* Cm. 2281 (1993), Chap. 10 and s. 14 Police and Magistrates' Courts Act 1994 which amends s. 21 Police Act 1964 empowering the Secretary of State to make alterations in force areas.
[3] The legal basis of the Metropolitan and City forces is different to that of provincial forces. The Metropolitan force is set up under Metropolitan Police Act 1829 and the City of London force under Metropolitan Police Act 1839.
[4] Her Majesty's Inspectorate of Constabulary (1992) *op. cit.* Of that figure, 1,730 were from

52,775 civilians.[5] The proportion of police officers to the population is 1:401 whereas in the nineteenth century, that ratio was not permitted to exceed 1:1000.

Table 2.1[6] Police Personnel 1960–1992, England and Wales

Year	Total Police Strength*	Authorised Establishment
1960	72,252	79,966
1970	94,312	108,306
1980	117,423	118,930
1990	127,090	125,646
1992	128,045	126,941

* This figure includes Home Office approved supernumeraries and secondments.

There are broad and narrow philosophies held about the function of policing; the narrow approach stresses crime control and evaluates the quality of policing in terms of response to crime reports, arrests, convictions and overall crime rates; the broader strategy encompasses community liaison work, multi-agency approaches and crime prevention. This latter philosophy was present in the Report of the Royal Commission on the Police in 1962[7] which saw the police providing a range of services to the public and to government:

(i) a duty to maintain law and order and to protect persons and property
(ii) a duty to prevent crime
(iii) responsibility for the detection of criminals and, in the course of interrogating suspected persons, a part to play in the early stages of the judicial process
(iv) some responsibility for the decision whether or not to prosecute persons suspected of criminal offences
(v) the duty of controlling road traffic
(vi) duties on behalf of Government departments

ethnic minorities compared with 1,105 in 1987. 15,862 officers were women compared with 12,754 in 1987.
[5] These figures do not include special constables (19,243), cadets (256) or traffic wardens (5,074).
[6] Her Majesty's Inspectorate of Constabulary: *Annual Reports* 1960 HCP 1960/61 248; 1970 HCP 1970/71 417; 1980 HCP 1980/81 409; 1990 HCP 1990/91 412; 1992 HCP 1992/93 679; Whitaker, B., *The Police in Society* (1982), p. 223.
[7] Royal Commission on the Police: *Final Report* (1962) Cmnd. 1728, p. 22.

(vii) a duty to befriend anyone who needs their help

The Report reflected a force that provides a 24 hour emergency service for the community, not only in the area of crime and public order but also in response to a wide range of requests. This "social work" function has become more visible since the 1960s. About 60 per cent of calls to a police station are not related to crime but to personal difficulties and problems—noise, disputes between neighbours, missing persons or lost property.[8] The force operates as a focus for and provides information about many other assistance agencies— the homeless, women's refuges or drug and detoxification centres. This broader philosophy of policing has led the police to become involved in a range of multi-agency initiatives.[9]

In the 1990s, that broader philosophy is under attack with increasing emphasis on crime detection and the maintenance of public order. One factor accelerating this is the increasing ethos of managerialism and especially the use of performance indicators.[10] Such indicators can provide desirable and objective measurement of a force's effectiveness but they also mean that resources are channelled towards the activity being measured. The indicators favoured by politicians and by the press are invariably crime-related—the most basic being the number of offences in relation to population and the clear-up rate.[11] The Police and Magistrates Courts Act in 1994 empowered the Home Secretary[12] to set objectives and performance targets for the police. A foretaste of this came in 1993 when Michael Howard published key objectives[13]:

- maintain and, if possible, increase the number of detections for violent crimes
- increase the number of detections for burglaries
- target and prevent crimes which are particular local problems in partnership with the public and other local agencies
- provide high visibility policing to reassure the public
- respond promptly to emergency calls.

Emphasising such factors does not provide an incentive to police managers to use resources on schools liaison, community work or even on general crime

---

[8] This figure (that 60% of total police effort is not related to crime) was suggested by (*inter alia*) Chatterton M., "Police in Social Control" in King M. (ed.), *Control Without Custody* (Cropwood Papers 7, Cambridge Institute of Criminology 1976). It has recently been confirmed by Audit Commission: *Helping With Enquiries* (Police Paper 12 1993). For discussion of the broader tasks of policing, see Uglow S., *Policing Liberal Society* (1988), p. 4 ff.
[9] Brake M. and Hale C., *Public Order and Private Lives* (1992), Chap. 4; Saulsbury W. and Bowling B., *The Multi-Agency Approach in Practice—the North Plaistow Racial Harassment Project* (Home Office Research and Planning Unit Paper 64) (1991); Uglow S., Dart A., Hale C. and Bottomley A., "Cautioning Juveniles—Multi-Agency Impotence" [1993] Crim.L.R. 632.
[10] Weatheritt M., "Measuring Police Performance" in Reiner R. and Spencer S. (eds), *Accountable Policing* (1993), p. 24.
[11] Though those used by the Audit Commission, HM Inspectors of Constabulary and the Association of Chief Police Officers are much broader and subtler—see Weatheritt (1993) *op. cit.*, Appendix, p. 45.
[12] s. 15 Police and Magistrates' Courts Act 1994.
[13] In a letter to Chief Constables dated December 3, 1993.

prevention, none of which will have a direct, short term effect on crime figures.

2.2 CONSTABLES AND CHIEF CONSTABLES

In theory, however, neither the Chief Constable nor the Home Secretary can instruct a constable on how or what to police. Constitutionally each police officer, having been sworn in in front of a justice of the peace, is the holder of an unpaid and independent Crown office recognised by the common law as the office of constable,[14] although now they are also employed by a local police authority.[15] Constables were historically subordinate to JPs—and these origins can still be seen in the fact that Chief Constables and Commissioners are themselves sworn in as justices—but officers exercise their authority and their powers independently by virtue of the common law,[16] as amended by statute.[17] However, the modern reality is that there is little independence and the "contemporary police officer is less a descendant of the nineteenth century constable than a distant cousin several times removed".[18]

There is a contradiction here since an officer at street level operates independently of direct control, exercises a discretion on whether to stop, search and question. This is of low visibility and almost impossible to supervise.[19] But above street level, there is a tight and hierarchical chain of command, culminating in the Chief Constable. The officer's autonomy disappears and there is a military quality to policing which is seen at its extreme in the control of public disorder, when the officer works as part of a squad, directly responding to an officer's commands and where individual discretion is non-existent.

Traditionally officers are assigned to police stations which were the lowest level of management but with two intermediate tiers (sub-divisions and divisions) with final control at force headquarters. Over the past few years, most forces have swept away this intermediate management with the development of Base Command Units (BCUs), designed to be small enough to maintain effective management control and sensitive to local community interests but large enough to meet normal policing needs. The superintendent in charge of a BCU is likely to have responsibility for a devolved budget and to be immediately accountable to headquarters. The modern force HQ provides policy, financial and personnel management but also specialist services beyond the BCU resources—drugs squads and training facilities, for example.[20]

---

[14] Lustgarten L., *The Governance of Police* (1986), Chap. 2; Jefferson T. and Grimshaw R., *Controlling the Constable* (1984).

[15] Local authorities are not responsible at common law for the acts of constables (*Fisher v. Oldham Corporation* [1930] 2 K.B. 364) although Chief Constables are treated as joint tortfeasors by statute (Police Act 1964, s. 48(1)).

[16] Although such common law powers differed little from those of the private citizen—Lustgarten, *op. cit.* p. 26.

[17] Their powers are significantly codified in the Police and Criminal Evidence Act 1984.

[18] Lustgarten, *op. cit.*, p. 29.

[19] Maguire M. and Norris C., *The Conduct and Supervision of Criminal Investigations*, (Royal Commission on Criminal Justice Research Study No. 5) (1992).

[20] The BCU concept was advanced in Audit Commission, *Reviewing the Organisation of*

"Introducing the (B)CU reduces the need for police hierarchies by flattening police management structures. Smaller police units will maximise service delivery and, by cutting overheads, offer a more cost effective service. (B)CUs may also release resources from a traditionally centralised service and are expected, if properly resourced and made coherent in terms of service responsibility, to form the basis of a regionalised system of policing. This would offer the opportunity of reducing the overhead costs of numerous headquarters, staffs and bureaucracies. With devolved budgeting and performance measurement, a reduced number of small police headquarters could be made responsible for general policing policy and inspection supporting a large number of (B)CUs."[21]

The Chief Constable[22] is the director of these services.[23] However his position is quite different in kind from that of the other directors of public services such as health, welfare or education. Such directors would normally be answerable, in terms of planning and performance, initially to local authorities themselves, then to regional and national levels of management and through secretaries of state to Parliament. Contrary to this, the Chief Constable's operational control is to a large extent autonomous and does not accord to the normal principles of local democratic scrutiny or parliamentary accountability. This is extraordinary considering that a chief officer controls a large force of trained, militarily organised and armed personnel with broad legal powers. The capacity to intervene in the life of civil society is considerable and can encompass involvement in industrial disputes, scrutiny of political groups, monitoring of "New Age" travellers or the surveillance and investigation of organised crime.

The statutory and constitutional position of the Chief Constable is laid down by the Police Act 1964, s. 5 as amended by the Police and Magistrates' Courts Act 1994, s. 5 where he[24] is given "direction and control" of the police force. That power is constrained as the Chief Constable is seen as part of a tripartite system of control with the Home Secretary and the Local Police Authority (LPA) being the other parts. But the Chief Constable is not subject to direct control by either of these. He can only be dismissed by the LPA in the "interests of efficiency" and only then with Home Office approval.[25] He has the power of appointment, conditions of employment, discipline and dismissal of all the constables and civilian personnel within the force. He is responsible for the operational deployment of the force and its financial management.

Despite recent inquiries,[26] the constitutional position of the police will remain anomalous in comparison to the provision of other public services.

Provincial Police Forces (Police Paper No. 9 1991); Her Majesty's Inspectorate of Constabulary (1992), op. cit., pp. 18–19.
[21] Loveday B., "Local Accountability of Police: Future Prospects" in Reiner R. and Spencer S., (eds.) (1993), op. cit., p. 55 at p. 63.
[22] In the Metropolitan and City forces, the chief officers are known as Commissioners.
[23] For a study of modern chief constables, see Reiner R., Chief Constables (1991).
[24] As yet there are no women Chiefs although the first deputy Chief was appointed in July 1994—there is clearly both discrimination against women (Halford v. Sharples [1992] 3 All E.R. 624) as well as unacceptable sexual harassment—see Her Majesty's Inspectorate of Constabulary (1992), op. cit., pp. 8–9.
[25] Lustgarten, op. cit., pp. 75–77 but now see procedure under s. 5 Police and Magistrates' Courts Act 1994.
[26] Audit Commission: Police Papers (Nos. 1–12) (1989–93) Inquiry into Police Responsibilities and Rewards (1993) (the Sheehy Report) (Cm. 2280); White Paper: Police Reform (Cm. 2281) (1993).

Why do we derogate from the normal constitutional mechanisms when it comes to the police?

2.3 THE DEVELOPMENT OF THE POLICE[27]

Although the office of constable has a long history going back to Anglo-Norman times,[28] it was low status and, until the nineteenth century, law enforcement remained the province of the middle and upper classes. How it was used, against whom and when it was enforced were not matters for state initiative but for the aggrieved private citizen. This operated well within a status-based, homogeneous, essentially rural society but the transition from a feudal to a capitalist economy in the 1700s brought changing forms of economic organisation and wealth. The criminal justice system evolved to protect these directly through new statutory and common law offences[29] and, indirectly, it brought about changes of attitude towards the idea of "property".[30] Yet in terms of procedures, institutions and enforcement, the eighteenth century showed little in the way of development in the criminal justice system. The patterns of social control were still largely centred in civil society and regulation of behaviour was frequently a personal matter, involving the propertied classes in their roles as squire or master as well as magistrate, member of the militia or sheriff. In the counties, the land-tie touched all points of existence, encompassing the worker not merely during working hours but also involving family relationships, the Church, leisure and politics. The use of the criminal law, where needed, reinforced the bonds of authority and deference, bonds which themselves rested on property relationships.

The nineteenth century saw the disappearance of the local, personal and voluntary basis of law enforcement with the creation of an organised and disciplined force with responsibilities for public safety and the prevention of crime. The idea of a patrolling force with the objective of preventing crime had been taking root during the latter half of the eighteenth century in the writings and actions of men such as the Fielding brothers and Colquhoun— the former as Bow Street magistrates had been responsible for the Bow Street Runners and the latter for the Dock Police, a force put on a statutory footing in 1800, the purpose of which was to protect the property of the West Indian sugar merchants from pilfering. These practical experiments fitted in well with the utilitarian social philosophy of Bentham and the reformist ideas of the Italian, Beccaria, whose ideas, expounded in 1764 in his *Essay on Crime and Punishment*, swept across Europe and influenced criminal justice reform in many countries. Alongside the need for clear and well-publicised laws, proper procedures at trial, proportional punishment and a humane prison system was highlighted the need for a police force with the aim of preventing and detecting crime.

[27] The standard history of the police is Critchley T., *A History of the Police in England and Wales* (1978). A more critical account is to be found in Reiner R., *The Politics of the Police* (2nd ed., 1992).
[28] Lustgarten, *op. cit.*, Chap. 2; Jefferson and Grimshaw, *op. cit.*, Chap. 2.
[29] Hall J., *Theft, Law and Society* (2nd ed., 1952).
[30] See Thompson E. P., *Whigs and Hunters* (1975); Hay D., "Property, Authority and the Criminal Law" in Hay D. (ed.), *Albion's Fatal Tree* (1975).

What is surprising is that reform along these lines was delayed so long—various Parliamentary committees studied proposals during the period 1770–1822 but they all opposed the creation of a police force. As the 1822 committee put it:

"... it is difficult to reconcile an effective police force with that perfect freedom of action and exemption from interference which are the great privileges and blessings of society in this country."

This constitutionalist and libertarian opposition remained strong, particularly among the Whigs but in 1829, Parliamentary opposition collapsed and the political acumen[31] of Peel steered the Metropolitan Police Act through Parliament with relatively little trouble.[32] The new police even survived the election of a Whig administration in 1832.

The social and economic reasons for the creation of a police force are apparent. The old techniques of social control were no longer appropriate in the new industrial towns where the propertied classes were less eager to turn out as militia men and saw it as the Government's job to protect them and their property. The contract of employment in the factory or mill counted for much less than the reciprocity of social obligations implied in the land-tie. Social control problems were exacerbated by major shifts of population from the country into the town and the acute unemployment and poverty which was suffered in the early decades of the nineteenth century. While the growth of a large and flexible pool of cheap labour was of great utility for industrial capital, such a population would scarcely remain docile. Crime and disorder arising from poverty was an obvious consequence. There was also the increasing capacity of the working class to mobilise politically. Peterloo, Captain Swing, the Chartists were all clear threats to the "social harmony" of the market place necessary for the new mode of production and for capitalist accumulation. Class conflict was much nearer the surface of everyday life.[33]

State intervention in the form of police forces was a reaction to the problems of urban order but not merely that; police were to be seen as independent and neutral, thereby legitimating not only themselves but also the law itself. The removal of the law and the state from close identification with the capitalist class was a necessary step for the establishment of capitalist hegemony.

Outside London, the extension of the franchise in 1832 and the subsequent democratisation of the boroughs led to the Municipal Corporations Act 1835 which required 178 boroughs to form Watch Committees for the creation of police forces. Few boroughs actually did so. In 1839, the County Police Act permitted (but did not require) the formation of forces in rural areas, a move hastened by the spread of the Chartist movement. Consolidation and compulsion arrived in 1856 when Palmerston forced through Parliament the

---

[31] *e.g.* Peel had to exclude the City of London from the provisions of the Act in order to secure its passage. But the City had its own police within 10 years.

[32] See Lyman J., "The Metropolitan Police Act 1829" 55 *Journal of Criminology, Criminal Law and Police Science* (1964) 141.

[33] This can best be seen by reading realist novels of this period such as those by Elizabeth Gaskell, *North and South* and *Mary Barton*, both of which deal with factory life in Manchester in the 1840s.

County and Borough Police Act which required all areas to form a police force and by 1857 there were some 239 forces operating in England and Wales. Apart from the Metropolitan police which was directly accountable to the Home Office, all other forces were free of national government interference— it was the "local state" which supervised the police. Indeed it was this element of local control that helped to reconcile the middle classes to this new phenomenon. Each force was controlled either by the Watch Committees in the towns or (after 1888) by the Joint Standing Committees in the counties.

Table 2.2 Commissions and Legislation affecting the police

Year	Report/Statute
1829	Metropolitan Police Act (creates London police force)
1835	Municipal Corporations Act (178 new boroughs required to form watch committees)
1836–39	Commission on the Rural Police
1839	Metropolitan Police Act (provides for wide-ranging police powers)
1839	County Police Act ("permits" formation of forces in rural areas)
1856	County and Borough Police Act (Palmerston's compromise—all local authorities required to create police forces)
1888	Local Government Act (gets rid of domination of JPs in shires—creates "joint standing committees" similar to boroughs' "watch committees"; Exchequer bearing half the cost of policing)
1919	Desborough Committee Report; Police Act (prohibits police from joining a union; established Police Federation; more central guidance from Home Office)
1964	Royal Commission Report (1962); Police Act (establishes modern structure for policing)

2.4 CONSTITUTIONALISM AND CONSENT

In Victorian England, the middle classes accepted the police, not only because they provided useful services but because they were seen as a legitimate mechanism for upholding the law. Consent to policing was a consent to the rule of law. However this was contingent upon police practices and the police could never depend on the fact of consent.[34] On the street and in working class areas, that consent was constantly negotiated and renegotiated. This carries on nowadays and was shown in the public disorders in the 1980s where for some communities with their "accumulation of anxieties and frustrations", the police were seen as representing an establishment which was "insensitive to their plight".[35]

Acceptance and legitimacy has always depended on the police exhibiting various characteristics which can been seen as positive attributes or conversely as negative constraints on the physical power of the state:

(a) independent of the state: this is linked to a convention that the government of the day does not identify itself with particular policing policies.[36]

(b) local and decentralised: the structure emphasises that policing arises out of the community rather than being imposed from above. There is a strong belief in local policing, shown, for example, by the continuous demands for more officers patrolling the beat or in the opposition to the changes to local police authorities when these are mooted by the government.[37]

(c) accountable to law: police actions and decisions are reviewable by the courts.

(d) governed by principles of fairness: in particular the police should be non-partisan in regard to class, gender or race.

(e) restricted in their capacity to interfere in everyday life: there are limits on the legal, economic and technical resources available to them.

(f) constrained by a doctrine of minimum force: the police are not generally armed and can only use "reasonable force" when effecting an arrest.[38] Such a principle places the constable on the same level as the citizen.

(g) providing services which go beyond the area of crime control: the police help and advise people with difficulties.

Although needing reassessment, such principles as the basis for policing still provide physical and visible representation of constitutional values. Liberal

---

[34] Storch R., "A Plague of Blue Locusts" (1975) 20 *International Review of Social History* 61; Storch R., "The Policeman as Domestic Missionary" (1976) *Journal of Social History* 481.

[35] Scarman, Lord, *The Brixton Disorders 10–12 April 1981* Cmnd. 8426, (HMSO 1981), para. 2.36.

[36] The significance may be seen in the police's continued resentment at the charge of being "Maggie's boot boys" during the miners' strike of 1984–85.

[37] Such changes were suggested in the debates on the Police and Magistrates' Courts Bill 1994 and provoked opposition from two former Home Secretaries, the Conservative, Lord Whitelaw, and the Labour, Lord Callaghan.

[38] Criminal Law Act 1967, s. 3.

society perceives itself as an aggregation of individuals with certain collective interests (mutual defence, regulation of economic and social relationships, provision of basic services). Of course, state agencies intervene constantly into the life of an individual—education, health, welfare and tax. But all these agencies possess clear limits to their powers and rights of intervention and they are restrained[39] by their own specific purposes. The constitutional significance of the police is that they possess no such defined boundaries to their work and in addition exercise the state's monopoly of physical force in civil society.[40] By its very nature police work can invade many aspects of individual lives, up to and including physical confrontation.

Policing is invariably more sensitive in terms of constitutional theory than that of the teacher or tax-collector and thus should possess essential characteristics which we perceive as representing the relationship between ourselves as citizens and the state. Any breach of those principles or constraints reflects not simply on the police but also upon the government. At its most basic, the characteristics reside in the physical image of the officer which is peculiarly evocative: the anachronistic uniform and the bike reflect the timelessness and continuity in the "rule of law" itself and indirectly the stability and natural quality of our social order.

2.5 THE "NEW" POLICE IN THE 1990S

The police not only have important practical functions to perform but also a symbolic function, constantly rehearsing and reinforcing beliefs that we hold about constitutional relationships. Those beliefs have traditionally been liberal in content although political demonstrators or inner city youth might harbour considerable scepticism about this, seeing a more authoritarian force inextricably linked to government policy. Certainly the 1980s saw increasing economic liberalism linked with increasing authoritarianism in social matters.[41] and these changes have coincided with fundamental alterations in policing.

2.5.1 *Local or National: the structure of the Force*

British policing has always been part of the local state but the 1950s saw criticism about its relationship with local government: there were several scandals, not least in Nottingham where the Watch Committee sought to block police investigations into local government corruption. This concern led to the Royal Commission[42] and the Police Act 1964. Although the Report rejected the idea of a national force and endorsed local independence, the subsequent legislation broke with the idea of the small decentralised force. Although there were still 120 in existence in 1960, the result of subsequent

[39] Although draconian powers can lurk in specialist legislation such as the search and seizure powers in the Customs and Excise Management Act 1979.
[40] Perhaps more important in this country than in other jurisdictions such as the USA which recognises the citizen's right to bear arms.
[41] Edgar D., "Bitter Harvest" *New Socialist* (September 1983), p. 19.
[42] For the background to the setting up of the Royal Commission, see Critchley (1979), *op. cit.*, p. 270 ff.

amalgamations was the emergence of 43 larger forces. Although these are still "local" forces, responsible to an LPA, there has been the weakening of local ties, coupled with the strengthening of the roles of Chief Constable and of the Home Office. Professor Goodhart's note of dissent to the Willink Report[43] pointed out that if local connection was unnecessary to preserve individual rights and if the local authority was not to have power to control the police, the logic was to create a national force. The rejection of this argument has had the predictable result that the Chief Constables and the Home Office who exercise power over the police are, by and large, unaccountable whereas local councillors on LPAs who are democratically elected and accountable have no power but are simply advisory.

There are no moves to organise the force on a national basis despite an increasing identification between government policy and policing. The current situation suits senior police management and the Home Office, leaving the former with operational autonomy and the latter with indirect control. That influence comes from providing various national facilities, overseeing the inspection of forces and laying down guidelines for operational and financial management. The Police and Magistrates' Courts Act extends Home Office influence by enabling the Home Secretary to set national objectives for policing, to require performance indicators to be set for measuring the achievement of those targets, to issue Codes of Practice for the performance of LPA functions and to require reports from the LPA on any matter concerning the policing of that area.[44]

The need for co-ordination between individual forces has long been recognised. Mutual assistance between forces was first given statutory recognition in 1890.[45] The power of a Chief Constable to provide assistance to other forces is now governed by Police Act 1964 s. 14. Although such mutual aid has the appearance of voluntary collaboration, the Home Secretary has powers to require that such assistance be given.[46] Such mutual aid can be temporary, providing extra officers for public order duties, or permanent when personnel are seconded to regional or national specialist squads. The oldest of these, dating from 1965, have been the eight[47] regional crime squads (RCS). RCS responsibilities are to identify and arrest those responsible for serious offences which transcend force boundaries, to co-operate with regional criminal intelligence officers in generating intelligence and to assist in the investigation of serious crime, usually for a limited period.[48] The squads are staffed by detectives from adjacent forces. Further the National Crime Intelligence Service (NCIS) was set up in 1992, to develop along the lines of the FBI.[49] Such co-ordination can be seen in the area of drugs, where every force has a dedicated Drugs Squad and these also exist

[43] Royal Commission on the Police, *op. cit.*, paras. 157–79; Lustgarten, *op. cit.*, p. 51.
[44] s. 15—although House of Lords opposition meant that the Home Secretary has been frustrated in attempts to appoint chairmen of LPAs and to ensure a majority of non-councillors (including Home Office appointees) on LPAs.
[45] Police Act 1890, s. 25.
[46] Police Act 1864, s. 14(1) and s. 13(5)—for a discussion of the legal basis of mutual aid, see Lustgarten, *op. cit.*, Chap. 8.
[47] Soon to be reduced to five—Her Majesty's Inspectorate of Constabulary (1992), *op. cit.*, p. 30.
[48] The current terms of reference are set out in Home Office Circular No. 28/1987. For a discussion of RCS work, see Maguire M. and Norris C. (1992), *op. cit.*, p. 73.
[49] Her Majesty's Inspectorate of Constabulary (1992), *op. cit.*, p. 30.

at RCS and NCIS level. This also occurs in areas such as immigration, terrorism or political surveillance through the work of Special Branch.[50]

Collaboration and close identification with government is also seen in the changing role of the Association of Chief Police Officers (ACPO), who have been described as a "focal part of the policy-making scene" and the "vertebrae of more centrally co-ordinated policing"[51] and who are an influential lobby group on all matters of criminal justice policy.[52] Operationally they have developed their own operational manuals on topics such as public order tactics and also set up in 1972 the National Reporting Centre, based in New Scotland Yard, to organise the provision of mutual aid, co-ordinating the movement of constables between forces in times of emergency. It has been activated on occasions such as the prison officers' dispute of 1980–81, the inner city disturbances in 1981, the papal visit in 1982 and, most controversially, the miners' strike in 1984–85.[53] During that latter dispute there was, at least, the appearance of co-ordination between government, Coal Board and police. It was a time which revealed how easily the police could be organised on a national basis and put under political control.

Despite such centralising tendencies, local forces are anxious to maintain their own identity and their independence from both local and national government. This ambition is reciprocated by the Home Office—the 1993 White Paper[54] foresees reductions in the number of forces[55] but nowhere suggests the creation of a national force. The local element is to be strengthened by giving LPAs responsibility for identifying policing priorities as well as greater autonomy from local authorities.[56] But alongside enchanced powers, the LPA's local democratic identity is to be decreased by the appointment (by the Home Secretary) of independent members, although not of the chairman. The Home Office's interest in keeping close, if not direct, control over policing has not diminished.

Such centralisation is about control over national policing strategies. The Home Office is content to see operational policing decentralised to the level of BCUs while general policing policy is centralised in the hands of relatively few Chief Constables who will be susceptible to government influence.

2.5.2. Beat Patrols and Specialist Squads

To the public, local and national organisation is less significant than the sight of the individual police officer patrolling the beat. The traditional idea was that officers were trained to be omni-competent at all facets of police

---

[50] Bunyan T., *The Political Police in Britain* (1977).

[51] Reiner R., *op. cit.* (1991), p. 367—see Appendix C on the history and structure of ACPO.

[52] A recent example is the restrictions on the right to silence incorporated in the Criminal Justice and Public Order Act, ss. 34–37.

[53] Kettle M., "The National Reporting Centre" in Fine B. and Millar R. (eds.) *Policing the Miners' Strike* (1985) Lustgarten, *op. cit.*, p. 109; Reiner (1991), *op. cit.*, p. 186; Uglow (1988), *op. cit.*, p. 43.

[54] *Police Reform, op. cit.*

[55] *ibid*, Chap. 10; provisions for simplifying current arrangements for force amalgamations are contained within the Police and Magistrates' Courts Act, s. 14.

[56] *ibid*, Chap. 4, provisions for these reforms are contained within the Police and Magistrates' Courts Act, s. 4 and ss. 27–31.

work and that the front line was the beat officer. The introduction of unit beat policing in the 1960s was designed to reorganise patrolling with the beat officers supplied with personal radios, acting as the "eyes and ears" of patrol cars and the detectives.[57] Policing became increasingly reactive, responding to crime reports, often as a result of phone calls from the public and even less need was seen for individual patrolling constables. Patrol cars rather than home beat officers became used for general patrolling. Officers were increasingly distanced from the community, whether behind the wheel of a car or seconded to specialist squads.

Police culture has always stressed "crimebusting", and beat patrolling, despite its importance to the public, was low status, undertaken by the younger, less experienced or less successful officers. Specialisation was demanded and although debates on community policing[58] in the 1980s saw some increase in foot patrol and in community liaison officers, patrolling was never seen as a specialist function and there is little training for beat work. Promotions and commendations tend not to go to beat officers[59] and the status of the ordinary constable has been reduced as "real" policework is left to the specialist. It is still the beat that will be denuded of manpower in order to fill gaps elsewhere.

The ambitious officer looks for career opportunities elsewhere,[60] to be found in specialist squads, especially with traffic and CID. Such squads are not a recent phenomenon—the earliest was perhaps the Special Irish Branch,[61] organised to deal with the Fenian campaigns in the 1880s and the most famous, the Met's Flying Squad. All forces will have a drugs squad and many have squads dealing with, *inter alia*, robberies, public order, child protection as well as tactical firearms units. Some might be long term, others for a very specific problem—one force set up a "Bogus Official" section in response to a number of such offences. Normally run from headquarters, there are obvious managerial justifications for such squads since they allow for the development of special knowledge and skills, the co-ordination of effort over a broad geographical area and the approach can be very effective in proactive, intelligence-driven policing.

But such policies have costs especially where such activities impinge directly on BCU territory. First, in public order work, local communities will experience specialist squads as more coercive and the local officer's expertise can be overridden and work at building up community confidence in the police can be destroyed.[62] Secondly, the internal objectives of a squad will invariably be narrow: drugs or robbery squads will measure their performace in terms of offences cleared up and convictions obtained, a crime-centred approach which may be appropriate but when it involves aggressive searches in sensitive communities, may undo much liaison work.

There are more general dangers as concentration on detection rates can

[57] The system was recommended by Home Office: *Police Manpower, Equipment and Efficiency* (Home Office, 1967); Holdaway S., *Inside the British Police* (1983), pp. 134–138, 159–163.
[58] Alderson J., *Policing Freedom* (1979).
[59] Jones M. and Winkler J., "Policing in a Riotous City" (1982) 9 J. Law and Soc. 103 at 110–111.
[60] Jones M., *Organisational Aspects of Police Behaviour* (1980).
[61] The "Irish" was later dropped as it became known as Special Branch.
[62] One area where this happened was in Brixton in 1981—Scarman (1981), *op. cit.*

encourage officers into unethical conduct. The methods alleged against the West Midlands Serious Crimes Squad included fabricated confessions, flawed identification procedures, inconsistent timings and accusations of attempted bribes by the accused's solicitors.[63] Squads such as that in West Midlands can even threaten central management by operating quasi-autonomously.[64] That autonomy can also mean lack of proper supervision and many corruption scandals[65] have involved specialist squads. Recently improved management has apparently lessened these risks.

Strategies of policing continue to change: beat and community, although liked by the public, are expensive; reactive policing through CID and the squad system is being overwhelmed by the volume of crime reports. The 1990s will see greater emphasis placed on crime management, intelligence, proactivity and crime prevention.[66] BCUs will use crime desks to filter crime reports and by initial telephone investigation, decide on the level of response. By not reacting to every crime report, resources become freed up and intelligence teams will collate information and present "targets" of known offenders or problem offences for proactive teams. Such an approach is a positive step away from reactive policing, especially when it is integrated into community liaison in identifying objectives and into crime prevention through analysis of crime patterns and through victim support work.

2.5.3 *Police Powers*

The common law placed strict limits on the legal powers of intervention by the executive and the police.[67] In mapping the relationship between the State and the citizen, police powers are very visible. Although other public agencies such as education, health or the Child Support Agency exercise such powers, the criminal justice system is the most dramatic rendering of that relationship because the police, the courts and the prisons have the power to detain people against their will. Concern about the extent of such powers and the conditions under which they are exercised has to be a measure by which civilised society judges itself.

For the police, legal powers are as much a resource as personnel, money or equipment. The fight for increased powers is not only an instrumental one but also a symbolic measure of their status.[68] Police organisations such as the Police Federation[69] and ACPO have fought for extra police powers. Their

---

[63] Kaye T., *Unsafe and Unsatisfactory* (Civil Liberties Trust 1991), Appendix B.

[64] West Midlands Chief Constable, Geoffrey Dear, recognised that the squad was beyond normal management control when he disbanded it in August 1989.

[65] The preponderance of these in modern times have been in the Metropolitan force in the 1970s—Cox B., Shirley J. and Short M., *The Fall of Scotland Yard* (1977).

[66] This is the thrust of the Audit Commission's report, *Helping with Enquiries, op. cit.*, certain ACPO reports and recent research commissioned by the Police Research Group in the Home Office.

[67] *Entick v. Carrington* (1765) 19 State Tr. 1029; Leigh L., *Police Powers* (2nd ed., 1985), Chap. 2.

[68] For a discussion of the instrumental and symbolic functions of legislation, see Carson W., "Sociology of Crime" in Rock P. and MacIntosh M. (eds.) *Deviance and Social Control* (1974).

[69] After the police strikes in 1918, the Desborough Committee was set up and recommended a ban on unions in the police. This was promulgated in the Police Act 1919 and a representative organisation, the Police Federation, was set up.

objectives often coincided, although not necessarily so, with those of Home Office ministers and civil servants.[70] They have been successful: the innovation in 1967 of majority verdicts[71]; the extended powers contained in the Police and Criminal Evidence Act 1984[72] and, more recently, provisions to abolish the right of silence in the Criminal Justice and Public Order Act 1994.[73]

Such constant tinkering with police powers should not occur, not least because there is no evidence that such extra powers improve police efficiency. The principles and scope of police intervention should be clearly laid out and, in general criminal investigation, there is now such a basic framework contained in a single statute, namely the Police and Criminal Evidence Act 1984 (PACE). This provides a general, comprehensive and comprehensible code of the powers of the police, *inter alia*, to stop people, search them, arrest them, hold them in police custody and interrogate them. It also lays down the suspects' rights.[74]

However, in the field of public order, there is no such framework. The police possess wide discretionary powers that are not constrained by positive and entrenched rights of speech or assembly.[75] The central statute, the Public Order Act 1986, is neither a "comprehensive systematisation" nor "an attempt to create a code of public order law".[76] It extended significantly the powers of the police to intervene in, impose conditions on and prohibit meetings and demonstrations.[77] The Criminal Justice and Public Order Act 1994 continues this piecemeal extension creating new powers against "raves",[78] hunt saboteurs,[79] squatters[80] and travellers,[81] all modern folk devils. The police, for example, now possess powers to stop those (within five miles) whom they suspect of going to a rave or to disrupt a hunt. These are unnecessarily broad powers to deal with minor nuisances but powers which possess the potential for being transformed into more general use at a later date.

---

[70] Lustgarten, *op. cit.*, Chap. 7; Reiner R., (1991) *op. cit.*, *passim*.

[71] Criminal Justice Act 1967—now Juries Act 1974, s. 17. See Mark R., *In the Office of Constable* (1979), p. 280 ff.

[72] Christian L., *Policing By Coercion* (1983), p. 8 ff.; de Gama K., "Police Process and Public Prosecutions: Winning by appearing to Lose" (1988) 16 Int.J.Soc. Law 339.

[73] ss. 34–37—although much desired by the police, this was against the recommendations in July 1993 of the Royal Commission on Criminal Justice and the research undertaken for that report: Royal Commission on Criminal Justice, Report (HMSO 1993) Cm. 2263. Chap. 4 and Recommendation 82; Leng R., *The Right to Silence in Police Interrogation* Royal Commission on Criminal Justice Research Study 10 (1993); McConville M. and Hodgson J., *Custodial Legal Advice and the Right to Silence* (Royal Commission on Criminal Justice Research Study 16) (1993); *infra*, para. 3.8.7.1.

[74] The background to general police powers, the history of PACE and the extent of police powers are examined in detail in Chap. 3.

[75] e.g. *Duncan v. Jones* (1939) 1 K.B. 218.

[76] Smith A. T. H., *Offences Against Public Order* (1987), p. 6.

[77] Smith, *op. cit.*, pp. 132–141.

[78] ss. 63–66.

[79] ss. 68–69.

[80] s. 73.

[81] s. 78.

2.5.4 *Physical Force*

The constable's unarmed status was part of Peel's campaign to separate his police from the military, representing the prohibition on the arbitrary use of force by the state. Historically, weapons such as truncheons and sabres for mounted police were issued even for Peel's police. The police themselves were issued with firearms[82] although often the army would be called in to control crowds.[83] But police stations would only have a limited stock of weapons, issued rarely. Even the most minor assaults alleged against a police officer might provoke parliamentary attention.[84]

Over the last 20 years, that position changed and there have been a number of incidents which suggested that the police had redefined the threshold of "minimum force"; in 1973, the Special Patrol Group shot dead two Pakistani youths holding hostages with artificial firearms in India House; in April 1979 the same unit was responsible for the death of Blair Peach in Southall[85]; 1983 saw the shooting of Stephen Waldorf in London, mistaken for an armed and dangerous criminal while five year old John Shorthouse was shot by officers on a "routine" house search in the West Midlands; in 1985, there was the accidental shooting of Cherry Groce in Brixton and in the same year Mrs Cynthia Jarrett died of a heart attack during a police search of her home at Broadwater Farm, both factors in the subsequent riots. Shootings, whether of armed criminals or in the course of sieges or of unarmed civilians, have become almost routine over the past decade.

"Minimum force" is no longer interpreted as last resort, defensive response. Such an interpretation is in accord with the concept of self-defence in the criminal law which accepts that people are justified in reacting if they believe that they are in imminent danger and that their response is reasonably proportional to that danger.[86] Armed police need not wait to be attacked before responding nor do they have to have objectively reasonable grounds that they are in imminent danger, although they must have an "honest belief" that this is the case.

In the late 1980s, there was a change of policy, away from increasing the numbers of officers who were "authorised shots" and away from the increasing regularity with which ordinary divisional officers were issued with firearms. The Home Office encouraged forces to set up specialist tactical firearm units such as D11, the Blue Berets of the Metropolitan force,[87] although other units such as those on royal and diplomatic protection duty and tactical support units are still routinely armed.[88] Police in Britain still use firearms rarely in comparison with any other country.

[82] Lee Enfields were used in the siege of Sydney Street in 1911.
[83] In the miners' strikes of 1910 and 1911, there were fatal shootings by soldiers at Tonypandy and Llanelli. In 1980, the SAS were used to end the Iranian Embassy Siege.
[84] Critchley, *op. cit.*, pp. 273–274.
[85] Dummett M., *Southall 23 April 1979* (1980).
[86] For the law on self defence, see Smith J. and Hogan B., *Criminal Law* (7th ed., 1992), pp. 253–261; *Gladstone Williams* (1984) 78 Cr.App.R. 276; *Scarlett* [1994] Crim.L.R. 288.
[87] Judging from TV documentaries ("Police" BBC 1982; "Scotland Yard" Carlton 1993), the tactics for such units involve saturation of an area regardless of the level of risk. Only when all risk has gone are weapons holstered!
[88] Many forces that have responsibilities for patrolling motorways are likely to have an armed patrol vehicle operating at all times.

2.5.5 Public Order

The tactics surrounding the policing of public order has also witnessed this change in the threshold of "minimum force". Since the end of the First World War, there was a marked decline in violent confrontation.[89] Unlike the soldier, constables were trained to operate independently and to enforce the law on their own responsibility. The unarmed constable required a flexible approach, working to defuse situations rather than relying on defensive equipment or firepower. Crowds responded in kind: "[disputes] were characterised by order rather than disorder. On the whole, strikers refrained from rioting, destroying property and even ... violent picketing".[90] A certain constitutionalism evolved in which violence was rare, police intervention minimal and although the legal basis of marching and assembly was obscure, the right to do so within a political consensus seemed well established.

That consensus disappeared in the early 1970s when there was a re-assessment of public order strategy following the mass picketing that led to the closure of a coking works at Saltley in 1972 by striking miners. All forces have a proportion (10 per cent) of officers trained in crowd control techniques—although such officers will be on normal duties, they can be mobilised rapidly to deal with disorder either within their own force boundaries or for adjacent forces. This latter function is under the mutual aid provisions of the Police Act 1964.[91] Thus there is a capacity to mobilise large numbers of officers to confront strikers or demonstrators[92] and to prevent a demonstration from taking a particular route or workers from closing a particular plant. The officers themselves are trained to act in concert on command, either defensively with long shields or offensively with round shields, baton rounds and water cannon. They operate in squads in a military fashion, a far cry from the notion of the "independent office holder" or the "citizen in uniform".

Such strategies have been supplemented by specialist public order squads, mobile reserves able to be moved quickly to the scene of any disturbance. The first of these, set up in 1965, was the Metropolitan Force's Special Patrol Group, replaced and renamed in 1987 as the Territorial Support Group. These exist in the majority of forces and are on permanent standby with their transit vans containing weaponry and riot gear. This history has not been uncontroversial[93]—the Scarman Report[94] is a detailed account of the SPG operations against street robberies in Lambeth especially in 1981. Codenamed "SWAMP '81", the aggressive and confrontational policing used arbitrary roadblocks, stopping and searching of pedestrians and mass detention—there were 943 stops, 118 arrests and 75 charges, only one of which was for robbery. It left police—community relations in a shambles and had little if any effect on crime figures.

[89] This is charted in industrial disputes by Geary R., *Policing Industrial Disputes* (1985).
[90] Geary, *op. cit.*, p. 66.
[91] s. 14—see discussion *supra*, p. para. 2.5.1.
[92] At Orgreave on May 29, 1984 there were 1,700 officers from 13 different forces confronting 1,500 pickets. A similar approach was seen during the Poll Tax demonstrations in the early 1990s.
[93] Dummett, (1980) *op. cit.*; Scarman, Lord, *Report of Inquiry into the Red Lion Square Disorders* Cmnd. 5915 (1974); generally Brake and Hale (1992), *op. cit.*, p. 46 ff.
[94] Scarman (1981), *op. cit.*

2.5.6 High Technology and Police Work[95]

Less visible than policing the streets but equally important is the impact of a range of technologies on police work. The means of gathering information has expanded: telephone calls can be easily monitored; video cameras are commonplace in many public areas[96] as well as on major roads where number plates can be scanned and recorded. Storage and retrieval of information through computerisation has changed the police job with the policeman on the beat having access to a range of local and national police data bases.

The managerial needs for new technology are undoubted in areas of activity analysis and resource management. As the police strategy moves emphasis to a more proactive approach, information technology plays a critical role. The increase in the use of informants and of intelligence requires the establishment and manipulation of sophisticated databases as does crime pattern analysis, especially when linked to geographic information systems. Eventually all BCUs will have intelligence units.

An aspect of police legitimacy is that policing should remain in the public sphere and not intrude into the private. Such a statement is axiomatic for the liberal democrat who sees all citizens as entitled to privacy, that is, that domain of thoughts, beliefs and behaviour which is unregulated by the state. Many jurisdictions possess constitutions specifically protecting rights to privacy. But it remains difficult to identify the criteria that marks a boundary between the public and the private. State intervention is everywhere and the language of privacy provides no obvious boundaries. This leads some theorists to conclude that the concept of privacy is simply ideological, an abstract concept which masks a concrete reality, thereby precluding certain forms of intervention and reinforcing inequalities of power. In this way O'Donovan sees privacy as masking male dominance within the family.[97]

But notions of privacy are part of our everyday language which takes for granted personal, internal worlds, and our relationships with others rests on the recognition of those worlds and of our own private identity. To erode the domain of the private is to legitimate and encourage state intervention with all the consequent dangers and to that end liberal theory would restrict the role of the state which should be constrained as to the amount of information it can gather about individuals.

Such large databases holding information on people's private lives pose problems. There are few legal limits on police work in this sphere and difficulties arise: first, there is the question of evaluation of the intelligence since not only must the information received be reliable, the quality of analysis must be high before it is of value otherwise individuals will be the object of unjustified surveillance; secondly, there are ethical issues since if an individual is "targeted", then there should be a proper level of evidence against him or her, such as reasonable suspicion of involvement in organised or persistent or serious criminal activity, already in existence; thirdly the sheer capacity to gather, store and retrieve large quantities of data on every

[95] Manwaring-White S., *The Policing Revolution* (1983), Chap. 4; Bunyan, (1977), *op. cit.*; Uglow, (1988), *op. cit.*, Chap. 6.
[96] And can play a major role in detection—the two young boys convicted in 1994 of murdering James Bulger were caught on video in the shopping centre.
[97] O'Donovan K., *Sexual Divisions in Law* (1985), p. 181.

individual in the country, regardless of whether they have committed offences or not. This is already the case in Northern Ireland. In 1994, there was a plan to mount a joint operation to monitor the movements of all "New Age" travellers by tracking their vehicle movements and thus maintain a database enabling them to intervene more easily in the event of trespasses at Stonehenge or the holding of music festivals. Such an operation would have been impossible without new technology and contains disturbing implications for all dissident groups, whether environmentalists, anti-nuclear protestors, animal rights activists, hunt saboteurs, trade unionists, left or right wing splinter groups and whether they operate within the normal channels of political and industrial protest or not.

2.6 ACCOUNTABILITY AND CONTROL

Obviously there should be mechanisms through which the community has an input into the operations of the police. These can be retrospective in getting a body to account for certain decisions and actions or prospective in seeking to impose positive policy and financial control. Reiner[98] suggests that there are certain basic questions about this issue:

(a) what type of decisions do the police make? Different types may require different mechanisms of accountability. Perhaps a democratic forum is required where there are issues of general policy. These can vary from questions as to whether to buy British cars for the force, to an initiative against burglary or guidelines for hot pursuit. Alternatively there are decisions to be made, often at street level, about individual cases. These often themselves require an investigative process.

(b) to whom should the police be accountable? In many cases an officer is responsible to some other part of the legal process, whether a superior officer, the Crown Prosecution Service or the courts. In others, it might be an external body such the Police Complaints Authority or the LPA.

(c) what remedies may be sought?—a change of policy, disciplinary action against an officer, exclusion of evidence or compensation through damages.

(d) what sort of accountability should we look for? Marshall developed a distinction between "subordinate and obedient" and "explanatory and co-operative".[99] Historically the police were controlled by the Watch Committee but active Labour local authorities in the 1980s attempted to get greater say in the policing of their communities with little success.[1] Indeed these authorities were abolished by the Local Government Act 1985 and replaced by less radical joint boards. Marshall suggests that the "explanatory and co-operative" style underlies the Police Act 1964, not just with LPAs but also with the Home Office. Despite the latter's considerable financial and policy

---

[98] Reiner R., "Police Accountability" in Reiner and Spencer, (eds.) (1993), *op. cit.*, p. 1.
[99] Marshall G., *Police and Government* (1965), p. 61.
[1] Simey M., "Police Authorities and Accountability: The Merseyside Experience" in Cowell D., *et al.* (eds.), *Policing the Riots* (1982).

influence, policy is formulated only after significant consultation with ACPO. Reiner suggests that a third mode, "calculative and contractual", will be the result of current government policies such as the setting of performance objectives and the isolation of "core" policing tasks and the possible privatisation of ancillary jobs.[2] In this scenario, while formal constabulary independence is preserved, the Home Secretary will have unprecedented control over police decision-making.[3]

Police behaviour is heavily scrutinised and police failings are highlighted where similar failings by other professions would go unremarked. That scrutiny can take many forms:

2.6.1 *Media and Public Attention*

Most of us will glean our knowledge of the police and the criminal justice system at second hand through newspapers or TV. The quantity of coverage is extraordinary and 25 per cent of newspaper copy is about crime.[4] Television coverage is also extensive in both documentary and fictional formats.[5] The bulk of such coverage is supportive of the police, presenting them as necessary and in the main effective. This is especially so in those programmes which reconstruct offences such as *Crimewatch*. These help to maintain and reinforce a perception of a force battling with a "law-and-order" problem. However the caricature of the good bobby in *Dixon of Dock Green* has moved on to recognising the police as flawed, fallible people undertaking a difficult job. Certainly this evolution can be seen from *Z Cars* and *The Sweeny* to the confrontation of sexism, racism and homophobia in the force in *Prime Suspect*.[6] There are, more occasionally, critical investigations by newspaper, radio or TV programmes such as *World In Action*'s investigation into the Birmingham Six.

Many police forces are sensitive to public opinion—Kent, for example, regularly take public opinion surveys. Public satisfaction with police performance in a range of matters features among the key performance indicators.[7] That sensitivity ensures that the police pay attention to media coverage.

2.6.2 *Accountability Through the Courts*

The police argue that they are first and foremost accountable to the law and the courts. However, as will be seen, their powers and decisions are often low visibility and are characterised as much by discretion as by rules. Discretion, such as the decision based on "reasonable suspicion" to stop and search a

[2] *The Guardian*, November 7, 1994, pp. 1–2.
[3] Reiner, (1993), *op. cit.*, pp. 19–20.
[4] Chibnall S., *Law and Order News*, (1977).
[5] Reiner, (1992), *op. cit.*, Chap. 5 gives a detailed analysis of media presentations of the police.
[6] ITV's *The Bill* has consistently and effectively covered difficult issues, providing a realistic view of policing to a prime time audience.
[7] Weatheritt, (1993), *op. cit.*

person under section 1 PACE, is often not justiciable. But three broad categories of court action can influence the police:

2.6.2.1 CRIMINAL AND CIVIL ACTIONS

Individuals do have redress through the criminal and civil courts. Police officers might commit criminal offences in the course of an investigation such as assault or perversion of the course of justice. "Law enforcement" cannot as yet be argued as a defence were an officer to be charged. However, recent Law Commission thinking appears to be moving in that direction.[8]

Alternatively, there can be civil actions[9] against officers and their Chief Constable[10] for compensation for assault or wrongful detention. In addition, there may be actions for trespass to land or goods and, possibly, breach of confidence. Civil remedies are often preferred by many solicitors who advise their clients to ignore the formal police complaints machinery.

However, such remedies are available to those whose injuries are caused directly by the police. If the harm is caused indirectly, for example, those who become victims of crime because the police negligently fail to apprehend the criminal, such persons do not have any right of action against the police.[11] The limits of police liability in negligence were shown in *Osman v. Ferguson*,[12] a "stalker" case where a schoolteacher formed an unhealthy attachment to a 15 year old male pupil. The level of harassment was high and known to the police. Eventually the man followed the boy and his family to their flat and shot and severely injured the boy and killed his father. The mother brought an action alleging negligence in that, although the police had been aware of P's activities, they failed to apprehend or interview him, search his home or charge him. The Court of Appeal held that as the family had been exposed to a risk over and above that of the public, the existence of a general duty on the police to suppress crime did not carry with it liability to individuals for damage caused to them by criminals whom the police had failed to apprehend when it was possible to do so. It would be against public policy to impose such a duty as it would not promote the observance of a higher standard of care by the police and would result in the significant diversion of police resources from the investigation and suppression of crime.

2.6.2.2 EXCLUSION OF EVIDENCE

One important influence on police behaviour is the court's power to exclude improperly obtained evidence and thereby often to ensure the acquittal of the accused. In the United States, the Supreme Court has actively policed the police through these methods. In the United Kingdom, the common law power to exclude confessions was quite restricted but the passage of PACE and the Codes of Practice promulgated under its provisions has led the Court of Appeal to adopt a much more active role. This is particularly the case in the Court's interpretation of section 78 PACE.[13]

---

[8] Law Commission Consultation Paper No. 131, (1993) at pp. 120–122.
[9] Clayton R. and Tomlinson H., *Civil Actions against the Police* (2nd ed. 1992).
[10] Police Act 1964, s. 48.
[11] *Hill v. Chief Constable of West Yorkshire* [1988] 2 All E.R. 238.
[12] [1993] 4 All E.R. 344.
[13] This will be examined in detail *infra*, para. 3.8.7 ff.

2.6.2.3 JUDICIAL REVIEW OF POLICE ACTION

An important means of redress for people who are adversely affected by a general policy or a particular decision of a public agency is to have that policy reviewed by the Divisional Court of Queen's Bench under its power of judicial review.[14] By the orders of mandamus, prohibition and certiorari, the court can order an inferior court or public body to take action where it has failed to do so or to desist from action or it can quash a particular decision. By the writ of habeas corpus, the court can review the conditions under which anyone is held in detention. By seeking a declaration, a litigant can obtain an authoritative ruling on the law.

The courts are reluctant to interfere in police decisions. In *Blackburn*[15] the applicant was seeking an order to compel the police to enforce the law against illegal gaming in London. The Divisional Court, while accepting that the Commissioner was ultimately answerable to the law, stated a doctrine of constabulary independence from democratic control which went well beyond precedent[16]:

> "No minister of the Crown can tell [the Commissioner] that he must, or must not, keep observation on this place or that; or that he must, or must not, prosecute this man or that one. Nor can any police authority tell him so. The responsibility for law enforcement lies on him. He is answerable to the law and to the law alone."[17]

The court's conclusion was that the Commissioner exercised a discretion as to operational matters and so long as he stayed within the broad parameters of that discretion, the court would not interfere. Those parameters would include a decision not to prosecute for attempted suicide or for sex with girls under 16 but, apparently, a decision not to prosecute for thefts under a certain value would not be included. As Lustgarten says, "Why?"

Mr Blackburn was not yet beaten. In *Blackburn No. 3*,[18] he sought an order to ensure that the Metropolitan Police enforced the Obscene Publication Acts. Again the court decided that it would not normally interfere in the exercise of a chief officer's discretion. This approach can also be seen in *Ex p. CEGB*[19] where the applicant sought mandamus against the Chief Constable who had refused to order his officers to clear a site of demonstrators protesting peacefully and with the landowner's consent in order to prevent a survey of the land for a planned nuclear power station. The court stated what the police powers were in such a situation and clearly felt that they should be exercised but refused to order the Chief Constable to exercise them.

[14] For an introductory account of the court and its powers, see Spencer J., *Jackson's Machinery of Justice* (8th ed., 1989) p. 48ff.; de Smith S. and Brazier R., *Constitutional and Administrative Law* (6th ed., 1989) Chap. 30.

[15] *R. v. Metropolitan Police Commissioner, ex p. Blackburn* [1968] 2 Q.B. 118.

[16] e.g. *Fisher v. Oldham Corporation* [1930] 2 K.B. 364.

[17] *per* Lord Denning at p. 136. For a compelling and destructive analysis of errors of law and logic contained in this judgment, see Lustgarten, *op. cit.*, pp. 64–65.

[18] [1973] Q.B. 241.

[19] *R. v. Chief Constable of Devon and Cornwall, ex p. Central Electricity Generating Board* [1981] 3 W.L.R. 961. It is also a clear expression not only of the chief officers' discretion but also that of the individual constable—he or she can be ordered to a particular site but could not be told to "Arrest that man!". That discretion to arrest is granted by statute and cannot be taken away by superior officers.

But the court will review the substance of the policy complained of—in *Ex p. Levy*,[20] after riots in Toxteth, the Chief Constable had instructed officers not to enter that area of Liverpool in police vehicles. The applicant had had property stolen and the thieves were being pursued by a police car which stopped at the border. Although resolved on different issues, Watkins L.J. concluded that the policy was in line with Scarman recommendations on inner city policing and decided that the Chief Constable of Merseyside was justified in issuing the instructions.

2.6.3 *Relations with the Crown Prosecution Service*

After investigation, the initial decision whether to charge a suspect lies with the police. There are a range of dispositions—the police could decide to take no further action or to issue an informal caution. Research suggests that no further action was taken in about 26 per cent of cases of arrested adults and that a caution was issued in 14 per cent of such cases.[21] There is no further scrutiny of police decisions not to prosecute.

If the decision is to prosecute,[22] the file will be sent to the Crown Prosecution Service (CPS) who will review that decision. When the CPS was set up in 1985, they were given the power to discontinue prosecutions[23] without further reference to the police. The Code for Crown Prosecutors[24] sets out the evidential and public interest criteria on which continuance or discontinuance may be based.

How effective a check the CPS is on police decisions is moot. Discontinuance of evidentially weak cases or those where there has been a breach of the PACE Codes of Conduct might lead the police to consider methods of disposal other than prosecution. Alternatively they might review their investigative and interrogation procedures to prevent the difficulties re-occurring.

The advent of the CPS was expected to lead to consistent application of national guidelines in relation to prosecutions. Patterns of prosecution as opposed to caution still vary across forces.[25] Sanders has argued[26] that the CPS are ill-placed to judge the propriety of individual prosecutions and whether such prosecutions are in the public interest. But it remains CPS responsibility and yet the CPS seem too willing to defer to the police on matters of policy.[27] Apart from discontinuance, the CPS possesses no effective sanctions, either for breaches of the Codes or for ill-considered prosecutions.

An alternative view is that the CPS will not be content to be the subordinate

---

[20] *The Times*, December 18, 1985.

[21] McConville M., Sanders A. and Leng R., *The Case for the Prosecution* (1991), p. 104.

[22] Such a decision might also be the subject of judicial review. *R. v. Chief Constable of Kent, ex p. L.* [1993] 1 All E.R. 756.

[23] Prosecution of Offences Act 1985, s. 23.

[24] *The Code for Crown Prosecutors* (CPS June 1994)—it is also published in the CPS Annual Reports. For further discussion of the discretion to prosecute, see *infra*, para. 4.8.

[25] Only 10% of those adult males found guilty of or cautioned for an indictable offence are cautioned in Lincolnshire, whereas 34% are cautioned in Devon—*Criminal Statistics 1993* Cm. 2680, Tables 5.4–5.7, p. 104 ff.

[26] Sanders A., "Controlling the Discretion of the Individual Officer" in Reiner and Spencer, (eds.) (1993), *op. cit.*, p. 96 ff.

[27] McConville *et al.* (1991), *op. cit.*, p. 142.

partner in the criminal justice system, occupying an obscure space between the police and the courts. The 1985 legislation does not define the relationship with the police but the power to discontinue prosecutions is significant. A more active CPS, requiring further and better investigation or demanding equal status with the police in laying down policy guidelines for prosecutions, is a viable scenario. It is a role that prosecutors have adopted in other European jurisdictions.[28] Regrettably the Royal Commission on Criminal Justice had the opportunity to define and clarify the relationship between the CPS and the police but their Report merely suggests that the police should seek CPS advice in a greater number of cases in accordance with guidelines to be agreed between the two services.[29] To that extent, the possibility of the CPS acting as an effective check on police decisions seems to have been shelved for the immediate future.

2.6.4 *Local Police Authorities*[30]

The central plank of police accountability is the so-called tripartite structure, the three-cornered relationship between the Chief Constable, the Home Office and the LPA. Under the 1964 Police Act, local government was given some say in the management of the local police force through the creation of the "local police authorities", replacing the Watch Committees and Joint Standing Committees. The composition of an LPA was two-thirds local councillors and one-third magistrates.[31] Under the provisions of the Police and Magistrates' Courts Act, the composition of the new police authorities will normally be 17 with 9 members from the relevant councils, 3 local magistrates and 5 independent members appointed by the Home Secretary.

There will still be differing forms of LPA:

(a) in London, there is no local input and the Commissioner of the Metropolitan force is directly responsible under the Metropolitan Police Act 1829 to the Home Secretary. The City of London police have the Common Council of the City of London as their police authority. There were plans to end this 160 year old anomaly and create a London police authority. However, the Police and Magistrates' Courts Act does not include provisions for this but there will be a non-statutory 12 member advisory body.[32]

(b) the standard model will be found in the provinces where the force is based on a county or group of counties (such as Devon and Cornwall

---

[28] See Downes D., *Contrasts in Tolerance* (1988), p. 13 for contrast with Dutch prosecutors. *infra*, para. 4.2.
[29] Royal Commission on Criminal Justice, *op. cit.*, para. 5.18.
[30] On LPAs, see Lustgarten, *op. cit.*, Chap. 6; Reiner, (1992), *op. cit.*, Chap. 6. Newburn T. *et al.*, Democracy and Policing (1994).
[31] The presence of magistrates is described by Lustgarten (p. 80) as an "indefensible anachronism". Critics of the legislation in 1888 (which set up joint standing committees with half the members being magistrates) and in 1964 suggest that the main motive for the inclusion of J.P's was the distrust of elected members. In 1994, the move in the Police and Magistrates Courts Act towards Home Office appointees on LPAs attracts the same criticism, especially in the light of the very few local authorities under Conservative leadership.
[32] *The Guardian*, December 18, 1994, p. 9.

or Thames Valley). The LPA was a sub-committee of the county council, consisting of county councillors and magistrates. But although questions could be put[33] in the full council, that latter body had very little power to interfere with LPA decisions, except on financial matters. Where the authority was combined between a group of counties, that political accountability was reduced still further. That accountability is now further diminished—under the Police and Magistrates' Courts Act 1994, an LPA will become autonomous, a "body corporate"[34] with fewer responsibilities to the full council and greater financial powers.[35]

(c) In 1985, many metropolitan councils (as in London or Manchester) were abolished and district councils set up in their place.[36] The LPA for such areas will remain a joint board[37] comprised of nominees of the local councils. The budget and establishment has to be approved by the Home Secretary.

The present powers of LPAs have proved quite limited—under section 5 of the Police Act 1964, the Chief Constable is given "direction and control" of the force while under section 4[38] the LPA is responsible for the maintenance of an "efficient and effective" force. Those terms were undefined and until the 1970s, LPAs were quiescent about their powers.

The LPA and the relevant council are responsible for the amount spent on local policing. However 51 per cent of the cost is met from central government—indeed the remainder also attracts rate support grant. Thus for every pound of local money spent on policing, approximately three will be spent by central government. Lustgarten points out that it is probable that this stimulates a permissive attitude towards policing costs.[39] The exent to which the LPA can make significant decisions on finance is very limited—police pay and pensions comprise some 85 per cent of expenditure and these do not require council or LPA approval.[40] Of the residue, the budget may simply represent a ceiling within which the Chief Constable operates at his discretion. Alternatively an authority might specify maxima for certain categories of expenditure or indeed require the Chief Constable to seek approval before any expenditure over a particular amount. At this point there is an obvious overlap between financial and operational policy. Certain LPAs adopted this latter approach as a tactic to enable them to debate the merits of certain expenditures—whether to purchase contentious equipment such as plastic bullets or CS gas would be examples. However even in such a case, the LPA had little power. In *ex p. Northumbria Police Authority*[41] the courts held that in exercise of prerogative powers, the Home Secretary can supply equipment to a force without the consent of the LPA.

[33] s. 11, Police Act 1964 and now s. 12, Police and Magistrates Courts Act 1994.
[34] s. 2.
[35] ss. 27–31.
[36] These metropolitan authorities were all Labour-controlled and the LPAs were active and critical of the police—Simey, *op. cit.*.
[37] Loveday B., "The New Police Authorities" in 1 *Policing and Society* (1991) 3.
[38] As amended by the Police and Magistrates' Courts Act 1994, s. 4.
[39] Lustgarten, *op. cit.*, p. 116.
[40] Police Act 1964, s. 8(1)(a).
[41] [1987] 2 All E.R. 282.

The limits of the LPA's financial control was shown during the miners' strike of 1984/85.[42] The LPAs in mining districts found that they were unable to prevent their Chief Constable from spending above the budgetary ceiling. The strategy chosen to police the dispute was to confront picket lines with equal or superior numbers of police, utilising the "mutual aid" provisions in the Police Act 1964. "Receiving" authorities found themselves faced with bills for overtime payments for officers from other forces. "Providing" authorities found that they initially had to foot the bill after their own forces had been decimated to provide assistance in other parts of the country. For many councils, this was a particular problem because it also involved local authorities in exceeding "rate-capping" levels imposed by central government and thereby attracting additional penalties. South Yorkshire's refusal to pay for billeting the officers involved in policing at the Orgreave coking plant was met with court action by the Attorney-General although further financial assistance from central government was forthcoming and the issue was never litigated. Another tactic of cutting expenditure in other areas also brought the threat of court action from the Home Office when South Yorkshire announced the abolition of its mounted police squad. What the legal basis of such an action might have been was never revealed.[43] It was a period which raised, but did not resolve, issues over the tripartite structure.

LPAs have the power to appoint senior officers.[44] However, they do so from an authorised short list drawn up by the Home Office. They may call on him to retire in "the interests of efficiency"[45] but this still requires the approval of the Home Secretary. The Chief Constable's sole duty is to present an Annual Report to the LPA and the LPA can require reports on other matters but the Chief Constable can refuse to produce such a report, if he and the Home Office thinks fit. Ultimately the LPA is unable to force the police to do anything which they are unwilling to do. However under the Police and Magistrates' Courts Act, the Chief Constable must have "regard to the local policing plan issued by the police authority".[46]

Under the Police and Magistrates' Courts Act, it is envisaged that the new authorities will be much more powerful than the old, not only producing local policing plans and objectives but acting independently of local government, able to employ, to contract for goods and services and many of the other functions of local government.[47] However, no change in the relationship between the Chief Constable and the police authorities with regard to operational matters is envisaged.

---

[42] Spencer S., *Police Authorities During the Miners' Strike* (1986); Lustgarten, *op. cit.*, pp. 118–125.

[43] Spencer, *op. cit.*, pp. 40–41.

[44] Police Act 1964, ss. 4(2) and 6(4), as amended by s. 5, Police and Magistrates' Courts Act 1994.

[45] *ibid.* s. 5(4), as amended by s. 5, Police and Magistrates' Courts Act 1994.

[46] s. 5 creates a new s. 5(2) of the Police Act 1964.

[47] See ss. 9, 10, 27–33 and Sch. 4.

2.6.5 The Home Office

In 1928, Sir Edward Troup[48] wrote:

"The central government should have complete control of the police in the seat of government. It would be intolerable that the legislature or executive should be at the mercy of a police force controlled by a municipal authority which might come into violent conflict with the national authority."[49]

Such sentiments have not changed. The decline in local influence has been matched by an accompanying shift of power to senior police officers and the Home Office. The Home Secretary has a dual role: first, he is the police authority for the Metropolitan force and, under the Metropolitan Police Act 1829, responsible for its size, the governing regulations and can order the Commissioner to undertake specific operations. In this, the Home Secretary has a formal accountability to Parliament. However, this authority over London's policing policy is not exercised on a routine basis. There is no department within the Home Office solely responsible for the Metropolitan Force and the Commissioner, with substantial consultation, is left to manage. The reasons why the Home Secretary should nowadays assume responsibility for the Metropolitan Force include the width of their national functions including royal and diplomatic protection as well as security work, the policing of national demonstrations and a range of services, both records and forensic, that are provided to other forces. However, Londoners who contribute large sums to the policing of the capital, have no democratic input into how those services are provided.[50]

The Home Secretary's other role is in regard to provincial forces under the Police Act 1964. He has the power to make regulations concerning the "government, administration and condition of service of police forces",[51] by which he is able to impose conformity and limit local autonomy. Furthermore, under section 28 it is his duty to promote police efficiency but if a force is failing to do its job, there is no residual control to take over the financial or operational management of a force.[52] However there are still powerful sanctions as the Home Secretary has the power to withhold the central government grant from forces deemed to be "inefficient" by HM Inspectorate of Constabulary.[53] In June 1992, the HMI refused to grant a certificate of efficiency to the Derbyshire force although the reason appears to have been a lack of money. The consequence appears to have been that the

---

[48] Until 1928, for 14 years the Permanent Under-Secretary in the Department.
[49] Troup E., "Police Administration, Local and National" (1928) 1 *Police Journal* 5, p. 9 (quoted in Lustgarten, *op. cit.*, p. 95).
[50] See Lustgarten, *op. cit.*, pp. 94–99 for a discussion of the possible alternatives.
[51] Police Act 1964, s. 33(1).
[52] This is unlike other public services such as education. However, under s. 15 Police and Magistrates' Court Act, the Secretary of State can direct police authorities to take such measures as he might specify when a force has been found inefficient or ineffective by the Inspectorate of Constabulary.
[53] Both the power to withhold the grant and the HMI itself were set up by the County and Borough Police Act 1856.

force's progress has been closely monitored by the county council, the LPA, Home Office and the HMI.[54]

The Home Secretary's eyes and ears are the HMI which has the statutory duty to inspect and report to the Secretary of State on the efficiency of all the police forces.[55] The form and content of the inspections has never been defined although the HMI provides guidance in the shape of 400 policy statements and 300 questions in relation to seven key areas: personnel and organisation; technology; operational performance; quality of service; community relations; complaints and discipline; counter-terrorism and war planning. Reports on individual forces have been published since 1990.[56] Each of the five inspectors (all ex-chief officers) has his own administrative staff and is attached to a particular region, not only inspecting the forces but also acting as convenor and chairman of regional conferences and promoting co-operation. Local forces are inevitably influenced by the HMI, a crucial conduit between them and central government, by which the policy concerns[57] of the Home Office are communicated as well as being the means by which the Home Office gains information on how those policy priorities are being implemented in the field.[58]

That process of communication and influence is also carried on through the Home Office's series (about 100 per year) of "advisory circulars" that it issues to forces on management, financial and operational issues. These are frequently the product of consultation between the Home Office and ACPO. LPAs are not consulted even when the advice might impinge directly on the LPAs' financial responsibilities nor do the LPAs have a right to see them nor Parliament to discuss them. One key recent document has been Circular 114/83 which applied the government's financial management initiative to the police since when, through HMI inspections, there has been a steady tightening of financial and managerial accountability. Weatheritt sees this circular as marking the beginning of the police identifying policing problems, setting themselves objectives, deploying resources to meet those objectives and reviewing performance, developing a much more "performance conscious culture" within forces.[59]

The growth of this culture has been accentuated by the entry of the Audit Commission onto the policing scene—created by the Local Government Finance Act 1982, the auditors have a brief to satisfy themselves that the resources are being used economically, efficiently and effectively. Since 1988, the Commission has published a series of studies on the police, developing performance indicators which are not simply financial but seek to identify the quality of service being provided by the police.[60]

The Home Secretary can inform himself by other means: section 30 of the Police Act 1964 allows him to require a Chief Constable to provide a report on any matter. By section 32 of the Police Act 1964 the Home Secretary is able

---

[54] Her Majesty's Inspectorate of Constabulary: *Report* (1992) HCP 1992/93 679, p. 14—the certificate was refused for a third year in 1994.
[55] s. 20, Police and Magistrates' Courts Act includes the words "and effectiveness".
[56] This will be made statutory by s. 21, Police and Magistrates' Courts Act 1994.
[57] *e.g.* the establishment of specialist drugs squads or tactical firearm units in each force.
[58] Weatheritt, *op. cit.*, p. 29.
[59] Weatheritt, *op. cit.*, pp. 25 ff.
[60] Weatheritt, *op. cit.*, p. 32.

to institute an inquiry into policing matters such as the Scarman Report into the Brixton disturbances[61] or the investigation into the brick-planting techniques of Detective Sergeant Challenor in London in the 1960s.[62]

Although the decisions on the appointment of senior officers are finally made by LPAs, the shortlist of candidates is provided by the Home Office and under section 29 the Home Secretary has to approve the dismissal of a Chief Constable but can also require it.

The Home Office also provides a range of forensic, computing and training[63] both for probationers[64] and for higher command.[65] Personnel can also be provided at a national level since section 14 of the Police Act 1964 allows the Home Secretary to order a Chief Constable to provide mutual aid.

The tripartite structure has in fact only two full partners and the extent of democratic involvement in policing policy is very limited. Despite his remarkably wide powers and influence, the Home Secretary is not responsible to Parliament for the police—he is entitled to refuse to answer parliamentary questions about provincial police forces and will also refuse to answer any questions about the Metropolitan force which are on "operational" issues. The reforms promulgated in 1994, although designed to give more power to police authorities, were also intended as a further centralising measure by replacing councillors with Home Office appointees. There seems little prospect of genuine local democratic accountability with police authorities having the power to discuss and decide operational priorities, to exercise proper financial controls, to supervise a local complaints machinery or to establish links with the HMI.

2.6.6 *Community Liaison*

Under section 106 of PACE, the LPA was responsible for making arrangements to obtain the views of local people living in the area about matters concerning local policing and for obtaining their co-operation with the police in preventing crime. This was a recommendation of the Scarman Report.[66] If the arrangements are inadequate, then the Home Secretary retains the power to require a report from the LPA. While consultative arrangements may provide a forum for local people to express their genuine feelings on crime and policing, Lustgarten points out[67] that there is a fundamental problem for democratic theory in interposing a non-elected body between the police and elected representatives.

The development of consultative committees in the 10 years since PACE seems unconvincing and they often operate as little more than talking shops

[61] Scarman (1981), *op. cit.*
[62] *Report of Inquiry by A. E. James Q.C.*, Cmnd. 2735 (1965).
[63] Under s. 23, Police and Magistrates' Courts Act, the Home Secretary cannot only provide such facilities but charge for them and compel forces to use them.
[64] Following the Audit Commission's *The Management of Police Training* (Police Paper No. 4 1989), such training has become concentrated in regional centres following a national curriculum.
[65] All those of ACPO rank will have passed through the Senior Command Course at the Police Staff College at Bramshill.
[66] Scarman (1981), *op. cit.*, paras. 5.55–5.66.
[67] Lustgarten, *op. cit.*, pp. 89 ff.

dominated by a police agenda.[68] However as police organisation stresses the base command unit as the fundamental element of policing, such consultative bodies will provide a more natural link with BCUs and a forum for the articulation of views on policing objectives and police performance in a locality. Local consultation is likely to become more significant because the 1994 legislation imposes a statutory duty on LPAs to publish key objectives for policing and local policing plans.

2.6.7 *Police Complaints Authority*

The basic machinery for investigation of complaints against the police was under section 49 of the Police Act 1964. The basic objection to that machinery was that it left the investigation and adjudication of the complaint to other police officers, often from the same force. Originally the only independent element was the Director of Public Prosecutions who had to decide whether or not an allegation of crime against an officer should be prosecuted. However there has been reform, initially through the Police Act 1976 which introduced the Police Complaints Board (PCB), an independent body which looked at all reports of investigations into complaints except those involving possible criminal charges which still went to the DPP. The Board had neither the power nor the staff to carry out its own inquiries but they could request further information and advise that disciplinary action be taken.

The system did not inspire great public confidence. A 1981 survey[69] revealed that as many as 3 per cent of respondents believed that they had been the victims of illegal police behaviour but had not made a complaint. Police resentment at the PCB died away as it became apparent that the Board almost invariably supported police disciplinary decisions. The DPP's office also gave the police little cause for concern, recommending prosecutions in only 2 per cent of the cases referred to them. Unpublished Home Office research suggested that those entrusted with investigating complaints of assault were too often concerned with the criminal guilt or untrustworthiness of the complainant.

There was further demand for an increased independent element and criticism of the requirement that all complaints had to be recorded and an investigating officer appointed. This led to a host of trivial matters being dealt with formally. In 1984 there was further reform under PACE whereby, although all complaints are recorded, an investigating officer is not appointed if it is possible to resolve the matter informally by way of explanation or apology. If it is pursued formally then an officer will be appointed, normally from the same force but from other forces if the complaint is serious, a matter of public concern or if it concerns an officer of the rank of superintendent or above. Investigations are supervised by the Police Complaints Authority (PCA), successor in title to the PCB. The powers of the PCA include approval of the investigating officer and the appointment of a supervisor from within

[68] Morgan R., "Policing by Consent—Legitimating the Doctrine" in Morgan R. and Smith D. (eds), *Coming to Terms with Policing* (1989).
[69] Tuck M. and Southgate P., *Ethnic Minorities, Crime and Policing* (Home Office Research Study No. 70), 1981.

the PCA itself. All complaints within certain categories (including death and assault) will be referred to the Authority but it also has the power to deal with other categories of complaint and indeed with matters that are not subject to complaint at all. However the ambit of the Authority still excludes[70] matters of operational policy.

The effectiveness of the PCA is still dubious.[71] Very few complaints succeed and the level of withdrawal is still high. The PCA only supervises in the most serious of cases and is in the position of evaluating the police's work on the basis of the police's own paperwork. The Authority still only publishes annual reports and not detailed reports on individual incidents. One example was the investigation into the Manchester Tactical Aid Group's operation at Manchester University Students' Union in 1985 on the occasion of the visit of Leon Brittan, then Home Secretary. There was a 15 month inquiry into 33 individual complaints and 71 general complaints. Fifty-six police officers were interviewed under caution and 700 statements taken. In 1987 an eight page summary of the report was published which revealed that only three officers were to be prosecuted, two for perjury and one for assault despite videotape evidence of officers throwing students down stone steps. The PCA's main finding was of serious management failings but the DPP prevented detailed publication claiming it would prejudice the trial of the officers. The main outcome was that the Authority's "critical view" of the affair was discussed with the two senior responsible officers! It is hard to disagree with Sanders;

> "... it is not that investigators wish to exonerate officers who 'overstep the mark' but that policing norms create 'codes of silence' which are almost impossible to penetrate and that 'the mark' is not a clear or unchanging line. It depends more on police culture and informal working rules than it does on law or official policy. Thus the complaints system will be unreformable until police culture and working rules are fundamentally changed which is not at all likely ...."[72]

---

[70] PACE, s. 84(5).
[71] Maguire M. and Corbett C., *A Study of the Police Complaints System* (1991).
[72] Sanders (1993), *op. cit.*, p. 102.

CHAPTER THREE

The Police—Crime and Investigation

3.1 CRIMEFIGHTERS

In the public imagination, the police are predominantly crime fighters, protecting the public against physical violence, burglaries, vandalism and thefts of all kinds. The police share this perception and see other activities as not proper "police" work.[1] This image of proper policing exists not only in the "canteen" culture[2] of constables but also underpins the arguments of senior officers for enhanced resources (personnel, legal powers, equipment) which quote rising crime figures and draw on the "war"[3] imagery of the "fight against crime". It is also the focus of politicians who regard clear-up rates as the key performance indicator.[4] It is a narrow philosophy of policing that affects the attitude towards the job which the ambitious junior officer will absorb.

---

[1] Punch M., "The Secret Social Service" in Holdaway S. (ed.), *The British Police* (1979).

[2] Reiner R., *The Politics of the Police* (2nd ed. 1992) Chap. 3.

[3] Such language is often employed but has little to commend it, not least because it leads to confrontation, stereotyping and depersonalising of those involved.

[4] White Paper: *Police Reform*, Cm. 2281 (1993), Chap. 7 esp. para. 7.7.

3.2 MEASURING CRIME

Our first question must be "how much crime is there?" In the nineteenth century, crime was measured through using statistics from the courts and the prisons but such figures merely reflected the activities of those institutions and not the amount of crime on the streets. Nowadays the Criminal Statistics published by the Home Office take notifiable offences recorded by the police as their source. Even these, for the reasons discussed below, are of limited value and understate the level of crime. An alternative approach recently has been to conduct victim surveys especially the British Crime Survey[5] (BCS) which surveys households rather than uses official statistics and gives a more accurate overall picture.

Recorded crime has increased steadily since the war[6] although the rate of increase slowed down in the late 1970s and again in the late 1980s.

Table 3.1 Recorded Crime 1950–1993

Year	Number of Offences	Offences per 100,000 population
1950	479,400	1,094
1955	462,300	1,040
1960	800,300	1,742
1965	1,243,500	2,598
1970	1,568,400	3,221
1975	2,105,600	4,283
1980	2,520,600	5,119
1985	3,426,400	6,885
1990	4,363,600	8,630
1993	5,317,100	10,369

This can be broken down by the type of offence and the figures for 1983 and 1993 compared with the following results[7]:

---

[5] There have been four such surveys—Home Office Research Studies Nos. 76, 85, 111 and 132.
[6] *Criminal Statistics 1993* Cm. 2680, Table 2.2, p. 38. The figures exclude criminal damage offences under £20.
[7] *Criminal Statistics 1993, op. cit.* Table 2.1 p. 37. The totals include all criminal damage.

Table 3.2 Recorded Crime by Offence Categories—1983 and 1993

Type of Offence	1983	1993	Average annual % increase 1983–93
Serious violence	6,700	18,000	10.4
Less serious violence	111,300	205,100	6.3
Rape	1,300	4,600	13.2
Indecent assault on female	10,800	17,400	4.8
Other sex offence	8,200	9,300	1.3
Robbery	22,100	57,800	10.1
Burglary	808,300	1,369,600	5.4
Theft of or from vehicle	749,900	1,523,300	7.3
Other theft or handling	956,000	1,228,600	4.9
Fraud and forgery	121,800	162,800	2.9
Arson	17,100	32,300	6.5
Other criminal damage	426,200	874,500	7.5
Drug dealing	5,000	14,800	11.5
Other	8,800	26,100	11.5
TOTAL	3,247,400	5,526,300	5.5

3.3 UNREPORTED CRIME AND UNRELIABLE STATISTICS

These official statistics reveal a pattern of crime. The media, professional groups and politicians analyse them, derive conclusions about the nature of our society and formulate policy, whether legislation, additional police resources or changes in sentencing practice. But there are important qualifications about such statistics: the majority of crime is discovered by the public who report it to the police and thus the statistics only measure the behaviour of the public in reporting offences and of the police in recording them. It does not directly measure "crime". The measurement of a "real" crime rate is probably impossible because, as will be seen below, only a relatively small proportion of incidents that could be labelled as criminal are ever reported to the police.

This hidden "dark figure" of crime contains many offences that, first, neither the public nor the police know about or, secondly, do not regard as crime or, thirdly, choose not to report or record. It is this figure that makes analysis of the criminal statistics difficult, particularly when faced with increases in recorded crime. Obviously there are some categories of offence where there is a high rate of reporting—car theft is one—and conclusions can be drawn confidently from any increase recorded in the statistics. But there are few crimes which are invariably reported and thus increases are as likely to reflect changes in reporting or recording behaviour as any increase in the actual amount of the crime. There are many reasons why people do not report an incident[8]:

  (i) although the incident is technically a crime, the individual might not share that perception. Students might not report cannabis smoking nor employees report thefts from the workplace that are seen as "perks" of the job.
 (ii) the incident might be regarded as too trivial or indeed too common— how many of us ever report road traffic offences? However even serious offences are not necessarily reported.
(iii) the police might be viewed as ineffective—the victim, aware of the low clear-up rate, might not report a domestic burglary unless there was a positive reason such as a potential insurance claim.
 (iv) the matter might be regarded as a private affair and not the business of the police. Close-knit groups (families, workplaces, schools, small communities) often choose to deal with the incident themselves.
  (v) groups might be united by race, age or class in their hostility to the police
 (vi) people might be discouraged from reporting offences where they are aware that being a witness entails a considerable degree of personal inconvenience, and sometimes personal risk.
(vii) with some crimes, such as blackmail, the sheer embarrassment for the victim might ensure the crime is never reported.

Less research has been done on the positive reasons why we report an incident. Is there a sense of civic duty and does that lie behind the proliferation of neighbourhood watch schemes? Or are we more utilitarian, looking for personal benefit? The police may be seen as protection for yourself from, say, the assault occurring again. With property offences, the report may lead to recovery of stolen property (especially with cars) or at least be a preliminary step to making an insurance claim. The rise in home ownership and in insurance cover thus leads to more reported offences.

[8] Mayhew P., *et al., The 1992 British Crime Survey* (Home Office Research Study No. 132) (1993) Chap. 3, henceforth BCS.

Just because the public choose to report an "offence", does not mean that the police will record it as such. If they decide that there is insufficient evidence that a crime has taken place, the incident may be "no-crimed". Less legitimately, if the offence is minor and there is no hope that the offender will be caught, the officer might just decide to lose the report in the wastepaper bin, a practice that aids the clear-up rate and is known as "cuffing". The BCS concluded that only 60 per cent of reported "crime" was actually recorded by the police as crime.[9]

The BCS has revealed that more offences are being reported, 50 per cent of those known to the public in 1991 compared to 36 per cent in 1981.[10] Many of these are less serious but it would be an error to assume that the Criminal Statistics record serious crime and that unreported crime is merely a mass of trivial incidents not worth the effort to report, record or investigate. First, those offences which are reported and prosecuted can be trivial: several years ago a child was tried at the Old Bailey for theft of an iced bun. To an extent, this might also be seen in the burglaries recorded in the Criminal Statistics, 25 per cent of which involve no loss of property at all and 45 per cent involve loss under £100.[11] Secondly, while the official crime figures inevitably contain much minor crime, it is clear that these figures ignore much serious crime, especially in the areas of violence against women (particularly domestic violence and sexual assault), racial assaults and white collar crime. By under-recording the amount of such crimes, it has been argued that official statistics present a skewed picture as to the real threats to property and person that we face.[12] Finally the "dark figure" contains many serious offences—the 1992 BCS found that only 40 per cent of the "most serious" assaults were reported.

The problems of using the official statistics are illustrated by looking at residential burglary involving loss— between 1972 and 1991, the Criminal Statistics revealed an increase of 189 per cent, from 166,000 to 480,000. However the data from the combined BCS/General Household Survey[13] shows a rise from 379,000 in 1972 to 612,000 in 1991, a 61 per cent increase. One explanation of such different figures would be to assume a greater willingness on the part of the public to report burglaries. In 1991, 94 per cent of burglaries involving loss are reported to the police compared with 78 per cent in 1972. There is also the spread of household contents insurance; only 19 per cent of incidents were covered by insurance in 1972 whereas the 1992 BCS figure was 58 per cent. Thus although burglaries increased, the rise was much less than suggested by official figures.

There is a second point which can be illustrated by looking at the burglary figures and by comparing the results of the BCS with the Criminal Statistics. The BCS estimated that there were 612,000 burglaries in 1991 and that the public reported 575,000 (94 per cent).[14] However in the Criminal Statistics only 480,000 (78 per cent) are recorded. How can this be? There are several

[9] BCS, *op. cit.* Table A2.6, p. 116.
[10] BCS, *op. cit.*, p. 16.
[11] *Criminal Statistics 1993, op. cit.* Table 2.18, p. 53. However the harm suffered by victims in the invasion of their home is not necessarily measurable in terms of property loss. Morgan J. and Zedner L., *Child Victims* (1992), pp. 54–55.
[12] Box S., *Power, Crime and Mystification* (1983).
[13] BCS, *op. cit.*, Chap. 4.
[14] *Criminal Statistics 1992*, Cm. 2410, Table 2B, p. 30.

explanations. First, the police might re-define the event: the victim would not know how the law distinguishes a theft from a burglary from a robbery—the police might re-classify so that if money is taken from a gas meter, it might be seen by the victim as a burglary but the police are likely to record it as theft from a dwelling. Secondly, the police might decide that there is insufficient evidence that a crime has taken place at all—the incident can be no-crimed. Finally, if it is a less serious incident, it might be ignored altogether.

The final point arising from the burglary statistics is that what appear to be dramatic increases in the level of burglaries feed anxieties about crime.[15] The fear is one of high risk (but only 4 per cent of homes are burgled in any year), of confrontation with the burglar and damage (but there are very few aggravated burglaries). The crime is normally committed by a young male (29,100 of the 50,900 males convicted or cautioned in 1992 were under 21 and 17,900 were under 17),[16] who spends little time in the house, takes property of little value, commits little damage and less violence.

3.4 THE PATTERN OF CRIME

Despite the fluctuations in the volume of crime, there remains a steady pattern in which property offences are predominant: burglary, theft, criminal damage and fraud accounted for 5.3 million or 94 per cent of offences in 1993. The increase in recorded crime between 1983 and 1993 was 2.25 million offences, 2.08 million of which were property offences, especially theft of and from cars, and shoplifting. Such figures reflect the increased opportunities for crime with 24 million vehicles on the road and the open shelves and marketing strategies of large retailers. The 1992 BCS found that 1 in 5 car-owners were victims of crime in 1991, nearly 5.5 million offences, although most were not reported to the police.[17] Despite this huge amount of recorded property crime, the figures still exclude a large amount of employee-related theft and white collar crime generally.[18]

England and Wales are relatively peaceful societies—675 offences were initially classified as homicide in 1993, a rise from 552 in 1983.[19] In the United States, New York alone has close to 2,000 killings a year.[19a] In the United Kingdom there has been a rise—in 1970, there were 7·0 homicides per million population; in 1993 there were 11.8.[20] The killer and the victim will be blood relatives, spouses, lovers or other acquaintances in 70 per cent of cases. The cause of the killing is usually a quarrel, revenge or loss of temper with only 5 per cent being in furtherance of gain.

Recorded assaults have increased by 80 per cent in the past decade although assaults frequently go unreported and the level of violent offences is much higher than that given in the official statistics. The BCS[21] suggests that there are over 0.5 million domestic assaults, 0.5 million street assaults and

---

[15] Maxfield M., *Fear of Crime* (Home Office Research Study No. 78) (1984).

[16] *Criminal Statistics 1993: op. cit.* Table 5.12 at p. 114.

[17] BCS, *op. cit.*; Light R. *et al.*, *Car Theft: The Offender's Perspective* (1993) (Home Office Research Study 130); NACRO: *Car Crime* (Briefing Paper 65, 1994).

[18] Henry S., *Informal Economy* (1978); Ditton J., *Part-Time Crime* (1977).

[19] *Criminal Statistics 1993: op. cit.*—these figures are taken from Tables 4.1–4.11, p. 76 ff.

[19a] Criminal statistics for U.S. cities can now be found on the internet—telnet sled. alaska. edu.

[20] The child under 1 year old remains most at risk—46 deaths per million.

[21] BCS, *op. cit.*, Chap. 6 for discussion of violent offences.

250,000 "muggings" a year as well as offences that were work-based, home-based and in and around pubs/clubs. Again assailant and victim were likely to be (at least) acquaintances and the most likely victim was the young (16–29) male—although women were predominantly the victims in domestic assault. However the BCS concluded that such offences had risen by only 24 per cent between 1981 and 1991, a low rate of increase and one that indicated that there was now less tolerance of domestic violence which was more likely to be reported to and recorded by the police. There were also changing perceptions about assaults at work, the number of which had doubled over the past decade. Firearms were used in 13,951 offences in 1993[22] although many of these are trivial. In 6,332 cases air weapons were used, typically for criminal damage. However, armed robberies, a category of offence which is unlikely to be under-reported,[23] rose from 1,957 in 1983 to 5,918 in 1993, with the preferred weapon being a pistol or shotgun.

The figures for rape and sexual assault are very difficult to interpret. With such a large number of unreported offences, the increase is as likely to reflect a greater willingness on the part of women to go to the police as an increase in male sexual violence. Although there has been a significant increase over the past 10 years, the vast majority of sexual attacks still go unreported, not least because the victim often finds herself victimised again. This can be through the loss of social reputation based on the "myths" of rape that "nice girls don't get raped" or that the assault must have been "victim-precipitated" because of the victim's dress or because she was in the wrong place at the wrong time. Alternatively the victim is unwilling to go through the ordeal of police investigative procedures (although these have improved with the recognition of rape trauma syndrome which have led to special investigation units for sexual assault). However women often conceal the crime rather than put themselves in the ambivalent positions of rape victims. This pattern of reporting leads to the perception of the stereotypical rape as an assault by a stranger in a public place whereas it is more likely to be committed by person known to the victim, often in the victim's home or workplace.[24] Although more mundane, this scenario indicates that men pose a more general threat of sexual assault to women than is suggested by the "official" picture of assault by the psychopathic stranger.

Drugs have been a major problem for law-enforcement agencies since the 1960s, with considerable resources devoted to preventing importation and dealing in proscribed drugs. The criminalisation of drugs has produced many unwanted side-effects, providing fertile ground for organised crime. The cost of drugs has led to many addicts financing their habit by property crime especially burglaries, auto-theft and shoplifting. There is also a serious public health risk. Such factors have led senior police officers and right wing thinkers[25] to argue that decriminalisation and regulation, as is the position with alcohol and gambling, is a more sensible policy. More humanely, legalisation could only have beneficial effects for drug-users themselves.

[22] *Criminal Statistics 1993, op. cit.*, Table 3.3, p. 66.
[23] BCS suggests only 62% of the "most serious" robberies are in fact reported—BCS, *op. cit.*, Table 3.2, p. 61.
[24] Temkin J., *Rape and Legal Process* (1987); Box, *op. cit.*, Chap. 4.
[25] Stevenson R., *Winning the War on Drugs: To Legalise or Not?* (Inst. of Economic Affairs 1994).

3.5 CRIMEFIGHTING—REACTIVITY VS PROACTIVITY

This chapter is now concerned with how the police investigate crime reports. Police tactics are essentially reactive: an offence is reported by a member of the public to the police who (resources permitting) investigate the incident and, if successful, take some form of action against the perpetrator. As a broad strategy, this has not succeeded in containing recorded crime which has increased steadily since the war. The alternative approach is proactive policing: by "proactive" is meant the gathering of intelligence, the analysis of that information and of crime patterns with the purpose of targeting of specific, "criminally-active" individuals to monitor their activities and to obtain evidence for a successful prosecution rather than "accidental" convictions of such people for offences which happen to come to police attention. Proactivity also implies strategic initiatives against particular categories of offences which are identified as problematic in a particular area.[26] Some specialist squads, for example, dealing with drugs or robberies, have adopted such an approach but overall the police still rely on the public to report crime to them. The beat officer whether on foot or in a car is unlikely to stumble across a crime in progress—it has been suggested that an officer would walk a beat for 14 years before intercepting a street robbery in progress.[27]

Under the reactive model, the police are receivers, recorders and resolvers of crime. How effective are they at this latter task? The most immediate measures are the overall crime rate and the clear-up rate. It has been said that the increase in the volume of crime is not a measure of police performance (and thereby a criticism of reactive policing) but of demand for its services.[28] Crime is discovered by the public who report offences. As the police react to such reports, the police workload is thus dictated by public demand. That demand for police services had increased to such an extent that there are now 620 crimes recorded every hour by the police in England and Wales, a 74 per cent increase since 1982.

The public dictate not only the amount of crime that comes to the attention of the police but also the type. The "dark figure" of unreported crime includes much serious crime, especially in the areas of violence against women, racial assaults and white collar crime. Demand policing is not an adequate mechanism to cope with such problems. It may be argued that reactive policing:

(a) encourages public demand for police services since reactive policing increases reporting and recording. The public have become more willing to report offences. One proposal is to give the police "ownership" of the volume of crime in order to encourage them to adopt more proactive and preventative strategies, dampening that demand.

(b) discourages the police and the public from adopting longer term,

---

[26] *e.g.* Operation Bumblebee against burglary in the Metropolitan police force area.
[27] This was the conclusion in the USA of the Presidents' Commission on Law Enforcement and the Administration of Justice.
[28] Audit Commission, *Helping With Enquiries* (Police Paper 12, 1993), p. 31.

strategic views which would involve defining "seriousness" in crime and identifying community and police priorities.

Reactive policing has not stemmed the rise in recorded crime but is it successful in the investigation and detection of crime? The yardstick is the clear-up rate but there must be caution in using this as a headline measure, not least because "detected" crime includes not merely those offences ending in caution or conviction but also those regarded as cleared-up other means such as being "taken into consideration" or admitted to by a prison inmate.

In national terms, the clear-up rate is running at 25 per cent having declined from 45 per cent in 1974[29]:

Table 3.3 Offences Cleared Up 1983 and 1993

Offence group	1983 (%)	1993 (%)
Violence	83,700 (75)	156,600 (76)
Sexual offences	14,800 (73)	23,400 (75)
Robbery	5,300 (24)	12,500 (22)
Burglary	241,100 (30)	266,400 (19)
Theft and handling	631,700 (37)	694,000 (23)
Fraud and forgery	84,500 (69)	82,900 (51)
Criminal damage	69,300 (26)	113,500 (16)
Other	12,800 (93)	39,000 (95)
TOTAL	1,143,300 (37)	1,328,200 (25)

This decline does not indicate a reduction in police efficiency. Recorded crime rose by over 70 per cent between 1982 and 1992 while the number of police officers rose by some 6 per cent. Recorded crimes per officer rose from 26 to 42 while the absolute numbers of crimes solved, as well as the number of crimes solved per officer, have increased. Thus productivity as measured by clear-ups per officer rose by 16 per cent in the period. Yet the clear-up rates do provide a measure of comparative efficiency: the Metropolitan Force clear up under 20 per cent of recorded offences whereas Greater Manchester achieves double this figure.

As a headline measure of police efficiency, the clear-up rate is very limited, failing to distinguish between the seriousness of offences (an assault can be

---

[29] *Criminal Statistics 1993, op. cit.* Table 2.8, p. 43.

life-threatening or relatively minor) or between the relative ease or difficulty of detection:

(a) the overall rate varies dramatically from offence to offence: 75 per cent of sexual and violent crime is cleared up compared with under 25 per cent of property crime. Specific offences vary widely—the clear-up rate in murder is high (95 per cent plus) as it is in shoplifting while fewer than 15 per cent of pickpocketing offences will be solved.

(b) even on a narrow basis, these figures are scarcely an adequate measure of police effectiveness. Certainly the high clear-up rate for homicides reflects the effort and resources put into such investigations but the assailant is likely to have been known to the victim. Identify the family and close friends of the victim and you have a small group probably containing the attacker. The same is true of offences of violence generally. Ease of detection also exists with shoplifting which is rarely reported unless there is an immediate suspect. High clear-up rates are more to do with the factors surrounding particular offences than with good police work. Sensible use of police resources, effective strategies or intelligent analysis of information only marginally affects crime rates at the present time.

(c) Not only do the public report crimes to the police, they are also mainly responsible for solving them. Clarke and Hough[30] have suggested that there are four categories of action which equally contribute to the clear-up rate:

   (i) where the offender is clearly identified by a witness or detained at the scene either by a member of the public or as a result of police observation.

   (ii) where the offence is cleared up by being "taken into consideration" at a subsequent court hearing. In other words, a suspect arrested for another offence admits this offence for the purpose of wiping the slate clean, at the risk of some additional punishment. Although offenders will be unlikely to ask for violent or sexual offences to be taken into consideration, nearly 40 per cent of burglaries are dealt with in this fashion. The Oxford Penal Research Unit discovered a Sheffield defendant who asked for over 1,000 other offences to be TIC'd.[31]

   (iii) where the case is resolved as a result of information from the public, usually identifying the offender.

   (iv) where the police undertake their own investigations through informants, plants, vigilance, special inquiries.

(d) the over-exposure of the "clear-up rate" in the media encourages a narrow conception of both police work of concentrating on offences after they have occurred rather than a more proactive response which emphasises liaison work in the schools and community as well as increased resources and status for crime prevention units.

[30] Clarke R. and Hough J., *The Effectiveness of Policing* (1980); McConville M., *et al.*, *The Case for the Prosecution* (1991) Table 1, p. 19.
[31] The Home Office and police now distinguish between "primary" and "secondary" clear up rates—the former being seen as a more reliable performance indicator while the latter includes TICs and offences admitted to by prison inmates.

Pauline Morris[32] suggested that an analysis of police detection methods such as that of Clarke and Hough calls into question the effectiveness of patrolling systems and of criminal investigation strategies. Changes in organisation or increasing the resources available to the police are unlikely to do more than marginally affect clearance rates. However Morris's conclusions were based on considering what refinements might be made to the traditional reactive style of police work. The arguments for more proactive and preventative police work can first be put in terms of the failures of that system:

(a) reactive policing is an inevitable part of police work but is short-term and obstructs a strategic approach to tackling crime, either in terms of volume or in terms of priorities.

(b) that short-term perspective encourages a narrow view of police work in terms of crime and inhibits a broader (although nonetheless crime-related) philosophy of policing.

(c) in reactive policing the stress is on detection of a particular incident— this is "victim friendly" so long as demand remains low and resources remain high. As demand increases, resources fail to keep pace, time devoted to any case falls, there is less detection and victim-satisfaction is reduced.

(d) as this scenario unfolds, the weaknesses of reactivity emerge—instead of dealing with all crimes, only some crimes can be allocated time. These would include the obviously serious (HOLMES inquiries) and perhaps the easily-resolved but elsewhere there are no means of identifying which offences should be investigated because there are no links with the community, no internal procedures or crime management system and no systematic storage or analysis of intelligence.

(e) as police try to react to all crime reports, this involves wasteful use of resources.[33]

Stressing investigation and detection as the primary concerns of a crime strategy means that reactive policing has encouraged the police into eschewing responsibility for the volume of crime and into failing to set priorities or allocate resources rationally. Overwhelmed by the sheer volume, it also contributes to police criticisms of, and alienation from, other criminal justice agencies. A reminder of first principles is in order:

> The principal object to be attained is the prevention of crime.
> To this great end, every effort of the police is to be directed.

In 1829, the first Commissioners of the Metropolitan Police, Rowan and Mayne, identified prevention as the core objective of the police. From this, two strategies suggest themselves: putting greater resources into crime prevention; giving greater emphasis to proactive intelligence-based approaches.

This is a strategic approach to crime and requires an integrated package of

[32] Morris P. and Heal K., *Crime Control and the Police* (Home Office Research Study No. 67), (1981).
[33] Audit Commission (1993), *op. cit.*, exhibit 15 "Response to Burglary" at p. 22.

measures, both on a local and national level.[33a] For example, the targeting of drugs importers and major suppliers can be linked to initiatives within schools as well as the phased decriminalisation of drugs. Although there will always be opportunist and casual crime for the police to react to, a proactive policing strategy as a part of an integrated approach to tackling crime has several positive attributes:

(a) it can lead to community input into priorities for prevention and prosecution,

(b) the building up of reliable information about problems, the careful analysis and constructive response to them, must be in the long term interests of policing and the community,

(c) constructive responses to crime are not necessarily arrest and prosecution, an expensive option and one that is encouraged by the reactive approach. Proactivity must involve multi-agency work with a range of local agencies—education, health, social services, planning and other council departments, victim support groups, probation and prisons.

3.6 PRE-PACE POLICE POWERS OF INVESTIGATION

The police constable is an officer whose,

"... authority is original, not delegated, and is exercised at his own discretion by virtue of his office; he is a ministerial officer exercising statutory rights independently of contract ... ."[34]

Although the nature of modern policing has made the constable's job more akin to a squaddie than this ideal of autonomy, the basic powers of a police officer still flow from the status of constable,[35] not from his or her contract of employment nor from any para-military aspects of the job. The constable is the holder of an office under the Crown, recognised by the common law, as a person lawfully invested with powers to keep the peace. Prior to 1964, the constable was under a statutory duty to obey the orders of J.P.s and Watch Committees,[36] although the local authority were not liable for his tortious acts.[37]

But the original powers of a constable to keep the peace and to intervene without judicial supervision were essentially those of a private citizen. There were no special powers for the constable and no special immunities. Nor indeed were there special powers for the state and even ministers could not authorise arrests or searches unless the legal grounds for such action existed.

[33a] Following experiments in Kent and Northumbria, the proactive model is being adopted in many forces. For the impact on organisation in the BCU, *supra*, para. 2.5.2.

[34] *Attorney-General for NSW v. Perpetual Trustee Company* [1955] A.C. 477 at 489.

[35] The powers are the same regardless of rank (except for limited exceptions under Police and Criminal Evidence Act 1984, *e.g.* s. 42 gives superintendents the power to extend periods of detention). Police ranks do not exist at common law but are created by statutory regulations—Critchley T., *A History of the Police* (1978), p. 125.

[36] Or the Joint Standing Committees with the county forces.

[37] *Fisher v. Oldham Corporation* [1930] 2 K.B. 364—nowadays the Chief Constables are liable for the torts of their officers under s. 48 of the Police Act 1964.

State necessity did not suffice.[38] The basic powers of the constable are now contained within the Police and Criminal Evidence Act 1984 (PACE) but first we will examine the common law nature and history of those powers.

3.6.1 Arrest

At common law,[39] a person is under no duty to assist the police by answering questions, providing information[40] or allowing a search of person, property or premises. Unless a person was willing to assist voluntarily, the constable would have to use powers of arrest if he wished to detain that person. A lawful arrest required that the officer possessed "reasonable suspicion" that a felony had been, was being or was about to be committed, that the officer (normally) physically touched the person to be arrested and that words indicating an arrest were spoken. The constable must also inform the accused of the grounds for arrest and a failure to do this or the giving of the wrong reason could make the arrest unlawful.[41] On lawful arrest a person's freedom of movement is curtailed. Arrest was for breach of the peace or for a felony but the constable was unable to arrest for misdemeanours unless they involved a breach of the peace which took place in the constable's own view. The officer could not arrest for assault or obtaining by false pretences but could arrest for theft of 6d.

The original purpose of arrest was to bring the offender before the courts. It was not to detain for the purposes of interrogation which was not the constable's function. The common law has never recognised the power of "detention for questioning". Arrest was thus quite a late stage in the investigative process. In 1929 the Royal Commission on Police Powers stated that a constable should not question a prisoner after arrest but should take him to a police station for formal charging.[42] Despite this, arrest soon became the mechanism for the police to hold people while further investigation and interrogation took place. This practice was approved by the House of Lords in *Mohammed-Holgate v. Duke*[43] when it was held that an officer was not acting unreasonably when arresting someone against whom there existed reasonable grounds for suspicion because it was more likely that the suspect would confess in the police station than elsewhere.

These limited powers of arrest were extended by statute, sometimes extravagantly, for example section 6 of the Vagrancy Act 1824 enabled the arrest of a suspected person in a public place while a similar wide power in section 64 of the Metropolitan Police Act 1839 gave a wide power of arrest but created no offence. By the 1970s there were some 70 statutes detailing powers of arrest. The general power of arrest was codified by section 2 of the Criminal Law Act 1967. This statute also abolished the categories of felonies and misdemeanours and created a broad category of "arrestable offence". A lawful arrest without a warrant required that the police had to have

---

[38] *Entick v. Carrington* (1765) 19 State Tr. 1029.
[39] For the development of police powers, Leigh L., *Police Powers* (2nd ed., 1985), Chap. 2.
[40] Nowadays there are statutory obligations to provide information in relation to road traffic offences, terrorism and serious fraud.
[41] *Christie v. Leachinsky* [1947] A.C. 573.
[42] Royal Commission on Police Powers and Procedures: *Report* (1929), Cmd. 3297, para. 137.
[43] [1984] A.C. 437.

reasonable suspicion that the suspect had committed an arrestable offence (basically one which carried a maximum sentence of five years imprisonment or more) or that the statute creating the offence gave a power of arrest. This has now been replaced by sections 24–25 of PACE.

3.6.2. *Search of Persons and Premises*

At common law, this was very limited. A search of the person could only take place on arrest. There was no general power for a constable to detain a person temporarily for the purpose of a search, although again there were some statutory exceptions. Under section 66 of the Metropolitan Police Act 1839, a constable could stop and search a person believed to be in possession of stolen property and there are similar powers under the Misuse of Drugs Act 1971.[44]

The power to enter and search premises was also restricted.[45] If a constable made an arrest, then the premises immediately under control of the suspect could be searched. In almost all other cases, a magistrates' warrant made under the relevant statute[46] was required although some statutes permitted entry and search on the authority of senior police officers.[47] Even then, the police could only search for the property specified in the warrant. A warrant to search for stolen goods could not justify a general rummage through the filing cabinets. Those statutory powers regarding the issue and execution of warrants must now be exercised in accordance with sections 15–23 of PACE.

3.6.3 *Detention and Interrogation*

The supervisory role of J.P.s over the issuing of warrants is a relic of a period when J.P.s played a much wider role in the administration of criminal justice than their purely judicial role today. They interrogated suspects and made decisions as to whether to discharge, release on bail or remand to prison. From the Summary Jurisdiction Act 1848, their supervision of investigation was restricted. This change of role may have been responsible for the considerable uncertainty, not to say hostility, with which nineteenth-century judges regarded police powers to detain and to question suspects. Judges took divergent attitudes towards statements made to the police while in police custody, some happy to admit such statements as evidence while others excluded them. Generally arrest signalled the end of police interrogation. The courts sought to limit the police powers of interrogation and insisted that a suspect should be taken before a magistrate with all speed, normally within 24 hours.

Eventually it was the judges themselves who took the initiative to resolve this uncertainty by issuing the "Judges' Rules" in 1912 to regulate police procedure over the treatment of detained persons. Although these Rules had

---

[44] There is a list in Annex A to the Code of Practice A which details statutory stop and search powers.
[45] Leigh, *op. cit.*, pp. 199–201.
[46] For a list, see Leigh, *op. cit.*, Appendix p. 288.
[47] *e.g.* Licensing Act 1964, s. 45 (to inspect premises); Official Secrets Act 1911, s. 9 (on suspicion that an offence is about to be committed) and Prevention of Terrorism Act 1984, Sched. 3, Part III, para. 4 (to search for evidence justifying an exclusion order).

neither the authority of common law nor of statute and thus in legal theory possessed no legal force, they remained as influential guidelines until 1984 and a basis for the courts to decide on whether to admit incriminating statements into evidence. Originally they prohibited police questioning after arrest, still reflecting the nineteenth century distrust of the "new" policing arrangements. It was not until the revision of the Rules in 1964 that the police power to question while the suspect was in custody was recognised. However by the 1960s, the judicial attitude towards breaches of the Rules had become very permissive—rarely did police misconduct lead to the exclusion of the evidence.[48] By the 1970s, although police powers appeared quite restricted as a matter of law, in practice they were relatively wide: the power to stop, search and question on the streets was exercised de facto; premises were often searched without the "technicality" of a warrant; people "assisted the police with their enquiries" at police stations (although the courts did not recognise the legal concept of "detention for questioning"); suspects were held for extended periods without access to legal advice. The Judges Rules provided no barrier to miscarriages of justice and many of the most notorious cases date from this period.[49]

3.7 THE PACE OF REFORM

There is now a single statute, namely the Police and Criminal Evidence Act 1984 (PACE), which codifies pre-trial procedures including the powers of the police to stop people, search them, arrest them, hold them in police custody and interrogate them. It also lays down the suspects' privileges. The statute's history was tortuous.[50] The need for reform had been recognised for many years but the spark came in Catford, South London in April 1977 where Confait, a homosexual, was found strangled with electric flex in a burning house. Three boys (fourteen, fifteen and eighteen and in one case, educationally subnormal) were arrested, interrogated and, as a result of their confessions, charged with murder. Three years later, they were all released after the Fisher Report concluded that they had nothing to do with the killing.[51]

The Labour government set up the Royal Commission on Criminal Procedure (RCCP) to examine police procedures. The establishment of the Commission was claimed as a victory for civil liberty groups but it rapidly became apparent that the most coherent evidence and proposals were coming from the police and Home Office. The Police Federation and ACPO were able to alter the Commission's focus, away from the abuses of police powers and onto the artificial restrictions on those powers that were alleged to hamper the police's fight against the rising crime rates.[52] It was an argument that was to find favour with the new Conservative administration.

[48] See *Jeffrey v. Black* [1978] Q.B. 490 where evidence resulting from an illegal search was admitted.
[49] Stefan Kiszko, Judith Ward, the Maguires, the Guildford Four and the Birmingham Six were all 1970s investigations.
[50] de Gama K., "Police Process and Public Prosecutions: Winning by Appearing to Lose" 15 Int.J.Soc. Law (1988) 339.
[51] Fisher Sir H., *The Confait Case: Report* HCP 1977/78 90.
[52] There is no evidence that changes in police powers affect crime rates in any way.

3.8 POST-PACE POLICE POWERS[53]

The recommendations in the Commission's Report[54] were presented as balancing the "interests of the community" (sufficient police powers to tackle the crime problem) with the "liberties of the individual" (providing safeguards for suspects in the police station). The left-wing libertarian commentators[55] criticised the Report and the subsequent Act as unjustifiably extending police powers, especially in the areas of stop and search, arrest and detention at the police station. The critics were answered:

    (a) the old rules were never adhered to as people were stopped and searched on the street or detained at the station for excessive periods. This could not be eradicated and thus it was better to legalise the old (mal)practices and to regulate their exercise, mainly by compelling adherence to the Codes of Practice.[56] Although this argument has its merits in relation to low-visibility, street searches, it does not justify the extension of powers of detention in a police station, where abuses were very visible and easily controllable.

    (b) the new powers would affect very few people. Few people are detained for longer than two or three hours, although stop and search powers have affected hundreds of thousands. However it is strange to see central values of criminal justice, in relation to powers of detention, disposed of by a statistical rather than an ethical argument.

    (c) there were new controls especially upon the custody officer and documentation procedures, tape-recording of interviews, access to legal advice, a duty solicitor scheme, an independent prosecution service and a revamped Police Complaints Authority. But the imperative for such controls came about because of the abuse of the old powers and such safeguards were not in themselves justification for new powers. Since the implementation of PACE, the police have fought a campaign to reduce the effectiveness of these new protections, especially on the issue of the right to silence but also on the more mundane ground that they involve excessive bureaucracy.

Prior to PACE, there were no obvious gaps in police powers, the filling of which would significantly affect crime rates. Although clarification and codification of those powers was undoubtedly long overdue (as were the safeguards on provisions of legal advice, proper monitoring of interviews, etc.), the fight for the extension of those powers was more symbolic than instrumental, charting the status and authority of the police rather than any demonstrable effect on the incidence of crime.

[53] For a detailed account of police powers, see Bevan V. and Lidstone K., *The Investigation of Crime* (1991) or Leigh, *op. cit.*

[54] Royal Commission on Criminal Procedure: *Report* (1981) Cmnd. 8092.

[55] Opposition was widespread especially amongst groups such as the GLC's Police Committe— Christian L., *Policing by Coercion* (1983).

[56] There are five statutory Codes promulgated under s. 66 of PACE. They do not bind the courts nor do breaches automatically lead to disciplinary action for the officer involved. However, as will be seen, used in combination with s. 78, breaches of the Code have been treated by the courts as justification to exclude evidence.

3.8.1 Stop and Search[57]

Prior to 1984, over most of the country,[58] the police had no power to stop pedestrians in order to question them or to search them. Indeed if they sought to do so, they might easily find themselves sued for assault.[59] The police argued that this power was important for crime detection since possession of prohibited articles could only be detected by such a measure.[60] Despite studies which suggested that existing stop and search powers were already being used arbitrarily and with limited success,[61] section 1 of PACE provided a general power that the police could, on reasonable suspicion that any person or vehicle was carrying stolen goods or other prohibited items, stop that person or vehicle and conduct a desultory search (checking pockets, looking in bags, etc). There are also such powers under other statutes such as the Sporting Events Act 1985.[62]

The concept of reasonable suspicion is the key element in the exercise of these powers.[63] The Code of Practice,[64] outlining how these powers should be exercised, does not define it positively but does seek to prevent officers from exercising their powers on the basis of ethnicity, age or clothing. An officer should be able to identify an objective basis for the stop which should not include a refusal to answer questions but would include attempting to run away. The courts have not addressed this directly but have accepted a low minimum threshold for the definition of a similar ambiguous phrase in other areas.[65]

The decision to stop is often based on the officer's own informal norms, the three most important of which are; first, previous convictions known to the officer, secondly, the maintenance of order and of police authority and finally general suspiciousness, being in the wrong place at the wrong time.[66] Officers rely on instinct and this can lead to class and race bias[67] in making stops and in turn, that can lead to a group's perception that they are harassed by officers.

Searches must be recorded[68] and be available to a suspect on request unless they are "voluntary". Forces publish statistics for such searches in their annual reports. In 1990, there were 256,900, with 39,200 (15 per cent) of

[57] Leigh, op. cit., pp.154–163.
[58] For Londoners, there was such a power under s. 66 of the Metropolitan Police Act 1839.
[59] Where the person resisted, was arrested and charged with assault on a constable, frequently the court had to decide whether that officer was acting outside the execution of his or her duty—Collins v. Wilcock [1984] 3 All E.R. 374.
[60] The effectiveness of such measures was demonstrated in Willis C., The Use, Effectiveness and Impact of Police Stop and Search Powers (HMSO 1983) (Home Office Research and Planning Unit Paper No. 15).
[61] Smith D. and Gray J., Police and People in London (PSI 1983) Chap. XI.
[62] s. 7—for a full list, see Code of Practice A, Annex.
[63] See Bevan and Lidstone, op. cit., Chap. 2 for a helpful discussion.
[64] Code of Practice A—for the exercise by police officers of statutory powers of stop and search.
[65] See Ward v. Chief Constable of Avon and Somerset Constabulary, The Times, June 26, 1986.
[66] Sanders A., "Controlling the Discretion of the Individual Officer" in Reiner R. and Spencer S. (eds), Accountable Policing (1993), p. 83.
[67] Smith and Gray, op. cit.
[68] ss. 3 and 5.

these resulting in arrests.[69] Research suggests that policing practice before and after PACE has changed little,[70] and that there is little supervision of the individual officer's discretion either by superiors or by the courts.[71]

The stop and search provisions have been broadened by section 60 of the Criminal Justice and Public Order Act so that a superintendent, believing that serious violence is likely in an area, can authorise officers to stop and search persons and vehicles regardless of whether the officer has any grounds for that search.

3.8.2 *Road Blocks*

Prior to 1984, this was an area of uncertainty: although section 163 of the Road Traffic Act 1988 gave a constable power to require a vehicle to stop, there was considerable doubt as to whether this could be exercised for purposes other than those under the Road Traffic Act itself. There may also have been a general common law power to detain vehicles, deriving from a constable's general duty to prevent crime.[72] However any such doubts were resolved by section 1 of PACE which entitled a constable in uniform to stop and search vehicles and section 4 which gives the police, for the first time, statutory powers to conduct road blocks.

An officer of superintendent rank or above may authorise a road block if there are reasonable grounds to believe that it will lead to:

  (i) the apprehension of a person who has committed a serious arrestable offence—a bank robbery might justify setting up checks on all exits from the scene

or

  (ii) the apprehension of someone who is about to commit such an offence—targeting drug dealers in an area could lead to wide-scale checks especially since vehicles may be stopped using "any criterion" (section 4(2))

or

  (iii) the tracing of witnesses to such an offence—a murder might be followed by a road check at the same time and place a week later

or

  (iv) the detention of someone unlawfully at large.

Between 1986–90 the police mounted 1,545 road blocks, detaining several hundred thousand people. This produced 331 arrests, 159 (48 per cent) of which were unconnected with the reasons for setting up the road block[73]:

---

[69] Research suggests that PACE has not really affected previous informal police practice— Skogan W., *The Police and Public in England and Wales* (Home Office Research Study No. 117) (1990).

[70] Smith and Gray, *op. cit.*; McConville M., Sanders A. and Leng R., *The Case for the Prosecution* (1991).

[71] Sanders, (1993), *op. cit.*, p. 87 suggests that to impose more controls in an area of low visibility policing would have negative effects.

[72] *Steel v. Goacher* [1983] R.T.R. 98.

[73] Home Office Statistical Bulletin 14/91.

Table 3.4 Road Blocks by Reason and Result 1986–1990

Year	No. checks	Reason i)	Reason ii)	Reason iii)	Reason iv)	Arrest Link	Arrest No Link
1986	377	195	24	148	26	34	30
1987	349	178	25	116	54	36	42
1988	294	153	19	103	39	52	27
1989	227	96	11	84	39	32	27
1990	298	167	15	97	22	18	33

Under section 65 of the Criminal Justice and Public Order Act, an officer can stop anyone on their way to a "rave" and direct them not to proceed. Similar powers exist under section 71 in relation to trespassory assemblies which may include the Druids at Stonehenge or hunt saboteurs. This draconian power can be exercised within five miles of the rave or assembly.

3.8.3. *Searching Suspects*

The power to search suspects on arrest is provided for under section 32 of PACE: a constable may search an arrested person at a place other than a police station if there are reasonable grounds for believing there might be evidence or anything that might assist escape or present a danger. The constable can also enter and search the premises where the accused was at the time or immediately before the arrest.[74] But once the suspect is at the police station, the power to search has been removed by section 53, and such searches of detained persons must be carried out by the custody officer[75] under the provisions of section 54 and the relevant Code of Practice.[76] The custody officer must ascertain what personal property the person possesses and to that end may search him or her, including a strip search if deemed necessary but the search must be carried out by someone of the same sex. The custody officer may withhold any evidence of crime and also any personal effects if the officer believes that the person might cause harm with them. The details of the property will be entered on the custody record as well as the reason for withholding any item.

In a further extension of police powers, sections 55 and 62 of PACE confer the right to conduct intimate searches and also to take intimate samples (including blood, saliva or semen) from a suspect. The intimate search (of body orifices) requires the authorisation of a superintendent who must have reasonable grounds for believing that a weapon or drug is concealed. Only qualified doctors or nurses can carry out the search.

[74] PACE s. 32(2)(b).
[75] The functions of the custody officer are explained *infra*, para. 3.8.6.
[76] Code C 4.

Intimate samples can be taken from a suspect but only with consent in writing under the provisions of section 62[77]—a refusal to consent allows a court or jury to draw inferences which may be used as evidence against that person.[78] Non-intimate samples such as hair or nail clippings can be taken from a suspect compulsorily under section 63 although again it must be authorised by a superintendent in writing and recorded on the custody record.

3.8.4 *Searching Premises for Evidence*[79]

Part II of PACE (sections 8–18)[80] provides the police with statutory powers to enter and search premises[81] for evidence. These powers can either be executed with or without a warrant; prior to PACE, only a small proportion (17 per cent) of searches were carried out under magisterial warrant[82] and post-PACE research suggests that the effect of sections 18 and 32 has reduced this to 12 per cent.[83] Searches of premises are governed by the Code of Practice[84] which states that searches should be made at a reasonable time, that only reasonable force should be used and that due consideration for the property and privacy of the occupier should be shown. The extent to which these standards are observed might be doubted by those accustomed to news footage of Operation Bumblebee[85] where the images of the sledgehammer through the door at 6 a.m., accompanied by TV cameras to record a bemused youth in boxer shorts, are scarcely conducive to the dignity of the individual.

A search of premises without a warrant can be based either on the consent of the occupier or on statutory powers. The police to a large extent rely on consent which need not be that of the owner but can be that of an occupier, including a squatter or a child of the family but probably not that of a mere visitor. The officer should explain the reason for the search and get the consent in writing, if that is practicable.[86] The advantage of consent is that it is not hedged in with the restrictions of the statutory powers and once a police officer is lawfully on any premises, then under section 19 of PACE, he or she is able to seize and retain any item that is evidence of a crime.[87]

Where no consent exists, a police constable in uniform has a wide power under section 17 to enter and search without warrant for various purposes; to execute a warrant of arrest; to make an arrest without warrant; to capture a person unlawfully at large; to protect people from serious injury or prevent

---

[77] Code D 5—these provisions will also apply to people not in custody under ss. 54 and 55 Criminal Justice and Public Order Act 1994.
[78] *Smith, The Times*, May 20, 1985, s. 62(10) Criminal Justice and Public Order Act 1994.
[79] For a detailed review, see Bevan and Lidstone, *op. cit.*, Chap. 4.
[80] As well as the Code of Practice B.
[81] "Any place" is the definition in s. 23 which seems sufficiently broad.
[82] Royal Commission on Criminal Procedure, *op. cit.*—supplementary volume on Law and Procedure Appendix 7.
[83] Bevan and Lidstone, *op. cit.*, 4.07.
[84] Code B 5.
[85] A proactive campaign by the Metropolitan Force against residential burglars in the early 1990s.
[86] Code B 4.
[87] ss. 19–23 spell out the broad powers that the police possess to seize and retain evidence. *Quaere* whether they can also retain goods with a view to returning them to their rightful owner—*West Mercia Constabulary v. Wagener* [1982] 1 W.L.R. 127.

serious property damage. Although other common law powers are abolished, the power to enter and remain on premises "to deal with or prevent a breach of the peace" is retained.[88] This is based on *Thomas v. Sawkins*[89] where police entered and forcibly remained in a hall where a political meeting was taking place. The police argument was that they had reasonable apprehension of a breach of the peace based on their experience of previous similar meetings. Thus in domestic disputes, an officer could lawfully remain in the house even where the occupier insists he or she leave.[90]

Under section 18, after an arrest for an arrestable offence, an officer can lawfully search premises occupied or controlled by the suspect if he or she reasonably suspects that there is evidence of the immediate offence or other offences on the premises. This can be done immediately[91] without authorisation but if it is delayed, then the search must be authorised and recorded in writing by an inspector or above.[92]

Under section 32, after an arrest for an arrestable offence, an officer can lawfully enter and search premises in which the person was when arrested or immediately before he or she was arrested[93] if the constable reasonably suspects that there is evidence relating to the offence in question on the premises. This should be done close to the point of arrest[94] although section 18 powers do provide a fallback.

The powers for justices of the peace to issue search warrants are contained in PACE (sections 8–16) as well as in other statutes. An application is made in writing to the magistrate by a constable. It is *ex parte*—that is, there is no right for the owner or occupier of the premises to be notified of, or to be present at, the application. Under section 15, the constable must state the grounds of the application, the premises to be searched and the articles being sought. The magistrate must act in a judicial manner and consider whether the evidence does show reasonable cause that a serious arrestable offence has been committed and that there is material[95] on the premises that is likely to be evidence in the investigation of the offence.[96] The magistrate must also be satisfied that entry by warrant is necessary to ensure access to the evidence.[97] Although there are procedures to ensure the reliability of the information,[98] there are still suspicions that warrants are too easily obtained with the standard formula "... as a result of information received from a previously reliable source ..." being too hastily accepted by the magistrate.[99]

---

[88] s. 17(6).
[89] [1935] 2 K.B. 249; Goodhart A.L., "*Thomas v. Sawkins*, A Constitutional Innovation" 6 Camb.L.J. 22 (1936–38).
[90] *Lamb v. DPP* (1989) 154 J.P. 381.
[91] s. 18(5) but the officer must later inform his inspector who shall make a record of the search.
[92] s. 18(4) and (7).
[93] s. 32(2)(b).
[94] *R. v. Badham* [1987] Crim.L.R. 202.
[95] Not being items subject to legal privilege, excluded material or special procedure material— s. 8(1)(c); Bevan and Lidstone, *op. cit.*, 4.51–4.78.
[96] s. 8(1)(a) to (e).
[97] s. 8(3)(a) to (e).
[98] Code B 2; Leigh, *op. cit.*, pp. 210–211.
[99] Bevan and Lidstone, *op. cit.*, pp. 99–100.

3.8.5 *Powers of Arrest*

Arrest, "the beginning of imprisonment", can be either under warrant from a magistrate[1] or without a warrant. Under PACE, the traditional requirements for a lawful arrest still apply: first, that it requires "reasonable suspicion" that an arrestable offence has been, is being or is about to be committed; secondly, that there is a physical touching of the person to be arrested; thirdly, this is accompanied by words indicating an arrest which can be colloquial ("You're nicked."). However section 28 of PACE makes it clear that not only must the suspect be informed of the fact of arrest but also the grounds for arrest either immediately or as soon as practicable. A failure to do this or the giving of the wrong reason can make the arrest unlawful.[2] Reasonable force can be used under section 3 of the Criminal Law Act 1967 and this depends on such factors as the nature of the suspect's reaction, the gravity of the offence and the possibility of effecting the arrest by other means.[3]

There are now three categories of arrest without warrant[4]:

(a) the first or summary arrest power comes under section 24 which largely codifies the earlier law relating to arrestable offences so that an officer can arrest where there are reasonable grounds for believing that such an offence has taken place and that the suspect has committed it. Arrestable offences in essence[5] are those for which a previously unconvicted offender over 21 could be sentenced to imprisonment for five years or more.

(b) the second or general arrest power is provided for by section 25 which gives a wider power of arrest for all criminal offences whether they are arrestable or not but where process through service of a summons is deemed inappropriate or impracticable. Section 25(3) specifies the "general arrest conditions" any of which can be satisfied—for example, the police officer doubts that the suspect has given his correct identification or address.

(c) the third category is under section 26 which repeals all statutory powers of arrest except those expressly preserved.[6] These are situations where a power of summary arrest is thought necessary and the approach through the general arrest conditions of section 25 inappropriate.

PACE did not abolish existing common law powers of arrest—this means that a fourth category, the power to arrest for breach of the peace still exists.[7]

[1] Especially under s. 1 Magistrates' Court Act 1980 and this can be for any offence—see Leigh, *op. cit.*, p. 91.
[2] *Christie v. Leachinsky* [1947] A.C. 573.
[3] See discussion *supra*, para. 2.5.4.
[4] See Bevan and Lidstone, *op. cit.*, 5.06 for a detailed description of arrest powers.
[5] s. 24 includes some specially listed offences where the penalty is less.
[6] Police and Criminal Evidence Act 1984, Sched. 2. These have been extended by the Criminal Justice and Public Order Act 1994 so that a constable is able, under certain conditions, to arrest ravers, squatters, hunt saboteurs and druids, without warrant. See ss. 65(5), 69(5), 71(4), and 73(6).
[7] *DPP v. Orum* [1989] 1 W.L.R. 88; *Howell* [1982] Q.B. 416 for a definition of breach of the

There is no substantive offence of breach of the peace[8] but a person may be taken in front of a magistrates' court and be bound over to keep the peace.[9]

Whether PACE simplified the law of arrest is moot. But the police still rely heavily on this power, not as a prelude to charging necessarily but as a technique of investigation. In 1986 1.37 million people were arrested. By 1988 this had increased to 1.44 million—about 33 per cent of those arrested are released without charge. The decision to arrest, as with stop-and-search powers, is low-visibility and the law is sufficiently vague and flexible to allow an officer considerable discretion using police criteria which are not necessarily legally relevant ones.[10] Factors such as previous involvement with the police, not recognising police authority[11] or general lifestyle will be significant. Such powers are "not exercised randomly or representatively across society"[12] and it is the young adult working class male, frequently black, that is the likeliest object of police attention. That in turn means that that group is more likely to be charged, prosecuted, convicted and imprisoned than other sections of society although crime is widely spread across age, gender, class and race.[13]

3.8.6 *Powers of Detention*

Arrest is the power to detain a person against their will. In origin it was the step immediately before charging and bringing before a court. That is no longer the case. Although the Royal Commission in 1981 recommended that a person should only be detained when it was "necessary",[14] that threshold was never incorporated into law and is ignored by the police who regard arrest and detention as a prelude to gaining supplementary evidence, mainly through interrogation.[15] On arrest a suspect must be taken to a police station.[16]

The arrested person is taken before the custody officer.[17] In brief the custody officer must decide whether sufficient evidence exists either to charge the person or to warrant further detention for the purpose of obtaining

---

peace. This power is nearly co-terminus with the powers of arrest under the Public Order Act 1986, s. 4(3) and s. 5(4).

[8] There are several related offences for the imaginative prosecutor such as s. 5 Public Order Act 1986 and under Criminal Justice and Public Order Act 1994 Part V.

[9] *Blackstone's Criminal Practice* (1991), pp. 1618–1620.

[10] McBarnett D., *Conviction* (1983), p. 36 ff.; McConville *et al.*, *op. cit.*, Chap. 2; Black D., *Manners and Customs of the Police* (1980).

[11] Piliavin I. and Briar S. "Police Encounters with Juveniles" (1964) 70 Am.J.Sociol. 206.

[12] McConville, *op. cit.*, p. 17.

[13] Box, *op. cit.*

[14] Royal Commission on Criminal Procedure, *op. cit.*, para. 3.77.

[15] McConville, *op. cit.*, p. 39.

[16] This must be a designated police station under s. 30 of PACE. s. 35 requires chief officers to designate certain stations to be used for the purpose of detaining arrested persons which will be stations which have the necessary personnel and resources for interviews, cells for detention, etc.

[17] s. 36 outlines the role of the custody officer; s. 37 defines the custody officer's duties before charge; s. 38 defines the custody officer's duties after charge and s. 39 outlines the custody officer's responsibilities to the arrested person. The custody officer will not be involved in the investigation.

evidence through interview.[18] The custody officer must ensure that the person is aware of their rights to legal advice, to notify someone of the fact of their arrest and to see the Codes of Practice. Throughout the period of detention, it is the custody officer's responsibility to monitor the conditions of the custody: how long and how often a person is interviewed, whether medical advice is required; whether proper sleep and refreshment has been provided. All of this should be recorded on the custody record,[19] an essential source of information for the defendant and the court in the event of, say, a disputed confession. Proper documentation was seen by the Royal Commission to be a critical safeguard for both police and suspect, not just the custody record but also a proper interview record.[20] However research[21] has suggested that over 10 per cent of custody records are falsely compiled.

The custody officer is initially responsible for the length of time that a person is detained in a police station. That detention must be periodically reviewed.[22] Prior to the Act, the police probably had to bring a suspect before a court within 24 hours.[23] Now, with some safeguards, they can hold people without charge for up to four days. Although section 41 lays down the principle that a person should not be held without charge for more than 24 hours, this can be derogated from in certain circumstances. Continued detention for a further 12 hours can be authorised by a senior officer (superintendent or above) if the detention is necessary to secure or preserve evidence, if the offence is a serious arrestable offence[24] and if the investigation is being conducted "diligently and expeditiously".[25] Further periods of continued detention up to 96 hours are possible with approval from the magistrates' court.[26]

Although the custody officer is conceived in PACE as a quasi-judicial figure, removed from the immediate imperatives of the investigation, it is difficult for the officer to distance himself or herself from the dominant police objectives, collaborating with and assisting the arresting officers.[27] Not to detain a suspect would mean undermining the authority of colleagues and detention thus becomes a matter of routine. However prolonged detention is rare with only 5 per cent detained for more than 18 hours and 1 per cent for more than 24 hours. In absolute figures, however, it is estimated that over the

---

[18] In practice, detention is almost never refused—McKenzie I. *et al.*: "Helping the Police with their Enquiries" [1990] Crim.L.R. 22.

[19] PACE, s. 37(4). In Kent there are five copies; for the station record, for the suspect, for case papers, a transit copy and finally for the local intelligence liaison officer.

[20] A major complaint by the police has been the bureaucracy engendered by PACE—see Audit Commission, (1993), *Helping with Enquiries* (Police Paper No. 12). Exhibit 17 "The Paper Chase", p. 29 indicates that some 40 forms need to be completed after arrest for even a minor offence.

[21] Sanders A. and Bridges L., "Access to Legal Advice" in Walker C. and Sturner K., (eds.), *Justice in Error* (1992).

[22] s. 40 PACE—the extent to which such reviews are carried out is doubtful—Dixon D. *et al.*, "Safeguarding the rights of the accused ..." 1 *Policing and Society* p. 115 (1990).

[23] In the 1970s there were several instances of the police holding suspects without access to legal advice for considerable periods before bringing them to court.

[24] These are listed in PACE, Schedule 3.

[25] PACE, s. 42.

[26] *ibid.* s. 43.

[27] McConville, *op. cit.*, p. 42 although see Irving B. and McKenzie I., *Police Interrogation: The Effects of PACE* (Police Foundation 1989).

course of a year about 5,000 will have been held for more than a day and that 747 of these will have been released without charge.[28]

3.8.7 *Interrogation—Confessions as Evidence*

Interrogation is the essential investigative tool. Compared to other forms of acquiring evidence, it is cheap and the end result, a confession, is evidence that is seen as reliable and convincing. Despite the (much reduced) right of silence and the privilege against self-incrimination, most suspects (especially those detained in the police station) talk to the police and many make either complete or partial, verbal or written admissions of guilt.[29]

An admission of guilt by the defendant is crucial evidence. Normally neither prosecution nor defence can rely on hearsay,[30] that is, a witness repeating an out-of-court oral or written statement in order that the court should rely on the truth of that statement. But this is exactly what a police officer does when he or she repeats a defendant's confession (whether that confession has been taped, written down or merely remembered by the officer). However there are a large number of exceptions to the hearsay rule, the most important of which is that confessions (statements by a party to a case which are against the party's interest) are admissible evidence. Indeed all statements made by a suspect to the police, whether exculpatory or inculpatory, are accepted into evidence.[31] Once admitted, such statements are deeply prejudicial since juries will often not bother to look for other independent evidence which supports the confession.

The rationale for the rule against hearsay[32] is twofold: first, it is unreliable and of less probative value; secondly, it denies the defendant the opportunity to confront his or her accusers,[33] in other words to cross-examine those giving evidence which is adverse to you. Both carry less weight when considering confessions; first, confessions are more reliable and therefore probative since people are unlikely to admit a state of affairs which is contrary to their own interests unless it is true; secondly, all the relevant people are in court so defendants are able both to confront the officer who allegedly took the statement and to testify on their own behalf.

However, although confessions may be theoretically more reliable, in practice reliance on them is very dangerous. The young as in the Confait Case,[34] the disturbed,[35] the mentally subnormal[36] let alone those subject to brutality and intimidation[37] are obviously vulnerable but under hostile interrogation in the psychologically intimidating environment of a police

---

[28] See Maguire M., "Effects of the PACE Provisions" 28 Brit.J.Criminol. (1988) p. 19; Irving and McKenzie, *op. cit.*; McConville *et al.*, *op. cit.*, p. 46.

[29] Mitchell B., "Confessions and Police Interrogation of Suspects" [1983] Crim.L.R. 596.

[30] Zuckerman A., *The Principles of Criminal Evidence* (1989), Chap. 15.

[31] *Sharpe* [1988] 1 All E.R. 65.

[32] Zuckerman, *op. cit.*, Chap. 11.

[33] See 6th Amendment to the United States Constitution.

[34] *Lattimore* (1976) 62 Cr.App.R. 53.

[35] *Ward* [1993] 2 All E.R. 577.

[36] Timothy Evans confessed to killings of his wife and child committed by John Christie—Kennedy L., *Ten Rillington Place* (1961).

[37] The Birmingham Six were seriously assaulted before they made any statements—Mullin C., *Trial and Error* (1989).

station, even non-vulnerable people are likely to make admissions which are not true,[38] not realising that once a statement had been made, there is great difficulty in retracting it.

A central question for the Runciman Commission was whether independent corroborative evidence should be required for all confession cases. An independent study suggested that 95 per cent of such cases had such supporting evidence[39] which indicated that a rule requiring corroboration would lead to few additional acquittals. However, although three members of the Commission felt that there should never be a conviction based solely on a confession, the majority were satisfied with a recommendation that the judge in all cases should give a strong warning that care was needed before convicting on the basis of the confession alone,[40] explicitly referring to reasons why people might confess to crimes that they did not commit.[41]

At common law, the judge had the discretion to exclude a confession if it was involuntary.[42] Substantial misconduct on the part of the interrogators was needed before confessions were excluded. Mere breaches of the Judges' Rules were insufficient. The overall attitude of the courts was that if the evidence was relevant and reliable, then it should be admitted[43] since it was not the task of the courts to police the police.[44] This was illustrated in *Jeffrey v. Black*[45] when, having arrested the accused for the theft of a sandwich, the police illegally searched his flat for drugs. The evidence was admitted—the test was whether the evidence was relevant and reliable and the means by which it was procured, however unfair, was irrelevant.

Currently the position is regulated by sections 76–78 of PACE. Section 76(2) requires the prosecution to prove beyond reasonable doubt that a confession was not obtained:

(a) by oppression—defined in section 76(8) as torture, inhuman or degrading treatment or the use or threat of violence, or
(b) in circumstances likely to render the confession unreliable.

Section 77 lays down special provisions for those with a mental handicap and section 78 allows the court to refuse evidence (of any kind) if it appears to the

---

[38] Irving B. and Hilgendorf L., *Police Interrogation: The Psychological Approach*; Irving B., *Police Interrogation*; Irving and McKenzie, (1989), *op. cit.*; Gudjonsson G., *Persons at Risk during Interviews in Police Custody* (Royal Commission on Criminal Justice Research Study No. 12 1992); McConville, *et al.* (1991), *op. cit.*, p. 56 ff.

[39] McConville M., *Corroboration and Confessions: The Impact of a Rule Requiring that no Conviction be sustained on the Basis of Confession Evidence Alone* (Royal Commission on Criminal Justice Research Study No. 13 H.M.S.O. 1993). Corroboration is not a panacea against wrongful conviction—in the Birmingham Six case, there were confessions to the pub bombings and there was independent forensic evidence, later proved fatally flawed, that the defendants had handled explosives.

[40] Such a development does not need legislation and has been implemented in the case of identification evidence by the Court of Appeal in *Turnbull* [1977] Q.B. 224—see *infra*, para. 3.9.

[41] Royal Commission on Criminal Justice: Report (1993) Cm. 2263, paras. 4.56–4.87.

[42] *Ibrahim* [1914] A.C. 599.

[43] *Sang* [1979] 2 All E.R. 1222.

[44] "It is not part of a judge's function to exercise disciplinary powers over the police or prosecution ..." *per* Lord Diplock in *Sang, supra*, at p. 1230. Perhaps that failure to realise that the reliability of evidence is immediately linked with police malpractices led directly to the self-inflicted wounds that the criminal justice system suffered in the 1980s.

[45] [1978] Q.B. 490.

court that the admission of such evidence would have such an adverse effect on the fairness of the proceedings that the court ought not to admit it.[46]

These provisions have been used to exclude incriminating statements allegedly made by the accused, when the statement has been obtained in breach of the Codes of Practice, in particular Code C which governs the detention, treatment and questioning of suspects. The police have been made to follow a set procedure in the Codes with strict conditions to be adhered to before the transcript of a police interview would become admissible evidence. This had been the concern of the Royal Commission in 1981 to ensure that the transcript was valid evidence both in terms of reliability and in terms of fairness.[47] While many other countries use a judicial intermediary to compile this record, the Royal Commission was unwilling to take this step towards a more inquisitorial role for the courts.[48] Instead it is the police who have been placed in a quasi-judicial role in interrogating suspects inside the police station.

Tape-recording[49] of interviews back up this process but even Codes of Practice and recordings have their limits since the courts still do not automatically exclude anything said by the suspect outside the interview room, thus allowing "spontaneous" admissions to occur in the patrol car as it takes the scenic route to the station.[50] Informal interviews[51] prior to the recorder being switched on is another ploy. However the police still seem willing to use oppressive questioning with the recorder switched on.[52] There is also the problem of tape summaries which are prepared by officers but which are rarely checked by defence lawyers.

This combination of the Codes of Practice and sections 76 and 78 has brought a sea-change in appellate courts' attitudes. The previous strategy was a "crime-control" model for the courts since the end (convicting the guilty by accepting any relevant evidence regardless of its provenance) was more important than the means (failing to protect suspects' rights). There is now a limited "due-process" model whereby violation of the defendant's rights may lead to the exclusion of the evidence. The courts have been driven in particular by the phrase "adverse effect on the fairness of the proceedings" contained in section 78 so that there is more concern that suspects' rights are not infringed and that the prosecution should not profit from their own wrongdoing. Thus if the evidence, however reliable, was obtained in circumstances which would make it unfair on the accused to admit it, then it is excluded. However this is not a solely rights-based approach—any breach

[46] s. 78 did not appear in the original bill but was the result of an amendment tabled by Lord Scarman enabling courts to exclude evidence on the basis of police malpractice. The government accepted the need for such an exclusionary clause but watered down the original with the eventual, rather obscure, text.

[47] Royal Commission on Criminal Procedure, *op. cit.*, paras. 4.2 *et seq.*

[48] Such as the *juge d'instruction* in France—see the Royal Commission on Criminal Procedure, *op. cit.*, para. 6.25 ff.; any move to an inquisitorial system was also rejected by the Royal Commission on Criminal Justice, *op. cit.*, paras. 1.11–1.15.

[49] PACE, s. 60—this is now nationwide practice.

[50] Sanders (1993), *op. cit.*, p. 91; Maguire M. and Norris C. *The Conduct and Supervision of Criminal Investigations* (Royal Commission on Criminal Justice Research Study No. 5).

[51] McConville *et al.* (1991), *op. cit.*, p. 60.

[52] *e.g.* the Cardiff Three whose convictions were quashed in December 1992. The Royal Commission on Criminal Justice, *op. cit.*, para. 1.22, were concerned at the endless repetitive questioning that the tapes revealed. *Paris* [1994] Crim.L.R. 361.

of the Act or the Codes of Conduct must be serious and substantial[53] so that the suspect's right to a fair trial would be put in jeopardy.

3.8.7.1 THE RIGHT TO SILENCE

Fundamental to any discussion of interviewing is the concept of the right to silence. Until 1994, this right consisted of a conglomerate of different ideas:

(a) there was the requirement of a caution—that is, that the police warned a suspect that he or she need not say anything and that whatever was said might be used in evidence. This had to be given initially when[54] the investigating officer had grounds for suspecting that that person had committed an offence and the purpose of the questions was to obtain evidence to use in court. A caution had to be given on arrest.[55] If the person was then interviewed at a police station, the interviewer had to remind the interviewee at the start and after every break that he or she was still under caution. The caution was repeated at formal charge.

(b) there was also the evidential rule that placed a burden of proof on the prosecution that they should prove the defendant's guilt beyond reasonable doubt,[56] in other words, a presumption of innocence.

(c) the most irksome aspect for the police and prosecution was that they were not permitted to comment on the defendant's decision to remain silent in the police station[57] or not to testify.[58] There were some limited exceptions—the prosecution could adduce evidence of silence when accusation was made by victim[59] or parent[60] or where the accused was on "level terms" with police.[61]

(d) although the judge could comment,[62] he or she had to do so in measured terms and had to warn the jury that they must not assume guilt from the defendant's silence.

(e) there also existed a privilege against self-incrimination.[63]

Much of this remains valid but as a result of sections 34–37 of the Criminal Justice and Public Order Act 1994, paragraphs (a), (c) and (d) above require reconsideration.

The background of this debate is that, despite this "right", most suspects

[53] *Walsh* (1989) 91 Cr.App.R. 161—denying access to a solicitor would usually mean denial of a fair trial (*cf. Oliphant* [1992] Crim.L.R. 40) but a technical breach of detention rules would not.
[54] Code C 10.1—there is no need to caution a person if questions are being put prior to a search or in exercise of stop and search powers under s. 1 of PACE.
[55] Code C 10.3—unless it is impracticable or if the person has been cautioned immediately before in accordance with Code C 10.1.
[56] *Woolmington* [1935] A.C. 462.
[57] *Hall* [1971] 1 W.L.R. 298.
[58] Criminal Evidence Act 1898, s. 1(b)—the failure of any person charged with an offence to give evidence shall not be made the subject of any comment by the prosecution now repealed.
[59] *Horne* [1990] Crim.L.R. 188.
[60] *Parkes* [1976] 1 W.L.R. 1251.
[61] *Chandler* [1976] 1 W.L.R. 585.
[62] *Bathurst* [1968] 2 Q.B. 99; *Sparrow* (1973) 1 W.L.R. 488 see Rupert Cross's forthright comments on "gibberish" [1973] "A Very Wicked Animal ..." Crim.L.R. 329 at 333.
[63] Zuckerman, *op. cit.*, Chap. 15; Keane A., *The Modern Law of Evidence* (3rd ed., 1994), p. 446 *et seq.*

talk to the police. Confessions have always been viewed by courts and juries as compelling evidence. Yet unreliable confessions have so frequently been identified as the cause of miscarriages of justice that it seems extraordinary that there have been constant campaigns to reform the "right to silence". These started with the Criminal Law Revision Committee in 1972[64] whose arguments were rejected by the Royal Commission on Criminal Procedure in 1981.[65]

After PACE, the police argued that the safeguards introduced, especially the suspect's access to legal advice, had tipped the balance in favour of suspects. The suggestion was that there were more serious cases which were being discontinued or else there were more acquittals, especially because of "ambush" defences. This latter term meant that, at trial, the defence relied on significant facts which had not been mentioned to the police at the time of the investigation and which the prosecution were subsequently in no position to rebut. A Home Office Working Group[66] again favoured the idea of abolition, only for its arguments to be rejected in their turn by the Royal Commission on Criminal Justice in 1993 which commissioned two separate reports.[67] The empirical evidence[68] put forward does not suggest that there is either an unacceptable acquittal rate or "no further action" rate for those few defendants, charged with serious crimes, who choose to remain silent.[69] Nor was there any serious problem of "ambush" defences.

The Royal Commission Report did suggest that the defence should be under an obligation to disclose aspects of its case but stood firm against the wholesale abolition of the right to silence. Despite this, the Criminal Justice and Public Order Act 1994 now allows juries to use silence as evidence against the accused. This is very similar to position in Northern Ireland[70]:

(a) article 3 and section 34 are aimed at "ambush defences" and at forcing disclosure of the defence, by allowing a court to "draw such inferences as appear proper" from a failure to mention a relevant fact relied on in the defence when it might reasonably have been mentioned during police questioning. Such inferences can only be drawn where the prosecution have supplied substantial evidence linking the accused with the offence and on which a reasonable jury could convict. A jury would thus be told to attach less weight to a defence which has only been revealed at the trial and logically is correspondingly less credible.

Such a provision will place pressure on the accused to disclose his or her defence at an early stage. Advance disclosure of the defence case was a key recommendation of the Royal Commission Report.[71] The

---

[64] Criminal Law Revision Committee: *11th Report* (HMSO 1972) Cmnd. 4991, paras. 28–52.
[65] Royal Commission on Criminal Procedure, *op. cit.*, paras. 4.33 ff.
[66] Zuckerman A., "Trial by Unfair Means" [1989] Crim.L.R. 855.
[67] Leng R., *The Right to Silence in Police Interrogation* (Royal Commission on Criminal Justice Research Study 10); McConville M. and Hodgson J., *Custodial Legal Advice and the Right to Silence* (Royal Commission on Criminal Justice Research Study 16).
[68] This is summarised in Leng, *op. cit.*, Chap. 2.
[69] Zander M., "The investigation of crime: a study of cases tried at the Old Bailey" [1979] Crim.L.R. 203.
[70] Criminal Evidence Order (No. 1987 of 1988); for its impact, see Jackson J., "Curtailing the Right of Silence: Lessons from N. Ireland" [1991] Crim.L.R. 404.
[71] Royal Commission on Criminal Justice, *op. cit.*, paras. 57–73 (but see note of dissent by Zander, p. 221, paras. 1–12).

majority defended this on the grounds that it might lead to discontinuances by the prosecution, early guilty pleas by the defence and thus allow earlier fixing of trial dates and permit accurate estimates of trial lengths. Dissentients have pointed out that likely defences are usually apparent on the face of the witness statements,[72] that trials might degenerate into issues as to why the accused failed to mention a particular fact and that genuine "ambush" defences are so infrequent that they provide no justification for making such a fundamental change.

(b) article 4 and section 35 apply where the prosecution have satisfied court that there is a case to answer and a defendant declines to testify in his or her own defence. The judge, in the presence of the jury, is empowered to tell the defendant that the stage has been reached at which he or she can give evidence and to issue a warning that if he or she remain silent, that it will be permissible for the jury to draw whatever inferences appear to be proper. Although this can only come into play once the prosecution have supplied substantial evidence, evidentially this seems suspect. Whereas the other sections relate to credibility or to a refusal to account for one's presence or possession of articles, the main result of a refusal to testify, whatever the reason, would be a jury presuming guilt.

There are strong constitutional arguments here since the right to silence is the final guarantee of the autonomy of the individual. There are ethical considerations whether the state should ever use such evidence as the basis of a conviction. It undermines a principle of the rule of law that the prosecution should prove guilt and thereby undermines the presumption of innocence. Technically, there is an old common law rule that if the prejudicial effect of a piece of evidence outweights its probative value, then it should be excluded.[73] Here, the prejudicial effect on the jury of the failure to testify must far outweigh any probative quality and section 35 necessarily infringes that rule. To an extent this has been recognised by the caution shown in Northern Ireland where failure to testify has been taken into account only where the prosecution case just rests on the brink of the necessary standard of proof.[74]

(c) article 5 and section 36 apply where the suspect gives no explanation to police about certain specific facts such as objects, substances or marks on clothing which tend to suggest the accused's participation in the offence.

(d) article 6 and section 37 where the suspect gives no explanation to the police of his presence at a particular place which again would tend to suggest participation in the offence.

Both these latter sections require the accused to have been arrested and to be warned about the consequences of the failure to answer. Although this indicates that the objective threshold of "reasonable grounds" for arrest should have been satisfied, as we have seen, the police often have a lot of suspicion and very little hard evidence. They

---

[72] These are often ignored by the police—"It is routine police work not to follow up evidence raised by an accused which may support a defence." McConville *et al.* (1991), *op. cit.*, p. 77.
[73] *Sang* [1980] A.C. 402.
[74] Jackson, *op. cit.*, pp. 410–412.

already use arrest as a technique to gain that evidence by putting pressure on a suspect, through interrogation. These sections will encourage this practice, putting even greater pressure on the suspect since a refusal can be part of the prosecution's case, contributing to proof beyond reasonable doubt.

Both these sections will encourage the over-use of arrest by the police. Is this balanced by probative weight of the defendant's refusal to co-operate with the police?[75] While it is possible to argue that a failure to account for your presence at a particular spot or your possession of a particular item has some weight since it does raise a presumption of guilty knowledge about a specific element of the offence, that presumption is very far from conclusive. There are defendants who are confused and vulnerable, defendants who wish to protect others, let alone those who are just unwilling to co-operate. Can a jury ever regard silence as sufficient to quash a reasonable doubt they might harbour about the prosecution case?

These changes will increase the pressure brought on people detained in police stations to answer questions. Although Bentham bears the burden of suggesting that the right to silence only protects the guilty and the criminally sophisticated when he wrote:

"Innocence claims the right of speaking as guilt invokes the privilege of silence."

he did so at a time when the right to silence as we know it did not exist, when the defendant was not permitted to testify in his own defence and when police interrogation did not exist. The pressure to answer police questions will necessarily bear on the innocent as well as the guilty. The controversy surrounding the right to silence encompasses empirical questions and evidential problems but ultimately it should be a decision based on concepts of due process of law and proper constitutional principles. It is another of those important markers which define the relationship of state and citizen, delineating constraints on the state and our moral choice that prosecution and punishment should not be based on evidence from the accused.

3.8.7.2. ACCESS TO LEGAL ADVICE[76]

Within the police station, PACE supports the right to silence by various provisions:

- section 56 provides for a right for a person to be informed of the fact of your arrest.[77]
- section 57 provides additional rights for young persons
- section 58 gives a right to legal advice.[78]

---

[75] Compare these reforms with the U.S. Constitution's 5th Amendment which provides a right against self-incrimination.

[76] Royal Commission on Criminal Justice, *op. cit.*, paras. 3.46–3.64; Baldwin J., *The Role of Legal Representatives at the Police Station* (1992) (Royal Commission on Criminal Justice Research Study No. 3); McConville and Hodgson, *op. cit.*

[77] Previously Criminal Law Act 1977, s. 62.

[78] Access can be delayed (but never refused altogether) under s. 58(6) and (8) if the person is

- section 59 provides for a duty solicitor scheme

A detained person will be given a notice stating these rights as well as the opportunity to consult the Codes of Practice and a copy of the Custody Record.

The right to legal advice was previously enshrined in the Judges' Rules and has recently been acknowledged as a right in common law.[79] The irony was that previously the right was more honoured in the breach[80] with few convictions being overturned as a result. The PACE provisions recognised that the isolated suspect was vulnerable and manipulable by interrogators even without malpractice on their part.[81] This was especially so given that the police have no obligation to reveal the nature of the case against the suspect. The police remain very hostile to a solicitor's intervention which is seen as increasing a suspect's resistance to questioning and reducing their control.[82]

Despite these provisions and the fact that custody officers did advise suspects of their rights,[83] there was a low take-up rate of legal advice of under 20 per cent in the immediate post-PACE years. However after the Codes were revised in 1991, take-up has risen to nearly 30 per cent.[84] The extent of protection is still limited and it has been suggested[85] that defendants are not always given the leaflet advising them of their rights, that they are told to "sign here" on the custody record without realising that they are waiving their right to see a solicitor or that they are told that a solicitor will not be available for some hours and it may be necessary to be detained in a cell. The alternative of a cosy chat and then going home seems attractive. The Royal Commission's recommendations included the video-recording of events in a custody suite and interviewers both reminding suspects of their rights to legal advice at the beginning of an interview and asking for their reasons for waiving those rights which would be recorded on tape.[86]

Even where advice is given, it can be over the telephone. The police can interview before or after a lawyer's visit, thus negating the value of the advice. Further doubts have been raised[87] about the quality of the legal work and advice given, with solicitors or their representatives failing to obtain information from the investigating officers, often failing to acquire important facts from their own client, and intervening in the interview on the client's behalf in less than one-third of cases.

---

suspected of a serious arrestable offence and access might lead to interference with evidence, alerting of accomplices or hindering recovery of property. Similar provisions apply for s. 56.

[79] *R. v. Chief Constable of South Wales, ex p. Merrick* [1994] 2 All E.R. 560—s. 58 does not apply to a prison held on remand in police cells but there is a common law right to legal advice which must be allowed by the police if reasonably practicable.

[80] Zander M., "Access to a Solicitor in the Police Station" [1972] Crim.L.R. 342; Baldwin J. and McConville M., "Police Interrogation and the Right to See a Solicitor" [1979] Crim.L.R. 145.

[81] Softley P., *Police Interrogation* (Royal Commission on Criminal Procedure Research Study No. 4) (1980).

[82] McConville *et al.* (1991), *op. cit.*, pp. 47–54.

[83] Irving B. and McKenzie I., *Police Interrogation* (Police Foundation 1989): Sanders A., *et al.*, *Advice and Assistance at Police Stations* (Lord Chancellor's Dept. 1989).

[84] Sanders and Bridges, (1992), *op. cit.*

[85] Sanders, *et al.* (1989), *op. cit.*

[86] Royal Commission on Criminal Justice, *op. cit.*, para. 3.47.

[87] Royal Commission on Criminal Justice, *op. cit.*, paras. 3.56 ff. Baldwin (1992), *op. cit.*; McConville and Hodgson, (1993), *op. cit.*

Despite such shortcomings these provisions in PACE have proved a more substantial safeguard than those in the Judges' Rules. Failure to observe the correct procedure in the Code of Practice, especially in relation to the provision of legal advice, can lead to the evidence obtained from the subsequent interview being excluded. In *Absolam*[88] the accused was arrested for threatening behaviour and taken to a police station. He emptied his pockets but the custody officer, knowing that the defendant had previously been arrested for possession of cannabis, said "Put the drugs on the table". The accused took a packet from inside his trousers and also admitted selling the drugs. Only then was he reminded of the caution but no written record was made until later when the accused refused to sign it. Nor was he advised of his rights under section 58 until a later stage. The conviction was quashed on appeal since not only was the defendant denied legal advice but the custody officer's questions constituted an interview and Code C 3.1 specifies the sequence of events which should not be overridden. The Court of Appeal considered this to be a "serious and substantial breach" and that the evidence ought not to be admitted as it produced an "adverse effect on the overall fairness of the proceedings" under section 78.[89]

Access to a duty solicitor was the issue in *Vernon*[90] where the accused nominated a solicitor who was unavailable as it was late at night. She agreed to be interviewed but was not told of the availability of the duty solicitor. The record of the interview was deemed inadmissible under section 78 as she would not have consented to be interviewed but for this breach. *Walsh*[91] involved an allegation of robbery. There was an interview in the cell which was not contemporaneously recorded and there had been no legal advice. Again the conviction was quashed. But a breach of section 58 does not lead to the automatic exclusion of the statements—the breach must be significant and substantial which affects the reliability of the statement (section 76) or adversely affects the fairness of the proceedings (section 78). Thus in *Dunford*[92] there was a breach but the accused was seen as thoroughly conversant with his legal rights.

The police are empowered to delay access to a solicitor under the serious arrestable offence provisions of section 58(8).[93] Delaying access to a solicitor requires that the police believe that this individual solicitor would alert other suspects or hinder the recovery of evidence, albeit inadvertently. Such a belief could only be rarely held. The police cannot refuse to allow a suspect access to legal advice on the grounds that legal advice will be to remain silent. In *Samuel*,[94] there was an allegation of robbery. The suspect had asked for a solicitor but this was denied under section 58(8). After 24 hours, he admitted involvement in two burglaries and was charged with those. Relatives and lawyers were informed at this point but police continued questioning until the accused confessed to the robbery as well. The Court of Appeal quashed the robbery conviction under section 78 because although the initial refusal of

[88] [1988] Crim.L.R. 748.
[89] See also *Williams* [1989] Crim.L.R. 66 and *Sanusi* [1992] Crim.L.R. 43.
[90] [1988] Crim.L.R. 445.
[91] [1989] Crim.L.R. 822.
[92] [1991] Crim.L.R. 370; also *Oliphant* [1992] Crim.L.R. 40.
[93] Bevan and Lidstone, *op. cit.* 7.49 ff.
[94] [1988] 2 All E.R. 135; see also *Parris* [1989] Crim.L.R. 214.

access to a solicitor was justified, that refusal could not be justified after charging D with the burglaries.[95] Legal advice was seen as a "fundamental human right".

A different approach was seen in *Alladice*,[96] again an armed robbery case. While *Samuel* adopts a "rights" approach (so that the accused's rights should be protected by putting him into a position that he would have been in if his rights had been observed), *Alladice* displays a slightly harder Court of Appeal line. The nature of the right interfered with and the causal link between that interference and the evidence obtained are factors to be taken into account under section 78 in reaching a solution which reflects "justice". In *Alladice* the suspect was accustomed to police interviews and thus the court felt that a solicitor's presence would not have made a difference.

Such cases suggest that the Court of Appeal is weaving a rather uneasy road between the two rationales for excluding evidence. Although they have turned their backs on the strict "reliability" approach (which would test the quality of the statement regardless of the infringement of the defendant's rights), they find it hard to embrace the full American "fairness" model which would lead to exclusion whenever the suspect's rights are infringed. The pragmatic approach in *Walsh* appears preferable as it seeks to measure the significance of the breach and to assess the effect that breach has on the fairness of the proceedings created.

3.8.7.3 INTERVIEWS OUTSIDE THE STATION

The Codes of Practice were intended to eliminate the damning verbal admission by focusing on the "interview" as the central stage—the central safeguards were the caution, notification of the right to legal advice and the recording of interviews. Where practicable, the interview of an arrested person should always take place at a police station.[97] If a suspect is questioned outside the station[98] or makes a spontaneous statement, these may well be admissible. In *Parchment*[99] the suspect was discovered naked in the cupboard in a flat. Arrested and cautioned over some burglaries, he made spontaneous admissions which were only written up later. At that point the record of these statements was shown to the accused but by then he was denying the offences. The Crown Court admitted the statements arguing that, while the police operated within PACE and its Codes, they could not be said to be operating unfairly under section 78. When there has been an arrest, there will have been a caution and the interview must be recorded as soon as practicable with the suspect given the opportunity to read the record and sign it as correct.[1] But outside the station there will have been no notification of any right to see a solicitor nor will the record have been taped or been contemporaneous.

However an officer must be able to ask questions which do not comprise an

---

[95] The Court of Appeal is quite strict on further questioning once charged although if the suspect makes voluntary statement, then that can be admitted—*Pall* [1992] Crim.L.R. 126.
[96] [1988] Crim.L.R. 608.
[97] Code C 11.1.
[98] The exceptions are in Code C 11.1—interference or harm to evidence or other people, alerting others or hindering the recovery of property.
[99] [1989] Crim.L.R. 290.
[1] Code C 11.5 and C 11.10.

"interview". An interview is defined[2] as the questioning of a person regarding his involvement in an offence. Questioning only to obtain information or an explanation or in the ordinary course of an officer's duties do not constitute an interview.[3] Nor do questions which are confined to the proper conduct of a search.[4] In addition, a person not under arrest might make unprompted statements. If courts permit such statements to be admitted into evidence, the PACE safeguards are largely by-passed, as "verbals" will move from the police station to the scene of crime and police car, before the Code of Practice starts to run.[5] In *Maguire*,[6] where the PC advised the suspect in the police car to "tell the truth" and he said that "... we were only going in to have a look around ... for anything, for money, whatever." The charge was attempted burglary and the Court of Appeal held that although the Code did not apply only to interviews in police stations, in this case, this questioning did not constitute an "interview" since there were no questions asked and thus the unverified police statement was admitted into evidence.

Although there is no obligation to record and verify such exchanges, courts do exclude the statements where this has not been done as in *Maloney and Doherty*[7] where a stipendiary magistrate excluded evidence of pocket book interviews undertaken at the scene, unseen and unsigned by defendants. In *Sparks*,[8] there was an informal chat at the social services office which an officer attended and yet the rules relating to recording and verifying still applied. But the inconsistency can be seen since the courts have reached different conclusions[9] as to whether to admit evidence in cases where substantial interviews have taken place outside the police station.

The Royal Commission found that about 30 per cent of suspects report being questioned prior to arrest and there was evidence that negotiations took place off-record as to what was to be said on the record.[10] Despite the dangers involved in the use of such unverified information obtained outside the police station, the Royal Commission did not consider its total exclusion but contented themselves merely with discussing the possibilities of extending tape-recording to all transactions between officer and suspect.

3.8.7.4 INTERVIEWS INSIDE THE STATION

General breaches of Code C other than those relating to legal advice[11] might lead to the exclusion of evidence. Custody officers must be aware of the special provisions regarding the mentally handicapped, those with sight or

[2] Code C 11A.
[3] But Code C 11A is self-contradictory since seeking information in the course of duties might well be questioning about a person's involvement in an offence—*Cox* [1993] Crim.L.R. 382; *Marsh* [1991] Crim.L.R. 455.
[4] *Langiert* [1991] Crim.L.R. 777; *White* [1991] Crim.L.R. 779; *Chung* [1991] Crim.L.R. 622.
[5] Royal Commission on Criminal Justice, *op. cit.*, para. 3.7; Moston S. and Stephenson G., *The Questioning and Interviewing of Suspects Outside the Police Station* (Royal Commission on Criminal Justice Research Study No. 22) (1993); McConville *et al.* (1991), p. 83.
[6] [1989] Crim.L.R. 815.
[7] [1988] Crim.L.R. 523.
[8] [1991] Crim.L.R. 128.
[9] *Keenan* [1989] Crim.L.R. 720; *Brown* [1989] Crim.L.R. 500.
[10] Irving B. and Dunnighan C., *Human Factors in the Quality Control of CID Investigations* (Royal Commission on Criminal Justice Research Study No. 21) (1993).
[11] Bevan and Lidstone, *op. cit.*, Chap. 8.

speech impediments, the ill, foreigners and juveniles. There are general provisions regarding conditions of detention, relating to heating, lighting, proper food and exercise.

The basic rights[12] of a suspect being interviewed allow for a minimum eight hour continuous period of rest without interrogation in any twenty-four hour period with properly heated, ventilated and lit interview rooms, with no requirement to stand and with proper breaks for refreshment at recognised mealtimes. The interview will be tape-recorded under the provisions of Code of Practice E.[13] Breaches of the Code might lead to the exclusion of any admissions by the defendant but these must be significant and substantial and not merely technical. In *Taylor*,[14] there was a breach of length of detention regulations as a result of delay in organising an ID parade. It was a minor delay and a technical infraction would not lead to the exclusion of evidence.

But presence in the police station does not mean that all the safeguards are observed. In *Mathews*,[15] the accused was remanded in police cells where she was alleged to have made incriminating statements. Although such unverified police statements should not be admitted, it is a matter for the trial judge's discretion and as long as the judge addresses his or her mind to the correct issues under section 78, then the appellate court will not interfere with the decision. As a result Court of Appeal decisions are difficult to fit into a clear pattern—in *Trussler*[16] the suspect was a drug addict who was arrested 9 a.m. and he eventually made a statement at 2 a.m. the following morning. A doctor had been provided and the suspect had talked to his lawyer on the phone but there were long periods of questioning without adequate rest periods and the statements were eventually excluded as potentially unreliable under section 76(2)(b). But in *Crampton*[17] where the defendant was again suffering from withdrawal symptoms, the Court of Appeal emphasised that the trial court must look for potential unreliability.

The discretion to exclude evidence is exercised freely with regard to vulnerable defendants. In *Lamont*,[18] the interrogation was of a mentally retarded suspect with an IQ of 73 and acting under section 77 of PACE, the Court of Appeal excluded evidence of a confession which provided the only evidence of intention in an attempted murder case. But in *Clarke*,[19] the accused admitted attempted theft while being taken to the police station. A record of the conversation was made and signed but at trial the defendant alleged that he was deaf and thus there had been a breach of the Codes.[20] On appeal, this argument was rejected. There was no breach of the Codes if the officer was unaware that the suspect was deaf but if shown as fact that the

---

[12] Code C 12.
[13] The major problems with taping appears to be the inadequate summaries of the tapes produced by the police—Royal Commission on Criminal Justice, *op. cit.*, para. 3.73; Baldwin J., *Preparing the Record of Taped Interview* (Royal Commission on Criminal Justice Research Study No. 2) (1992).
[14] [1991] Crim.L.R. 541.
[15] [1990] Crim.L.R. 190.
[16] [1988] Crim.L.R. 447.
[17] [1991] Crim.L.R. 277.
[18] [1989] Crim.L.R. 813.
[19] [1989] Crim.L.R. 892.
[20] Code C 13.5 which specifies that if a person appears to be deaf, he must not be interviewed in the absence of an interpreter.

defendant was deaf, it could still be excluded under section 78. Exclusion of evidence is not predicted on proof of police misconduct as could be seen in *Brine*,[21] where the suspect was properly interviewed but the interview was excluded after medical evidence that the accused was suffering from a mild form of paranoid psychosis.

When the police do act unethically, the Court of Appeal again fails to give a clear guide. In *Fulling*,[22] the police told the defendant that her lover had been unfaithful to her with another woman (being held in the next cell). The accused made a statement which was not excluded since this was not "oppressive" behaviour under section 76. The conviction was upheld but some questions remain. Could the statement be said to be "reliable" in such circumstances for the purpose of section 76? Or could it be said that deliberately (but not illegally) undermining the willpower of a suspect in this manner has an "adverse effect on the fairness of the proceedings"? This can be contrasted with *Mason*[23] which involved arson of a car—the police alleged falsely that they had fingerprints of the defendant on a fragment of glass and as a result, he made incriminating statements. The conviction was quashed with the Court of Appeal stressing the need to balance the gravity of the charge, the public interest, the position of the defendant and the nature of the police illegality. This was regarded as a significant deception on a minor charge, not merely to deceive the defendant but also his lawyer. General oppressive conduct can lead to exclusion—*Beales*[24] where the officer "hectored and bullied" and fabricated evidence.

3.8.7.5 INADMISSIBLE STATEMENT FOLLOWED BY PROPER INTERVIEW

If a statement is excluded because of a breach of the Codes, this does not automatically lead to exclusion of a second statement occurring in course of a properly conducted interview.[25] But if the grounds for impugning the first statement still exist, when the second statement suffers the same fate. In *Canale*,[26] the officers deliberately broke the rules and the court will then prevent prosecution from gaining an advantage. In *McGovern*,[27] the suspect had an IQ of 73 and it was felt that the impact of the first statement could not be excluded from affecting reliability of the second statement even though this latter was in the presence of a solicitor.

3.8.7.6 ENTRAPMENT AND SURVEILLANCE

Although the appeal courts have concentrated on scrutinising interview evidence, the text of section 78 permits a broader application. Police practices such as the use of agents provocateurs or of entrapment are common but

---

[21] [1992] Crim.L.R. 122.

[22] [1987] Crim.L.R. 492.

[23] [1987] Crim.L.R. 757 but *cf. Bailey* [1993] Crim.L.R. 681 where play-acting by the police convinced the suspects that their cell had not been bugged and they made incriminating statements.

[24] [1991] Crim.L.R. 118.

[25] *Y v. DPP* [1991] Crim.L.R. 917.

[26] [1990] Crim.L.R. 329.

[27] [1991] Crim.L.R. 124.

provide no defence known to English law. In theory a similar result may be reached if the court can be persuaded to exclude evidence gained by the use of an agent provocateur. At common law, the key decision is *Sang*[28] in which the House of Lords held that although the fact that evidence was obtained by the use of an agent provocateur, this was not a ground on which the trial judge could exclude evidence.

Section 78 apparently has made little difference. In *Marshall*,[29] the police purchased alcohol from the respondent who were charged with selling liquor without the requisite licence. The evidence of police officers who had made test purchases was not regarded as having an adverse effect on the fairness of the proceedings. In *Christou*,[30] an undercover police operation in London set up a shop to buy and sell jewellery commercially. It was staffed solely by undercover officers purporting to be shady jewellers willing to buy stolen property. Discreetly sited cameras and sound equipment recorded all that occurred over the counter. The evidence was admitted and the court held that such operations were not against public policy.

The issue of the agent provocateur was raised in *Smurthwaite and Gill*[31] where it was alleged that S had solicited another to murder his wife and similarly that G had solicited another to murder her husband. In each case an undercover police officer was introduced to the defendant by a third party and pretended to be a contract killer. Conversations incriminating the defendant were then recorded by a tape recorder concealed by the police officer. The Court of Appeal upheld the judges' decisions to admit the conversations but suggested some factors to be taken into account:

- was the officer acting as an agent provocateur in the sense that he was enticing the defendant to commit an offence he would not have otherwise committed?
- what was the nature[32] of the entrapment?
- how active or passive was the officer's role in obtaining the evidence?
- is there an unassailable record of what occurred, or is it strongly corroborated?
- did the undercover officer abuse the role to ask questions which ought properly to have been asked as a police officer and in accordance with the codes?

An entrapment which fell very close to this boundary can be found in *Wilson et al.*,[33] where convictions for a massive forgery of American Express traveller cheques only led to suspended sentences for the accused who had been enticed into the operation by a police informer.

There exist, in strict law, no police "powers" of surveillance and information gathering. These activities are not carried out under any direct

---

[28] [1980] A.C. 402.
[29] [1988] 3 All E.R. 683.
[30] [1992] 3 W.L.R. 228.
[31] [1994] Crim.L.R. 53 and 1 All E.R. 898.
[32] In the Rachel Nickell murder case, it was reported that an undercover police officer sought admissions from suspect, Colin Stagg, by offering sexual favours.
[33] *The Guardian*, December 15, 1994.

statutory or common law authority and are, in effect, based upon the common law principle that whatever is not expressly forbidden by law is permissible.[34] Such activities are not forbidden because they do not, in general, infringe interests of the citizen which are recognised by the common law, and Parliament has shown itself reluctant to extend those interests. There is a limited protection provided by recent legislation such as the Interception of Communications Act 1985 and the Data Protection Act 1984. The most effective remedy appears to be an application under the European Convention on Human Rights.

There are thus few legal constraints on the police and correspondingly considerable legal and practical difficulties in obtaining remedies against them. Common law has never recognised a right to privacy as such. The practice of intercepting letters under the Home Secretary's warrant is very long-standing although the authority for doing so is obscure. The Home Secretary's power to authorise telephone tapping was challenged in *Malone v. Metropolitan Police Commissioner*[35] when the plaintiff failed in his domestic action when he sued after the prosecution [in a criminal trial] had admitted tapping his telephone. The Interception of Communications Act 1985 now regulates interception of the post, telephone tapping and any communications sent by a public[36] telecommunications system.[37] It is now a criminal offence for a person to intentionally intercept a communication unless he was doing so under a warrant issued by the Secretary of State or he had reasonable grounds to believe that the sender or recipient of the communication consented.[38]

In *Effik*,[39] it was held that a cordless telephone operated through a base unit which is connected to the public telecommunications system is not part of that public system but is instead a private system connected to the public system. Accordingly, the interception by the police of telephone conversations on a cordless telephone is not subject to the Interception of Communications Act 1985 and evidence at a criminal trial of such conversations is not rendered inadmissible under s.9(1) of the Act by reason of the fact that the interception has taken place without a warrant.

In *Preston*,[40] five defendants were arrested and charged with conspiracy to import drugs from Holland. During the course of the trial, it became apparent that the defendants' telephones had been tapped, and defence requested the prosecution to produce evidence of the material obtained from telephone tapping, in the hope that the telephone intercepts would establish that S had acted under duress and/or that the importation had been arranged by an informer and that the defendants had, in fact, nothing to do with it. Section 9 of the Act provided that no evidence could be adduced and no question asked in cross-examination which tended to suggest that a warrant had been issued. The judge ruled that no evidence could be given about the matter and no questions asked. He also refused to exclude the evidence of the telephone calls

[34] See *Malone v. Metropolitan Police Commissioner* [1979] Ch. 344 at 366.
[35] *supra.*
[36] As defined in s. 9 of the Telecommunications Act 1984.
[37] As defined in s. 4(1) of the Telecommunications Act 1984.
[38] Interception of Communications Act 1985, s. 1(1) and (2).
[39] [1994] 3 All E.R. 458.
[40] [1993] 4 All E.R. 638.

under section 78(1) of PACE although the defence had argued that it would be unfair for the prosecution to be allowed to invite the jury to draw inferences from that evidence while refusing to disclose information from the intercepts which might show that the inferences were unfounded. This was upheld by the House of Lords.

The police can also rely on the product of other listening devices: in *Khan*,[41] the Court of Appeal gave firm approval for bugging as a technique used in targeting known offenders. The test for admissibility is relevance and the product is admissible if relevant. In other cases, there may well be more compelling considerations of invasion of privacy or even of tort through trespass and of criminal damage. But such considerations must be weighed against the probative value of the evidence and judicial discretion exercised under section 78 of PACE:

> " ... no crime was incited; no deliberate deceit was practised on the appellant; no misleading information was advanced or pressure placed upon him to induce him to speak; the police did not act oppressively towards him; at the time the conversation was taped the appellant had neither been arrested, interviewed, nor charged; the tape provided a clear record of what was admittedly said by the appellant; and no question arose of the breach of any PACE Codes of Practice"

The significant restraints on police surveillance are likely to be the result of applications under the European Convention which protects a variety of "human rights". United Kingdom police practices of "visual and aural surveillance" are very likely in breach of Article 8 as they are regulated only by administrative guidelines and therefore contravene the Convention of it as they are not clearly formulated and accessible.

3.9 IDENTIFICATION EVIDENCE

Apart from the interrogation of suspects and the search of persons, vehicles and places for objects and traces as evidence of crime, the other main source of evidence for the police is the eye-witness and one of the most obvious aspects of eye-witness testimony is the identification of suspects. As with the confession, identification is treated in court as possessing considerable probative weight; as with confessions, its probative value is over-estimated.

Identification evidence can be very strong, especially when it is recognition of a person already known to the witness. This is commonly the case with offences of personal violence. But the identification of strangers, perhaps glimpsed for a moment at the scene of a crime can be extremely weak, depending upon a range of factors which may not be taken into account at trial.[42] Unfortunately the jury's and the judge's perception of the weight of identification evidence is less likely to be affected by "scientific" factors (duration, range, visibility) than by the credence that is given to the witness (the witnesses's demeanour, the coherence of the testimony). The prejudicial effect of such testimony is strong since it is hard to doubt the impartial witness

---

[41] [1994] Crim.L.R. 830.
[42] Clifford B., "The Relevance of Psychological Investigation to Legal Issues in Testimony and Identification" [1979] Crim.L.R. 153; Jackson J., "The Insufficiency of Identification Evidence Based on Personal Impression" [1986] Crim.L.R. 203.

who clearly identifies the accused. Yet as psychological research has suggested, the odds on the witness being right are at best evens, odds which are difficult to square with proof "beyond reasonable doubt".

Where the identification evidence is simply corroborative of other testimony implicating the accused, there is less concern. But often the conviction is based wholly or mainly on such evidence. Figures in this area are hard to come by. The Devlin Report[43] suggested that in 1973, 347 people were prosecuted and 258 convicted solely, or mainly, on identification evidence. Naturally there have been many notorious cases of miscarriages of justice as a result of misidentification—the most famous of these was Adolf Beck in the early years of the century who was wrongly identified by 12 women.[44]

Safeguards can exist either at the point of investigation (the manner in which the police gather identification evidence) or at the point of trial. This latter approach would require stricter conditions before a court would accept identification evidence. Such conditions might have involved:

(a) that corroboration,[45] in the form of other independent evidence linking the accused to the crime, should be a requirement so that there could be no conviction based solely on identification evidence, or

(b) that the jury should be warned to look for corroboration but it should not be a bar to conviction if none were found, or

(c) (the Devlin Report's preferred option) that there should be legislation for a special warning which explained to the jury that identification alone did not comprise probable cause for a conviction unless there were special circumstances—namely, familiarity; where the accused was a member of a small group, one of whom had committed the crime; where the defendant had failed to counter evidence with his own story.

None of these materialised as a result of the Devlin Report. The significant controls were introduced at the point of trial by the Court of Appeal's decision in *Turnbull*.[46] The Court was against any rule which prevented convictions from being based on identification alone and argued that the crucial element was the quality of that identification. But it was not a rule which required corroboration. Instead the jury should be warned of the special need for caution before convicting the accused in reliance wholly or mainly on identification evidence, and they should be told to examine closely the circumstances in which the identification came to be made. Where this warning is not given, then the conviction will normally be quashed.

Initially some controls at the point of investigation were introduced,

---

[43] *Report of Departmental Committee on Evidence of Identification in Criminal Cases* (1976) (HCP 1975/76 338)—this report was set up after the convictions of Virag and Docherty had been quashed—the former was quashed since the defendant had been on a coach trip at the time. Only calling two witnesses, one failed to turn up and the other failed to convince the jury!

[44] Glanville Williams, "Evidence of Identification" [1976] Crim.L.R. 407 gives several other examples.

[45] The concept of corroboration is discussed *infra*, Chap. 6. However, legislation has reduced the scope of rules relating to corroboration very significantly over the past five years. It is unlikely that they will be expanded again.

[46] [1977] Q.B. 224.

especially when the Home Office issued a 1978 circular to police forces tightening up procedures in identification parades.[47] In 1981, the Report of the Royal Commission called for such procedures to be made statutory[48] but instead there is a Code of Practice under which there is a pecking order of methods of identification; a parade, a group identification, a video film and finally confrontation. It is only if a parade is not practicable or the suspect refuses to attend, that a group identification should be arranged.[49] A parade should be held where the suspect requests it or where the police feel it would be useful *and* the suspect consents.[50] The suspect is entitled to take legal advice and to have a lawyer or friend present.

ID parades[51] have been in common use throughout this century. It was and remains a voluntary system and if the suspect chooses not to take part or to disrupt it (perhaps by refusing to wear some item of clothing or to speak certain words), there are no sanctions.[52] Any parade must be conducted by a uniformed officer, inspector or above, not concerned with the case.[53] The suspect must be told of his rights not to participate and asked whether he wants a solicitor or friend present.[54] If no lawyer or friend is present, then the parade has to be photographed or videoed. The places are numbered and if the witness makes a positive identification, it is by number. The witness can be behind a screen to see but not be seen but a representative of the suspect must be present. Everything relevant should be recorded on the custody record.

There should be a minimum of eight[55] others on the parade, resembling the suspect as far as possible.[56] The suspect is able to make objections to the arrangements and such objections should be met, if practicable. The suspect is allowed to stand where he likes and to change position. Once the parade has started, everything that happens should take place in sight and hearing of the suspect or his representative.

The witness should not be shown or reminded of photos or other descriptions prior to the parade and should be isolated from other witnesses. The witness should be encouraged to walk up and down a couple of times, to identify by touch as well as number (but unambiguously). The witness can ask for particular clothing to be worn, gestures to be made or words to be spoken.

Failure to observe the Code of Practice can lead to the identification evidence being excluded under section 78 of PACE. In *Ladlow*[57] there were

[47] These much revised procedures are now contained in Code of Practice D under PACE.
[48] Royal Commission on Criminal Procedure, *op. cit.*, para. 3.138.
[49] Code D 2.6—similarly if group ID is impracticable, then video may be used and if that proves impossible, the last resort can be confrontation.
[50] Code D 2.3.
[51] Bevan and Lidstone, *op. cit.*, p. 379; Leigh, *op. cit.*, p. 233.
[52] There is some authority that the judge can comment on the fact that the suspect has refused to take part in a parade, drawing on analogy from *Robert William Smith* (1985) 81 Cr.App.R. 286. It would appear that in the USA, the suspect can be forced to participate—*US v. Wade* (1967) 388 US 218.
[53] Code D 2.2.
[54] For the detailed conduct of a parade, see Annex A to Code D.
[55] A minimum of 12 if there are two suspects of similar appearance—normally separate parades should be held for each suspect (Code D Annex A, para. 9).
[56] But see Clifford, *op. cit.*
[57] [1989] Crim.L.R. 219.

21 suspects and 11 witnesses so the police held confrontations having decided that 232 parades were impracticable. The evidence of identification was excluded. Similarly in *Gaynor*[58] where the suspect asked for a parade to be held but the police decided (wrongly in the court's opinion) that it was impracticable.

If the suspect does not consent to a parade, if it is impracticable or if it is more satisfactory than a parade[59] then the police can arrange for a group identification[60] and can use their discretion to proceed even though the suspect does not consent. Here the suspect to be identified will be in a group of people, not in the police station[61] unless this is dictated by reasons of security.

Showing the witness a video of a suspect is a possibility where a parade or group identification is not possible or the police consider the video to be the most satisfactory course of action.[62] In essence this is an identification parade conducted on video.

Then, as a last resort, when no other method of identification is practicable, the suspect can be confronted by the witness. The dock ID appears no longer to be admissible—*Eatough*.[63]

---

[58] [1988] Crim.L.R. 242.
[59] Code D 2.7 suggests one reason might be fear on the part of the witness.
[60] See Code D 2.6—2.9.
[61] Code D 2.9 suggests an underground station or shopping centre.
[62] Code D 2.10 and Annex B.
[63] [1989] Crim.L.R. 290.

CHAPTER FOUR

The Prosecution Process

4.1 PRE-TRIAL JUDICIAL SUPERVISION

There is a critical disjuncture between police investigation and prosecution of the offence. Once a suspect is identified, there is a series of decisions shared between the police and the Crown Prosecution Service (CPS). This is a grey area. The autonomy of the police disrupts any coherent "system" since they do not see themselves as part of the criminal process. The narrow policing philosophy sees the courts simply as a mechanism of validating police decisions. The police only bring people before the court for valid reasons and acquittals are defeats. They see little purpose and none of the values in "playing by the rules" or in the intricacies of the judicial process. These are merely "technicalities". This is a blind spot as officers can see the public interest in the detection and punishment of offenders but fail to recognise the equally compelling public interest in ensuring that the power to prosecute is exercised in a manner constrained by social and moral values. Although the police constantly refer to their own accountability to the law, police culture possesses little belief in the principles of legality. Even the liberal police officer finds it difficult to excavate the values embedded in legal technicalities. Those values get hidden behind the formalities which are the province of the lawyers, bureaucratic trivia of no interest to police or public.

But the police do not embrace a wholly neutral stance in the pre-trial process and adopt an adversarial approach with suspects; they are unlikely to follow up possible lines of defence raised by an accused and will seek to undermine exculpatory statements.[1] In contrast, an investigative strategy would see the police gathering evidence for others to make the relevant

[1] McConville M., et al., The Case for the Prosecution (1991), p. 77.

102

decisions. The adversarial role can affect decisions: the level or number of charges might be designed to encourage negotiation over an eventual plea of guilty; police bail might be contingent on making a statement. Adversarialism should imply some level of supervision but the English system sees no need for intervention by CPS, judge or court[2] to ensure the quality of these decisions which are of great significance for both the victim and for the offender: whether to investigate[3] or take no further action (NFA); whether to caution or prosecute; whether to charge or to summons; what offence to charge the suspect with; whether to grant bail. Despite their legal[4] nature, all these decisions rest initially with the police although in many other jurisdictions this is reversed and the police are under much stricter administrative and judicial control.

We justify the lack of pre-trial supervision by pointing to the adversarial nature of courtroom proceedings, the formal equality of the parties and the idea of the "day in court". All contribute to the illusion that the trial cures any pre-trial injustice. But by then it is too late for any consideration of whether the charges are at the right level of seriousness and of the appropriate number to reflect the events, whether there is adequate and admissible evidence to support those charges or whether it is in the public interest to proceed. Reformers such as Lord Scarman have argued for the introduction of an intermediate judicial officer, supervising the decision to prosecute, the nature and level of charge or the need for remands in custody, while giving due weight to principles of legality, due process and the public interest.

4.2 ALTERNATIVE APPROACHES

This lack of supervision in England and Wales is unique. The Scots have a procurator fiscal[5] who has responsibility at common law for the investigation of offences and may instigate and supervise police investigation, especially in cases of sudden death. However the fiscal rarely gets involved in such primary investigation although statements will be taken from all witnesses in serious cases, even when these have already been seen by the police. The fiscal must be satisfied that there is a prima facie case for the prosecution. Although in 1981, the fiscal's approval was seen as simply a formality ("His is an extra door that has to be passed through in getting to court and in general it is readily opened")[6] a decade later the non-prosecution rate in Scotland has risen from 8 per cent to 47 per cent as part of a continuous process in the re-assessment of what constitutes prosecution in the public interest.[7]

---

[2] With the exception of bail decisions—some magistrates' courts also hold pre-trial reviews and until 1994 all magistrates' courts held committal proceedings for cases that were to be tried in Crown Court but the majority of these involved no consideration of the evidence and were merely "paper" committals under Criminal Justice Act 1967, s. 1. See *infra*, para. 5.2.2.2(b).

[3] The basic options are that a complaint may be investigated first, over the telephone, secondly by the attendance of a uniformed officer or thirdly by mobilising CID. Alternatively the complaint may not be investigated at all.

[4] Such decisions are also discretionary and are often affected by non-legal factors such as age, class and ethnicity.

[5] Moody S. and Tombs J., *Prosecution in the Public Interest* (1982); Tombs J. and Moody S., "Alternatives to Prosecution: The Public Interest Redefined" [1993] Crim.L.R. 357.

[6] Royal Commission on Criminal Procedure: *Report* (1981) Cmnd. 8092, para. 6.35.

[7] Tombs and Moody, (1993), *op. cit.*

Many continental countries have an officer analogous to the French *juge d'instruction*,[8] in theory, a neutral figure representing the public interest. In eighteenth century France, the monarchy had at its disposal a centralised police force, regarded by Englishmen with horror.[9] That image of the French *mouchard* both delayed and shaped the form of the British police. But the Napoleonic reforms (which introduced the *juge d'instruction*) were a reaction to those self-same abuses of the *ancien regime* and the *juge* was to be a check on the police function, superior in power and status.[10] The role of *juge* was a natural focal point as a symbol of legalism, a concept of legalism that the French police with their links to despotic monarchy could not represent. In contrast in Britain, it was the local independent police that became that constitutional symbol, representing the limits of state power and public service.

In modern France,[11] the judiciary is a career choice for lawyers rather than a reward for distinguished or long-serving lawyers as it is here. This professionalism means that law school graduates progress through a competitive exam to the *Ecole Nationale de la Magistrature* (ENM) where a two year course leads to qualification as a judge. The ENM graduate can choose initially between the prosecution service (*parquet*), being an examining magistrate (*juge d'instruction*) or a trial judge (*juge du siege*). The *juge d'instruction* in law can exert strong control over the police forces[12] and indeed there is a separate *police judiciaire* to carry out investigations into serious cases under the immediate direction of the *juge*. The *parquet/juge d'instruction* in France are frequently charismatic civil heroes, initiating inquiries into anything that troubles *l'ordre publique* and pursuing the rich and powerful as well as the run-of-the-mill offender. The French often say of the "juge" that "... *il etait l'homme le plus puissant de France* ..."![13]

In the Netherlands, the public prosecutors' functions include the following[14]:

(a) they alone decide who shall be prosecuted in court and have the power to waive prosecution. The principle is that prosecutions should only

[8] Ploscowe M., "Development of Inquisitorial and Accusatorial Elements in French Procedure" 23 *Journal of Criminal Law, Criminology and Police Science*, pp. 372–390 (1932); Tomlinson A., "Non-adversarial Justice: The French Experience" (1983) *Maryland Law Review* 42, p. 131 at 146 ff.; Brouwer G., "Inquisitorial and Adversary Procedures—a Comparative Analysis" (1981) *Australian Law Journal* 55, p. 207.
[9] For an excellent comparison of the French and English police between 1750 and 1850, see Emsley C., *Policing and Its Context* (1983).
[10] For a short history of the French police, Le Clere M., *Histoire de la Police* (4th ed., 1973).
[11] Leigh L. and Zedner L., *Report on the Administration of Criminal Justice in the Pre-Trial Phase in France and Germany* (Royal Commission on Criminal Justice: Research Study No. 1 1992).
[12] In reality, of course, interference is limited, formal approval for police actions is readily forthcoming, often over the telephone. There is involvement in some 10% of cases—Royal Commission on Criminal Justice, Report (1993) Cm. 2263, p. 3, n.3.
[13] Larguier, J., *La Procedure Penale* (6th ed., 1987), p. 21.
[14] Downes D., *Contrasts in Tolerance* (1988), *passim*—in particular see pp. 13–15; also see Lensing H. and Rayar L., "Notes on Criminal Procedure in the Netherlands" [1992] Crim.L.R., p. 623.

take place when the public interest demands it.[15] There is a high level of such waivers.[16]

(b) they have the power to release suspects on bail or indeed to extend periods of detention at their discretion.

(c) they recommend to the court the level of sentence and the judge is bound to take this into account. Senior prosecutors issue national guidelines on both this and on waivers of prosecution.

Although there is also an equivalent to the "juge d'instruction", the Dutch public prosecutor exercises a dominance across criminal justice. In the United States as well it is the prosecutor, the District Attorney, who can exert influence over the course of investigations, making the decision whether to prosecute and on what charge. Several DA's offices have investigative teams attached to them.[17] Recently major investigations have been conducted by special prosecutors; the Watergate allegations during Nixon's presidency; the Iran arms scandal during Reagan's; the Whitewater scandal during Clinton's. One might speculate that in the United States, the history of law enforcement with its tales of gun-slinging sheriffs and rough-and-ready justice meant that the police were unlikely to fit comfortably into symbolic rule of law clothing. Violence and corruption is still linked in the American public imagination with law enforcement. It is the crusading District Attorney who plays the symbolic role.

Here the CPS is in the position to exercise pre-trial supervision although it is unlikely to evolve in that direction in the short term. In 1981, the Royal Commission stressed the importance of different agencies being responsible for investigation and prosecution.[18] The CPS was created by the Prosecution of Offences Act 1985 but it is not empowered to supervise the investigation, make the original decision whether to prosecute or decide on the nature and level of charges. They do not even have the power to require the police to make further inquiries. However they are able to modify charges or to discontinue the prosecution altogether. The Royal Commission's model of two autonomous agencies with overlapping powers and responsibilities has led to an uneasy relationship.

The prosecutor has an immediate interest in the building of casefiles (interviewing witnesses, suspects, scene-of-crime reports) and the nature of the charges. Furthermore the CPS has *locus standi* as guardians of the "public interest" when making decisions as to whether to prosecute, caution or take "no further action". Such pre-trial decisions require coherent criteria, consistently applied on a national basis. Disparities in cautioning and bail rates reveal that this does not happen. Such disparities of treatment would be unacceptable within the courtroom and are equally unacceptable outside. The development of the CPS in a quasi-judicial role could prevent this.

In 1993 the Royal Commission had the opportunity to clarify the

[15] In the U.K. the Code for Crown Prosecutors (CCP) (CPS 1994) para. 7 could be interpreted in this way but the examples given in para. 8 go the other way, detailing negative factors where prosecution is not required and not positive factors indicating that prosecution is required.
[16] Nearly a half of burglaries and a fifth of rapes—see Downes, *op. cit.*, Tables 2.1 and 2.2, pp. 38–49.
[17] Royal Commission on Criminal Procedure, *op. cit.*, para. 6.33.
[18] *ibid.* Chap. 6 and para. 7.3.

relationship between the CPS and the police, either to move towards greater prosecutorial control or to reduce CPS interference in police decisions, emphasising their role as a junior partner. This nettle was not grasped and the status quo was affirmed. It was not desirable that the CPS should be put in charge of police investigations[19]; it was "impracticable" that they should be responsible for the initiation of prosecutions[20]; there would be no fall-back power to require further inquiries but instead a formal system of consultation.[21] Inevitably the interface between CPS and police will remain murky.

4.3 PRE-TRIAL DECISIONS—CAUTION, CHARGE AND BAIL

In this country, we exhibit remarkable haste, especially when a person has been arrested, in deciding whether to prosecute and, if so, the nature of the charge. This decision will be taken by a police officer, not legally qualified and relatively junior, at a very early stage of the proceedings, usually within hours of the suspect arriving at the station. Only rarely will the police seek CPS advice before charging.[22] When a suspect has been brought to the station, the police options are:

   (i) whether to prosecute and if so, whether to charge or to proceed by summons. If the outcome is to charge, there are further decisions as to whether to release on bail.
  (ii) whether to caution the suspect, whom they do not intend to prosecute on this occasion, that they will prosecute if there are future offences.
 (iii) whether to take no further action.

The police retain this discretion in all cases, even serious offences.[23]

4.3.1 *Cautioning*

It has been a penological truism for many years that one of the most effective and efficient disposals of offenders is to divert them from the courts altogether.[24] This has been recognised in the growth of formal cautioning[25] by the police, particularly when dealing with juveniles.[26] The Home Office cautioning guidelines[27] lay down the criteria on which the decision to caution should be made:

[19] Royal Commission on Criminal Justice: *op. cit.*, paras. 5.16–5.17.
[20] *ibid.* para. 5–21.
[21] *ibid.* para. 5–26.
[22] Moxon D. and Crisp D., *Termination of Cases by the CPS* (Home Office Research Study—forthcoming) suggests that national average is about 4%. Cited in Royal Commission on Criminal Justice, *op. cit.*, para. 5.17.
[23] In 1992, 1,735 cautions were issued for offences triable only on indictment including rape and attempted murder—*The Guardian*, March 16, 1994.
[24] If this is not possible, the system should divert them from custodial sentences wherever possible.
[25] A formal warning by an officer of the rank of inspector or above as to the person's future conduct.
[26] Cautioning juveniles is discussed *infra*, Chap. 9.
[27] Home Office Circulars 14/1985, 59/1990 and 18/1994.

- a caution can only be administered where there is a realistic prospect of a successful prosecution.
- the offender must admit guilt.
- in the case of a juvenile, the offender's parents or guardian must consent to a caution being administered.

If these criteria are met, other factors to be taken into account are: the seriousness of the offence and the extent of the damage done; the interests and desires of the victim; the previous conduct of the offender; family background as well as the subsequent conduct of the offender such as a willingness to make reparation. The guidelines emphasise that, in respect of juveniles, prosecution is a last resort. Formal cautions are recorded and, if there is a subsequent conviction, can be cited as part of the offender's record.

In 1993, 311,300 people were cautioned, 209,600 for indictable offences, almost double the numbers in 1983 when 165,500 were cautioned, 114,900 for indictable offences.[28]

Table 4.1 Persons Cautioned for Indictable Offences 1983 and 1993

Type of offender	1983	1993
All offenders	114,900 (10%)*	209,600 (41%)
All male offenders	82,700 (18%)	153,600 (37%)
Males 10–13	na (74%)	19,900 (90%)
Males 14–17	na (32%)	48,600 (63%)
Males 18–20	na (3%)	24,500 (32%)
Males 21 +	na (4%)	60,600 (26%)
All female offenders	na (34%)	55,900 (60%)
Females 10–13	na (90%)	7,500 (97%)
Females 14–17	na (58%)	18,000 (84%)
Females 18–20	na (5%)	6,700 (52%)
Females 21 +	na (13%)	23,600 (46%)

* In brackets, offenders cautioned as a percentage of offenders found guilty or cautioned.[29]

Over the past decade, police cautioning has risen in both absolute numbers and in the percentage of offenders cautioned. The risk of prosecution has not necessarily lessened since the development of diversionary techniques leads to

[28] *Criminal Statistics 1993* Cm. 2680 Table 5.1, p. 100.
[29] *Criminal Statistics 1993, op. cit.,* Tables 5.1–5.3, pp. 99–102.

"net-widening", that is, people are brought within the formal system when previously no formal action would have been taken.[30] Despite this, the rise in cautioning adult offenders has been remarkable. It is no longer an option reserved for juveniles. However the cautioning rate varies according to the seriousness of the offence, age, gender and ethnicity. It also varies according to police force area—the adult male is more than twice as likely to be prosecuted in Cumbria with a cautioning rate of only 13 per cent than in another rural area, Devon, where 35 per cent are cautioned rather than prosecuted.[31]

A caution cannot be administered unless the person admits the offence. A person might thus admit responsibility even when there is some doubt, for example the existence of the requisite criminal intent. Frequently the evidence on which a caution is based would not measure up to court scrutiny.[32] Despite this, the caution can be retailed to a court if the person is convicted of a subsequent offence, normally within three years. Cautioning is administrative justice, wholly within the control of the police and with no possibility of external challenge.[33]

But the positive characteristics of cautioning are many: it keeps offenders out of the courts, reduces the courts' workload with consequent economic benefits. The social benefits are significant as there is less stigmatisation and disruption to the person's life. It is also effective—87 per cent of those cautioned in 1985 were not convicted of a "standard list" offence within two years of the caution. Eighty per cent of those cautioned had no previous cautions or convictions but for those who had been previously convicted, there was a much greater likelihood that they would re-offend.[34]

Prosecution and conviction is the most expensive option in dealing with offenders. The value of diversionary schemes was recognised by the Runciman Commission which felt that the limits of cautioning had yet to be reached for petty offenders. However the disparities in cautioning rates across the country led them to recommend that cautioning should become statutory with national guidelines. The decision whether to caution should remain in the hands of the police although the CPS should be able to require the police to caution in lieu of prosecution.[35] Despite this, the new national guidelines[36] are more restrictive, removing any presumption that juveniles should be cautioned, discouraging repeat cautions and cautions for serious offences.

Even when the police choose not to caution but to prosecute, the CPS can review the case file to decide whether a caution would be a more appropriate course of action. In making such decisions, a Crown Prosecutor is governed by the Code for Crown Prosecutors (CCP), issued by the Director of Public Prosecutions and approved by the Attorney-General.[37] The CCP lays down

---

[30] Pratt J., "Diversion from the juvenile court" 26 Brit.J.Criminol. (1986), p. 212.

[31] *Criminal Statistics 1993, op. cit.*, Table 5.4, p. 104 and pp. 92–93 for discussion.

[32] McConville *et al.* (1991), *op. cit.*, pp. 78, 81–83.

[33] The decision *not* to caution a juvenile is reviewable—R. *v. Chief Constable of Kent, ex p. L* [1993] 1 All E.R. 756.

[34] Home Office: *Statistical Bulletin* (Issue 20/92).

[35] Royal Commission on Criminal Justice, *op. cit.*, para. 5.57.

[36] *The Guardian*, March 16, 1994; Home Office Circular 18/1994; Evans R., "Cautioning: Counting the Cost of Retrenchment" [1994] Crim.L.R. 566—see infra para. 9.4.

[37] In accordance with s. 10 Prosecution of Offenders Act 1985.

two criteria in assessing whether a prosecution is called for—that of evidential sufficiency and that of the public interest.[38] In particular the Code notes that when dealing with young adults, consideration should be given to the harm that a conviction can do to a young person's future prospects and that the public interest may be best served by a caution. Until 1993, the section on juvenile offenders stated: "The objective should be to divert juveniles from court wherever possible."[39] It also required that the Crown Prosecutor should be satisfied that the spirit of the Home Office guidelines on the cautioning of offenders have been followed and that all the agencies relevant to the welfare of the individual offender have been consulted.[40] All this has now been changed: "Young offenders can sometimes be dealt with without going to court. But Crown Prosecutors should not avoid prosecuting simply because of the defendant's age."[41] This inevitably means more prosecutions and more young offenders serving custodial sentences.

Where the Crown Prosecutor is not satisfied that a prosecution is appropriate, they can refer the case back to the police for them to administer a caution. If the police are unwilling to do this, the CPS can simply discontinue the prosecution.

4.3.2 *Charging*

When an officer considers that there is enough evidence for a successful prosecution, the suspect should be taken before the custody officer who must decide whether the person should be charged.[42] Custody officers will rarely refuse a charge.[43] The charging officer must identify clearly the offence which the suspect is alleged to have committed, both in factual and legal terms. The suspect will be cautioned[44] and asked if he wishes to say anything. The charge[45] will then be recorded in the police charge book.

Having been charged, the accused must not be questioned any further in relation to the offence with which he or she is charged[46] and must be brought before the court as soon as possible.[47] The Runciman Commission considered this former requirement as too restrictive and would permit further questioning provided there has been a further caution and the opportunity to take legal advice.[48]

But what is a charge? Its legal significance is obscure. Sanders argues[49] that

---

[38] See *infra*, 4.8.

[39] CCP (pre-1993), para. 21 (in CPS, Annual Report 1992–3 HCP 1992–93 748 App.)

[40] *ibid*. para. 22.

[41] CCP, para. 6.8.

[42] PACE Code of Practice C 16.1.

[43] McConville *et al.*, *op. cit.*, p. 118.

[44] In the sense of PACE Codes of Practice that the suspect is warned that he does not have to say anything but that anything he does say will be recorded and may be used in evidence.

[45] The word "charge" is open to several different meanings, dependent on context—Pearson J. in *R. v. Norfolk Quarter Sessions, ex p. Brunson* [1953] 1 Q.B. 503.

[46] There are limited exceptions in PACE Code of Practice C.16.4 and 16.5—for example where the questions are necessary to prevent harm or loss, to clear up ambiguities or to comment on information which has come to light after charging.

[47] PACE, s. 46(2).

[48] Royal Commission on Criminal Justice, *op. cit.*, paras. 2.39–2.42.

[49] Sanders A., "Arrest, Charge and Prosecution" (1986) 6 *Legal Studies* 257.

police charging is a nineteenth century development from their power to arrest and then to grant bail. The charge was simply the writing down of the allegation so that the court, police and the defendant could be sure of the precise nature of the allegation when the case came to court. As magistrates withdrew from investigation and interrogation, the police used the charge procedure more frequently. It took on a quasi-legal status as if it were the beginning of the legal process against the accused.

But does a charge "institute proceedings"? If it does, then only a court may halt those proceedings. If it does not, the police can "uncharge". Although this is a technical issue, it highlights the obscurity of the boundaries between and the responsibilities of the police, the CPS and the courts. At common law it is only the bringing of suspects before magistrates and laying information as to an offence that initiates proceedings.[50] The legal implications of police charging were thus minimal since charging did not compel further proceedings. Yet within the police station, the charge was an important stage for the old Judges' Rules and now is even more significant for PACE and for the PACE Codes of Conduct. Administering cautions and regulating periods of detention depend on it.

Its legal status appears to be changed under section 15(2)(c) of the Prosecution of Offences Act 1985 which states that proceedings are instituted when "... a person is charged with an offence after being taken into custody without a warrant, when he is informed of the particulars of the charge." This would appear to limit police discretion to withdraw charges although the CPS still have statutory powers to discontinue prosecutions.[51]

The charge has a quality of being an irrevocable step. The police rarely "uncharge".[52] It does mark the point at which the police cease to have an immediate interest and the papers are passed on to the Crown Prosecution Service. But even the CPS will rarely drop or amend the charge on their own initiative. The Runciman Report considered the suggestion that the CPS should have responsibility for framing the initial charge but saw practical difficulties in having prosecutors posted to police stations and felt it would add to delay.[53]

4.3.3 *Bail*

After arrest, the defendant's liberty can only be restored by a decision of the police or the courts to grant bail. This is discussed later[54] but in outline, the police powers are as follows:

(a) if the suspect is in police custody but has not been charged and if the custody officer is unwilling to authorise further detention for questioning, then the officer can release either unconditionally or conditionally on bail to report back to the police station at some point.[55]

---

[50] *Hill v. Anderton* [1982] 2 All E.R. 963, *per* Lord Roskill at 971.
[51] Prosecution of Offences Act, s. 23(4) enables the CPS to discontinue prior to a court being informed. Sanders A. (1986) *op. cit.*, regards this as conceptually irreconcilable with s. 15(2)(c).
[52] Sanders A., "Police Charging and the Prosecution of Offences Act" 149 J.P. 662 (1985).
[53] Royal Commission on Criminal Justice, *op. cit.*, para. 5.21.
[54] *infra*, para. 5.3.1.
[55] PACE, s. 37(2) and s. 40(8).

(b) if the suspect is in police custody and has been charged, the officer has the power[56] to release on bail subject to the condition that the suspect appear before the magistrates' court on a certain date. The police can impose other conditions.[57]

(c) where the suspect has been arrested by magistrate's warrant, this warrant may already have the terms of bail endorsed on it—it is "backed for bail".

(d) if none of these apply, the custody officer can detain the suspect and take him or her to the next sitting of the magistrates' court. Although the court may hear the case at that point, this is rare and the accused may make an application for bail at this point.

4.4 PERSPECTIVES ON PROSECUTION

Historically and culturally, prosecution and trial have more significance than the straightforward disposal of those identified by the police as committing a crime. In previous centuries the public interest in the detection of crime and the private interest of the victim were more interwoven and the prosecutor was far from an invisible figure. In the eighteenth century, he was the initiator and controller of events. The trial was a ritual which depicted, in a microcosm, the social relationships prevailing in that society. Hay[58] has demonstrated how class authority and legal ideology can be represented through the criminal prosecution. Through prosecution, a private citizen exercised a control over punishment (and thus over the life and death of others) that is extraordinary to modern eyes—"If I succeed, I shall certainly hang the culprit" wrote a 1796 prosecutor.[59] The power may have been indirect but nonetheless it was an important constituent in both personal and class relationships.

But the judicial process ensured that such prosecution and punishment were not seen too directly as the vengeance of an individual. Instead it was the law at work. The crime was represented as an attack on the "body politic" and the public good and not as damage to specific and personal interests or to an individual's power or authority. The interests of the powerful may have been masked but not so obscurely as to prevent the message filtering through. In the eighteenth century, private prosecutors manipulated the pomp and ritual of the trial. The Assize was not just a set of trials as sittings of the Crown Court might be today—it was one of the social occasions of the year, to see and be seen and not merely by social equals. It was the visible representation of a class's cohesion, identity and characterisation of themselves as rulers. Through the minutiae of punishment, through the capacity to use and abuse

[56] PACE, s. 38 which also specifies the situations where bail may not be granted—that the name and address of the suspect cannot be ascertained, that custody is necessary to prevent harm to others or that there are reasonable grounds for believing that the suspect will not answer to bail.
[57] The power to impose conditions both for release on bail before and after charge is recommended by Runciman—Royal Commission on Criminal Justice, *op. cit.*, para. 5.22 and was introduced by s. 27 Criminal Justice and Public Order Act 1994.
[58] Hay D., "Property, Authority and the Criminal Law" in Hay D., *et al.* (eds) *Albion's Fatal Tree* (1975); "Controlling the English Prosecutor" in 21 *Osgoode Hall Law Journal* p. 165 (1983); "The Criminal Prosecution in England" (1984) 47 M.L.R. 1.
[59] Hay, (1983), *op. cit.*

the bodies of others, the relationships of power and the pattern of social order were visibly and regularly re-enacted.[60] Why? Foucault, among others, would argue that the use of the body as an object of punishment has always been a measure of individual and political power. To humiliate, to flog, to main or to kill are emphatic symbols of power. Allied to the legitimacy conferred by the processes of the court, these are the ultimate symbol of political authority.

In feudal times, the king and barons fought over the rights to hang thieves. In modern times, although we neither whip nor execute, the trial and the social debate is still about what is to be done *to* the accused. The focus on the body means that the criminal trial can be seen as an important site for symbolic struggles. This is exemplified by the continuing campaign to restore capital punishment or by feminist groups who campaign to increase punishment for domestic violence or sexual assault. There is little evidence that murder or rape declines as a result of increasing judicial punishment. For such campaigners there is a hidden agenda, meanings to be communicated through the official rituals of trial and punishment.

The mounting of a trial, its abandonment or successful conclusion—all these have meanings which are publicly negotiated. There is a significance which goes beyond the efficient processing of offenders.[61] Whether viewed by historians,[62] political scientists[63] or anthropologists,[64] the criminal trial becomes a complex social and political ritual, perhaps mystifying class relationships, perhaps symbolising constitutional ideals or, on a deeper level, a reaffirmation of order in the face of the irrational and the unknowable.

4.5 THE DEVELOPMENT OF THE PUBLIC PROSECUTOR

In eighteenth century England, the capacity to mobilise the criminal courts and to mould the punishment on your own behalf was a significant *private* right/rite. The state provided the legal and administrative mechanisms but the power to prosecute lay in the hands of private individuals who, in the main, were members of the propertied class. To the eyes of the working classes, the victims of the criminal justice system, the law was a mechanism of social discipline. The middle and upper classes had privileged access to and leverage over forms of punishment.

However, the criminal law was not just barely-concealed class aggression. The ideology of justice and law played a major part nor was this mere mystification; as Thompson has put it, men are not mystified by the first man who puts on a wig. "If the law is evidently partial and unjust, then it will mask nothing, legitimise nothing, contribute nothing to any class's hegemony."[65]

[60] Foucault M., *Discipline and Punish* (1977), Chaps. 1, 2.
[61] *e.g.* Garfinkel H., "Conditions for Successful Degradation Ceremonies" 66 Am.J.Sociol. (1956), p. 420; Carlen P., "Remedial Routines for the Maintenance of Order in Magistrates' Courts" (1974) 1 Brit.J. Law and Soc., p. 101; McBarnet D., *Conviction* (1983).
[62] Hay D., (1975), *op. cit.*
[63] Arnold T., *Symbols of Government* (1962), Chap. 6.
[64] *e.g.* Gibbs J., "The Kpelle Moot" 33 *Africa* (1963), p. 1; Ottenberg S., "Ibo Oracles and Intergroup Relations" 14 Southwest. Jour. Anth. (1958); Bohannan P., *Justice and Judgement Among the Tiv* (1957).
[65] Thompson, E. P., *Whigs and Hunters* (1975).

To be effective, substance had to be given to the values of neutrality, universality and equality. In that context, private prosecution should have withered away and a public prosecution service taken its place.

There were several moments in the nineteenth century[66] when it appeared as if this would happen. There were reports and parliamentary inquiries, all of which backed the idea. There was even government support. All that emerged was the 1879 Prosecution of Offenders Act and the new office of the Director of Public Prosecutions[67] (DPP). This proved a damp squib and five years later the office was *de facto* merged with that of the Treasury Solicitor, not to re-emerge until 1908. Even then there was no statutory definition of functions nor even public prosecutions to direct. The only identifiable group of day-to-day prosecutors were the Treasury counsel, retained by the DPP for prosecution work in the Central Criminal Court and Middlesex and Surrey Sessions. Yet they were merely barristers on whose services the DPP had first call and they also had large practices outside the prosecutorial function.

Can we explain why there was no development of an autonomous prosecution service at that time or why such a service should materialise a century later? One explanation lies in the constitutionalist position that the state and the executive must remain shackled at all times. Although the "new police" had been accepted, it was done reluctantly and they provided a service which individuals, even wealthy individuals, could not provide for themselves. Private prosecution was another matter entirely. For the nineteenth century liberal, let alone the Tory squirearchy, access to the courts by the private subject signified that the law was not merely a weapon of the state and, to ensure that, its mobilisation should remain vested in private hands.

A complementary but contradictory answer lies in the development of the "rule of law" conception later to be enshrined by Dicey. This stressed certainty, neutrality, universality and equality. These qualities were certainly not part of the make-up of the private prosecutor who was to be found pursuing self-interest, discretionary and subjective justice, perhaps most notably with the Societies for the Prosecution of Felons.[68] But equally there was a seamier side to the public prosecutor. Parliamentary committees had heard of the "low attorney" consorting with and bribing constables to obtain fees for prosecution. To what extent did this image tarnish reform movements pressing for public prosecutors? From the viewpoint of legal ideology of the "rule of law", class conflict was to be masked and the workers co-opted into the parliamentary road. Did the prospect of a new breed of corrupt public officials freeze the reforming zeal?

The private prosecution was neither abolished nor did it expand. It withered away with its tradition of private interest inimical to liberal rule of law. This process was aided by the practical problems of travel, cost and

[66] There were earlier possibilities of such developments especially in the 16th century with the Marian statutes—see Langbein J., *Prosecuting Crime in the Renaissance* (1974).

[67] For a detailed account of these developments and the history of the DPP, see Edwards J.Ll.J., *The Law Officers of the Crown* (1964); for an outline, see Uglow S., "Independent Prosecutions" Brit. J. Law and Soc. (1984), p. 233.

[68] Shubert A., "Private Initiative in Law Enforcement" in Bailey V. (ed.), *Policing and Punishment* (1981).

general inconvenience which led to a deepening reluctance to become involved. It was a slow process as prosecution was regarded as an inalienable right of the citizen. Even after the First World War, the DPP, Archibald Bodkin, talked of the police's role as one of giving "reasonable assistance by way of investigation to the prosecutor".[69] Today under the 1985 Prosecution of Offences Act, it still remains possible for the private citizen to undertake criminal prosecution.

It was the success of the "new" police that must have contributed to the decline of the private prosecutor and the still-birth of any public successor. All too easily the police were seen not only as investigators but as prosecutors. Indeed the juridical basis for the prosecutions undertaken by the police was as if they were private citizens. From 1887, the Metropolitan Police routinely used a private firm, Wontners, to run prosecutions on their behalf. Outside London, where the control of the police was firmly vested in the local Watch Committees, the middle classes must have watched contentedly as prosecutions were *de facto* delegated to the police and their own responsibilities declined. Most police forces developed prosecuting solicitors' departments and they, although often referred to as "County" prosecutors, looked to the Chief Constable as their "client". In many magistrates' courts, it was not just the police agents who were the prosecutors, in many cases it was a police inspector.[70]

4.6 THE MODERN PROSECUTION SYSTEM

Reform came about as the result of the Report of the Royal Commission on Criminal Procedure (RCCP) in 1981. The Report highlighted a range of problems[71]:

(a) there was a lack of uniformity with differing procedures and standards applied across the country on such matters as whether to prosecute or caution, so that while Cheshire cautioned 2 per cent or fewer of adults for indictable offences, Suffolk cautioned 22 per cent.[72]

(b) the system was inefficient especially in the preparation of cases since many acquittals were the result either of the judge stopping the trial at the end of the prosecution case or directing the jury to acquit.[73]

(c) in principle, investigation and prosecution should be separate processes.[74] It was wrong for the prosecuting lawyer to have the investigating officer as a client. The goals of investigation and of prosecution were incompatible although a complete separation was in practice impossible.

[69] Sir Archibald Bodkin, "The Prosecution of Offenders" (1928) 1 *Police Journal* 353.
[70] Royal Commission on the Police, *Report* (1962), Cmnd. 1728, paras. 380–381.
[71] Royal Commission on Criminal Procedure, *op. cit.*, Chap. 6.
[72] *ibid*. para. 6.40.
[73] *infra*, para. 4.9.
[74] Royal Commission on Criminal Procedure, *op. cit.*, para. 6.23.

(d) there was no executive or democratic accountability or control over the existing system.[75]

The RCCP's recommended that a Crown Prosecution Service be established. The recommended structure was decentralised and modelled on the police, with a separate CPS for each police force area with a Chief Crown Prosecutor responsible locally to a supervisory body and nationally to the Director of Public Prosecutions.[76] But this local option was rejected by the Government[77] and in the Prosecution of Offences Act 1985 a national structure was created. Although the new service was independent of the police, only 31 areas were set up compared to 43 police forces. The areas are directly answerable to the DPP whose role is to provide national guidelines and procedures, to intervene in difficult or complex cases, to appoint and supervise personnel and to manage resources generally. The Attorney-General is responsible in Parliament for general policy but not for individual cases.

These areas were reorganised in 1992 and reduced to 13, placing increased emphasis on the 111 branches as the basic operational units. Such re-organisation parallels that occurring in the police where locally operational control has moved downward and fewer forces are envisaged.[78] The prospect is of a criminal justice system managed by a few powerful Chief Constables and Chief Crown Prosecutors. Financially the CPS cost £283 million in 1993–94, mainly on salaries[79] and accommodation but also involving prosecution costs, a figure which covers fees and expenses for lawyers acting on behalf of the CPS and witnesses' expenses.[80]

Has the new system addressed the problems identified by the RCCP in 1981?

(a) the central objection to the old system was the lack of objective fairness because of the institutional overlap between the investigative and prosecution stages. The relationship between the police and CPS remains ill-defined and this was not resolved by the Runciman Report.[81] In itself, such ambiguity does not affect the objectivity of case review of the CPS. But they are reliant on the police for the quality of the evidence supplied[82] and for co-operation.[83] This lack of a clear identity for the CPS is a major weakness for the criminal justice system since there is a residual sense of subordination to the police, which is accentuated by sharing a common adversarial culture.

(b) the second problem was one of disparities in standards, especially in cautioning rates in different parts of the country. Cautioning remains

---

[75] *ibid.* para. 6.48.
[76] For further discussion, see Uglow S. (1984), *op. cit.*, pp. 237–238.
[77] *An Independent Prosecution Service* (1983), Cmnd. 9074.
[78] White Paper *Police Reform*, Cm. 2281 (1993), Chap. 10.
[79] Currently the CPS employs over 2,000 lawyers and 4,000 administrative staff in 100 offices.
[80] CPS *Annual Report 1993–94*, HCP 1993/94 444, para. 6.3.
[81] Royal Commission on Criminal Justice, *op. cit.*, paras. 4.3.1 and 4.3.2.
[82] See McConville *et al.* (1991), *op. cit.*, and McBarnet D., *Conviction* (1981) for discussions on the police "construction of a suspect population".
[83] This is sometimes not present—see Block B., Corbett C. and Peay J., *Ordered and Directed Acquittals in the Crown Court* (Royal Commission on Criminal Justice Research Study No. 15), (1993), p. 14 and Chap. 6, Recommendation 1.

the province of the police and the unfairness inherent in the discrepancies still exists.

(c) the third problem was the inefficiency of the system, both in terms of non-jury acquittals (which is explored below) and also in terms of delays. One of the agency's key targets is to reduce the average processing delay in magistrates' courts to three months. It has achieved that figure.[84] This target is still higher than that achieved in January–March 1988 when the delay was two-and-a-half months.[85]

(d) the lack of accountability, identified by the RCCP, remains. Although there is ministerial responsibility to Parliament through the Attorney-General for the performance of the CPS, there is a notable absence of any form of local accountability for prosecution policies and performance. It illustrates again the lack of cohesion in the system. The Police and Magistrates' Courts Act 1994 obliges local police authorities to produce policing plans, identifying areas of concern and key objectives. Such plans necessarily impinge on the work of the CPS but there is no local body with whom the LPA can agree a joint strategy. The agencies, be they the police, CPS, courts, probation officers or prison governors, all work autonomously at a time when there is an obvious need on a local level for broad and co-operative strategies to be developed.

4.7 THE CROWN PROSECUTOR

The role of the state prosecutor is still not 10 years old and still far from the lynchpin around which the system of criminal justice rotates. Sandwiched virtually to vanishing point between the two symbolic reference points of the police and the judge, the new Crown Prosecutors or even senior Treasury counsel are faceless, certainly in terms of personal identity[86] and status. In Germany as well, although the prosecutor has theoretical mastery over pre-trial process, he has no discretion as to whether to prosecute and cannot engage in plea-bargaining.[87] As in the United Kingdom, it is a low status office. Such anonymity also reflects an equivalent public ignorance of their function. What, after all, do prosecutors do?

The CPS receives files of individual cases from the police. On a day-to-day basis, these may require immediate action as the files refer to people arrested, charged and detained by the police who wish to see the accused remanded into custody. The prosecutor will present the case for remand to the magistrates, often with little time to consider whether remand into custody is justified. Once immediate problems are resolved,[88] the file is handed to the

---

[84] CPS *Annual Report 1993–94, op. cit.*, para. 5.2.

[85] CPS *Annual Report 1987–88*, Annex B, Figure B.3. Is it significant that the CPS Reports do not show year-on-year performance or that delay in Crown Courts (around five months in 1987–88) is no longer a key aspect of performance?

[86] For example, there is a dearth of information or research on the Treasury counsel but see Tudor Price J., "Treasury Counsel at the Old Bailey . . ." [1985] Crim.L.R., p. 471, Even the DPP has had a low profile, although recently Sir Alan Green brought some unwelcome notoriety to the job. His successor, Barbara Mills, as the first woman DPP, has had a higher profile.

[87] Langbein J., *Comparative Criminal Procedure: Germany* (1977), pp. 11–13, 87.

[88] Here and elsewhere in this section, I draw upon the valuable summary of CPS operations in

team leader for the court concerned who assigns it to a prosecutor[89] to review the information contained in it. A case file will contain details of the offender, of the offences with which she or he has been charged, details of witnesses and arresting officer, witness statements. The prosecutor will ask a number of questions[90]:

(a) is the nature and level of charge appropriate given the evidence? This might involve discussion with the investigating officer, who might have sought advice prior to charging, as well as defence lawyers.
(b) in the case of mixed offences,[91] what mode of trial (magistrates' or crown court) would be suitable? The seriousness of the offence and whether magistrates possess sufficient sentencing powers are factors but the prosecutor's preference for summary trial might be overridden either by the magistrates or the defendant.
(c) what is the quality of the evidence? Is there relevant, credible and substantial evidence going to all the facts in issue? Is there a realistic prospect of conviction? Again discussions might be needed with the police about additional evidence. Police forces use civilian teams (known as Administrative Support Units or Crime Support Units) supervised by a detective to provide liaison. The CPS rely on such units to provide them with evidence against the accused but also with all unused material for disclosure to the defence.[92]
(d) is there any reason in the public interest why this prosecution should not proceed?

The case is prepared for the first hearing at the magistrates' court. If it is a summary offence and the accused pleads guilty, then the prosecutor[93] reads out brief facts and that is the end of the matter. If there is no plea or an indication of a not guilty plea, there will be an adjournment to prepare the case for trial, allowing time for obtaining witness statements and exhibits. There may be several preliminary hearings and the prosecutor at some stage will need to disclose the prosecution case.[94]

If the matter is indictable or jury trial has been chosen, then the prosecutor used to prepare for committal proceedings. These proceedings dated from 1848[95] since which date justices of the peace had to hold a preliminary hearing to ascertain whether there was a prima facie case against the accused.

Block B., Corbett C. and Peay J., *Ordered and Directed Acquittals in the Crown Court* (Royal Commission on Criminal Justice Research Study No. 15, 1993) Chap. 2.

[89] It is rare for a prosecutor to have sole charge of a case throughout. The CPS has a Working Group on Pre-Trial Issues to secure improvements in case management but also are emphasising "team working" and "file ownership" so that the team remains responsible throughout the life of a case file.

[90] These are given in outline here and considered in more detail *infra*, para. 4.8.

[91] *i.e.* offences triable either summarily in the magistrates' court or on indictment in the Crown Court. See *infra*, para. 5.2.1.

[92] *Maguire* (1992) 94 Cr.App.R. 133; *Ward* (1993) 96 Cr.App.R. 1; *Edwards* [1991] 1 W.L.R. 207—this is discussed *infra*, para. 5.3.3.1.

[93] The CPS still use agents (local private lawyers) in some 25 per cent of magistrates' courts sittings—Royal Commission on Criminal Justice, *op. cit.*, para. 5.7 although CPS *Annual Report 1993–94: op. cit.*, para. 6.3 suggests that this has been reduced to 16 per cent.

[94] Magistrates' Courts (Advance Information) Rules 1985 (S.I. 1985 No. 601).

[95] Indictable Offences Act 1848 although the use of committal hearings can be traced back to the Marian statutes in 1554.

If there was, the defendant could be "committed for trial" to a higher court, nowadays the Crown Court. Committal proceedings were abolished by section 44 of the Criminal Justice and Public Order Act 1994 so that there is now "transfer for trial" proceedings which allow the prosecutor to serve notice on the accused that the case will be held in Crown Court. The accused can apply for a dismissal of the case and that application will then be heard by the magistrates.[96]

After transfer, the Crown Prosecutor or, more likely, a law clerk must prepare the brief (consisting of all statements, interviews, tape transcripts, exhibits, etc.), for independent counsel. CPS barristers do not as yet have rights of audience in the higher courts.[97] It is extraordinary that responsibility for a serious prosecution is transferred not just once (from the police to the CPS) but inexplicably for a second time from the CPS to a private barrister. There are obvious weaknesses; there is no machinery in barristers' chambers for allocating cases to appropriately experienced counsel[98]; there is no requirement for a preliminary written assessment by counsel of the strengths and weaknesses of the prosecution case[99]; counsel will rarely offer advice to the CPS without first being asked; although counsel will be selected for particular cases, it is possible that on that day, they will not be available; at the trial itself, the CPS is often represented by an unqualified law clerk so that counsel assumes full responsibility for the conduct of the case, even offering no evidence on his or her own initiative (although such a course of action is more likely to be after CPS instructions or pressure from the judge).[1]

The lack of a proper line of responsibility at this point can only be wondered at. The trial is a natural focal point of the whole process here investigators, prosecutors, defenders, the courts and penal measures intersect. The criminal justice system suffers from the diffusion of responsibility and the lack of authority existing at the heart of the English criminal process.

4.8 THE DECISION TO PROSECUTE AND THE CPS CODE

The prosecutor's first action is to review the police case, not simply to decide whether to take court action but also to confirm the nature and level of the charge against the accused and whether the mode of trial is appropriate. We have seen the police acting as a preliminary filter, removing cases from the conveyor-belt of justice, by NFAs or cautions. The CPS act as a second filter using their power to discontinue prosecutions. The criteria they use are to be found in the Code for Crown Prosecutors (CCP).[2]

There are two basic issues, the first evidential and the second a matter of

---

[96] There is further discussions on committal proceedings and transfer for trial, *infra*, at 5.2.2.2.
[97] CPS *Annual Report 1993–94, op. cit.*, para. 4.1.
[98] Royal Commission on Criminal Justice, *op. cit.*, para. 5.39.
[99] The Royal Commission would require counsel to inform the CPS in writing that the case meets the criterion of the Code of Crown Prosecutors that there is a realistic prospect of conviction or that further evidence be required or that the case be discontinued—*op. cit.*, para. 5.39.
[1] Block *et al., op. cit.*, p. 22.
[2] Provided by the DPP in accordance with s. 10 of the Prosecution of Offenders Act 1985. The revised version was issued in 1994; Ashworth A. and Fionda J. "The New Code For Crown Prosecutors: Prosecution Accountability and the Public Interest" [1994] Crim.L.R. 894.

public interest. The first question is sufficiency of the evidence.[3] The Crown Prosecutor must be satisfied that there is a realistic prospect of conviction, namely would a bench of magistrates, properly directed, be more likely than not to convict? He or she must consider whether there is admissible, substantial and reliable evidence that the offence has been committed by an identifiable person. The prosecutor should be satisfied that there is no realistic expectation of an ordered acquittal or a successful motion of "no case to answer". He must have regard to obvious lines of defence.

The 1994 Code is much less detailed than its predecessor which directed the prosecutor to consider:

(a) the conduct of the police inquiry and interrogation especially with regard to breaches of the provisions of PACE Codes of Practice,
(b) in particular the reliability of the accused's admissions, having regard to the age and understanding of the suspect,
(c) the possibility of exaggeration, unreliability or bias on the part of a witness,
(d) the possibility of a witness lying,
(e) matters which might undermine credibility of witness,
(f) the quality of the witness—the impression that might be made, the ability to stand up to cross-examination and any physical or mental disability,
(g) conflicts between eye-witnesses and whether there is a suspicion that a false story might have been concocted,
(h) availability and competence of witnesses,
(i) the reliability of identification evidence,
(j) whether the public would consider the proceedings oppressive?
(k) if separate trials be ordered for joint defendants, would there still be a realistic prospect of convictions?

Having considered the evidential aspects, the prosecutor should consider whether the public interest requires a prosecution.[4] It is not the case that every suspected crime should automatically be prosecuted.[5] Bluntly this is rhetoric. Reading the revised Code leads to the conclusion that there is a presumption of prosecution. Under the old Code, the prosecutor was urged that, if undecided, he or she should abide by the spirit of the cautioning guidelines. That injunction has now been removed. Again the old Code stated "... the police decision to institute proceedings should never be met with passive acquiescence but must always be the subject of review."[6] That positive exhortation also has been removed.

The prosecutor is enjoined that, broadly speaking, the graver the offence, the more likelihood that the public interest required prosecution. The Code's constant refrain is the "seriousness" of the offence. As we shall see, this is consistent with the sentencing criteria laid down in the 1991 Criminal Justice Act.[7] With a serious offence, even where there are public interest factors

---

[3] CCP, para. 5.
[4] Ashworth A., "The 'Public Interest' Element in Prosecutions" [1987] Crim.L.R., p. 595.
[5] CCP, para. 6.1 quoting Attorney-General, Lord Shawcross, in 1951.
[6] CCP (pre-1993) *op. cit.*, para. 10.
[7] *infra*, Chap. 7.

against prosecution, the prosecution should often go ahead and those factors should be put to the court in sentencing.[8] The Code outlines the factors in favour of prosecution:

- the prospect of a significant sentence
- the use of weapons or violence
- whether the victim was in public service
- whether the accused was in a position of trust or authority
- whether the offender was the ringleader
- was there premeditation?
- whether the offence was carried out by a group
- was the victim vulnerable and was there significant harm or loss?
- did the motive involve discrimination?
- was there a difference in ages between victim and defendant or any evidence of corruption?
- was the offence committed while the defendant was under a court order?
- is the offence likely to be repeated or is it prevalent in the area?[9]

The factors to be taken into account[10] in considering waiver of prosecution are:

- would the likely penalty to be imposed by the court be purely nominal?
- was the offence committed as the result of a misunderstanding?
- was the harm minor and the result of a single incident?
- does the delay in bringing the case to court make the case "stale"? The rule of thumb was "was the offence committed 3 years before the date of trial?" This is less relevant where there is likely to be a substantial custodial sentence, the investigation has been complex or the accused has contributed to the delay.
- is the defendant old or infirm? In such cases there should be prosecution only if the offence is very grave or there is a real danger of repetition.
- was the accused mentally disordered at the time of the offence or would prosecution have an adverse effect on the mental health of the accused? In such cases prosecution is rarely appropriate.[11]
- has the defendant put right the loss caused?
- could disclosure at the trial harm sources of information or national security?

Where the public interest factors are in favour of waiving prosecution, the CPS have statutory power[12] to discontinue. Discontinuance should involve consultation with the police but the final decision rests with the prosecutor exercising an independent judgement as guardian of the public interest. The Runciman Committee found that the CPS did exercise that judgement

---

[8] CCP, para. 6.2.
[9] CCP, para. 6.4.
[10] CCP, para. 6.5.
[11] See Home Office Circular: *Provision for Mentally Disordered Offenders* No. 66/1990.
[12] Prosecution of Offences Act 1985, s. 23 but there is also a common law power to withdraw or offer no evidence even at a late stage—*Grafton* [1992] Crim.L.R. 826—even at Crown Court the judge cannot interfere even where this power is exercised after the trial has commenced. In such circumstances the judge can only direct an acquittal.

appropriately, citing one study[13] which suggested that nearly a third of discontinuances were dropped on public interest grounds. Of these, nearly half were discontinued because of the triviality of the offence or of the likelihood of a nominal penalty. The factors were the youth, age, previous good character or mental state of the accused, the attitude of the complainant or the offer of compensation.

To prosecute only where there is an identifiable need should be a central strategy for a criminal justice system. Ethically we should make only a minimal use of punishment. In resource terms, alternative strategies to prosecution are invariably cheaper and more effective. However, assessment of public interest is only possible where the necessary information has been collected. The police are unlikely to consider this in detail nor do the CPS have resources available for such investigation. An encouraging development has been that some probation services run schemes to expand the quantity and quality of that information. There has been a growth of public interest case assessment (PICA) schemes and the Royal Commission has recommended that these be put on a country-wide systematic basis.[14]

Discontinuance of all charges is not the only option since the defendant may well wish to plead guilty to a lesser charge while maintaining a plea of not guilty to more serious charges. The CPS can accept such "deals" but the Code's strictures are that the overriding consideration in considering acceptance of guilty pleas is that the court must not be left in the position where it is unable to pass a sentence consistent with the gravity of the actions. However, having accepted a plea, the CPS should not then argue that the case is more serious than appears in the charge. Administrative convenience should not take precedence over interests of justice.[15]

The review process should also ensure that the number of charges should be as few as possible so as not to obscure the nature of case. Specimen charges can be used where appropriate. However, the CPS should not use multiplicity of charges as a lever to put pressure on the defendant so that he or she pleads guilty to a few charges in exchange for others being dropped. The charges laid should reflect the gravity of conduct but again as long as court's sentencing powers are adequate, then factors such as the speed of trial and the mode of trial might permit a charge of lesser gravity.[16]

4.8.1 *A Reviewable Discretion?*

Earlier we examined the court's power to review police decisions not to enforce the law.[17] Reviews of a decision to prosecute are fewer but in *ex p. L*,[18] the applicant had been regarded as a suitable case for a caution by the local

[13] Moxon and Crisp, *op. cit.*
[14] Royal Commission on Criminal Justice, *op. cit.*, para. 5.61.
[15] CCP, para. 9.1.
[16] CCP, paras. 7.1–7.3.
[17] *supra*, para. 2.6.2.3.
[18] *R. v. Chief Constable of Kent, ex p. L* [1993] 1 All E.R. 756—see Uglow S., Dart A., Bottomley A. and Hale C., "Cautioning Juveniles—Multi-Agency Impotence" [1992] Crim.L.R. 632; Osborne P., "Judicial Review of Prosecutors' Discretion" (1992) N.I.L.Q., Vol. 43, p. 178; Hilson C. "Discretion to Prosecute and Judicial Review" [1993] Crim.L.R. 739.

multi-agency juvenile offender liaison team but this was ignored by the police who chose to prosecute and were supported by the CPS. The juvenile sought to review this decision. Lord Watkins accepted that it was the decision of the CPS that was judicially reviewable and not any prior decision of the police:

> "[The CPS] has unquestionably the sole power to decide whether a prosecution shall proceed. It is entirely dominant in that very important respect and all the erstwhile corresponding power of the police has been stripped away ..."

But can a CPS decision to continue proceedings against an individual be impugned in the Divisional Court at all? Some authorities[19] suggest that any body subject to statute such as the CPS would be subject to judicial review while others indicate that the prosecuting powers of the Attorney-General, under whom the DPP and CPS operate, cannot be controlled or supervised by the courts.[20] Since the lower criminal courts had the power to stop proceedings as an abuse of process,[21] judicial review was unnecessary but Watkins L.J. accepted that this power was too limited. A criminal court of trial was not an appropriate forum to test the merits of a decision to prosecute; first, because there was the general policy aimed at keeping juveniles out of the criminal courts; secondly, because individual juvenile defendants can scarcely argue that prosecuting them was an abuse of process since they had admitted guilt in order to be eligible for a caution. Judicial review was more appropriate and a CPS decision not to discontinue was open to challenge. However the Divisional Court concluded that in this instance there had been a proper exercise of discretion. It also restricted its decision to the discretion to prosecute children and stated that judicial review of decisions to prosecute adults was not available.

4.9 DISCONTINUANCE AND NON-JURY ACQUITTALS

One of the major concerns of the Royal Commission in 1981 was the inefficiency of the old system of County Prosecuting Solicitors.[22] The fact that 43 per cent of Crown Court acquittals in 1978 was the result either of the judge ordering an acquittal (19 per cent) or directing the jury to acquit (24 per cent)[23] suggested that cases were not properly reviewed prior to trial to check that there was sufficient evidence or that, where the evidence was present, there was a poor level of preparation of cases. A closer analysis was less damning since the commonest factors leading to a non-jury acquittal[24] were unforeseeable because either witnesses fail to attend the court or fail to testify satisfactorily. Despite this, the Royal Commission's research suggested that about 20 per cent of directed acquittals ought to have been foreseen and avoided because proper review of the evidence would have revealed doubt as to whether there was sufficient evidence to justify the initial decision to

---

[19] *R. v. Panel for Take-overs, ex p. Datafin* [1981] Q.B. 815.
[20] Following Lord Dilhorne in *Gouriet v. Union of Post Office Workers* [1978] A.C. 435.
[21] See *R. v. Derby Crown Court, ex p. Brooks* (1985) 80 Cr.App.R. 164 at 169 and *R. v. Bolton JJ., ex p. Scally* [1991] 2 W.L.R. 239 at 256.
[22] Weatheritt M., *The Prosecution System: Survey of Prosecuting Solicitors' Departments* (Royal Commission on Criminal Procedure Research Study No. 11) (1981).
[23] Royal Commission on Criminal Procedure, *op. cit.*, para. 6.18 drawing on McConville M. and Baldwin J., *Prosecution, Courts and Conviction* (1981).
[24] Block *et al.*, *op. cit.*, p. 42.

prosecute. By use of powers of discontinuance,[25] these non-jury acquittals could have been avoided.

The pattern over recent years is as follows:

Table 4.2 Acquittals in Crown Court[26]

Year	% of all defendants acquitted	% acquittals after "not guilty" plea	% non-jury acquittals as % of all acquittals	Ordered*	Directed*
1978	16	47	43	19	24
1980	18	50	42	22	20
1981	17	50	43	22	21
1982	17	49	43	23	20
1983	15	50	46	26	20
1984	16	51	47	26	21
1985	15	50	48	28	20
1986	16	49	52	37	15
1987	14	50	50	34	16
1988	13	55	52	36	16
1989	15	56	53	36	17
1990	15	57	58	40	18

* A judge orders an acquittal before the trial begins usually because the prosecution are unable to advance evidence. An acquittal is directed when the judge considers there is insufficient evidence at the end of the prosecution case.

Over the past decade, there has been a steady rise in the number of non-jury acquittals and this is accounted for by the rise in the number of ordered acquittals while directed acquittals have fallen slightly. Block[27] suggests that the ordered acquittal is much more likely to be CPS-initiated when a weakness in their case has been identified between committal and trial. Despite recognising this, the prosecution cannot be dropped since once a defendant has been committed for trial, all parties have to attend even where the CPS is not intending to offer evidence.[28]

[25] Now under s. 23 of the Prosecution of Offences Act 1985 but also at common law—*Grafton* [1992] Crim.L.R. 826.
[26] Block *et al.*, *op. cit.*, p. 12; Zander M., "What the Annual Statistics Tell Us about Pleas and Acquittals" [1991] Crim.L.R., p. 252.
[27] Block *et al.*, *op. cit.*, p. 13.
[28] Royal Commission on Criminal Justice, *op. cit.*, para. 5.37 recommends that the CPS be given

Block's study looked at 100 cases of non-jury acquittals and concluded that in only 45 per cent was the acquittal unforeseeable and that 27 per cent were clearly foreseeable with evidential deficiencies. They also noted instances of inadequate advice from prosecuting counsel. This study and Table 4.2 do not suggest any significant improvement since 1985 in directed acquittals, largely because these are the cases which are less foreseeable. But the weaknesses could be foreseen by closer liaison with witnesses and victims and the obvious way of achieving that is to allow CPS lawyers to have rights of audience and thus greater "ownership" of the case. However the rise in the numbers of "ordered acquittals" suggests that pre-trial assessment of the relative strength of cases has improved markedly. It is unfair to regard this sector as part of an acquittal rate which suggests inefficiency.

The CPS surveyed discontinuances in magistrates' courts in November 1993.[29] Of the prosecutions discontinued:

- 43 per cent were for insufficient evidence. In a quarter of these cases, weak identification evidence was the reason for discontinuance
- 31 per cent were for public interest reasons[30]
- 9 per cent were where the defendant eventually produced the relevant motoring documents
- 17 per cent were where the prosecution were unable to proceed mainly because an essential witness was missing but also where the offence had been taken into consideration by another court or simply the prosecution were not ready.

4.10 SENTENCING

It has always been a convention that, after conviction, the prosecution's job was over and there was no involvement in the sentencing of the offender. It is still the case that CPS do not make any recommendation as to type or length of sentence (although this can be affected indirectly by the decision on the nature of the charge and acceptance of plea). There have been proposals for reform in this area but the only change has been under section 36 of the Criminal Justice Act 1988 which permits the CPS to ask the Attorney General to refer unduly lenient sentences to the Court of Appeal.[31] There have been such references when courts have imposed non-custodial sentences for rape[32] and for conspiracy to supply drugs.[33] In some driving cases where death had been caused, fines have been replaced by prison sentences.

Prior to the trial, the CPS do have the power to discontinue and recommend that the police administer a formal caution. The procurator fiscal in Scotland

---

the power to discontinue proceedings up to the beginning of trial in both magistrates' and Crown courts.

[29] CPS *Annual Report 1993–94: op. cit.*, para. 3.3.

[30] These results resemble those in Moxon and Crisp, *op. cit.*

[31] There were 59 applications in the first three years—Hansard, H.L., Written Answers 85, December 19, 1991; Henham R., "Attorney-General's References and Sentencing Policy" [1994] Crim.L.R. 499.

[32] *Attorney-General's Reference* (No. 3 of 1993) [1993] Crim.L.R. 472.

[33] *Attorney-General's Reference* (No. 16 of 1992) [1992] Crim.L.R. 456.

can go further and make an offer to the accused to discontinue proceedings if the offender pays a fixed penalty.[34] There were 15,599[35] in 1991, and it is an alternative to prosecution that the Royal Commission would like introduced in England and Wales.[36]

4.11 THE TWENTY-FIRST CENTURY PROSECUTOR?

Comparative and historical examples suggest that the CPS may evolve into a major force in the criminal process. The Prosecution of Offences Act does not specify in detail CPS functions—in section 3 it talks of instituting or taking over the "conduct" of proceedings or giving "advice" to police forces. Now the teething problems over efficiency have been overcome, the CPS inevitably will fight for its own institutional autonomy. In legal terms, it already occupies the high ground. Through the discretion as to whether to proceed with prosecutions, the CPS can develop the power to censor police actions or to take a more pro-active role in investigation and interrogation before the trial. This conclusion flows from the prosecutor's discretion whether to proceed in any particular case. Guidelines also ensure that prosecutors must take the overall public interest into account alongside "evidential sufficiency".

There are further proposals to add to CPS functions. Most importantly is the suggestion that the prosecutor should suggest an appropriate sentence to the trial judge. Such a radical reform would bring the prosecutor out of the shadows. If the British press's first priority are the details of the offence, close behind comes the punishment. Prosecutor's suggestions (and necessarily the prosecutors themselves) would inevitably come under close scrutiny in major cases. It would give a specificity and visibility of function that has always been lacking. Section 36 of the 1988 Criminal Justice Act now permits the Attorney-General to refer cases to the Court of Appeal where the sentence is considered to be "unduly lenient". Although the need for referral to the Attorney-General means that such prosecution "appeals against sentence" have not become routine, this reform inevitably give a greater depth to the prosecution involvement. Although the image of "neutral presentation of the facts" would be tarnished were the prosecution seen to aim for a particular sentence, the dominant prosecution image would be as guardians of the "public interest".

We may see the emergence of an institutional "competitor" to the police. There is a vacuum between investigation and trial in this country which the CPS might fill. There is a need for co-ordination and direction in the criminal justice system. This is particularly the case in difficult inquiries which involve various agencies.[37] This function is recognised as important in other jurisdictions which realise that the goals and values of other agencies such as social workers or the police need to be mediated by the ideas of justice and of legal values.

---

[34] Criminal Justice (Scotland) Act 1987, s. 56.

[35] Toombs and Moody, *op. cit.*, at p. 362.

[36] Royal Commission on Criminal Justice, *op. cit.*, para. 5.63.

[37] Sexual abuse of children is an obvious example—see the criticisms about the lack of co-ordination in the investigation made by Lord Justice Butler-Sloss in *Report of the Inquiry into Child Abuse in Cleveland* Cm. 413 (1987).

CHAPTER FIVE

Courts and Trials

5.1. HISTORICAL ORIGINS OF ADVERSARIAL SYSTEM

As a representation of moral and rational government, the trial is one of the major constitutional institutions of the common law. Naturally its composition, jurisdiction and procedures are significantly the product of its history. In its origins, a central question of any hearing lay in discovering the truth of an accusation.[1] Truth was not a matter of witnesses and evidence but instead might be found through ordeal, trial by battle[2] or by compurgation.[3] However, in 1166, the Assize of Clarendon provided for a "jury of presentment"[4] which was a group of local people put on their oath to tell the truth about local crimes. This was not a trial jury but one of accusation. The allegations were tested through the ordeal of water[5] which was the only means of proof for those indicted by the presenting jury.

The ordeal was the *judicium dei*, its legitimacy came from God and as such the proceeding required the presence of a priest. But at the Lateran Council in 1215 the Church declared the ordeal to be mere superstition.[6] Without the religious imprimatur, other methods of proof had to be found. Continental Europe turned to the Roman-canonical law of proof[7] with its calculus of evidence ranging from the full confession to eye-witnesses down to mere circumstantial evidence or *indicia*. This approach did not take hold in England which had turned to the jury of trial. This was a petty jury, initially apparently the choice of the accused, who could decide on the truth of the allegations. Yet it slowly became the custom of the royal courts and after the Statute of Westminster in 1275, those who refused to "put themselves upon the country" could be imprisoned. The trial was still not a fact-finding forum, however, since the jurors were people who already knew the circumstances of the accusation.[8]

In small, rural, homogeneous communities, juries may well have been an effective means for the determination of the truth. As male landholders, jurors could probably also be relied on to uphold royal interests. In medieval England, the king dispatched justices to the provinces to inquire into matters affecting those interests, including felonies which involved the forfeiture of the felon's property to the king. But the right of the state to investigate and prosecute crime was rejected, whether by accident, design or by an "insular dislike for things foreign".[9] Criminal prosecution became very much a matter for private individuals to mobilise the machinery through accusation although how the accused was to confront or refute this (except through the knowledge of the local jury) remains shrouded in mystery:

> "Of the actual conduct of a trial we know almost nothing before the sixteenth century, not nearly enough until the eighteenth. How the jury informed itself or was

[1] Milsom S. F. C., *Historical Foundations of the Common Law* (1981) Chap. 14; Plucknett T. F. T., *A Concise History of the Common Law* (5th ed., 1956).
[2] Initially introduced after the Conquest for appeals of felony where a Norman was the accused.
[3] Suspicion was often the basis of accusation and proof by compurgation involved the accused producing a set number of neighbours to swear to his or her overall good character.
[4] This was later known as the grand jury which was not abolished in England until 1933 to be replaced by committal proceedings but it still survives in the USA.
[5] The accused was bound and lowered by a rope into a deep pool—if he sank to the level of a knot tied in the rope at the distance of his hair, he was declared innocent but if he floated, the water would not receive him and he was judged guilty. Warren W. L., *The Governance of Norman and Angevin England 1086–1272* (1987), p. 109.
[6] Warren, *op. cit.*, p. 213.
[7] Langbein J., *Torture and the Law of Proof* (1977).
[8] Milsom, *op. cit.*, p. 411. It is not until after the 17th century that personal knowledge of the case becomes a disqualification for a juror. Lord Justice Coke talked of trial being by jury and not by evidence.
[9] Spencer J., *Jackson's Machinery of Justice* (8th ed., 1989), p. 19.

informed, how rules of evidence emerged, when and in what detail directions were given by the justices, these are things we do not know."[10]

There was formal control of the criminal courts by the king with a monopoly of jurisdiction and of punishment over serious offences but contrasted with this is a local quality to justice, both through the jury system and by gentry exercising control over criminal courts. Legal doctrine remained unsophisticated and the extent of moral blame was dealt with by jury verdict rather than by technical rules of law. Equally throughout the thirteenth and fourteenth centuries, it is an illusion that all criminals would face the death penalty since relatively few were executed and composition in cases of violence was common.[11]

The absolutist monarchies of the Tudors and Stuarts led not just to savager punishment but to greater centralised control of the courts as well as to innovations in procedures. The "prerogative" court of Star Chamber, for example, operated without juries, on a basis of unidentified accusation and with the defendant interrogated by the judges under oath and perhaps under torture.[12] Political and popular reaction in the seventeenth century to such courts was to delineate the conditions under which the monarch or state has the power to restrict a person's freedom and to inflict punishment.

Adversarialism was the technique which emerged. The two basic building blocks were the two principles of natural justice. Progress was slow. In 1610 Chief Justice Coke might declare the first of these; that a man should not be judge in his own cause.[13] But even in the nineteenth century we find Lord Brougham citing the case of the Duke of Buckingham who heard a charge against a neighbouring farmer brought by his own gamekeeper and decided in the Duke's own home.[14] The second cardinal principle, that of *audi alteram partem*, was also recognised by the early eighteenth century.[15] But the criminal defendant had no means of getting his or her story heard since it was not possible to compel witnesses to testify (although they might do so voluntarily) nor was there professional assistance to examine witnesses or to speak on the accused's behalf until 1836. Furthermore the defendant could not give sworn testimony until 1898.[16] Even the "bulwark of freedom", the jury, could not be relied on to be impartial.[17] The central elements of the adversarial trial were legal representation, cross-examination of the prosecution witnesses, the ability to call and examine your own witnesses, to testify on your own behalf and to address the jury. These were in place by the

---

[10] Milsom, *op. cit.*, p. 412.
[11] Given J., *Society and Homicide* (1977).
[12] Radcliffe and Cross, *The English Legal System* (5th ed., 1971), p. 107; Milsom, *op. cit.*, pp. 418–419; Holdsworth W. S., *History of English Law* (1936–72), Vol. V, p. 155.
[13] *Dr Bonham's Case* (1610) 8 Co.Rep. 113b.
[14] Quoted in Manchester A. H., *Modern Legal History* (1980), pp. 161–162.
[15] *The King v. University of Cambridge* (1723), 1 Str. 557 cited in Wade H., *Administrative Law* (1961), Chap. V "Natural Justice".
[16] Criminal Evidence Act 1898, s. 1.
[17] After the acquittal of the Quakers, Penn and Mead, in 1670, for a "conspiratorial gathering", the jury were fined and imprisoned until eventually released by the Chief Justice who declared "the right of juries to give their verdict by their conscience". Harman H. and Griffith J., *Justice Deserted* (1979), p. 11.

end of the nineteenth century. A system of appeal was instituted in the early twentieth century.[18]

Adversarial trial places great significance on the day in court. At this point the information and argument from both sides is placed before the judge and jury, both of whom come to the courtroom with no prior knowledge or opinions. This might be contrasted to the inquisitorial method where there is a continuing judicial process of collecting evidence and interviewing witnesses. The common law trial is regarded as the single, public proceeding, both the beginning and end of the affair. It is difficult to explain why the adversarial process rather than the investigative process should have emerged in England: the relatively short period of absolutist monarchy and the impact of the puritan revolution in reaction to undiluted state power is one factor; the historical dominance of the local state over the national is another. Private prosecution correlated with the image of a society that was the product of the actions of its more powerful members, not of an interventionist government.

In the nineteenth century, adversarialism was not just a representation of the rule of law but of government itself; the agent of the state (the judge) sits above and apart from the individuals below. The competition of the courtroom mirrors the competition of the market place. Yet it is also the forum where the rights of the citizen are at their most inviolable.

5.1.2 *Characteristics of the Common Law Trial*

The three major characteristics of the trial are the independence of the court, the adversarial nature of the trial and the priority given to procedural fairness.

5.1.2.1 INDEPENDENCE

Constitutionally there is independence for the court and the judge. Decisions can only be challenged through appeal and review procedures. There is no interference by national[19] or local government and it is very difficult to remove judges[20] or magistrates[21] except for extreme misconduct. Even in relation to the other institutions of the criminal justice system, the courts operate autonomously.

The trial is separated from all the previous events and the judge, in common with the jury and the spectators in the public gallery, is hearing the evidence for the first time. It is solely on the evidence that is retailed in court, usually by formal oral testimony, that the decision is based. It is an autonomy which verges on quarantine; the court's decision is not allowed to be infected by

[18] Manchester, *op. cit.*, p. 180 *ff.*—often execution of sentence was carried out within a few days.
[19] The extent to which this is valued by J.P.s can be seen in the Magistrates' Association's adverse response to the Lord Chancellor's *Scrutiny of Magistrates' Courts* (1989) which suggested a rationalised and centralised system under the Home Office.
[20] Superior judges can only be removed after an address presented to the Queen by both Houses of Parliament. Circuit judges can be dismissed by the Lord Chancellor under powers given by the Courts Act 1971 for "incapacity or misbehaviour". See Spencer, *op. cit.*, p. 368, for some entertaining examples.
[21] Magistrates can be removed from the commission by the Lord Chancellor—Spencer, *op. cit.*, pp. 410–412.

information that derives from any source other than the formal rules of evidence, except the assistance that the court can obtain in interpreting the law from appellate court decisions; once the jury has retired, they remain together[22] and incommunicado and their discussions are absolutely privileged.[23]

Within the Crown Court itself, the judge is king. Once transfer proceedings have taken place, discontinuance of the action (for example, by offering no evidence) or amendment of the indictment is subject to the consent of the judge.[24] Although there is an over-riding power of the Attorney-General to stop a prosecution by entering a "nolle prosequi",[25] this judicial control over the indictment emphasises the role of the judge as representative of the monarch and of the conceptualisation of crime as an offence against the state; the Queen appears as the wronged party in the indictment and the juror swears an oath to try the issues between the Queen and the prisoner. The form of trial belongs as much to constitutional history as to a modern democratic state.

In France the trial judge will have a full *dossier* prepared by the *juge d'instruction*, including witness statements and the interrogation of the defendant. The examination of witnesses will be on the basis of these documents. There is judicial supervision of the process from the beginning of the investigation to the decisions in the prison itself on length of time to be served. This latter function is the province of the *judge de l'application des peines*. In contrast, the English judge will usually know nothing about the case before the trial, will not have been engaged in supervising any investigation, taking statements from witnesses or the accused or making bail decisions. Nor, except in the case of life sentences[25a], would he or she be consulted over decisions to release from prison.

Formal independence of the courts from the state is an essential check on the power of executive government. Independence from the other criminal justice agencies also makes the courts a neutral forum which is a key part both of the adversarial system and of due process. However, the costs of such isolation are that the judiciary are reluctant to be involved in formulation of criminal justice policy,[26] especially over sentencing policy. This detachment is slowly changing with the advent of national and local Criminal Justice Consultative Councils on which judges sit.[27]

---

[22] *Alexander* [1974] 1 W.L.R. 422.
[23] *Thompson* [1962] 1 All E.R. 65.
[24] *Broad* [1979] 68 Cr.App.R. 28 but see *Grafton* [1992] Crim.L.R. 826. The Crown Prosecution Service is able to discontinue prosecutions before they have reached this stage under s. 23 Prosecution of Offences Act 1985. In magistrates' courts, however, they appear to be able to halt proceedings at any time *R. v. Canterbury Justices, ex p. Klisiak* [1981] 3 W.L.R. 60.
[25] *Blackstones' Criminal Practice* (1991), para. D2.36.
[25a] *infra*, para. 8.7.4.
[26] Although judicial members of the House of Lords have involved themselves in debates on criminal justice—see Goddard L.C.J. opposing capital punishment reform H.L.: Vol. 157, col. 1030.
[27] Editorial in [1992] Crim.L.R. 141.

5.1.2.2 ADVERSARIALISM

The court (judge and jury) in making decisions, does not act as an investigative body, calling and examining witnesses on its own initiative. It plays a passive role, listening to evidence which is advanced by the prosecution and the defence. Both parties only call those witnesses likely to advance their cause and both parties are permitted to attack the credibility and reliability of the witnesses testifying for the other side. The case is prepared for trial by the CPS and defence lawyers and in court, the lawyers decide which evidence is to be produced and which witnesses are to be called. The judge should not interfere or act as an investigator. This is the major difference between common law countries and other European jurisdictions.[28]

One rationale for adversarialism is in the right to confront the accuser and the evidence.[29] Confrontation implies that the witness should be there in person in order that the reliability of the evidence and the credibility of the witness can be tested. This can lengthen trials because even where the evidence is uncontroversial, the witness is normally present. Criminal trials do not use pre-trial written pleadings,[30] as occur in civil cases, although this process would reduce trial length by concentrating on those matters in dispute.[31]

The judge acts as umpire, ensuring that the rules on procedure and evidence are followed, directing the jury on the law to be applied and reminding them of the evidence that they have heard. The jury's role is first, to decide questions of fact—that is, to make up their minds between conflicting accounts as to what happened—and then to decide on the guilt or innocence of the defendant.

One glaring omission from the trial is the victim; there is no right to speak, to be represented[32] nor even a place to sit. The crime is conceptualised as a wrong against society and once the complaint has been made, control is relinquished. The victim's wishes whether to prosecute or not may be taken into account by the police or the prosecution.[33] The lack of protection may be seen in sexual assault cases where the defence is often a thinly-veiled attack on the character of the victim. The need for representation can become acute when the defendant asks for leave to cross-examine the rape victim on her

---

[28] Tomlinson E. A., "Non-Adversarial Justice: The French Experience" in *Maryland Law Review* (1983), Vol. 42, p. 131. In Europe, several jurisdictions are considering reforms which would allow the defence lawyer to question prosecution witnesses directly—at present questions have to be asked indirectly through the presiding judge. This was one of the reforms in Italy's new Code of Criminal Procedure in 1989.

[29] It is one of the rights granted in the 6th Amendment of the American Constitution which provides for a fair and unbiased trial.

[30] One reason for this is that the plea of not guilty puts the entire prosecution case in issue. Criminal Justice Act 1967, s. 10 provides for formal admissions but is rarely used.

[31] Some magistrates' courts do use pre-trial hearings—Baldwin J., *Pre-Trial Justice* (1985).

[32] This is not the case in certain European jurisdictions where the victim has a right to legal representation. In France the victim can be joined to an action as *une partie civile* and has *locus standi* in all preliminary matters and at the trial is able to argue that the charge is insufficient, to object to a certain line of questioning or to ask that certain questions be put to a witness.

[33] Code for Crown Prosecutors (CPS 1994), para. 6.7 "... Crown Prosecutors must always think very carefully about the interests of the victim ..."

past sexual history.[34] In such situations, the tactical interests of the prosecutor do not necessarily overlap with those of the victim.[35] Further examples can be seen in homicide cases; where the plea is provocation involving an attack on the victim's character, the victim's relatives might wish to be independently represented in order to examine witnesses or even to object to the acceptance of a plea of "guilty" to manslaughter but of "not guilty" to murder.

5.1.2.3 FAIRNESS

A fight model requires rules of engagement which are essentially based on the idea of fairness. There are three types of fairness; of the rule, of the procedure or of the decision. The doctrine of sovereignty of Parliament meant that from the seventeenth century[36] the courts would not interfere in the substantive quality of a statute.[37] Nor is there intervention of any kind with jury deliberations or verdict. Fairness in the courtroom is about procedural justice. The assumption is that truth is more likely to emerge from due process of law. This is seen in the appeal system which is a review of process rather than of the decision. If the decision is one which could reasonably have been reached, then the Court of Appeal will not interfere.[38]

The root values of procedural justice are encapsulated in the House of Lords' decision in *Woolmington*[39] where Lord Sankey talked of the "golden thread" of justice that the prosecution has to prove every element in a criminal charge and that proof has to be beyond reasonable doubt. The defendant has to prove nothing. More specifically the elements of fairness are:

    (a) the right to know the nature of the charges and evidence,
    (b) the right to be represented by a lawyer,
    (c) the presumption of innocence including the right to silence and the burden of proof on the prosecution,
    (d) the standard of proof to be applied is proof beyond reasonable doubt,
    (e) the right to a public trial in a neutral forum,
    (f) the right to cross-examine and test the prosecution evidence,
    (g) the right to call evidence and give evidence on the accused's behalf,
    (h) the right to appeal.

Such rights underpin our perception of a "fair trial". This takes precedence over more pragmatic aims such as the determination of truth or law enforcement. Frank[40] argues that Anglo-American criminal procedure

---

[34] Sexual Offences (Amendment) Act 1976, s. 2. *infra*, para. 6.6.5.1.

[35] Temkin J., *Rape and the Legal Process* (1987), p. 162.

[36] Wade, *op. cit.*, pp. 128–129.

[37] Again this can be compared to the USA, where state and federal legislation is subject to judicial review of its constitutionality—see the recent debate on the constitutionality of various states' abortion laws.

[38] Criminal Appeal Act 1968, s. 2 allows for conviction to be set aside where they are "unsafe or unsatisfactory", where the judge has made a wrong decision on any question of law or where there was a material irregularity in the course of the trial. But the proviso to the section provides that the appeal may be dismissed if the court is satisfied that no substantial miscarriage of justice has occurred.

[39] [1935] A.C. 462.

[40] Frank J., *Courts on Trial* (1949).

detracts from the discovery of the truth. Were we to invent a mechanism to find out facts and allocate blame, the solution would not be an adversarial system, with partisan advocates, untrained judges, reliant heavily on cross-examination and where the final decision is left to 12 people plucked arbitrarily off the street. The goal of discovering the truth and making a reliable decision might require a trained chairperson with investigative powers, sitting with assessors expert in the relevant field and with the parties' representatives having a much lower profile.

Some commentators, especially Robert Mark,[41] ex-Commissioner of the Metropolitan Police, attack the ritual formality of the trial especially when the "guilty" are released because of some perceived technicality. A trial should keep its eye on the ball—that is, convicting the guilty (the substantive justice of the decision itself). But this ignores the symbolic force of the trial. Procedural justice emphasises the distinction between the trial as a logical function and the trial as a symbol. In its outward form, the trial is about the determination of truth and the application of that truth to legal rules. But compare the courtroom with a police station; what would be the public reaction if a court were to interrogate a defendant over days and nights with limited rest, no legal assistance, perhaps using the threat of violence or the inducement of release to obtain responses to questions?[42] In the court, the accused's rights are paramount because the covert function of the trial is its concrete illustration of a fair and just society.

5.1.3 *Rational Decision-making*

The predominant image of the courtroom is a plea of "not guilty" followed by trial by jury.[43] Any imperfections in pre-trial process can be swept away by the "day in court" which will ascertain the truth, ascribe responsibility and impose proper and proportionate punishment. The trial is rational decision-making within the overall values of the rule of law. However there are other elements which directly contradict and undermine this.

5.1.3.1 EFFICIENT MANAGEMENT

Rational management influences the courtroom as much as rational decision-making. Offenders are processed and disposed of as efficiently as possible in terms of time and resources. Key performance indicators relate to such issues as cost per case, the time taken between first appearance in magistrates' court and committal, or between committal and trial, or the backlog of cases for a particular court or petty sessional division. The publication of such KPIs create pressure to maintain efficiency. This leads to pressure to speed up cases and to the negotiation of outcome.[44] The defendant's role can be reduced to passivity especially where there are

---

[41] See Mark R., *Minority Verdict* (BBC—Dimbleby Lecture 1973).

[42] Only since the promulgation of the PACE Codes of Practice could defence lawyers be reasonably confident that a court would exclude confessions obtained in such circumstances.

[43] Although this is a popular image, most cases are heard by magistrates acting without a jury. As well, most cases are disposed of by guilty pleas—over 90 per cent in magistrates' courts and around 70 per cent in Crown Courts. Perhaps less than 5 per cent of cases that are eligible to be heard by a jury are so heard.

[44] *e.g.* the importance of a high percentage of guilty pleas to reduce delays. See *infra*, para. 5.3.5.

going professional relationships between the defence and prosecution lawyers, the police, probation services, court administration and judges. Thus there is a divergence between the official and articulated ideals of the courtroom and the organisational reality that exists behind them. Central values can be too easily ignored and the quality of the decision reached becomes of lesser significance.

5.1.3.2. RITUAL

Even when there is a contested trial, rational decisions can take a backseat to the high level of ritual in the formal procedures, dress and language which regulate the parties. On one level ritual contributes not only to the authority of the court but also to establishing the authoritative version of the events not merely in the courtroom but also for the outside world. But the ritualism is an appeal which is less than rational, reinforcing a view of the courtroom as a reified rather than a human process. For example, one American sociologist[45] has suggested that the trial is a process of recasting the defendant, away from his own identity and into a stereotyped social role (mugger, hooligan, drunk, vagrant). The trial becomes a degradation ceremony which reduces the defendant to a lower status and, through him, personifies broader patterns of social authority and of social power.

5.1.3.3 WORLD OF AUTHORITY

The courtroom is an imposed and imposing "world of authority"[46] with dominance and subordination clearly signposted. There is the deference shown by all the personnel towards the bench as well as those elements of "majesty"; the elevated bench, private access to judge's "chambers" and the judge's throne-like chair. The geography of the court carries this on; in the dock, the defendant is raised but on a lesser level; there is a rail surround, not to stop an escape attempt but representative of captivity. The public are well to the back of the court, segregated so that we are allowed to observe but not to participate. Carlen suggests that the organisation of space is such as to impede communication, especially for those who are not part of the routine cast and who are unfamiliar with a courtroom. Distances are much greater than one would normally use for disclosure of private or traumatic incidents or indeed for effective intervention. Communication is through the lawyers and there is also the sense of a play being carefully stage-managed, again maintaining the sense of domination, of the inexorability of the law.

The language employed, with its technical vocabulary and flowery and archaic forms of address, again put the uninitiated at a disadvantage. The defendant becomes "Smith" or "this person". The court insists upon the precise technical words,[47] again marginalising the accused. Any involvement by the defendant is essentially passive, responding to questions. Indeed the mode of discourse in the courtroom involves either interrogation or monologue, both of which are extraordinary (and resented) when they occur

---

[45] Garfinkel H., "The Trial as a Degradation Ceremony" (1956) 66 Am.J.Sociol. 420.
[46] Carlen P., "Remedial Routines for the Maintenance of Control in Magistrates Courts" (1974), 1 Brit.J. Law and Soc., p. 101.
[47] Carlen, *op. cit.*, p. 107.

in day-to-day conversation.[48] Even the intelligent and articulate defendant is ill-equipped to deal on an equal basis. Defendants feel confused, alienated and by-passed so that even the practice of asking the defendant if he has anything to say before sentence is now delegated to the lawyer.

Through the ritual, the geography and the language, there is a high level of situational control by the court and the lawyers. "After all, they're near enough mates in the same play. They're the cast of the play, you're just the casual one-day actor. It's just another day's work to them."[49] This control is experienced by all defendants but the workforce in a court is mainly white, middle-aged, middle-class and male. Defendants are often coloured, young and working-class. There is an inevitable clash of conflicting beliefs, attitudes and of social realities. In this context, the perception of the courtroom as imposing a social authority is as valid a perspective as that of rational decision-making.

5.1.3.4 TRIALS AS NARRATIVE

We might also think about the trial as story-telling. It is the party that puts together the most credible narrative that often wins. Narrative plays an important part in imposing order on our lives.[50] We see our own selves in terms of a biographical narrative, with the events of our lives moving in a connected flow, linked to some central theme. Similarly, narrative helps us to impose order on the external world. Thus we do not believe poor story-tellers since their narrative is often internally inconsistent, jumps from one point to another and does not link to central action. Whether we believe or disbelieve what people tell us is more related to their abilities as story-tellers than it is to the truth, or otherwise, of their story. This raises interesting questions about the human "need" for order and how narrative satisfies that need. But in the context of the trial, it further erodes the dominance of "legal rationality" as well as requiring re-assessment of the role of the lawyer and of the decision-making by the judges or jury.

5.2 SUMMARY AND INDICTABLE TRIAL

There are two systems of courts that hear and decide criminal cases; the magistrates' courts for minor, summary, cases and the Crown Courts for more serious cases heard on indictment. Decisions in these courts can be challenged through a number of channels. These structures can be seen in Figs. 5.1 and 5.2.

---

[48] Atkinson J. M. and Drew P., *Order in Court* (1979).
[49] Baldwin J. and McConville M., *Negotiated Justice* (1977), p. 85.
[50] Bennet W. and Feldman M., *Reconstructing Reality in the Courtroom* (1981).

Figure 5.1 Trial on Indictment

MAGISTRATES' COURTS
|
Committal proceedings
↓
CROWN COURT
|
Appeal by defendant against conviction or sentence[51]
Appeal by prosecution against unduly lenient sentence
↓
COURT OF APPEAL, CRIMINAL DIVISION
|
Appeal by either party on point of law of general public
importance
↓
HOUSE OF LORDS

Figure 5.2 Summary Trial

MAGISTRATES' COURT
| |
Rehearing for defendant only as of   Appeal by way of case stated for
right   either party
↓   ↓
CROWN COURT————————→   DIVISIONAL COURT OF QBD
|
Appeal by either party on point of
law of general public importance
↓
HOUSE OF LORDS

Quantitatively, 95 per cent of all criminal cases will be dealt with in the magistrates' courts. Even the remaining 5 per cent, the more serious cases, until 1994 had an initial hearing known as committal proceedings there. In magistrates' courts, cases are heard by justices of the peace who are local people with no legal background, taking time from their jobs to serve as unpaid judges.[52] In contrast the Crown Court has a judge who will have been a lawyer of some experience before being appointed to the judiciary.[53] The Crown Court trial takes place in front of a jury, a body of 12 people randomly selected from the local community.

---

[51] This includes appeals where the defendant has been committed for sentence to the Crown Court from the magistrates' court.
[52] There are paid and legally qualified stipendiary magistrates in major conurbations—*infra*, para. 5.2.2.
[53] *infra*, para. 5.2.3.2.

5.2.1 *Classification of Offences and Mode of Trial*

Magistrates and Crown courts deal with different levels of offence. There are three different categories[54]:

(a) **Summary offences:** these are the most minor crimes and are only triable "summarily" in the magistrates court. "Summary" does not refer to the speed or the lack of quality of justice in magistrates' courts (although often dozens of cases will be dealt with in a morning) but to the process of ordering the defendant to attend the court by summons, a written order usually delivered by post. This is the most frequent procedure adopted in magistrates' courts. However, McBarnett[55] suggests that too little concern is shown about summary justice and that the safeguards which exist in the higher courts are often absent. This is justified by an "ideology of trivia" and a belief that the law and facts involved in such cases are very simple. Although summary offences involve a wide range of trivial matters, often relating to road traffic or perhaps not possessing a TV licence, this category also encompasses other more serious crimes such as driving with excess alcohol, assault on a police officer or indecent exposure. Redistribution of business from the Crown Court to the magistrates' courts especially of offences of dishonesty and of public order crimes, has often been controversial.[56]

(b) **Indictable offences:** these are the most serious crimes, triable only on indictment in a Crown Court in front of a judge and jury. This category includes homicide, serious assault, rape, kidnapping, robbery, conspiracy and Official Secrets Acts offences. Magistrates will never try these cases. Prior to 1994, the accused always appeared in front of the magistrates' court in committal proceedings which were a preliminary check that the prosecution case was strong enough and that there was a "case to answer".[57] Committal proceedings have now been replaced by "transfer for trial" proceedings[58] by which the prosecutor simply serves notice of the prosecution case on the accused who can apply for dismissal. If there is such an application, there will be a hearing before magistrates who must decide whether there is sufficient evidence against the accused to put him or her on trial by jury.

[54] This was the result of rationalisation brought about by the Criminal Law Act 1977, following recommendations of the James Committee—*Report of the Committee on the Distribution of Criminal Business between the Crown Court and the Magistrates' Court* (1975), Cmnd. 6323.
[55] McBarnett D., *Conviction* (1981), Chap. 7.
[56] This could be seen with the recommendations of the James Committee (*Report of the Committee on the Distribution of Criminal Business between the Crown Court and the Magistrates' Court, op. cit.*) to make minor thefts only triable in magistrates' courts which attracted great opposition during the debates on the Criminal Law Act 1977.
[57] Committal proceedings frequently took some months to be heard. Magistrates will also make certain preliminary decisions, especially on the question as to whether the suspect is to be remanded in custody or released on bail. Where the accused is held in custody awaiting trial, then there will be regular hearings to renew the remand decision. Such functions will still be undertaken.
[58] Criminal Justice and Public Order Act 1994, s. 44 and Sched. 4.

er way: these are triable either in Magistrates Court or in ...rt. The most common examples are theft and burglary but ...ry also includes indecent assault, arson and criminal ...[58a] There is no clear conceptual boundary here; theft is triable ...vay whereas social security fraud is a summary offence. ...er, with some offences, the magistrates will hold a "mode of ...hearing[59] to decide whether the case is suitable to be heard summarily or not. Both parties can address the court. The prosecutor's preference cannot bind the court but magistrates tend to follow the CPS recommendation.[60] The general issue is the seriousness of the offence and whether a magistrates' court would have sufficient sentencing powers to deal with it. The detailed criteria are laid down in the Lord Chief Justice's guidelines.[61] Summary trial is only possible if both the accused and the magistrates[62] assent to it. The defendant has the right to insist on jury trial and if the magistrates consider summary trial inappropriate, they too can elect for trial on indictment.

Most defendants opt for summary trial,[63] not least because of the speed of the proceedings and the ceiling placed on the punishments which magistrates courts can impose (six months for £2,000 fine—12 months if the accused is convicted of more than one offence). But often either the magistrates decline jurisdiction or the defendants exercise their right to trial by jury.

Table 5.1 Crown Court Committals 1993–94[64]

Crown Court committals	91,748
Indictable only	19,545 (21.3%)
Triable-either-way	72,203 (78.7%)
Magistrates' direction	46,954 (51.2%)
Defendants' election	25,249 (27.5%)

Many cases are unnecessarily tried on indictment. Magistrates are

[58a] Where the value of the property damaged is under £2,000, the offence is only triable summarily.
[59] Magistrates' Courts Act 1980, ss. 18–21 lays down the procedure.
[60] Riley D. and Vennard J., *Triable-Either-Way Cases: Crown Court or Magistrates' Court?* (Home Office Research Study No. 98) (1988) where research showed that the magistrates disagreed with the CPS on 23 out of 623 occasions; Hedderman C. and Moxon D., *Magistrates' Court or Crown Court? Mode of Trial Decisions and Sentencing* (Home Office Research Study No. 125) (1992).
[61] *Practice Note (Mode of Trial Guidelines)* [1990] 1 W.L.R. 1439.
[62] The hearing (like committal proceedings) can be before a single magistrate—although it is more common to have a full bench.
[63] In 1993, 392,600 were proceeded against for triable-either-way offences, of whom 64,700 (16.5 per cent) were committed for trial—*Criminal Statistics 1993*, Cm. 2680, Table 6.5, p. 135.
[64] CPS *Annual Report* 1993–94 (H.C. Vol. 444), p. 29.

unwilling to accept jurisdiction despite the evidence that suggests that in 62 per cent of cases in which magistrates direct Crown Court trial, the judge imposes a sentence that would have been within the power of the magistrates.[65] Although defendants' elections have declined as a proportion over the past decade,[66] they opt for Crown Court trial for various reasons. If they are remanded in prison and a custodial sentence is inevitable, prolonging the period spent on remand has advantages since conditions are more favourable.[67] Defendants also consider that the trial at Crown Court is fairer and there is more chance of acquittal[68] but oddly most defendants (83 per cent) end up pleading guilty to all or some of the charges. They discover that Crown Court judges are more likely to impose a custodial sentence and that that sentence will be longer than magistrates would have imposed in a similar case.[69]

The ineffectiveness of the mode of trial hearings is apparent. There are defendants who might intend originally to contest the allegations but eventually plead guilty and there are magistrates who decline jurisdiction only for the Crown Court to impose a penalty within the magistrates' own powers. The result is increased pressure on the workload of the Crown Courts where there remain considerable delays in processing cases.[70] There are also financial costs—a contested case in a magistrates' court will cost around £1,500 and an uncontested case around £500, whereas the equivalent figures for the Crown Court are £13,500 and £2,500.[71]

In Scotland the choice of venue is a decision of the procurator fiscal, the equivalent of the CPS. The Runciman Report rejected that simple option but recommended that if the prosecution and defence agreed on venue, that would suffice. If there was a disagreement, then there would be a mode of trial hearing as at present but that, if the magistrates were to choose summary trial, defendants would no longer have the right to elect trial by jury.[72] A different and more controversial option would be to re-classify a range of minor property offences as summary offences. The Runciman proposal occupies the middle ground whereby the right is not automatically excluded and allows a defendant to argue that it is the appropriate form of trial in the circumstances of this particular case. Critics[73] have argued that the increasing derogation of this right to election is driven by economic considerations. Further, there is a widespread perception that the quality of Crown Court justice is more thorough and fair than that in magistrates' courts. The

[65] Hedderman and Moxon, *op. cit.*
[66] Riley and Vennard, *op. cit.*
[67] These include more visits, your own clothes and more money. The time spent on remand counts towards the eventual sentence.
[68] The chances of Crown Court acquittal (57 per cent) are considerably higher than acquittal in magistrates' court (30 per cent)—Vennard J., "The Outcome of Contested Trials" in Moxon D. (ed.), *Managing Criminal Justice* (1985).
[69] Hedderman and Moxon, *op. cit.*; see Royal Commission on Criminal Justice, *op. cit.*, para. 6.8.
[70] Committals to Crown Court have declined from 119,170 in 1991/92 to 91,748 in 1993/94 CPS *Annual Report 1993–94, op. cit.* In 1993, there were 86,000—*Criminal Statistics 1993, op. cit.*, p. 16.
[71] Royal Commission on Criminal Justice, *op. cit.*, para. 1.18.
[72] Royal Commission on Criminal Justice, *op. cit.*, paras. 6.12–6.14.
[73] Ashworth A., "Plea, Venue and Discontinuance" [1993] Crim.L.R. 830.

Commission do not address this sense of dissatisfaction nor does it prevent their recommending an increase in magistrates' courts work.

5.2.2 Magistrates and Clerks

The origins of the office of "justice of the peace" (J.P.)[74] can be found in 1195 when Richard I nominated country gentlemen as "keepers of the peace" but their duties appear to have expanded in the middle of the fourteenth century at the time of the Black Death. In 1361, the Justices of the Peace Act provided for the appointment of J.P.s in every county. Their function was the enforcement of the strict labour laws which prevented free movement of labour around the country as well as wage freeze legislation. Their role as the Crown's representatives meant not merely judicial activity but also a range of administrative functions, a role that only disappeared in the nineteenth century with the emergence of democratically elected local councils.

The forefathers of the modern magistrates were less content to sit passively in a courtroom but operated in a more proactive role empowered to "pursue, arrest ... and chastise" offenders. In 1554, the Marian statutes cast them as public prosecutors while in the eighteenth century, the Fielding brothers who were London magistrates, showed most unjudicial activity by organising the Bow Street Runners. The restriction of a J.P.s functions to predominantly judicial ones comes about with the Summary Jurisdiction Act 1848 which established the procedure to be followed by justices' courts.[75] However, the police still took their orders from J.P.s, either directly in the shire counties (until 1888) or through the Watch Committees in the boroughs.

In 1949, the title of the court was formally changed[76] to "magistrates' court" whereas before they were known as "summary courts" or, worse, as "police courts" suggesting undue influence. There are 30,054[77] Justices of the Peace in England and each is required to attend 24 sessions throughout the year. They are normally[78] appointed by the Lord Chancellor who acts on the advice of local advisory committees. There are about 100 of these but the names of the members (save for the secretary) are not published. Individuals and organisations can put forward candidates for consideration. Nomination is often done by local political parties. The bench should "reflect the community it serves"[79] but the problem that occurs is one of balance in terms of gender,[80] race and class. It has proved very difficult to appoint sufficient working class magistrates and less than 10 per cent of J.P.s are manual workers.[81] Magistrates are unpaid, although they do receive expenses. There is compulsory training before they are allowed to adjudicate as well as continuing refresher courses.[82]

A J.P.s' main work is crime—in 1992, 1,960,000 defendants were

---

[74] Moir E., *The Justice of the Peace* (1969); Milton F., *The English Magistracy* (1967), Chap. 1.
[75] Manchester, *op. cit.*, pp. 74–79 and p. 162.
[76] Justice of the Peace Act 1949.
[77] As of January 1, 1994—*Judicial Statistics 1993* Cm. 2623, p. 92.
[78] Except in Manchester, Liverpool and Lancashire where the appointments are made by the Chancellor of the Duchy of Lancaster.
[79] *Judicial Statistics 1993*, *op. cit.*, p. 92
[80] 54 per cent of J.P.s are men and 46 per cent are women.
[81] Spencer, *op. cit.*, p. 404.
[82] Spencer, *op. cit.*, p. 408.

proceeded against in magistrates courts and 83,000 were tried in the Crown Court.[83] J.P.s sit in groups of three in court for most hearings. They are assisted by the "clerk to the court"[84] who will advise the Bench on matters of law, procedure, evidence and sentencing.[85] The clerk is the focal point of the court with the J.P.s as a superior jury. Problems can arise when clerks are seen to be too involved in the decision-making, for example, retiring with the magistrates when they leave to consider their verdict. They should take care to give their advice in open court wherever possible.[86]

Nowadays the clerks (who number around 250) are fully trained and paid lawyers,[87] either a solicitor or barrister. Not only do they provide the legal input into court proceedings, it is also their job to manage the administration of the courthouse, listing cases for hearing; summoning witnesses; handling adjournments; collecting the fines; as well as managing the personnel of the court. Although the clerks are appointed by the magistrates' courts committees, there is no proper accountability to them. The 1989 Scrutiny[88] found that clerks have little control over the resources with which they worked, insufficient management information and no proper definition of their legal and management responsibilities.[89]

In the major conurbations, the work of the J.P.s is supplemented by a legally qualified and paid magistrate, known as a stipendiary magistrate.[90] They are appointed by the Queen on the advice of the Lord Chancellor and are drawn from the ranks of practising lawyers with relevant background. They normally sit alone. There are 78 such magistrates,[91] 46 in London and 32 in the provinces with a further 90 "acting" stipendiaries who are appointed to assist in magistrates' courts and to establish their own competence for a full-time appointment. However, the policy of successive governments has been to have larger court centres, more J.P.s, but not to rely on stipendiary magistrates; "The government is wholeheartedly committed to the concept of summary justice provided by law people drawn from their local communities."[92] The Webbs cite Sidney Smith:

"What in truth could we substitute for the unpaid magistracy? We have no doubt but that a set of rural judges, in the pay of government, would very soon become corrupt jobbers and odious tyrants, as they often are on the continent. But magistrates, as they now exist, really constitute a bulwark of some value against the supreme power of the state. They would not submit to be employed for base and criminal purposes. They are tools, perhaps, in some cases, but tools that must be respected."[93]

[83] *Criminal Statistics 1993, op. cit.,* p. 126 and p. 129.
[84] Darbyshire P., *The Magistrates' Clerk* (1983).
[85] A clerk might be asked what the normal range of sentence for such an offence might be amongst other local benches. The clerk could not suggest a suitable sentence for a particular case.
[86] *R. v. East Kerrier Justices* [1952] 2 Q.B. 719 although this has been held too restrictive. Where matters of law and fact are inextricably intertwined, the clerk may withdraw with the justices for virtually the whole period of their retirement—*R. v. Consett Justices, ex p. Postal Bingo* [1967] 2 Q.B. 9.
[87] Spencer, *op. cit.,* p. 415.
[88] Lord Chancellor's Department *Magistrates' Courts—Report of a Scrutiny 1989* (1989).
[89] *infra*, para. 5.2.2.1.
[90] Spencer, *op. cit.,* p. 412.
[91] As of January 1, 1994—*Judicial Statistics 1993, op. cit.,* p. 93.
[92] *A New Framework for Local Justice* Cm. 1829 (1992), para. 8, p. 4.
[93] Quoted in Manchester, *op. cit.,* p. 77.

The alternative would be to create a career judiciary similar to France or Germany. In France, for example, law graduates take a competitive public examination to enter the *Ecole Nationale de la Magistrature* where they undergo a two year period of training. Graduating from the ENM, they might start as examining magistrates, prosecutors or trial judges. Their career would involve promotion to the higher courts and offices.

Such a system might easily be introduced. In the justices' clerks, there is a highly qualified group that already fulfils many quasi-judicial functions. In one sense, it is the justices who are the jury but it is the clerk who directs them on law and procedure. Under the 1994 reforms,[94] there will be relatively few (circa 60) chief clerks, responsible for a significant number of individual benches, considerable administrative staff and a large budget. Giving more judicial functions and higher status to the career of clerks is a viable option. One scenario might be that clerks, with substantially more formal training behind them, sat as the presiding magistrate with two lay justices. Yet the implications of and opposition to such a change would be far-reaching, not least from the Magistrates' Association which has been a powerful force in resisting change to one of the oldest common law institutions.

Miscarriages of justice suggest that the need for a properly trained, professional judiciary is more apparent in the higher courts than in the magistrates courts. Criticisms of the justices of the peace are quite rare and their mistakes are more easily rectified through re-hearings in the Crown Court and by the supervision of the Divisional Court. Yet studies[95] would suggest that there is a level of routine injustice which attracts little attention because of the perception of magistrates' courts as dealing with trivia. "... the lower courts remain something to be laughed at or yawned over for the pettiness of their crimes, not watched with care for the marginality of their legality."[96]

5.2.2.1 THE ORGANISATION OF MAGISTRATES' COURTS

The organisation of the magistrates' courts is contained in the Justices of the Peace Act 1979[96A] and their jurisdiction and powers in the Magistrates' Courts Act 1980. Executive responsibility was split between the Home Office who to an extent controlled the finance, organisation and management of the courts, while the appointment and training was arranged by the Lord Chancellor's department. All responsibility was transferred to the Lord Chancellor in 1992. However, there is considerable local autonomy:

(a) the central element is the "commission area", the name of which comes from the "Commission of the Peace" which is the formal document from the Lord Chancellor setting out the powers and duties of the justices in a given area and authorising them to act. The commission areas are the counties and divisions of metropolitan districts. A court's jurisdiction is limited to offences allegedly committed within the area for which the court acts.[97]

[94] Police and Magistrates Court Act 1994, Part IV.
[95] McBarnett D., *Conviction* (1981), Chap. 7; Carlen, (1974) *op. cit.*
[96] McBarnett, *op. cit.*, p. 147.
[96a] As amended by the Police and Magistrates' Courts Act 1994.
[97] Magistrates' Courts Act 1980, s. 2(1).

(b) the commission area is divided into "petty sessional divisions" or bench. There are over 600 of these and that represents a reduction from 1,000 forty years ago. Each bench has its own courthouse and (normally) justices' clerk to which magistrates are assigned. Each bench is required to elect a chairman and deputies. Petty sessional divisions will vary considerably in size from a dozen J.P.s to over 100, some with only one weekly sitting while others have several courts sitting daily.

(c) each commission area is administered by a Magistrates' Courts Committees[98] (MCC) which appoints justices' clerks and other staff (there are over 10,000), provides court rooms and equipment and advises on the organisation of petty sessional divisions. The system costs about £200 million a year to run[99] which is provided by the Lord Chancellor's department.

Both benches and Magistrates' Courts Committees operate in an individual fashion, leading to a range of problems:

(a) there are divergent standards between courts: in the award of legal aid to defendants; in the use of bail as opposed to remanding in custody; most seriously, in sentencing—in 1985 one research study showed that Brighton imprisoned 30 per cent of those convicted of indictable offences whereas only a few miles away in Lewes, the comparable figure was 14 per cent.[1]

(b) court centres are still inconveniently sited. Eighty of the 600 plus centres have less than twelve J.P.s and many sit infrequently. The separate existence of small benches is a waste of resources.

(c) there is often lack of communication and distrust between magistrates and other agencies, especially the probation services.[2]

(d) there are difficulties in recruiting properly qualified staff. Local organisation means that staff are not interchangeable and that career prospects remain limited. Many justices' clerks have chosen to move into the CPS where pay and promotion opportunities are better.

The magistrates' courts' system still reflects its historical roots, looking anachronistic and with no clear management structure. This state of affairs led in 1989 to a Home Office-initiated scrutiny of magistrates's courts.[3] This concluded that:

(a) there was no coherent management structure for the service with no self-evident role for the Home Office and with 105 local services, each run by a committee of magistrates. Under these committees come 285 justices' clerks also occupying a semi-autonomous status. It is

---

[98] Justices of the Peace Act 1979, s. 20, as amended by s. 70, Police and Magistrates' Court Act 1994.
[99] These figures are for 1989. The total income from fines, fees and fixed penalties collected by magistrates' courts in 1990/91 was £269,088,000.
[1] Spencer, *op. cit.*, p. 188, n.2.
[2] The need to improve this can be seen in *Magistrates' Courts and the Probation Service* (Magistrates' Association 1989).
[3] Lord Chancellor's Department, *Magistrates' Courts—Report of a Scrutiny 1989*.

impossible "... to locate clear management, responsibility or accountability anywhere in the structure".

(b) there was little evidence of a planned relationship between work and resources, of review of performance or of scrutiny of efficiency.

(c) the arrangements were not delivering value for money with the funding authorities not providing effective budgetary control.

The Scrutiny pointed to the increase in the unit costs of dealing with cases and enforcing fines as well as to the delays and backlog of cases. What was suggested was a centralised government responsibility for the magistrates' courts service with the establishment of a "Magistrates' Courts Agency" responsible to ministers but operationally independent. There would be about 30 areas in the charge of a chief executive with the day-to-day management of the courts in the hands of court managers, qualified lawyers who are "... selected, trained and managed as managers".

These proposals were rejected by the Council of the Magistrates' Association who argued that J.P.s should continue to play a substantial role at every level of the service, that magistrates and their clerks should remain independent and superior to the administration of the service. These criticisms were reflected in the government's White Paper[4] and the 1994 Police and Magistrates' Courts Act which:

(a) seeks to streamline the system by giving the Lord Chancellor the power[5] to reduce unilaterally the number of commission areas from 105 to between 50–60 by combining MCCs of small counties or in metropolitan districts. These committees will be much smaller with an upper limit of 12[6] as compared with the current limit of 35, with up to 2 non-J.P. members,[7-8] and with their role and responsibilities defined by the Lord Chancellor.[9] The new MCC will need to adjust to the performance targets and measures encountered by other criminal justice agencies. However, an attempt to have the MCC chair a nominee of the Lord Chancellor was defeated.

(b) will provide each of the new commission areas with a head of all paid staff.[10] This will be a justices' chief executive who will continue a dual role of lawyer and manager. The chief executive would be responsible to the new inspectorate. However, the chief executives themselves will move to performance-related and fixed-term contracts of employment and would no longer be office holders.[11]

(c) would provide greater accountability through a magistrates' courts' inspectorate,[12] independent and reporting directly to the Lord Chancellor. Further review is provided by extending the Audit Commission's remit to include the magistrates' courts.[13]

---

[4] Lord Chancellor's Department *A New Framework for Local Justice* Cm. 1829 (1992).
[5] Police and Magistrates' Courts Act, s. 69.
[6] *ibid.* s. 71.
[7-8] *ibid.* s. 70.
[9] *ibid.* ss. 73 and 74.
[10] *ibid.* s. 75.
[11] *ibid.* s. 76.
[12] *ibid.* s. 86.
[13] *ibid.* s. 89.

These proposals have attracted criticisms,[14] not least because of the new funding arrangements which initiate a "value for money" regime. The courts will be funded on a formula basis[15]: 60 per cent will be allocated to workload, 25 per cent to "fine enforcement efficiency", 10 per cent to "time taken to deal with cases" and 5 per cent for "quality of service". Although the White Paper restates the independence of magistrates and the statute[16] makes it clear that the chief clerk is not subject to direction in respect of any legal advice given to the benches, such funding arrangements and the introduction of performance targets must inevitably affect decisions if income is related to cases processed. These arrangements could provide indirect control over other issues—for example, if the Government were to wish to restrict the granting of legal aid.

5.2.2.2 THE WORK OF THE MAGISTRATES' COURTS

Much of the criminal work[17] of a J.P. is done either in the magistrates' court (including the Youth Court[18]) or in the Crown Court. Yet their involvement goes beyond that:

(a) during the investigative stage, J.P.s issue warrants to search premises,[19] to arrest,[20] or to authorise continued detention in a police station.[21]

(b) prior to 1994, where the offence was serious enough to warrant trial in the Crown Court,[22] J.P.s sat as examining magistrates in committal proceedings. This was not a trial but a hearing to decide whether the prosecution evidence was substantial enough to justify the accused standing trial. There were two modes of committal proceedings:

    (i) Under section 6(1) of the Magistrates' Courts Act 1980, there was active consideration by the bench of the evidence, with the prosecution outlining its case and the defence arguing that there was "no case to answer", inviting the magistrates to reject the charge at this point. Such full committal proceedings were rare.

    (ii) Under section 6(2) of the Magistrates' Courts Act 1980,[23] the court could commit to trial without consideration of the evidence, known as a paper committal. Such proceedings were a formality[24] and 90 per cent of committals were of this type.

---

[14] Raine J. and Willson M., "Reforming Magistrates' Courts: A Framework for Injustice?" *Justice of the Peace* (1993), Vol. 157, p. 661; Editorial in *The Magistrate* (1994), Vol. 50, p. 2; *The Guardian* July 13, 1993.

[15] *A New Framework for Local Justice, op. cit.*, p. 11.

[16] *op. cit.*, s. 78.

[17] Away from criminal work, magistrates also sit as a Family Proceedings Court, ordering husbands and fathers to pay maintenance to wives and children but also able to make separation orders. There is a range of bureaucratic work—licensing pubs, betting shops.

[18] *infra*, Chap. 9.

[19] PACE, s. 8.

[20] Magistrates' Courts Act 1980, s. 1.

[21] PACE, s. 43.

[22] *i.e.* it is an indictable offence or is an offence triable either way and where either the magistrates have decided to commit for Crown Court trial or where the defendant has elected for Crown Court trial.

[23] This reform was first introduced by s. 1, Criminal Justice Act 1967.

[24] Once the mode of trial hearing has decided on Crown Court trial, then there was a period for

Committal proceedings were supposed to act as a further filter to ensure that evidentially weak cases did not come to trial. But, at most, 10 per cent of committals were "old style" committals and in 80 per cent of such cases, the result was that the defendant was committed for trial. In 1978, only 2,000 (2.38 per cent) out of 84,000 cases were thrown out at committal stage. In that year, some 27,900[25] out of 82,000 defendants pleaded not guilty and 47 per cent or 13,100 were acquitted. Of that 13,100, some 5,630 were non-jury acquittals of which a high proportion should have been picked up by any effective filtering system.

Such figures suggest that committal proceedings were an inefficient way of screening out weak cases[26] and were an irrelevance, a false focus.[27] The alternative was simple transfer to Crown Court with the option for preliminary argument before the judge that there is no case to answer. This reform was embraced by both Phillips and Runciman.[28] The new "transfer for trial" proceedings[29] provide for the prosecutor simply to serve notice of the prosecution case on the accused who can apply for dismissal. If there is such an application, there will be a hearing before magistrates who must decide whether there is sufficient evidence against the accused to put him or her on trial by jury.

(c) the traffic court takes up much of the J.P.'s time. About 1.2 million such offenders will be dealt with each year. Another 5 million will receive fixed penalty notices (mainly parking offences) and make payment direct to the court without any formal proceedings.

(d) J.P.s will try cases, both summary offences and offences triable either way. Such offences comprise small property offences (frauds, thefts, burglaries, vandalism), minor assaults and woundings and a bewildering array of regulatory crime.

(e) J.P.s will sit in the Crown Court when the Crown Court is hearing an appeal or when there is a committal for sentence from the magistrates' court. The court must consist of a professional judge and between two and four J.P.s. When the court is hearing guilty pleas, magistrates are permitted to sit with the judge. If they do so, they must play (and be seen to play) a full part in the decisions.[30-32] J.P.s are not permitted to take part when the case involves a contested first instance trial.

(f) the youth court has its own group of J.P.s and its own procedures. Its philosophy is one based on the welfare of the child.[33]

---

both sides to prepare papers for a s. 6(2) committal. When the parties returned for the formal committal, a justices' clerk could make the necessary order—S.I. 1993 No. 1183.

[25] I have derived these figures from the overall committal figures given by Jones P., Tarling R. and Vennard J., "The Effectiveness of Committal Proceedings as a Filter in the Criminal Justice System" in Moxon D. (ed.), *Managing Criminal Justice* (1985) and applying the overall acquittal rates in Crown Courts and the non-jury acquittal rates in Crown Courts given in Block B., Corbett C. and Peay J., *Ordered and Directed Acquittals in the Crown Court* (Royal Commission on Criminal Justice Research Study No. 15) (1993), p. 12, Table 2.

[26] Jones, Tarling and Vennard, *op. cit.*

[27] Block, *et al.*, *op. cit.*, p. 64ff.

[28] Royal Commission on Criminal Procedure, *Report* (1981) Cmnd. 8092, para. 8.24; Royal Commission on Criminal Justice, *op. cit.*, paras. 6.20–6.32.

[29] Criminal Justice and Public Order Act 1994, s. 44 and Sched. 4.

[30-32] *Newby* (1984) 6 Cr.App.R.(S.) 148.

[33] This is discussed further in Chap. 9.

5.2.3.1 THE INDICTMENT

When an offence is too serious for magistrates' court, an indictment is drawn up. The indictment is a formal document containing the alleged offences against the accused, supported by the briefest of facts.[34-35] This document supersedes all other accusations (the police charge or the information laid before the magistrates) and it is to the indictment that the accused pleads guilty or not guilty. It is the indictment that should provide the starting point for the judge and the jury.

There can be more than one offence specified in an indictment but each offence must be contained in a separate "count" or paragraph with a description of that particular offence and the facts supporting the accusation. More than one offence in a count will make the indictment bad for "duplicity". The rationale is is based on the principle of specificity.[36] Fairness requires that any accusation should be clear and specific in order that a defendant is able to answer it. An allegation that the defendant has "shoplifted in Canterbury High Street constantly" is more difficult to counter than one which specifies the time and place of the offence.[37]

There is derogation from this principle whenever more than one offence or more than one defendant are joined in a single indictment. However, separate trials for each defendant on each count are not practical. Yet the accused can be prejudiced by an indictment containing several offences, especially where evidence may be admitted on one count but not be admissible on another. For example, an offender charged with sex offences on small children is entitled to a judge's direction to the jury to the effect that the evidence from one child is not to be taken into account on the other charge. But it is extremely difficult to counter the prejudicial effect of that evidence on the jury.[38] The judge does have discretion to award separate trials, either on the different charges or for different defendants.

The formality and brevity of the modern indictment has been criticised by the Law Commission[39] who felt that there should be more and clearer factual allegations so that the document can act as a "practical agenda" for the jury in its deliberations. The Runciman Commission also felt that a "system of particularised indictments would be of benefit to the clearer and more efficient conduct of trials".[40]

5.2.3.2 THE CROWN COURT

Only the Crown Court has the jurisdiction to hear criminal trials on indictment.[41] Presiding in the Crown Court is a single "professional" judge who will be a lawyer of at least 10 years' experience. However there are different categories:

[34-35] Indictments Act 1915, s. 3—*Blackstone's Criminal Practice* (1991), D.8.
[36] Ashworth A., *Principles of Criminal Law* (1991), p. 59, esp. p. 64.
[37] Conspiracy charges often suffer from and can be criticised for this lack of specificity about the precise acts complained of.
[38] Evidence that a defendant has committed other offences or is of bad character is not proof that he has committed this particular offence—Chap. 6 at para. 6.7.3.
[39] Law Commission, *Counts in an Indictment* (1992).
[40] Royal Commission on Criminal Justice, *op. cit.*, para. 8.5.
[41] There is a rarely used alternative to indictment known as a Voluntary Bill of Indictment.

(a) High Court judges who normally would be attached to the Queen's Bench Division and when in Crown Court would hear only the most serious cases.

(b) Circuit judges those office was created by the Courts Act 1971. There are 491[42] full-time circuit judges. They may also undertake civil work in the County Court.

(c) Recorders who are equivalent to circuit judges but their appointment is only part-time. There are 813[43] recorders. They can be appointed, not only from the ranks of barristers, but also from solicitors of 10 years' standing. Recorders of three years experience can be appointed as circuit judges.

(d) The Lord Chancellor may appoint deputy circuit judges and assistant recorders[44] for fixed periods especially when backlogs of cases have arisen.

Technically the Crown Court is a single court[45] which sits in 90[46] different centres around the country. These centres are divided into six circuits (Midland and Oxford, North-Eastern, Northern, South-Eastern, Wales and Chester, Western). Each circuit will have a High Court judge as a "presiding judge". Each centre will be designated as a first, second or third tier centre. The first tier is attended by High Court and such centres will also hear High Court civil work. Second tier centres will have regular visits from High Court judges hearing criminal but not civil work. Third tier centres are not visited by High Court Judges. Circuit judges, Recorders and Assistant Recorders will sit at all three classes of centre.

The division of work between the High Court judges and the circuit judges rests on a Practice Direction by the Lord Chief Justice.[47] Offences are divided into four classes:

(a) Class 1 offences (for example, murder and Official Secrets offences) can only be tried by a High Court judge unless a particular case is released on the authority of the Presiding Judge to a circuit judge approved by the Lord Chief Justice.

(b) Class 2 offences (for example, other homicides, rape) must be tried by a High Court judge unless a particular case is released by the presiding judge for trial by a circuit judge.

(c) Class 3 offences (those not in the other classes such as aggravated burglary or causing death by reckless driving) may be listed by the listing officer for trial by any category of judge.

(d) Class 4 offences (for example, all offences triable either way, robbery, serious assaults) will normally not be listed for trial by a High Court judge but will be tried by a circuit judge.

The work of circuit judges also includes hearing committals for sentence and

---

[42] On January 1, 1994—*Judicial Statistics 1993, op. cit.,* Table 9.1, p. 89.
[43] *ibid.*
[44] There were 432 on January 1, 1994—*ibid.*
[45] Created by the Courts Act 1971 which abolished the old Assize Court and Quarter Sessions.
[46] *Judicial Statistics 1992,* Cm. 2268, p. 4 for a map of the centres.
[47] The Lord Chief Justice is empowered to make such directions by s. 75, Supreme Court Act 1981 and these are reported in [1987] 1 W.L.R. 1671.

appeals from the magistrates' courts. Such hearings are usually conducted by the judge sitting with two lay magistrates.

5.2.4 *Waiting Times and Hearing Times*

At common law there is no restriction on the time that may elapse between offence and prosecution although the prosecutor should take the staleness of the offence into consideration when exercising their discretion to prosecute.[48] There are some statutory time limits, in particular, for a summary offence the information must be laid within six months of the offence.[49] Apart from these exceptions, legally there is no bar on proceedings for indictable or triable either way offences being commenced at any time.[50]

There are, however, "custody time limits". These were introduced[51] experimentally in England in 1987 but from 1991 covered the whole country. These apply only to defendants held in custody and denied bail. If the prosecution is not started within these limits, the prosecution is not dismissed but the defendant should be released on bail unless the court agrees to an extension. The basic limits are:

(a) for summary trial, 56 days from first appearance in magistrates' court to trial. This may be extended to 70 days if the choice of mode of trial has not been made within 56 days.

(b) for trial on indictment, 70 days from first appearance to committal and 112 days from committal to arraignment.[52]

There is still a problem of delay[53] in criminal courts. This is of importance particularly for those defendants remanded in custody awaiting trial:

- in 1992, the average waiting time in Crown Courts between committal and trial was 16.2 weeks nationally, 12.9 weeks in Wales and 18.1 weeks on Northern circuit.[54] This period will be longer if the defendant is on bail rather than remanded in custody and if he or she is pleading "not guilty". Such figures do not include the period from first appearance to committal which can add at least 8–10 weeks on to the overall length.
- in 1992 in magistrates courts, it took 120 days on average to process an indictable case from offence to disposal,[55] showing a gradual increase from 98 days in 1985.

[48] *Code of Crown Prosecutors* (CPS 1994), para. 6.5—but the accomplices who aided the escape of George Blake, a Russian spy, were prosecuted (and acquitted) over 25 years later!
[49] Magistrates Court Act 1980, s. 127—for other statutory time limits, see *Blackstones Criminal Practice, op. cit.*, para. D.1.75.
[50] There is discretion for the examining magistrates to refuse to commit for trial—*R. v. Derby Crown Court, ex p. Brooks* (1984) 70 Cr.App.R. 164; *R. v. Grays JJ., ex p. Graham* [1982] Q.B. 1239.
[51] By the regulations made under s. 22, Prosecution of Offences Act 1985.
[52] Arraignment is the start of the Crown Court trial when the clerk reads the indictment to the accused and asks whether there is a plea of guilty or not guilty.
[53] The position is regarded as "most unsatisfactory" by the Royal Commission on Criminal Justice, *op. cit.*, para. 5.53 but the author's discussions with French and German judges would suggest that the position is considerably worse on mainland Europe.
[54] *Judicial Statistics 1993, op. cit.*, Table 6.14, p. 68.
[55] *Criminal Statistics 1993, op. cit.*, Table 6.3, p. 133.

Delay may be ascribed to many causes. The lack of urgency and overwork in the Crown Prosecution Service may be one. Decisions by the defence may be another especially where there is a late change of plea from "not guilty". The system also depends on a high proportion of "guilty" pleas and changes in that rate affect "productivity". But the very organisation of the system induces delays. Aspects of pre-trial procedure are absurdly over-elaborate, especially mode of trial hearings and (formerly) committal proceedings. A formal system of pre-trial review which would identify the substantial issues between the parties still does not exist. Worst of all is the practice whereby a legally-qualified Crown prosecutor prepares all the factual and legal aspects of a case but, as a result of a wholly unjustified restrictive trade practice, has to transfer responsibility to a barrister in private practice.

Once a contested trial begins, the average hearing time is 7 hours for a not guilty plea and 0.9 hours for a guilty plea. During the trial, the judge controls the procedure, rules on the evidence, will direct the jury on the law that is to be applied and will sentence the defendant if convicted. But the decision as to whether the accused is guilty or not guilty is taken by the jury in the absence of the judge. These issues are discussed later.

5.2.5 Appeals from the Magistrates' Court

From the magistrates' court, a defendant can appeal in two[56] ways:

(a) *Crown Court*—only the defendant can appeal against conviction or sentence. The prosecution cannot appeal against an acquittal. Furthermore only the defendant who has pleaded "not guilty" or who is appealing against sentence has the right to appeal. The defendant who has pleaded "guilty" cannot appeal against conviction unless the plea is shown to be equivocal or to be entered under duress.[57] If the defendant appeals on the grounds of an equivocal plea, then the Crown Court can remit the case to the justices for re-hearing on the basis of a "not guilty" plea.

The appeal takes the form of a complete re-hearing of the entire case, calling the original witnesses (although additional witnesses may be called) and hearing the legal arguments again. The case is heard before a circuit judge or recorder who is assisted normally by two J.P.s. They can uphold or quash the conviction or vary the sentence, including increasing it but only up to the maximum that could have been imposed in the original hearing.[58-59]

In 1993, there were 23,722 appeals dealt with by the Crown Court, less than 0.01 per cent of all cases heard by magistrates. Of those appeals, 7,998 (33.7 per cent) were allowed, 7,318 (30.8 per cent) were dismissed, 3,264 (13.7 per cent) were varied and 5,142 (21.6 per cent) were abandoned or otherwise disposed of.

---

[56] It is also possible to apply for judicial review (as opposed to appeal) of proceedings in magistrates' courts, seeking one of the prerogative orders—*certiorari, mandamus* or *prohibition*.
[57] This would include cases where the defendant who pleads "guilty" but at the time or later in the proceedings mentions matters that would have been the basis of a valid defence—*e.g.* a guilty plea of shoplifting followed by "... but I thought I'd put it in the basket" or "... but my husband threatened to beat me up".
[58-59] The powers of the Crown Court are defined by s. 48 Supreme Court Act 1981.

(b) *Divisional Court of Queen's Bench*

"... any person who was a party to any proceedings before a magistrates' court or is aggrieved by the conviction, order, determination or other proceeding of the court may question the proceeding on the ground that it is wrong in law or in excess of jurisdiction by applying to the [magistrates] to state a case for the opinion of the High Court on the question of law or jurisdiction involved."[60]

This allows either party (prosecution or defence) an appeal by way of "case stated" to the Divisional Court of the Queen's Bench Division. This is an ancient jurisdiction by which the Queen's Bench controls the actions and decisions of inferior administrative and quasi-judicial bodies.[61] However it is a supervisory jurisdiction and this is not a re-hearing of the facts of the case. Indeed there is no dispute about the facts which are presented to the Divisional Court in a "statement of the case" from the magistrates' court. Thus no evidence will be called at the hearing which will consist of legal argument that the magistrates applied the law wrongly, failed to apply it or acted in excess of jurisdiction.

The court can "reverse, affirm or amend" the magistrates' decision,[62] replacing the conviction with an acquittal (or vice versa), changing or imposing a sentence, remitting the case to the magistrates with a direction to acquit or convict, or ordering a retrial.[63] A decision of the Divisional Court may be appealed to the House of Lords.

In 1993 there were 199 appeals from magistrates' courts and 37 appeals from Crown Court by way of case stated to the Divisional Court. 222 were disposed of—86 (39 per cent) were allowed, 77 (35 per cent) were dismissed and 54 (24 per cent) were withdrawn.[64-65]

5.2.6 *Appeals from the Crown Court*

The defendant who has been convicted in the Crown Court or who has been sentenced in the Crown Court after committal from the magistrates' court may appeal against that conviction or sentence to the Criminal Division of the Court of Appeal and, following that, to the Judicial Committee of the House of Lords. Where the defendant has appealed from the magistrates' court to the Crown Court, that decision may be challenged by way of case stated to the Divisional Court of Queen's Bench.

5.2.7 *The Criminal Division of the Court of Appeal*

The Court of Appeal sits in London and consists of the Lord Chief Justice, the Master of the Rolls and 27 Lords Justices of Appeal. It is divided into the civil and criminal divisions. Until 1907 there was no formal appeal court for

[60] Magistrates' Courts Act 1980, s. 111(1).
[61] For a brief introduction, see Spencer, *op. cit.*, p. 48.
[62] Summary Jurisdiction Act 1857, s. 6.
[63] There is some controversy as to whether the Divisional Court has the power to order a re-trial but it has exercised this power in the past—*Jeffery v. Black* [1978] 1 Q.B. 490.
[64-65] *Judicial Statistics 1993, op. cit.*, Table 1.14, p. 16.

defendants.[66] In that year the Court of Criminal Appeal was set up, consisting of the Lord Chief Justice and puisne judges of the Queen's Bench. This jurisdiction was transferred in 1966 to the new Criminal Division of the Court of Appeal.[67] Queen's Bench Division judges are still able to sit in the reformed court. The administrative side of the court is under the auspices of the Registrar of Criminal Appeals who must be a lawyer of 10 years standing. For hearing appeals, the court normally consists of at least three judges[68] who can hear appeals against conviction and sentence.

A defendant can appeal as of right against conviction if the issue is purely a point of law or if the trial judge issues a certificate that the case is fit for appeal.[69] If it is a issue of fact or mixed law/fact, the appellant must ask for leave to appeal. Yet applications are not rejected because they fail to ask for leave or treat a pure point of law as a matter for leave. In either case, the Registrar of Criminal Appeals would amend the application.

Even where a defendant has pleaded guilty, he or she can appeal against conviction if there has been a misunderstanding as to the nature of the charge or the plea or where on the admitted facts, the defendant could not have been legally convicted of the offence.[70]

The procedure for applying for leave to appeal[71] requires:

(a) notice of application for leave to appeal to be served on the Crown Court, along with the grounds on which the appeal is based (although these are provisional at this point). This is forwarded to the Registrar for Criminal Appeals.

(b) the Registrar may either: refer it to the Court for summary dismissal, without a hearing[72] if the notice shows no substantial grounds; or directly to a full court for an expedited hearing; or normally he will refer it to the "single judge".[73-74]

(c) the appellant can request a transcript of those parts of the original trial that are deemed necessary. This is usually the charges, summing up and relevant parts of the evidence. With this transcript, counsel (or the applicant in person) can redraft the grounds of appeal and these will be

---

[66] From 1848, there was the Court for Crown Cases Reserved designed to hear issues which were specifically reserved for it by judges on assize or by the chairmen of quarter sessions—Radcliffe and Cross, *The English Legal System* (5th ed., 1971), p. 353.

[67] Criminal Appeal Act 1966. The jurisdiction, powers and procedure are now governed by the Criminal Appeal Act 1968 and the membership and composition for different sorts of hearing by the Supreme Court Act 1981.

[68] Five judges occasionally sit—in *Vickers* [1957] 2 Q.B. 664, the old Court of Criminal Appeal sat with five members to decide on the interpretation of s. 1(1) of the Homicide Act 1957. More recently, a five member court laid down guidelines for the receipt of identification evidence in *Turnbull* [1977] Q.B. 224.

[69] This happens very rarely—in 1986, 10 appellants out of 1,846 had a trial judge's certificate.

[70] Avory J., in *Forde* [1923] 2 K.B. 400. Thus in *Clarke* [1972] 1 All E.R. 219, the defendant pleaded guilty to shoplifting, having been told that her defence of lack of *mens rea* due to depression was a plea of insanity! Her conviction was quashed on appeal, despite the plea of guilty.

[71] The Registrar of Criminal Appeals has issued *A Guide to Proceedings in the Court of Appeal, Criminal Division* (1983) (reproduced in 77 Cr.App.R. 138).

[72] Criminal Appeal Act 1968, s. 20.

[73-74] See below—faced with 6,982 applications for leave to appeal in 1993, the Court of Appeal would be faced with an unmanageable task without this procedure; Malleson K., *A Review of the Appeal Process* (Royal Commission on Criminal Justice Research Series No. 17) (1993).

put in front of a single judge of the Court of Appeal—in the Criminal Division, this will often be a puisne judge.

(d) the single judge, on consideration of the papers, will grant or refuse leave to appeal. If it is refused, then the application can be renewed in front of the whole court. In 1993, 18 per cent of those initially rejected, renewed their application but with little success. Even where it is renewed, the case is normally decided without argument and on the papers.

(e) where the appeal is of right or leave is granted, there will be a hearing in front of the full court. The appellant will normally be represented and, if in custody, has a right[75] to be present unless the appeal involves an issue of law alone. If the appeal is against conviction (but not if it is against sentence) the Crown will also be represented.

Although the Court does not have the power to increase sentences, it has the power to direct that the time spent in custody between the commencement and

Table 5.2 Court of Appeal (Criminal Division): Summary of results of appeals and applications during 1992[76]

Applications for leave to appeal against conviction	2,134
Allowed by single judge	601
Dismissed by single judge	1,088
Applications for leave to appeal against sentence	4,848
Allowed by single judge	1,597
Dismissed	2,863
Applications* for leave to appeal against conviction renewed	372
Granted	73
Refused	183
Applications* for leave to appeal against sentence renewed	347
Granted	49
Refused	316

[75] Criminal Appeal Act 1968, s. 22.
[76] *Judicial Statistics 1993, op. cit.*, Tables 1.7 and 1.8, pp. 11 and 12.

Table 5.2—*cont.*

Appeals against conviction heard by the full court	926
Allowed	402
Dismissed	524
Appeals against sentence heard by the full court	1,909
Allowed	1,309
Dismissed	600
Re-trials ordered	20

* These are renewed applications to the Full Court following refusal by the Single Judge.

the hearing of an appeal shall not count towards service of a custodial sentence. This is supposed to have the effect of discouraging unmeritorious appeals.[77] However, this is rarely exercised and the maximum period in practice is 28 days. The Runciman Commission recommended an increase in the deterrent effect of this "time-loss" rule so that the maximum should be 90 days.[78]

At the appeal the defendant will invariably be legally represented. Legal advice should have been available immediately after the conviction and the defendant's legal representative should offer at least provisional advice on the possibility of appeal[79] which has to be within 28 days from the date of conviction or sentence.[80] Plotnikoff and Woolfson[81] found serious defects in the pattern of provision with 9 per cent of prisoners not visited in the cells, 23 per cent not being advised about appeal and nearly 90 per cent not receiving anything in writing about an appeal. Lawyers often were ill-informed about the powers of the Court of Appeal, believing that they had the power to increase sentences. Applicants who sought to appeal without the benefit of legal advice were, not surprisingly, less successful.[82]

The grounds on which an appeal may be based are laid down in section 2(1) of the Criminal Appeals Act 1968. The appellant must show:

(a) that the verdict of the jury should be set aside on the ground that under all the circumstances of the case, it is unsafe or unsatisfactory; or

(b) that the judgment of the court of trial should be set aside on the ground of a wrong decision on any question of law; or

[77] Criminal Appeal Act 1968, s. 29—this was challenged (unsuccessfully) in the European Court of Human Rights in *Monnell and Morris v. UK* (1988) 10 E.H.R.R. 205.
[78] Royal Commission on Criminal Justice, *op. cit.*, para. 10.26.
[79] Bar Council, *The Crown Court—A Guide to Good Practice.*
[80] Criminal Appeal Act 1968, s. 18(2).
[81] Plotnikoff J. and Woolfson R., *Information and Advice for Prisoners about Grounds for Appeal and the Appeal Process* (Royal Commission on Criminal Justice Research Series No. 18) (1993).
[82] Malleson, *op. cit.*; Royal Commission on Criminal Justice, *op. cit.*, para. 10.9 argues for more legal advice for appellants.

(c) that there was a material irregularity in the course of the trial

At the hearing, the burden of proof is cast on the appellant to establish one or more of these grounds. The standard of proof which must be reached appears to be low. Lord Widgery suggested that the court should set aside a verdict if there was a "lurking doubt" in the minds of its members as to whether an injustice had been done.[83] Sections 2(1)(b) and (c) are relatively clear, covering those situations where the judge has made an error in, for example, explaining the law to the jury, allowing the introduction of inadmissible evidence or some significant procedural error.

Section 2(1)(a) is more subjective and the appellant is arguing that there is a "lurking doubt" as to whether justice had been done. Yet despite the breadth of the wording ("unsafe or unsatisfactory") the court's practice is not to review the evidence in order to substitute their judgment for that of the jury. It is not a re-hearing of the case. For the appellant to create the necessary doubt appears quite a difficult task and the court frequently takes the view that what appears a flimsy prosecution when looked at through the case papers might well have appeared strong to a jury who had the opportunity to hear and assess the witnesses.

If the appeal is successful, the court can quash the conviction.[84] However, there is a proviso; the court may dismiss an appeal, even though they find the point of law to be in the accused's favour, if they feel that no miscarriage of justice has occurred. In other words, the Court of Appeal must be satisfied, even taking into account the error of law or procedure, that the only verdict that a reasonable jury could have reached was one of "guilty". Yet the normal course for the court is to quash the conviction; only 13 out of 118 dismissed appeals in Malleson's 1990 sample were dealt with on this basis.

After quashing the conviction or applying the proviso, the third option for the Court of Appeal is to order a re-trial. Under section 7 of the Criminal Appeal Act 1968, the court could only order a re-trial where they had allowed an appeal on the basis of fresh evidence. The Criminal Justice Act 1988[85] now gives much greater discretion to the court to decide whether to order a re-trial or not. The number of such re-trials has been growing from three in 1990 to twenty three in 1992.[86]

5.2.8 *The Court of Appeal and Miscarriages of Justice*

Wrongful convictions[87] can stem from police malpractice, from the prosecution withholding evidence, from trial judge bias, from faulty forensic evidence. It is the job of the Court of Appeal to ensure that such errors are rectified. They have proved inadequate for this task.[88] Even when cases are

---

[83] *Cooper* [1969] 1 Q.B. 267 at 271.
[84] Criminal Appeal Act 1968, s. 2(2). If the appeal is against sentence, then the court can quash any sentence and replace it with the sentence that it sees fit, provided that it is one that would have been within the power of the Crown Court and that the accused is not dealt with overall more severely than he or she was by the Crown Court—Criminal Appeal Act 1968, s. 11(3).
[85] s. 43.
[86] Royal Commission on Criminal Justice, *op. cit.*, para. 10.64.
[87] Greer S., "Miscarriages of Justice Reconsidered" (1994) 57 M.L.R. 58.
[88] Thornton P., *et al., Justice on Trial: Report of the Independent Civil Liberty Panel on Criminal Justice* (Civil Liberties Trust 1992); Woffinden B., *Miscarriages of Justice* (2nd ed., 1989); Zuckerman A., "Miscarriages of Justice and Judicial Responsibility" [1991] Crim.L.R. 492;

referred back by the Home Secretary,[89] the Court has been obdurate in upholding convictions. *Cooper and McMahon*[90] involved the murder of a Luton postmaster in the 1970s. They and a third man were convicted on the uncorroborated evidence of an accomplice. The accomplice was later shown to have been lying in the case of the third man but the Court still insisted that his evidence in relation to Cooper and McMahon was reliable. It was referred back to the Court of Appeal four times before eventually the Home Secretary had to remit the remainder of the sentences.[91]

In the 1980s there was growing anxiety about the performance of the Court of Appeal. Again and again cases have had to be referred back to the court by the Home Secretary.[92] The Birmingham Six originally appealed in 1976. The case was referred by the Home Secretary in 1987 and the appeals dismissed. Referred again in 1990, the DPP decided not to resist the appeal, thus pre-empting the court. However the court went ahead with the hearing and quashed the convictions in 1991.[93] The "fresh" evidence concerned the police methods of interrogation and the quality of the forensic evidence. This evidence had essentially been heard in 1987 but at that time the convictions were still upheld and it is hard to understand why the Lord Chief Justice, Lord Lane, and his colleagues were unable to discover a "lurking doubt" which was patently obvious to everyone.[94]

In 1985, the murder of P.C. Blakelock at Broadwater Farm in North London was committed by a group of perhaps 30 people. Six persons went on trial, including Winston Silcott who was alleged to be the leader of the attack. The judge excluded confession evidence against three defendants and directed their acquittal. The other three were convicted, including Silcott although the sole evidence against him was unverified police evidence that he had made an incriminating statement ("You won't pin this on me . . . nobody will talk"). Silcott had not signed this statement and denied making it. There was no identification evidence, no forensic evidence nor admissible evidence from alleged accomplices. Yet initially the court upheld the conviction feeling that presumably it was "safe and satisfactory".[95]

The Court of Appeal give due account to the fairness of the procedures at the trial. Malleson's study[96] showed that 80 per cent of successful appeals were on the basis of a wrong decision on the admissibility of evidence or alleged misdirection by the judge. They have also shown greater willingness to deal with pre-trial malpractice.[97] Despite this there has recently been substantial injustice. It is difficult to isolate the factors that seem to lead the court to such results:

Zuckerman A., "Miscarrages of Justice: A Root Treatment" [1992] Crim.L.R. 323; Buxton R., "Miscarriages of Justice and the Court of Appeal" (1993) L.Q.R.
[89] Criminal Appeal Act 1968, s. 17—there is rarely a reference back without compelling reasons.
[90] (1975) 61 Cr.App.R. 215.
[91] For the full story, see Woffinden, *op. cit.*, p. 171.
[92] In 1989–92, 28 cases involving 49 appellants had been referred, a sharp rise over the average of five cases a year since 1968.
[93] *McIlkenny* [1992] 2 All E.R. 417.
[94] For a disturbing account of this case, see Mullin C., *Error of Judgement* (1989).
[95] The conviction was eventually overturned—*The Times*, December 9, 1991.
[96] Malleson, *op. cit.*; Royal Commission on Criminal Justice, *op. cit.*, para. 10.35.
[97] Especially where there have been breaches of PACE Codes of Practice—*supra*, para. 3.8.7.2 FF.; Royal Commission on Criminal Justice, *op. cit.*, para. 10.47.

(a) the legal system has always placed considerable faith in jury verdicts, has been unwilling to lift the veil on how they are arrived at or to interfere with them.[98] If the jury has reached its verdict having heard all the relevant evidence and with no material irregularities, the Court of Appeal has been unwilling to substitute their verdict for that of a jury who have seen and heard the witnesses. However this has often placed too great a value on the truth-revealing qualities of the adversarial forum. An analysis of the evidence, away from the emotion of the trial, often reveals its circumstantial nature and its true probative value.

(b) until recently the prevailing belief, judicial and non-judicial, has been to take identification evidence and confessions at their face value. Jurors will still accord considerable weight to these items of evidence. Courts do not stress the need for independent supportive evidence.

(c) although the standard of proof required is proof beyond reasonable doubt, this barrier seems somewhat easy to cross and the appellate courts pay little attention to the sheer lack of weight of the evidence against defendants. In a conspiracy to murder case in 1988, the evidence included driving licences in false names, a list of prominent public figures, a second-hand car, a radio and a woolly hat. This scarcely compelled the conclusion that the accused had plotted to kill. In this case, the accused were freed by the Appeal Court in 1990.[99]

(d) although the court has a discretion to receive fresh evidence, it is only obliged to do so if that evidence:

    (i) appears likely to be credible.

    (ii) would have been admissible at the trial.

    (iii) was not adduced at the trial but there was a reasonable explanation for this failure.[1]

Frequently the court is reluctant to receive fresh evidence, seeing decisions as to the facts as the jury's function and unwilling to turn a process of review into a form of re-hearing. The Runciman Commission[2] saw these powers as adequate but judged the Court's interpretation of them to be too narrow and that the Court should take a more flexible approach to whether the evidence was available at the time of trial and to whether there was a reasonable explanation why it was not adduced at that time. If the new evidence is capable of belief and would have affected the outcome of the trial, a retrial should be ordered unless this is impracticable or undesirable in which case the Court should decide the matter for itself.

(e) finally, the Court of Appeal appear to give considerable weight to maintaining public confidence in the police, the courts and the criminal justice system as a whole over and above considerations of justice in the individual case.

The Runciman Commission highlighted two weaknesses of the Court of Appeal's performance, the first being technical and the second cultural. The technical issue was the drafting of section 2 of the Criminal Appeal Act 1968

[98] Royal Commission on Criminal Justice, *op. cit.*, para. 10.40.

[99] Woffinden R., "The Case of the Winchester Three" (1990) 140 New L.J., p. 164.

[1] Criminal Appeal Act 1968, s. 23(2).

[2] Royal Commission on Criminal Justice, *op. cit.*, para. 10.51.

where they considered the paragraphs over-complex and over lapping. The Report recommended a straightforward test of whether the conviction "is or may be unsafe". Such phrasing was felt to make the proviso redundant.[3] If the Court feels that the conviction is unsafe, then the conviction should be quashed. If it may be unsafe, then a new trial should be ordered. The Commission felt that retrials should be used more extensively.

The cultural change is that the Court should be willing to substitute its judgment for that of the jury. In reaching its verdict, the jury can err in assessing the true probative weight of circumstantial evidence, of confessions, of accomplices, of unverified police statements, especially given the publicity spotlight and emotion generated by terrorist and other high profile cases. What is required is recognition by the Court that there are cases where the evidence advanced does not reach the standard of proof required and a greater willingness to intervene.

The Commission rightly felt that such fine-tuning of the Court of Appeal was unlikely to ensure that wrongful convictions would always be rectified.[4] What is often required is the ability to instigate and supervise further investigation, a function which is ill-suited to a court. Currently the Home Secretary can refer cases to the Court under section 17 of the Criminal Appeal Act 1968. This work is done by the C3 division in the Home Office which has attracted considerable criticism over its record—in 1990, the division was asked to sift some 790 cases of alleged miscarriages of justice but between 1989 and 1992, the Home Secretary's power to refer back was used on only 28 occasions. Applicants were given the barest of information why their application had been turned down. However, this practice was ended by the High Court in *Hickey*[5] so that applicants will now have to be given both reasons for the refusal and disclosure of any new evidence that has emerged.

The Runciman Commission recommended that an independent Criminal Cases Review Authority[6] be set up which would take over the work of C3 and would be responsible for referring cases back to the Court of Appeal. Legislation for such a body is likely to be introduced in 1995.[7]

5.2.9 Appeals Against Acquittal

As a general rule, the prosecution has no right to appeal against an acquittal in the Crown Court.[8] However, there are two mechanisms which give the prosecution a limited right of appeal:

(a) Attorney-General's Reference: introduced in 1972 by section 36[9] of the Criminal Justice Act, this permits the Attorney-General to refer to the

---

[3] Royal Commission on Criminal Justice, *op. cit.*, para. 10.32.
[4] The BBC's series *Rough Justice* is still publicising worrying cases. The Carl Bridgewater killing is one seen as well as the 1977 "torso" murder case—Greer, *op. cit.*, p. 71, n.60.
[5] *The Guardian*, November 29, 1994, p. 1.
[6] Royal Commission on Criminal Justice, *op. cit.*, Chap. 11; Thornton P., "Miscarriages of Justice: A Lost Opportunity" [1993] Crim.L.R. 926.
[7] *The Guardian*, November 29, 1994, p. 2.
[8] The prosecution can appeal on a point of law by way of case stated to the Divisional Court of Queen's Bench either from a summary acquittal or from a successful appeal to the Crown Court following a summary conviction—Magistrates' Courts Act 1980, s. 111.
[9] Henham R., "Attorney General's References and Sentencing Policy" [1994] Crim.L.R. 499.

Court of Appeal any point of law even though it arose in a case where the defendant has been acquitted. However this does not affect the status of the original verdict and the defendant remains acquitted.

The Runciman Commission recommended that there should be the possibility of an appeal and a retrial where the jury can be shown to have been bribed or intimidated. However they rejected that route in cases of a "perverse" acquittal as well as situations where the accused is acquitted because of a mistake by a prosecution witness.[10]

(b) "unduly lenient sentences": by sections 35–36 of the Criminal Justice Act 1988, where a defendant has been convicted but in the eyes of the prosecution has been given an "unduly lenient" sentence, the Attorney-General may refer that sentence to the Court of Appeal who may substitute a more severe sentence, if they see fit. In *Major*,[11] two concurrent sentences of three years for robbery and possession of a firearm with intent to commit an indictable offence were quashed and a sentence of seven years was substituted. In *Hill-Trevor*,[12] the defendant had been convicted of causing death by reckless driving and had been fined £2,000, disqualified for three years and ordered to take a driving test. The fine was quashed and a 21 month custodial sentence imposed.

5.2.10 *The House of Lords*

This is not the legislative body acting as a whole but merely the Judicial Committee of the House of Lords. It is the supreme court of appeal. In 1992, there were 25 petitions, 23 of which were disposed of, six of which were allowed and 17 of which were refused. House of Lords judges are senior judges who have been given honorific titles for life, entitling them to sit as members of the House of Lords but really to form the membership of this committee. A House of Lords panel will consist of five such judges. Appeals from the Court of Appeal must involve a point of law of general public importance. The procedure involves the Court of Appeal certifying that it is a point of general public importance. Either the Court of Appeal or the House of Lords must give leave for the appeal to take place.

5.2.11 *Pardons and the European Court of Human Rights*

After all these appeals have been exhausted, then the defendant can apply to the Home Secretary for a pardon[13] which is granted by the Crown under the royal prerogative of mercy. This is rarely used after convictions on indictment since the Home Secretary can, as explained above, remit the case back to the Court of Appeal.[14] In 1992, there were 19 free pardons, 17 for motoring offences and two for convictions for failing to purchase a TV licence.

[10] Royal Commission on Criminal Justice, *op. cit.*, para. 10.72.
[11] *Reference No. 2 of 1989* (NACRO News Digest Nov. 1989 No. 59 p. 13). Other examples are also given of increased sentences under s. 36.
[12] *Reference No. 2 of 1989* (NACRO News Digest Nov. 1989 No. 59 p. 14).
[13] The effect of the pardon is to free the person from the imposed penalties. The conviction still stands until it is quashed by the Court of Appeal.
[14] Criminal Appeal Act 1968, s. 17.

There are also the remedies through the European Court of Human Rights. These are not considered here.

5.3 SETTING THE SCENE FOR TRIAL

As has been seen, proceedings against an accused start by his or her appearance in the magistrates' court. This can be as a result of:

(a) the accused being arrested by the police and either being brought to the court in police custody or being bailed by the police to appear at court.
(b) the prosecutor laying an information[15] before the magistrates which results either in the issue of a summons to attend the court or the issue of a warrant for arrest.

However before the trial, there are further preliminary issues to be considered.

5.3.1 *The Bail Decision*

Where a defendant has been arrested with or without a warrant, his or her personal liberty has been curtailed. It can only be restored by a decision of the police or the courts to release on bail. Technically the person remains under arrest but release is obviously important, both personally and for purposes of employment but also for the greater ease that the accused has in preparing a defence. Furthermore conditions for those held in remand prisons are the worst in the penal system.

Bail can be granted in the following situations:

(a) if the suspect is in police custody but has not been charged, the custody officer can release on bail either unconditionally or on a condition to report back to the police station or under the normal conditions of bail under section 3 of the Bail Act 1976.[16]
(b) if the suspect is in police custody and has been charged, the custody officer can detain the suspect and take him or her before the court. However, the officer has the power[17] to release on bail subject to the condition that the suspect appear before the magistrates' court on a certain date. The police can impose other conditions.[17a]
(c) where the suspect has been arrested by magistrate's warrant, this warrant may already have the terms of bail endorsed on it—it is "backed for bail".[18]
(d) where the accused is brought from the police station to the magistrates' court, the court may hear the case at that point but this is uncommon.[19]

---

[15] An information must be laid by a named and identified informant, with brief particulars of the offence and the statutory provision contravened.
[16] PACE, s. 37(2) and s. 40(8).
[17] *ibid*. s. 38 as amended by s. 28, Criminal Justice and Public Order Act 1994—this also specifies the situations where bail may not be granted; that the name and address of the suspect cannot be ascertained, that custody is necessary to prevent harm to others or that there are reasonable grounds for believing that the suspect will not answer to bail.
[17a] Criminal Justice and Public Order Act 1994, s. 27.
[18] Magistrates Courts Act 1980, s. 117.
[19] 21 per cent (31 per cent in 1985) of defendants charged with indictable offences are dealt with

Normally the hearing is adjourned prior to a summary trial or transfer proceedings but there will be a remand hearing.[20] The accused will either be remanded on bail or in custody during this period. The Bail Act 1976 provided that a defendant should be granted bail unless he or she is likely to abscond, commit a further offence, interfere with witnesses or otherwise obstruct the course of justice.[21] The court can initially remand in custody for no longer than eight days.[22] However the Criminal Justice Act 1982 permitted defendants to be remanded in custody for up to a month without attending court as long as they consented. Section 155 of the Criminal Justice Act 1988 goes further and permits remands in custody for up to 28 days whether or not the accused consents.[23]

The defendant has only a limited right to make repeated argued bail applications. In *R. v. Nottingham Justices, ex p. Davies*,[24] it was held that the defence were only permitted to make two fully argued bail applications. After those, a fresh hearing will be heard only if new considerations arise. This was given statutory effect by section 154 of the Criminal Justice Act 1988.

(e) Defendants may appeal from the refusal of magistrates to grant bail to the Crown Court or to the High Court. However, from June 1994, the CPS were given a right to appeal against a decision by magistrates to grant bail in cases which carry a maximum sentence of imprisonment of five years or more. The defendant would remain in custody until the hearing in front of a Crown Court judge who must decide within 48 hours of the original decision.[25]

In 1993:

- 94,000 people were arrested and held in police custody until their first court appearance.[26] (In 1983 the figure was 123,000.)

At the magistrates' court:

- 48,300 were remanded in custody by magistrates (the rest being bailed or dealt with immediately).
- 8,900 (18.4 per cent) were acquitted,
- 12,900 (26.7 per cent) were given a non-custodial sentence,
- 5,200 (10.7 per cent) were given an immediate custodial sentence.

---

on first appearance. On average, cases are listed 3.4 times—*Criminal Statistics 1993, op. cit.*, Table 6.3, p. 133.

[20] Generally see, White R., *Administration of Justice* (2nd ed., 1991), pp. 80–88.

[21] Bail Act 1976, s. 4 and s. 26 Criminal Justice and Public Order Act 1994 which gives magistrates the right to refuse bail if it appears to them that the offence was committed while the accused was on bail for a previous crime.

[22] Magistrates' Court Act 1980, s. 128(6) and s. 128(A).

[23] This power will apply in areas in respect of classes of offence specified by the Home Secretary in a statutory instrument. The initial trial started in four courts (Manchester, Nottingham, Croydon and Highbury Corner) in 1989. (NACRO Briefing No. 56, May 1989, p. 10).

[24] [1981] Q.B. 38.

[25] Bail (Amendment) Act 1993.

[26] *Criminal Statistics 1993, op. cit.*, Table 8.1, p. 190—the quality of the statistics in Chap. 8 is variable and only express an order of magnitude.

Of the rest, 16,900 (35.1 per cent) were committed for trial or sentence in custody, 3,500 (7.3 per cent) were committed for trial or sentence on bail and 900 failed to appear.[27]

Of 16,100 appearing at Crown Court who had been committed for trial and remanded in custody,

- 1,400 (8.8 per cent) were acquitted,
- 3,100 (19.6 per cent) were given a non-custodial sentence,
- 11,500 (71.6 per cent) were given an immediate custodial sentence,[28]

Of 1,300 remanded in custody awaiting sentence,

- 500 (36.6 per cent) were given a non-custodial sentence,
- 800 (63.4 per cent) were given an immediate custodial sentence.[29]

Despite the "right to bail" and statutory time limits,[30] we find that the use of pre-trial custody is still high.

Table 5.3 Remands in Custody 1987 and 1992[30a]

	1987	1992
Annual receptions	59,210	49,869
Average daily population	9,074	8,076
Average length of time for unconvicted male prisoner (days)	70	77

In 1992 the daily average prison population of unconvicted and unsentenced prisoners was 10,090,[31] constituting 22 per cent of the average prison population of 45,187. In 1982, the average daily number of remand prisoners was 7,432 or 17 per cent of the average prison population of 43,772.[32] The rise is explained by two factors; the increasing numbers of annual receptions and by the lengths of time spent on remand.

Is it justified to hold such numbers on remand? 60 per cent or all defendants remanded in custody are either acquitted or given a non-custodial sentence.[32a]

[27] *Criminal Statistics 1993*, op. cit., Table 8.6, p. 194.
[28] *Criminal Statistics 1993*, op. cit., Table 8.9, p. 196.
[29] *ibid.*
[30] Prosecution of Offences Act 1985, s. 22. The early experiments in time limits were satisfactory with only a small percentage over-running: Morgan P., *Pre-Trial Delay: The Implications of Time Limits* (Home Office Research Study 110) (1989).
[30a] *Prison Statistics 1992*, Cm. 2581, Ch. 2.
[31] This can be broken down: 8,076 (7,805 males and 271 females) awaiting trial; 2,014 (1,902 males and 112 females) awaiting sentence.
[32] The statistics in this section are taken from NACRO Briefing No. 32, *Remands in Custody* (December 1993).
[32a] *Criminal Statistics 1993*, op. cit., Ch. 8. *Prison Statistics 1992*, op. cit., Ch. 2.

Such figures speak for themselves. It is unjustifiable that defendants are remanded in custody when the nature of the offence with which they are charged would not justify a custodial sentence. It operates in a discriminatory fashion against women (who are even less likely to receive a custodial sentence) and against Afro-Caribbeans, a higher percentage of whom are remanded in custody.[33] But current government policies are to restrict access to bail[34] and Home Office projections anticipate a remand population in 2001 of 13,300, 26 per cent of a population of 51,600.

Much of the difficulty with bail comes with a lack of information in front of the court about the defendant. The VERA Institute of Justice in New York has developed bail information schemes which are now being widely copied in this country. Forty-five magistrates' court were serviced by such schemes in 1990. Such schemes provide the court with information about the character of the accused or the conditions under which he or she would be living if bailed. This information seems to encourage courts to release on bail more often, without any increase in the breach of bail conditions.

5.3.2 *Legal Representation*

Defendants were not permitted professional assistance to examine witnesses or to speak on their behalf until 1836 but legal representation nowadays is a central part of the due process model. The suspect in police custody is entitled to the advice of a lawyer as well as access to a duty solicitor scheme.[35] Outside court, an accused can consult a lawyer either privately or, much more likely, under the Green Form scheme or under the legal aid scheme for representation in criminal proceedings. But it remains difficult to get full representation at public expense. The Benson Commission[36] argued for a statutory right to legal aid for bail applications, committal proceedings and trial of "either way" offences. These recommendations have been rejected.

For most defendants, the cost of legal advice and representation would be prohibitive. The legal aid scheme allows for the costs of conducting the defence to be borne by the state and not by the defendant. For hearings in magistrates' courts, there is a Legal Aid Fund, which is administered by the Law Society. For Crown Court cases, the costs are paid through the Home Secretary. Legal aid is a means-tested benefit and the defendant might have to make a contribution.

The procedure is a matter for the court. Even if the trial is on indictment, legal aid can be granted by the committing magistrates. This is initially done through application to the magistrates' clerk, although this might be referred to a magistrate or the bench.[37]

In magistrates' courts, however, a substantial proportion of defendants will be unrepresented.[38] Although their function is judicial, magistrates'

[33] Home Office, *Race and the Criminal Justice System* (1992), para. 4.6.
[34] Criminal Justice and Public Order Act 1994, Part II.
[35] PACE, ss. 58 and 60; *supra*, 3.8.7.2.
[36] Royal Commission on Legal Services, *Final Report* (1979), Cmnd. 7648.
[37] For a deeper discussion of the problems of providing legal services, White R., *Administration of Justice* (2nd ed., 1991), pp. 74–80, 108–110 and Chaps. 15–16.
[38] Figures are somewhat imprecise—Zander M., "Unrepresented Defendants in Magistrates' Courts" (1972) New L.J. 1042 suggests less than 25 per cent are represented; Riley and

courts are much less adversarial than higher courts and a major problem is the extent to which normal legal standards exist within summary justice. In cases of unrepresented defendants, both the bench and the clerk often question the defendant to obtain the information that they need, whether for the purpose of the plea itself, mitigating circumstances before sentence or working out a suitable payment plan for the fine. In provincial courts, this may come over as benevolent paternalism but elsewhere:

> "To enter the lower courts is to be taken aback by the casualness and rapidity of the proceedings. The mental image of law carried into courts is shattered by observation. The solemnity, the skills of advocacy, the objections, the slow, careful precision of evidence, the adversarial joust, none of these taken-for-granted legal images are in evidence."[39]

It is only the defendant who is unrepresented. The CPS lawyer inevitably will be present. McBarnet charts the difficulties of the defendant attempting to refute the prosecution version of events, especially in the formulation of suitable questions for witnesses, as opposed to making statements;

Accused: (to the magistrate) "Well, all I can say is ..."
Magistrate: "It's him you ask the questions"
Accused: "No questions then[40]"

The unrepresented defendants are baffled both by such linguistic traps or else by legal terms such as hearsay that convey nothing.[41]

5.3.3.1 PROSECUTION—DISCLOSURE OF EVIDENCE

In trials on indictment,[42] the defendant is entitled to advance disclosure, not only of the prosecution evidence but also of "unused material". The interpretation of this was originally the subject of guidelines by the Attorney-General.[43] "Unused" material was information which had some bearing on the offence and the surrounding circumstances of the offence such as witness statements not included in the committal bundles. Its importance is illustrated in *Taylor*[44] where a senior policeman withheld information from the CPS that a witness identifying the defendants had made an earlier statement that one of the girls he had seen might have been black (neither defendant was) and that he had claimed a reward. The officer withheld the information fearing that it would be disclosed to the defence.

This has been extended by certain judicial rulings—in 1991, Mr Justice Henry at the trial of Ernest Saunders[45] ruled that "unused material" applied to almost all material collected during the course of an investigation and that whether it was "relevant" was not a matter for the prosecution. This ruling

---

Vennard, *op. cit.*, in a study of 909 cases triable either way, suggested that 20 per cent were unrepresented.
[39] McBarnet D., *Conviction* (1981), p. 123 and Chap. 7.
[40] McBarnet, *op. cit.*, p. 132.
[41] McBarnet, *op. cit.*, p. 127.
[42] In summary trials, there is no obligation on the prosecution to disclose but there is a duty in the case of offences triable-either-way—s. 48 Criminal Law Act 1977 and Magistrates' Courts (Advance Information) Rules 1985 S.I. No. 601.
[43] Reported in (1982) 74 Cr.App.R. 302.
[44] Reported in *The Independent*, June 15, 1993.
[45] A Serious Fraud Office prosecution arising out of the Guinness affair—see Royal Commission on Criminal Justice, *op. cit.*, para. 6.38.

was upheld in *Maguire*[46] and *Ward*.[47] The prosecution had also to disclose any matters against prosecution witnesses, for example, police disciplinary hearings.[48] These developments were bitterly resented by the police and prosecution on the grounds that they were either having to disclose sensitive and confidential material or having to discontinue prosecution.

Runciman[49] saw practical problems in the sheer volume of material especially since many major investigations nowadays will use computerised databases. However, there were also issues of principle. Should confidential and sensitive information contained in the material be so readily disclosed? This was seen as particularly acute where informants or undercover police officers were involved. Whereas the Attorney-General's guidelines left considerable discretion to the prosecution, *Ward* held that notice had to be given to the defence of any claim to public interest immunity (PII)—although this has been more restrictively interpreted in *Davis*.

Runciman's guidelines recommended a two-stage process[50]:

(i) Primary disclosure which is automatic. The prosecution would be under a duty to supply the defence with copies of all material relevant to the offence, the offender and the circumstances of the case. Schedules of other information held by the police or other key participants such as expert scientific witnesses would be supplied at this point.

(ii) Secondary disclosure which takes place after the defence have disclosed their case. The defence would be obliged to establish the relevance of the material sought, relating it to their disclosed case. Where the parties disagree on this aspect, the court could rule, after weighing the potential importance of the material to the defence.

Runciman looked to primary legislation to lay down this framework. Under *Davis*[51] and *Keane*,[52] new procedures have developed to allow such material to be placed before the court for a ruling on whether it should be disclosed without compromising its confidentiality. It is for the prosecution to take a view on the relevance of the material to the defence. Clearly they must err on the side of disclosing even the most marginal information.[53]

(a) If the prosecution wish to withhold the information on the grounds of PII, then this is an issue for the court but the prosecution must give notice to the defence, indicating at least the category of the material held and the defence must be given an opportunity of making representations.

(b) If the very indication of the category of material would reveal that which the Crown are arguing ought not in the public interest to be

---

[46] (1992) 94 Cr.App.R. 133.
[47] (1993) 96 Cr.App.R. 1.
[48] *Edwards* [1991] 1 W.L.R. 207.
[49] Royal Commission on Criminal Justice, *op. cit.*, para. 6.41.
[50] Royal Commission on Criminal Justice, *op. cit.*, para. 6.50; for comments, see Glynn J., "Disclosure" [1993] Crim.L.R. 841.
[51] [1993] 2 All E.R. 643.
[52] [1994] 2 All E.R. 478.
[53] *Winston Brown* C.A. June 20, 1994—an issue in the case must be construed broadly.

revealed, then the category need not be specified. Though the defence should still be notified, the application would be *ex parte*.

(c) If, on very rare occasions, even the disclosure of the fact that an *ex parte* application was to be made would tend to reveal that which the Crown are arguing ought not in the public interest to be revealed, then the prosecution can apply to the court *ex parte* without giving notice to the defence. At the application, if the court decides that notice ought to have been given to the defence, then it can so order. However these developments are linked to a more contentious issue.

5.3.3.2 DEFENCE—DISCLOSURE OF EVIDENCE

There has never been such an obligation on the defence to disclose evidence except in the case of alibi evidence,[54] expert evidence[55] and preparatory hearings in serious fraud cases.[56] The Runciman Commission,[57] while maintaining the defendant's right of silence at police station or trial, recommended that in all contested trials, the defence would have to indicate the substance of the defence or the fact that no evidence would be called. The arguments employed were pragmatic: defence disclosure would prevent the "ambush" defence; it would encourage better preparation as well as guilty pleas or prosecution discontinuances where appropriate; it would facilitate better estimates of length of trial and thus more efficient use of resources. Opposition to the proposal points to the lack of any evidence of the widespread use of defence "ambushes",[58] to the diminution of the burden of proof on the prosecution and argue that the "reform" would in fact increase delay and waste resources.

Obviously the shorter the notice that the prosecution have of a witness or item of evidence, the less able they are to counter it. Yet the principal function of a jury is to determine truth, a difficult task amongst the rhetoric and emotion of the courtroom. They should be entitled both to an indictment which lays out an agenda of the issues to be decided and also to both parties putting forward their own evidence as to those issues and how they intend to answer the other's evidence. Concealment of evidence until a late stage by either side necessarily leads to the jury being unable to assess the weight or probative quality of such evidence.

Such principles of proof argue for joint disclosure. Scotland has operated such a practice for several years with little dissent.[59] Yet despite such principles, the practical disadvantages of applying disclosure to simple cases seem to outweigh the benefits. There are arguments for restricting such a reform to complex cases where there is a need for narrowing of the issues.

---

[54] Criminal Justice Act 1967, s. 11.
[55] PACE 1984, s. 81 and Crown Court (Advance Notice of Expert Evidence) Rules 1987 (S.I. No. 716).
[56] Criminal Justice Act 1987, s. 9.
[57] Royal Commission on Criminal Justice, *op. cit.*, para. 6.57 (note of dissent by Professor Zander, pp. 221–223); Glynn J., "Disclosure" [1993] Crim.L.R. 841.
[58] Zander M. and Henderson P., *Crown Court Study* (Royal Commission on Criminal Justice: Research Study No. 19) (1993) suggests that prosecution counsel see such ambushes in 7 per cent of cases whereas for the CPS and the police, the figures are 10 per cent and 23 per cent respectively. Counsel only considered them a serious problem in 3 per cent of cases.
[59] Glynn, *op. cit.*, at 842.

The Criminal Justice and Public Order Act 1994 adopts a less subtle approach. Section 34 is aimed at forcing disclosure of the defence by allowing a court to "draw such inferences as appear proper" from a failure to mention a relevant fact relied on in the defence when it might reasonably have been mentioned during police questioning. To that extent, the section is justified in allowing a jury to attach less weight to a defence which is only revealed at the trial and logically is correspondingly less credible.

5.3.4 Pre-Trial Review

Arguments about disclosure reflect the emphasis on adversarialism in English courts. One party is unwilling to cede tactical advantages to the other. Does a better truth emerge from this process of presenting a jury with opposing and contradictory accounts? Regardless of the answer, the finder of fact, whether judge or jury, is entitled to a proper definition of the issues and clear exposition of the evidence. Pre-trial hearings are essential in achieving this.[60] Currently, save in serious fraud cases, there are no statutory provisions requiring the Crown Court to hold preliminary hearings. There is the possibility of such hearings[61] but the arrangement in the different Crown Court centres are ad hoc and haphazard[62] and their status is informal.[63]

A 1992 pilot study aimed at listing all cases for a "plea and directions" hearing[64] but the Runciman Commission recommended a broader scope. Currently the aim is to discuss and decide on plea, prosecution witnesses, facts which are admitted and which can be reduced to writing, the length of trial, probable exhibits, the medical or mental condition of any witness or defendant, the admissibility of evidence, any point of law and any legal authority on which a party intends to rely. If the hearing is in open court, the judge can rule on applications to sever a count or a defendant as well as those to amend or provide further and better particulars of any count in the indictment. The Royal Commission would widen this to include issues relating to the ethnic composition of the jury as well as issues on the anonymity of witnesses or the use of video-links.[65] The crucial recommendation is that the preliminary hearings should be treated as part of the trial, with the judge able to rule on such matters as the admissibility of evidence and that the trial judge, if different, should be bound by such rulings. Such proposals do move towards a system by which criminal trials will be properly and judicially supervised from the moment when proceedings are instituted.

---

[60] See Court of Appeal dicta in *Thorn* (1977) 66 Cr.App.R. 6; for a study of pre-trial review in magistrates' courts, Baldwin J., *Pre-Trial Justice* (1985).
[61] Practice Rules November 21, 1977—*Blackstones' Criminal Practice, op. cit.*, D.11.13.
[62] Zander and Henderson (1993), *op. cit.*; Royal Commission on Criminal Justice, *op. cit.*, para. 7.11.
[63] *Hutchinson* (1985) 82 Cr.App.R. 51, *per* Watkins L.J. at 56–57.
[64] Described in Royal Commission on Criminal Justice; *op. cit.*, para. 7.12.
[65] Royal Commission on Criminal Justice, *op. cit.*, para. 7.25.

5.3.5 *The Plea and Plea Bargaining*[66]

It is not the public procedures that predominate at a trial. The formal start is the arraignment, the reading of the charges and the defendant's plea. Immediately apparent is the all-pervasiveness of pleas of guilty. In 1992, 479,000 defendants were proceeded against in magistrates' courts for indictable offences of which 243,500 were tried summarily with about 48 per cent pleading guilty.[67] There has been a decline in guilty pleas in all categories of offences tried in magistrates courts over the last five years. Even guilty pleas in summary motoring offences have sunk from 76 per cent in 1985 to 59 per cent in 1993. In the Crown Court, there were 89,800 defendants dealt with—66 per cent of whom pleaded guilty.[68]

There is nothing sinister in this. Suspects are apprehended and charged because they are caught red-handed, are known to the victim, are easily identified by him/her or there has been a statement admitting some or all of the allegations. In such cases, a plea of "guilty" is to be expected. "Not guilty" pleas are more likely to occur in that smaller number of cases that have involved the painstaking gathering of circumstantial evidence and the drawing of deductions from such evidence.

For many defendants, however (although perhaps not a high proportion), the choice between guilt and innocence is not straightforward. To them the interpretation of the events and the consequent responsibility for those actions is likely to be much more complex. Often the defendant is unwilling to accept the bald statement of "facts" as advanced by the prosecution[69] or would like to introduce material which is legally irrelevant but which expresses the defendant's understanding of the incident.

To what extent is the plea the untrammelled choice of the defendant and to what extent does it rely on hidden pressures and informal negotiations? At an early stage, there are likely to be pressures during police interrogation to make a statement of some sort to the police, to "get it off your chest" or "clear the matter up". Yet any admissions at this point will be hard to refute later and will lead to pressure from legal advisors to plead guilty. Unjustified pressure by the police (for example, a suggestion that bail would be forthcoming after a statement was made) would almost certainly lead to the statement being ruled inadmissible.[70]

Pressure which is immediately pre-trial is of more concern. There are inconsistent pleaders; those who have pleaded guilty but still assert their innocence. Susan Dell's[71] study of 527 women in Holloway Prison, convicted in magistrates' courts, suggested that over 10 per cent (n=56) still alleged innocence despite having pleaded guilty. Baldwin and McConville[72]

---

[66] Royal Commission on Criminal Justice, *op. cit.*, para. 7.41; White (1991), *op. cit.*, pp. 110–115.
[67] *Criminal Statistics 1993, op. cit.*, Tables 6.1–6.3, pp. 131–133.
[68] *Judicial Statistics 1993, op. cit.*, Table 6.8, p. 65.
[69] Baldwin J. and McConville M., *Negotiated Justice* (1977), p. 87 where they give examples of the defendants who wish to plead guilty to the offence but challenge the prosecution's version of events.
[70] In *Middleton* [1974] 2 All E.R. 1190, the police threatened to keep a woman accomplice in custody unless the defendant made a statement. The resulting admission was later ruled inadmissible.
[71] Dell S., *Silent in Court* (1971).
[72] Baldwin and McConville, *op. cit.*

identified 150 defendants, about 10 per cent of the total guilty pleas and about 7 per cent of their sample overall, who had changed their pleas from not guilty to guilty at a late stage. The study discovered 121 late plea changers in their study. The defendants gave the following reasons for pleading guilty.[73]

Guilty as pleaded	35	(28.9%)
Plea bargain	22	(18.2%)
Tacit bargain	16	(13.2%)
Pressure from counsel	48	(39.7%)

What is significant from these figures is the large number of defendants who experience pressure from their own counsel to plead guilty. Such pressure is at a very late stage:

> "There were a million and one things that I wanted to say to the barrister if I only could have had the time. There was a lot to say but when the barrister only comes in a few minutes before you go into court there's not a lot you can say and, anyway, he just didn't want to know."[74]

Zander and Henderson's study[75] revealed a similar order of magnitude, concluding that each year there were some 1,400, possibly innocent, persons whose counsel felt that they had pleaded guilty in order to achieve a reduction in the charges faced or in the sentence. There are other factors to consider, not least that the defendants may be alleging innocence as long as possible in order to gain maximum advantage from the system.

In managerial terms the courts need to process a large number of defendants annually. Without guilty pleas, the backlog of trials would be intolerable. The figures suggest that there is a covert system of plea bargaining as a means of encouraging defendants to plead guilty but at the expense of unacceptable pressures being placed on defendants. Plea bargaining means that the defendant enters a mutually acceptable plea of guilty in return for some concession. These concessions were recognised by Newman in the United States[76] and would typically be a sentence concession on length of time to be served or the reduction or dropping of some of the charges. In the United States, plea bargaining is officially recognised whereas in England, it has remained much less obvious, perhaps due to the difference in role and status of the prosecution agencies and to the lack of a public defender system.

In addition, in England the judge retains control over the indictment and also has wide discretionary powers of sentencing.[77] Were the prosecution able to recommend a particular sentence,[78] this would significantly change the

[73] *ibid.* p. 28.
[74] *ibid.* p. 55.
[75] Zander and Henderson, *op. cit.*
[76] Newman D. J., "Pleading Guilty for Considerations: A Study of Bargain Justice" (1956) *Journal of Criminal Law, Criminology and Police Science*, Vol. 46, pp. 780–790.
[77] In England, the judge can normally make an order ranging from an absolute discharge to the maximum prison term specified in the statute. However, in the USA, many states have an indeterminate sentencing system so that the statute specifies a set sentence, say three to five years, for a particular offence and conviction for an offence automatically requires the judge to impose that sentence.
[78] This is already common practice in many civilian jurisdictions—see Downes D., *Contrasts in Tolerance* (1988), pp. 13–14 for the position in the Netherlands.

balance of power in plea negotiations. At present any bargain requires the active co-operation of the judge but the Court of Appeal has consistently set itself against any such involvement. In *Turner*,[79] the defendant was indicted for theft and pleaded "not guilty". His counsel strongly advised him to change his plea on the grounds that he might well go to prison if convicted but otherwise was likely to receive a non-custodial sentence. Counsel went to see the judge and on his return repeated his advice. Turner changed his plea but the Court of Appeal quashed the conviction on the grounds that, since the defendant felt the views had emanated from the judge, it was idle to feel that there had been a free choice. The Court stressed that although there should be freedom of access between the judge and counsel and that counsel could advise a client in strong terms, (any such discussion should involve both prosecution and defence) and should be limited to matters that counsel cannot, in his client's interests, mention in open court. The Court also stressed that the judge should never indicate what sentence he had in mind unless he is able to say that, regardless of plea, the sentence will not take a particular form.

The pressure on the accused emanates from the sentencing discount. A guilty plea attracts a lesser sentence with the discount amounting to about 30 per cent. The Court of Appeal has accepted that it was proper for the judge to ensure that the defendant was aware of the discount[80] although the same court has said[81] that it would be improper to extend a sentence because the defendant has pleaded not guilty or has run a defence in a particular way. The rationale for the discount is that a guilty plea shows contrition but since defendants rarely speak on their own behalf, this is more of a convenient presumption than a reality.

Late changes of plea can be regarded as the result of realistic and practical approaches being adopted by the police, defence and prosecution lawyers, judges and the defendants themselves. Such agreements can be expeditious and economical and a confrontation with "hard facts and realism".[82] Others are less convinced since the existence of the sentencing discount means that defendants are never confronted with a free choice. The pressure of the discount is experienced by all defendants, guilty or innocent.

The Runciman Commission was less concerned about the inconsistent pleader than with the "cracked" trial where the accused is listed as pleading "not guilty" but changes the plea at the last minute with the consequent administrative and economic costs. One study[83] found that of the total cases listed, 39 per cent were listed as guilty pleas and 57 per cent as not guilty pleas. Forty-three per cent of the not guilty pleas, (*i.e.* 26 per cent overall) cracked and became guilty pleas. The Commission's recommendation to avoid this and to encourage early pleas of guilty were twofold; first, the "graduated" discount so that only the accused who pleaded guilty at a

---

[79] [1970] 2 All E.R. 281. For an account of other Court of Appeal decisions, see Baldwin J. and McConville M., "Plea Bargaining and the Court of Appeal" (1979) 6 Brit.J. Law and Society 200.
[80] *Cain* [1976] Crim.L.R. 464.
[81] *Harper* (1967); 117 N.L.J. 1086.
[82] McCabe S. and Purves R., *By-passing the Jury* (1972); Purves R., "That Plea Bargaining Business: Some Conclusions from Research" [1971] Crim.L.R. 470.
[83] Zander and Henderson, *op. cit.*

relatively early stage would be entitled to the full discount whereas the accused who changed his or her mind at the trial would only receive minimal advantage[84]; secondly, they envisage[85] what is, in effect, a plea bargaining hearing although it is called a "sentencing canvass". There would be a preparatory hearing at which the judge would be able to indicate the maximum sentence that would be imposed on the basis of the facts available. This derogates from the *Turner* rule that the judge should not engage in such negotiations. Furthermore, the parties could discuss the possibility of the accused pleading guilty to a lesser charge so that there could be a "full and realistic discussion about plea and especially sentence."

Whether a criminal justice system should have elements of discretion and covert negotiation which legitimate past processes and future actions against the defendant is not a question to which the Runciman Commission addressed itself. Nor is the straightforward issue addressed as to whether a defendant should receive a more severe sentence just because he or she chooses to plead not guilty. This section of the Report has been castigated as its "nadir" in its inability to distinguish issues of principles from managerial expediency.[86]

Section 48 of the Criminal Justice and Public Order Act provides for the court to take into account the stage at which the accused indicated an intention to plead guilty and the circumstances in which that indication was given. If the court imposes a less severe punishment as a result, it must state in open court that it has done so. This will lead to caselaw on the levels of sentencing discount available to the accused for a prompt guilty plea as opposed to a tardy one. Defence counsel and the court will need to make defendants aware of this, and plea bargaining will inevitably become more overt, will involve the judge and will place more pressure on the accused.

5.3.6 *The Jury*

In any trial at Crown Court where the defendant has pleaded "not guilty" to a charge in the indictment and where that plea has not been accepted by the prosecution he or she will be tried in front of a jury. This will consist of 12 people between the ages of 18 and 70, registered as electors and resident in the United Kingdom for at least 5 years since the age of 13.[87] The function of the jury will be to listen to all the evidence relating to the charge, listen to the judge's direction on the law to be applied and then to make up their collective mind as to what they consider to be the facts of the case and to bring in a general[88] verdict of "guilty" or "not guilty" on the charge.

Numerically speaking, the jury has become less significant. In 1993, 65 per cent of Crown Court defendants pleaded guilty and that meant that there was a jury trial in some 30,000 cases. The right to jury trial has been slowly eroded. In 1977, the Criminal Law Act[89] removed the right to jury trial for

[84] This process has already been recognised by the Court of Appeal—*Hollington and Emmens* (1986) 82 Cr.App.R. 281.
[85] Royal Commission on Criminal Justice, *op. cit.*, para. 7.48.
[86] Ashworth A., "Plea, Venue and Discontinuance" [1993] Crim.L.R. 830.
[87] Juries Act 1974, s. 1.
[88] There can be a special verdict in certain cases such as an insanity plea.
[89] ss. 15–17.

some drink/driving offences, for public order offences under section 5 Public Order Act 1936 (now 1986) and for assault on a police constable. In the 1970s, the James Committee[90] made more far-reaching recommendations, for example that theft under £20 would become a summary offence. This was resisted at the time although Runciman would now take away the defendant's right to elect for jury trial subject to review by the magistrates.[91]

The jury is not a democratic part of the trial. Jurors are randomly selected, untrained amateurs from all sections of the population and are, in theory, the least controlled aspect of criminal justice. They are unpaid.[92] Trial by jury has been regarded as a paradigm of English criminal law, described as a bulwark against oppression, a safeguard of our liberties since the common sense of the ordinary person prevails when all else fails.[93] The acquittal of Clive Ponting represents that. He was a senior civil servant who had sent documents to an opposition M.P. These related to the sinking of the Argentinean battleship, the Belgrano, in the course of the Falklands conflict. Prosecuted under the Official Secrets Act 1911, he admitted passing the documents. The judge virtually instructed the jury to convict, yet they still acquitted.[94]

Whether the jury live up to this ideal is moot.[95] Jackson wrote that the only cure for admiration of juries is to read *Howell's State Trials*, for example, the account of the conviction by a jury in 1792 of Thomas Paine for writing *The Rights of Man*. What is undoubted is that it is the most ancient element of "the most ancient relic in any modern legal system",[96] dating from Anglo-Saxon and Anglo-Norman times. While the continental legal systems devised complex systems of logical proof, the English used the jury.[97]

Until the Criminal Justice Act 1972, the property qualification meant that juries were predominantly middle-class, middle-aged, middle-minded and male. The Morris Committee reporting in 1965[98] found that only 22.5 per cent of those on the electoral roll were entitled to be called up for jury service and that 95 per cent of women were ineligible. This was despite the fact that rate revaluation and inflation had increased numbers of those eligible to be jurors fourfold, to the extent that the Metropolitan Police Commissioner, Waldron, was already talking of a deterioration in the quality of jurors. Morris recommended that eligibility for jury service should be co-extensive with the franchise. Although this reform was brought in in 1972, the first 'reform' was the abolition of unanimous verdicts and the introduction of majority verdicts by the Criminal Justice Act 1967.[99] From that time, it was possible to convict or acquit if 10 jurors agree where the jury consists of 11 or

---

[90] *Report of Committee on the Distribution of Business between the Crown and the Magistrates Courts, op. cit.*
[91] This issue on classification of offences and mode of trial is discussed *supra*, 5.2.1; Ashworth (1993), *op. cit.*, at p. 832.
[92] There is a financial loss allowance, wholly inadequate for the self-employed—Royal Commission on Criminal Justice, *op. cit.*, para. 8.56.
[93] Devlin P., *Trial By Jury* (1956).
[94] *The Times*, February 12, 1985.
[95] See discussion in Spencer, *op. cit.*, p. 390.
[96] Milsom, *op. cit.*, p. 413.
[97] Milsom, *op. cit.*, p. 410.
[98] *Report of Interdepartmental Committee on Jury Service* (1965) Cmnd. 2627.
[99] s. 13 (now incorporated in s. 17 of the Juries Act 1974), s. 11 of the same Act introduced the "alibi warning", designed to protect the jury against "ambush" defences.

12 jurors; alternatively if nine jurors agree where the jury consists of 10 or 11 jurors.

After 1972, those excluded from jury service are:

(a) those ineligible by virtue of work concerned with the administration of justice but also including the clergy.[1]
(b) those disqualified by virtue of a criminal record. The disqualification can be for life or 10 years depending upon the seriousness of the offence.
(c) those excusable as of right such as M.P.'s, servicemen, doctors, vets.
(d) there is also a discretion to excuse; if you have served as a juror within the last two years or have been excused by a judge for a longer period; if there is any physical or mental disability; if there is an insufficient command of English. There is a general discretion to excuse for good reason,[2] with the initial decision being made by the Crown Court Officer with the possibility of an appeal to the judge.[3]

The panel for any particular week will be selected from the electoral roll randomly. In earlier times an official would read through the register picking each name. A consequence of this was discrimination. One study[4] discovered that only 1 per cent of Birmingham jurors were of Asian or West Indian origin whereas the proportion in the population as a whole would be at least 12 per cent. It was also true that generally men outnumbered women on juries. Computerisation has meant some form of statistical randomness.

5.3.6.1 VETTING THE JURY

The other factor which reduces the randomness is the vetting of jurors by the police and the security services. This is an honoured tradition.[5] The ABC Official Secrets trial[6] in 1978 showed that it still continued when it was disclosed that the whole panel had been vetted, two members of the jury had signed the Official Secrets Act and the foreman of the jury was a former member of the Special Air Services regiment. In November 1978, there was a trial of some Welsh Language demonstrators in Carmarthen. In a Welsh-speaking area, 10 out of 12 jurors had to listen through headphones since the defendants spoke Welsh and 11 out of 12 jurors had English surnames. The Home Office admitted that a junior officer had "without authority" conducted a check.

There were strong words, both for and against, by the Court of Appeal in *Brownlow*[7] where Lord Denning dubbed vetting "unconstitutional" and *Mason*[8] where Lord Lawton described it as "just common sense". Vetting jurors to obtain some tactical advantage in a minor case was an abuse of

---

[1] But why should the clergy be ineligible? Royal Commission on Criminal Justice, *op. cit.*, para. 8.57.
[2] Juries Act 1974, s. 9.
[3] Practice Direction [1988] 1 W.L.R. 1162.
[4] Baldwin J. and McConville M., *Jury Trials* (1979).
[5] Thompson E.P., "The State versus its enemies" *New Society* October 19, 1978.
[6] Spencer, *op. cit.*, p. 387; White, *op. cit.*, p. 117.
[7] *R. v. Sheffield Crown Court, ex p. Brownlow* [1980] Q.B. 530.
[8] [1981] Q.B. 881.

power. It was finally addressed by the Attorney-General in 1988 when a revised set of guidelines were published.[9] In these, the Attorney reiterates the principle of random selection and that only ineligible or disqualified jurors should be excluded. However, in cases of terrorists and national security, jurors' names will be checked at the Criminal Records Office, against Special Branch records and through local investigations. Such authorised checks require the personal authority of the Attorney-General acting on the advice of the DPP.

CRO checks may be carried out in any case and in an annexe to the guidelines, the Attorney-General specifies such cases: where there is reason to believe that a juror is disqualified; where there has been an attempt to interfere with a juror in a prior and related trial; where the DPP or Chief Constable considers it important that no disqualified person serves on this particular jury. Yet random, and apparently routine, sample checks are still continuing.[10] Since the essence of any check is its secrecy and since the information is passed only to prosecution counsel, there is considerable capacity for the manipulation of the jury, a clear abuse of due process.[11] Again it was not an issue considered by the Runciman Commission.

5.3.6.2. CHALLENGING JURORS

In the courtroom, the clerk selects 12 cards. The juror comes forward and is sworn. There is still some capacity to affect the composition of the jury:

(a) either party can now challenge for cause although the prosecution had no right of challenge whatsoever until 1307. Overall, the defence is in a poor position to affect the composition of the jury since they will have little information. Nor are they able to gain much at the trial itself. Prior to 1973, jurors' occupations were included on the jury list but the Lord Chancellor, Lord Hailsham, used his responsibility for the jury list to abolish this practice.[12]

One means of gathering information was the "voir dire" examination of jurors before they took the oath. In the United States, prospective jurors are examined by both prosecution and defence lawyers and there is no limit to the number that can be rejected. In England, the right to question jurors has been restricted since 1973. In the "Angry Brigade" trial of that year,[13] the judge permitted questioning of jurors to discover whether there was the likelihood of bias. Later a Practice Direction[14] laid down guidelines so that defence

---

[9] [1988] 3 All E.R. 1086—the earlier version is in [1980] 3 All E.R. 785.
[10] Royal Commission on Criminal Justice, *op. cit.*, para. 8.60 which does not mention the Attorney-General's guidelines or whether such checks are in line with them.
[11] Harman H. and Griffith J., *Justice Deserted* (NCCL 1979); East R., "Jury Packing: A Thing of the Past?" (1985) 48 M.L.R. 418; White R., *op. cit.*, p. 117.
[12] Harman and Griffith, *op. cit.*, p. 15.
[13] Dashwood A., "The Jury and the Angry Brigade" 11 W.A.L.R. 245.
[14] Practice Note [1973] 1 W.L.R. 134 now superseded by Practice Direction [1988] 1 W.L.R. 1162.

lawyers cannot question jurors except regarding connections with institutions in the case but not on the juror's beliefs or possible bias.

(b) until January 1, 1988, the defence had the opportunity to make a peremptory challenge to the potential juror and arbitrarily reject a number. This was originally 35 but in modern times had been reduced to seven. The 1977 Criminal Law Act reduced it to three before the right was abolished altogether in 1988.[15]

(c) the prosecution never had a right of peremptory challenge but established the right to "stand by for the Crown". The "stood by" juror only got on the jury if the entire panel had been used up. The Attorney-General issued guidelines[16] that the power should be used sparingly and never in order to gain a tactical advantage. The defence have never had the right to "stand by" jurors[17] and now can only challenge for cause.

The gender and racial balance of juries has improved. Zander and Henderson found that women were slightly under represented and that non-white jurors made up 5 per cent of jurors as compared with 5.9 per cent of the total population.[18] Yet this does not address the problem of ethnic balance in individual cases. It has been suggested that where there are defendants from ethnic minorities, judge and prosecutor should use their powers to "stand by" jurors to establish balance on the jury. In *Bansal*,[19] the judge in a case involving an anti-National Front demonstration ordered the jury panel to be drawn from an area which had a large Asian population. However in *Ford*,[20] the Court of Appeal held that race should not be taken into account in selecting juries and that any such change should be by statute.

The Commission for Racial Equality has argued that, where there is a racial dimension which results in a defendant believing that he or she cannot receive a fair trial from an all-white jury, there should be a specific procedure. The defence (or the prosecution on behalf of the victim) should apply to the judge to show that such a belief was reasonable because of special features in the case and that the judge should have the power to order that three jurors should come from the same ethnic minority as the defendant or the victim.[21]

5.3.6.3 JURIES AND ACQUITTALS

Do juries play the legal game or do they operate on different criteria? There are plenty of recent examples of juries who have acquitted against the weight of the evidence, especially in cases involving the Official Secrets Acts or drink/drinking charges.[22] This undermines the tidy structure of the judge directing the jury as to the legal rule to be applied and then the jury applying the rule to the facts as they decide them. One ex-juror[23] suggests that juries

---

[15] Criminal Justice Act 1988, s. 118(1).
[16] [1988] 3 All E.R. 1086.
[17] *Chandler v. DPP* [1964] A.C. 763.
[18] Zander and Henderson, *op. cit.*
[19] [1985] Crim.L.R. 151.
[20] [1989] 3 W.L.R. 762.
[21] This proposal was endorsed by Royal Commission on Criminal Justice, *op. cit.*, para. 8.63.
[22] Zuckerman A. A. S., *The Principles of Criminal Evidence* (1989), p. 36.
[23] Ely Devons, "Serving as a Juryman in Britain" (1965) 28 M.L.R. 561.

operate on other than purely legal criteria, in one case rejecting the evidence of the chief prosecution witness who was a "tinpot dictator" and "pipsqueak of a civil servant" and in another ignoring the fingerprint evidence before it. The main criticism directed at juries' performance[24] is in regard to the acquittal rate.

In 1993 in the magistrates' courts:

- 479,000 defendants were proceeded against for indictable offences
- 259,900 were tried summarily
- 124,750 (48 per cent) pleaded guilty
- 134,150 pleaded not guilty
- 16,400 (14 per cent) were acquitted.[25]

In the Crown Court

- 89,800 defendants dealt with
- 59,152 (66 per cent) of whom pleaded guilty
- 25,500 pleaded not guilty to all counts
- 14,800 (58 per cent) were acquitted
- 5,170 pleaded not guilty to some counts and 3,390 were acquitted.[26]

These figures can be compared with those produced by the Royal Commission on Criminal Procedure[27] which found that in 1978, 47 per cent of defendants pleading "not guilty" in the Crown Court were acquitted. Prima facie juries look generous in comparison with magistrates. However, the figures must be treated with considerable caution. To arrive at the 14 per cent acquittal rate in magistrates' courts, the figures exclude all "non-jury" acquittals[28] and other disposals such as committals for trial. This is not the case with the Crown Court figures. In 1981, the Royal Commission found that 43 per cent of acquittals were a result of the prosecution offering no evidence or the judge directing the jury to return a verdict of "not guilty" at the conclusion of the prosecution's case.[29] Thus the jury acquittal rate is approximately 25 per cent of contested cases. Recently CPS figures[30] show that rate to be higher since in 1992/93 there were 18,109 contested trials with 6,785 (37 per cent) acquittals.

However, when guilty pleas are taken into account, this figure means that under 8 per cent of all Crown Court defendants are ultimately acquitted by the jury. Furthermore, many of the acquittals will be justified given the nature and the weight of the evidence. Thus the number of "perverse" verdicts by juries (that is, verdicts which are against the weight of the evidence) are relatively few. McCabe's study of 173 acquittals in Oxford suggested that

---

[24] Assessing performance for researches is particularly difficult since s. 8 Contempt of Court Act 1988 makes it an offence to disclose or publish what goes on in a jury room.

[25] *Criminal Statistics 1993, op. cit.*, Tables 6.1–6.3, pp. 131–133.

[26] *Judicial Statistics 1993, op. cit.*, Table 6.8, p. 65—this relates to "cases" dealt with; the Criminal Statistics: *op. cit., supra*, p. 126 give 83,000 as the number of defendants whose trial was completed at Crown Court in 1993.

[27] Royal Commission on Criminal Procedure, *op. cit.*, para. 6.17.

[28] *supra*, para. 4.9.

[29] Royal Commission on Criminal Procedure, *op. cit.*, para. 6.18.

[30] CPS *Annual Report 1992–93, op. cit.*

only 15 (9 per cent) could be described as perverse.[31] Baldwin and McConville[32] suggested that their respondents (judges, police, prosecution and defence lawyers) considered as many as 25 per cent of jury acquittals were "questionable". However, they also found that the same respondents found 5 per cent of convictions also "questionable". Juries in the main play the legal game, following the judge's directions as to the law and applying the facts to applying that law.

5.3.6.4 FUNCTIONS OF JURIES

The jury's role is to listen to the testimony and other evidence provided by the prosecution or defence. It is their function to assess the credibility of a witness, to measure the weight that should be given to any piece of evidence and to determine the existence or non-existence of the facts in the case. The jury then have to apply their determinations as to the facts to the legal elements in the case. It is the judge's job to explain what those legal elements in any offence are. This clear demarcation between facts and law often becomes clouded—the definition of many offences include as "facts" concepts that are relatively imprecise in their definition. The key elements of theft, for example, are legal concepts of appropriation, property belonging to another and intent to deprive,[33] all of which can be defined legally by the judge. But then we encounter the central idea of "dishonesty" and whether community values would regard the accused's acts as "dishonest".[34] This can be seen as "some matter of degree on which opinions of reasonable men may differ ..." (*Stonehouse*[35] per Lord Diplock). In *Stonehouse* itself, the issue was whether the defendant's acts (faking his own suicide) were "sufficiently proximate" to his wife's obtaining the insurance money to form the *actus reus* of the offence of an attempt to obtain that money by deception. This idea of "proximity" was in itself a fact which needed to be proved and decided by the jury. *Stonehouse* and *Brutus v. Cozens*[36] are both authority for the proposition that it is for the jury to decide upon and apply the meaning of ordinary English words. In *Brutus*, the defendant had interrupted Wimbledon by blowing whistles and distributing leaflets. He was charged under section 5 of the Public Order Act 1936 with insulting behaviour and it was held that it was not for the judge to interpret "insulting", but for the jury.

Thus the jury have an interpretative common sense function but it only takes a cursory glance around the criminal law to see that these common sense concepts are frequently circumscribed by quite detailed legal definitions—in *Caldwell*,[37] the House of Lords took it on themselves to lay down the definition of "recklessness" for the jury to follow. We can see the same process in the appellate courts' definition of "intention" in *Hancock*[38] and *Nedrick*.[39]

---

[31] McCabe S., *The Jury At Work* (1972).
[32] Baldwin and McConville, (1979) *op. cit.*
[33] Smith J. and Hogan B., *Criminal Law* (7th ed., 1992), Chap. 16.
[34] *Ghosh* [1982] Q.B. 1053; Smith and Hogan, *op. cit.*, p. 536.
[35] [1977] 2 All E.R. 909.
[36] [1972] 2 All E.R. 1297.
[37] [1982] A.C. 341.
[38] [1986] A.C. 455.
[39] [1986] 3 All E.R. 1.

5.3.7 *The Role of the Judge*

Within the adversarial trial, the judge is the umpire ensuring that the procedural rules are followed. He or she exercises control over the indictment, over the taking of the plea, over the admission of evidence; acts as the ultimate arbiter of any issue of law; summarises the evidence for the jury; explains the law and draws their attention to the issues that have to be decided. Judges do not normally call or question witnesses. This can mean that the jury do not hear significant witnesses. Zander and Henderson found that in 19 per cent of trials, judges knew of one or more important witnesses who had not been called by either side.[40] An eyewitness might not be called by the prosecution because he is a friend of the accused. The accused might not call him because the witness has previous convictions which, when revealed in cross-examination, would harm the defendant's case. Adversarialism necessarily brings such considerations into play at the expense of a clear picture for the jury. The Royal Commission recommended a more proactive approach but spent little time on considering the philosophy of the trial that brings such a situation about.[41]

5.3.7.1 EXCLUSION OF EVIDENCE AND THE VOIRE DIRE

The judge exercises a general supervisory function over the trial but in particular needs to address the question as to whether the evidence adduced by one or other of the parties is admissible and whether it can be placed in front of a jury.[42] The judge acts as a preliminary filter of the evidence, initially considering whether the conditions for admissibility exist. Even when those conditions exist, judges can still exclude admissible evidence by use of their discretionary powers. However, although they can exclude otherwise admissible evidence, they do not have the discretion to admit otherwise inadmissible evidence.

That discretion may be exercised where the probative value of the evidence is negligible in relation to the time and trouble caused by its admission or, more significantly, where its prejudicial effect is so great as to outweigh the probative value. This was the result of the decision in *Sang*.[43] However, that case also held that there was no discretion to refuse evidence solely on the grounds that it was obtained improperly, by a trick or by use of an agent provocateur. In such situations the prejudicial effect is not outweighed by its considerable probative quality.

The decision as to whether evidence is admissible is normally quite straightforward. Sometimes the judge will have to conduct a hearing to determine the question. This is called a *"voire dire"*, taking its name from the special oath sworn by any witness. This hearing often needs to be conducted in the jury's absence although the defendant and his counsel will be present.

[40] Zander and Henderson, *op. cit.*
[41] Royal Commission on Criminal Justice, *op. cit.*, para. 8.18; for consideration of adversarialism, see para. 1.11.
[42] This is examined in more detail in Chap. 6.
[43] [1980] A.C. 402—although *Sang* is still good law, its effect has been lessened since judicial discretion to exclude evidence is largely governed by s. 78 PACE 1984—*supra*, Chap. 3.

Often the argument as to admissibility is purely legal but sometimes the judge will have to conduct a factual inquiry. For example with a young child, there may be an examination to decide whether the child is competent. In such cases, it is necessary for the jury to be present. *Dunne*[44] and *Reynolds*[45] both led to convictions being quashed because the jury were sent away and thus were denied the opportunity to gauge what weight they should give to the child's evidence when the child testified in the trial proper. It is only in situations where the jury might hear evidence which will later be ruled inadmissible that they should not be present.

More importantly a judge might be called upon to rule upon the admission of a piece of evidence such as an incriminating statement by the accused. If the accused alleges that it was obtained in breach either of section 76 or section 78 of PACE 1984, there are conditions precedent before it can be admitted into evidence. With regard to section 76, for example it is for the prosecution to prove beyond reasonable doubt that the statement was obtained without oppression and in circumstances that would not render the statement unreliable. Such a decision will be made by the judge in the absence of the jury. It is likely that a defendant would give evidence as to the circumstances in which the statement was made, testimony which might be very prejudicial. The defendant is protected in such hearings since he or she cannot be cross-examined on the truth or falsity of the alleged confession during the *voire dire*[46] nor are statements made at the *voire dire* admissible in the trial proper.[47]

If the judge admits the evidence, it is a matter for the jury as to what weight might be given to it. The judge might consider a confession admissible but the defendant could still adduce evidence (already advanced at *voire dire*) to seek to persuade the jury that it was not reliable. Tactically the defence must decide whether to reveal their hand at the preliminary *voire dire* in order to exclude the evidence altogether or to wait for the trial proper and thus not alert the prosecution.

5.3.7.2 WITHDRAWAL OF ISSUES

The judge also exercises control by his ability to withdraw issues, or the whole prosecution, from the jury. This can affect both prosecution and defence. At the end of the prosecution case, the defence might argue that there is no case for the defence to answer since the prosecution had failed to satisfy the burden of producing enough evidence for a particular element of the offence so that there is not enough evidence for a conviction. Although, as has been seen, under the Criminal Appeal Act 1966, convictions can be quashed if they are in all the circumstances "unsafe and unsatisfactory", the trial judge must not ask that question but:

(i) is there any evidence that the accused committed the crime?

(ii) is there sufficient evidence for a jury properly directed properly to convict?

[44] (1929) 99 L.J.K.B. 117.
[45] [1950] 1 All E.R. 335.
[46] *Wong Kam-Ming* [1979] 1 All E.R. 939.
[47] *Brophy* [1982] A.C. 476.

The judge is not permitted to look ahead to the appellate process.[48]

However, the judge may also withdraw a single issue from the consideration of the jury. For example, a defendant charged with murder might be arguing for a conviction for manslaughter on the grounds of diminished responsibility. The judge might well refuse to allow the issue of whether the defendant was suffering from diminished responsibility to go to the jury if he or she had not produced enough evidence on the issue.

5.3.7.3 SUMMING UP

After closing speeches from the prosecution and the defence, the jury will hear from the judge who should remind the jury of the evidence that has been put before them and explain to them the nature of the charge. He or she must put all aspects of the defence that have been disclosed by the evidence and must explain to the jury about the burden and standard of proof that must be applied. The judge cannot direct the jury to accept his version of any disputed facts nor can he direct a verdict of guilty. There may be directions as to evidential law, for example, warnings where there is a need for corroboration or where there is identification evidence.

Although judicial direction as to the substantive and evidential law is required, should judges sum up the facts?[49] The argument is that this inevitably influences the jury in one way or another.[50] Jurisdictions such as New York have written jury charges which seek to avoid reference to the facts of the case.

---

[48] *Greenfield* [1981] 2 All E.R. 1060; Pattenden R., "The Submission of No Case to Answer" [1982] Crim.L.R. 558.
[49] *Wilson* [1991] Crim.L.R. 838 where the judge told the jury that it was unnecessary (after a short case) for him to review the facts. The Court of Appeal did not interfere but disapproved of this course in *Gregory* [1993] Crim.L.R. 623 which said there must be a reminder of facts in all cases.
[50] Wolchover D., "Should Judges Sum Up on Facts?" [1989] Crim.L.R. 781.

Chapter Six

Evidence, Witnesses and the Course of Trial

6.1 INTRODUCTION

The plea of "not guilty" has been taken and the jury has been empanelled. There will be an opening speech by the prosecution, an overview of the evidence[1] supporting the allegations in the indictment but in an impartial manner. Whether such, often lengthy, openings are necessary was questioned by the Runciman Commission,[2] which supported the Law Commission's proposals for particularised indictments[3] which would remove the need for opening speeches in routine cases. Although Runciman accepted a need for an opening address in more complex cases, best practice should be to review the issues involved in the trial and not to provide a comprehensive rehearsal of the evidence to be given by each witness. It is much rarer for there to be an opening speech for the defence. This is an option where the defendant intends to call witnesses as to facts in addition to testifying himself or herself but not otherwise.[4] The defence in its closing speech does have the right to the last word[5] (other than the judge's summing up).

After the opening speech, the prosecution will advance witnesses and other forms of evidence to prove the case. Rules of evidence are central to contested trials. They also affect decisions to plead guilty or to discontinue the prosecution. The principles underlying rules of evidence are central to concepts of justice. These rules are concerned with how "facts" are established in a courtroom.[6] The only information for the trier of fact will be that called by the prosecution or defence and tested by cross examination by the opposing party. Parties are constrained by considerations of relevance, probative force and the need not to create undue prejudice against the defendant. Truth is seen as emerging from this counterpointing of differing accounts. It is a "fight" model[7] between interested parties rather than scientific investigation by a disinterested adjudicator.

6.1.1 *Relevance and Reasoning*

Confronted with an item of information, we might ask; "Is it evidence?". This question contains within itself two issues. The first concerns the logic of proof; is the information relevant and probative of whatever issue

---

[1] Omitting reference to any evidence where the defence has given notice that it will be contested as inadmissible, especially confessions—*Swatkins* (1831) 4 C. & P. 548.
[2] Royal Commission on Criminal Justice (1993), Cm. 2263, para. 8.7.
[3] Law Commission, *Counts in an Indictment* (1992).
[4] Criminal Evidence Act 1898, s. 2.
[5] Criminal Procedure Act 1865, s. 2.
[6] As opposed to uncovering or "constructing" facts during investigation—McConville M., Sanders A. and Leng R., *The Case for The Prosecution* (1991), p. 65.
[7] McEwan J., *Evidence and the Adversarial Process* (1991).

needs to be decided? Secondly, there are the lawyers' issues; even if we answer "yes" to that question, are there other reasons why we should not allow that information to be presented?

Items of information are presented to the court; oral testimony by witnesses; written documents; "real" evidence such as material objects, fingerprints; automatic recordings; a witness's demeanour. Such information is not proof but it is data from which we can draw inferences and come to conclusions. Conclusions to what? This is easily answered since it is a key principle of due process that an accused can only be tried for a recognised and specific offence. There must be proof of all of the legal elements required in that offence[8] and only evidence that is relevant to those elements can be used.

Is the evidence relevant? In a shoplifting case, there may well be testimony from the store detective as to the accused's actions in putting goods into her own shopping basket rather than a wire basket provided by the store. Is this relevant? If we define relevance as information which tends to make another fact more or less probable, then it is. This item of information renders the accused's dishonesty more probable. Yet this definition of relevance can encompass marginal circumstantial evidence and Runciman felt that the criterion of relevance was too widely interpreted by judges, allowing time-wasting by counsel and forcing juries to sit through evidence which adds little to what was already before them. A more "robust" approach would be encouraged by the powers under Rule 403 of the US Federal Rules of Evidence which empowers judges to exclude evidence if:

> "although relevant, its probative value is substantially outweighed by the danger of unfair prejudice, confusion of the issues or misleading the jury, or by considerations of undue delay, waste of time, or needless presentation of cumulative evidence."[9]

The process of drawing inferences from evidence is one of common sense logic: people who put supermarket goods into their own baskets normally are not intending to pay for those goods. However, there may be a conflicting interpretation put forward by the defence: "I like to keep the washing powder separate from the food and use my shopping basket. I forgot it was there." Often there are many relevant items of evidence, some supporting and others contradicting a particular inference and jurors must assess the weight that they are willing to place on any item. Furthermore, we may be dealing with chains of inferences. Evidence leads the jury to an inferred fact from which a further inference can be drawn and so on through a series of intermediate stages until we reach the ultimate issue[10] which had to be decided.

Overall, this is inductive reasoning, drawing conclusions from established facts. However, we do not draw inferences in a vacuum and juries often use an inarticulated generalisation: people who hide goods in shops tend to be dishonest. It is moot how far courts go to uncover such generalisations and to

[8] For example, with theft, the prosecution must adduce evidence to prove each of five elements—the defendant *appropriated property belonging to another, dishonestly and with the intention to permanently deprive.*
[9] Royal Commission on Criminal Justice; *op. cit.*, para. 8.13.
[10] An excellent short story illustrating this is Kemelman's "The Nine Mile Walk" in Anderson S. and Twining W., *Analysis of Evidence* (1991), p. 9. On the logic of proof, see *ibid.*, Chaps. 2 and 3.

assess their validity as opposed to their prejudicial quality. The shoplifter's previous convictions for theft, although relevant, are excluded. Any probative value such evidence might have is outweighed by the prejudice it would create in the minds of the jury. There is less protection from other stereotyping, based upon assumptions about race or nationality. This is illustrated by the disproportionate numbers of young blacks prosecuted, convicted and given custodial sentences.

6.1.2 *What is proof?*

Having heard the evidence, the trier of fact must come to a conclusion on the ultimate issue of guilt or innocence. This is a two stage process:

(a) who has to prove anything? Must the accused satisfy the jury of his or her innocence or must the prosecution convince them of his or her guilt? This is the question of the burden of proof. In a criminal trial, it rests upon the prosecution.

(b) what level of proof is needed? Total certainty rarely happens and proof is about the probability of a state of affairs existing. In a criminal trial with an individual's liberty is at stake, a high standard is required and that occurs when the jury is satisfied "beyond reasonable doubt". In theory this seems a proper formula but in practice there are significant inadequacies. For example, juries have been allowed to convict on uncorroborated confession, identification or accomplice evidence. The jury is not necessarily to blame. In many cases where justice has miscarried, the quality of evidence, accepted by the judge as evidence on which a reasonable jury might convict, has nowhere approached "proof beyond reasonable doubt". The ready acceptance of circumstantial evidence has meant that sometimes not only the quality but the quantity of the evidence is wanting.[11] The English legal system has always prided itself on its rules on proof of guilt but there remain real problems as to whether judicial supervision over the sufficiency of evidence is adequate.

6.1.3 *Burden of Proof*

There are two types of burden of proof; a legal burden and an evidential burden:

● the legal burden is where a party has to *prove* a particular issue. In a criminal trial the prosecution to prove all the elements of an offence for the defendant to be found guilty. The defendant has normally to prove nothing.
● the evidential burden is where a party had to adduce enough evidence for the judge to be satisfied that the issue should be left to the jury and might be referred to as the problem of "passing the judge".

---

[11] Woffinden R., "The Case of the Winchester Three" (1990) 140 New L.J., p. 164.

6.1.3.1 LEGAL BURDEN

The legal burden is straightforwardly the allocation of risk. The party shouldering the burden loses if there is no evidence at all or if the evidence does not satisfy the finder of fact. It is often called the probative or persuasive burden and it has various effects:

(a) in specifying the right to start calling evidence.
(b) in dictating who can make submissions of "no case to answer".
(c) in settling doubts for the trier of fact.
(d) in assisting appellate courts when considering the propriety of directions on burden.

The burden of proof exists in relation to specific issues. Although the prosecution will bear the burden in relation to most issues, the defence may bear it in respect of another. In a murder trial, the prosecution has to prove the fact of killing and the intent to kill but if the accused is seeking a verdict of "not guilty through reason of insanity"[12] or of manslaughter by reason of diminished responsibility,[13] the legal burden of proof of those issues rests on the accused.

The basic common law rule is that the burden of proof of particular facts rests upon the party who asserts those facts. In criminal cases, this was laid down by Lord Sankey in *Woolmington*[14]:

> "Throughout the web of English criminal law one golden thread is always to be seen, that it is the duty of the prosecution to prove the prisoner's guilt subject to what I have already said as to the defence of insanity and subject also to any statutory exception. ... No matter what the charge or where the trial, the principle that the prosecution must prove the guilt of the prisoner is part of the common law of England and no attempt to whittle it down can be entertained ...."[15]

In *Woolmington*, the accused shot his estranged wife. He claimed that the shotgun had gone off by accident. It was not for the accused to prove that it was an accident. He was not required to persuade the jury of that fact on the balance of probabilities.[16] It was for the prosecution to prove beyond reasonable doubt that he had intended to fire the gun and kill his wife. If the defendant chose not to testify, he would take a considerable risk but would not inevitably lose[17] because the jury might still not be convinced by the prosecution witnesses. Tactically the accused would wish to testify in order to implant a doubt in the jury's mind about whether the shooting was intentional or accidental. But such tactical decisions must be distinguished

---

[12] There is a presumption of sanity—the defendant must prove on the balance of probabilities that he or she is insane within the meaning of the *M'Naghten Rules* (1843) 10 Cl. & F. 200; Smith and Hogan, Criminal Law (7th ed. 1992), p. 205.

[13] Homicide Act 1957, s. 2(2); Smith and Hogan B., *op. cit.*, p. 210.

[14] *Woolmington v. DPP* [1935] A.C. 462.

[15] *ibid.* at pp. 481–482.

[16] If the defendant ever carries the burden of proof, the standard of proof would always be this lower one.

[17] There is no evidential burden on the accused here. Unlike self-defence, accident is not an additional issue but is merely a denial of intention—and proof of intent is undoubtedly the function of the prosecution.

from the concept of the legal burden of proof resting on the prosecution to convince the jury beyond reasonable doubt.

Sankey suggests that there are two exceptions to this rule, namely insanity and statutory exceptions which place a burden on the accused.[18] Yet these narrow limits have already been "whittled away" by an acceptance that Sankey's statutory exceptions were not limited to statutes which expressly cast the burden of proof on the accused but extended to those which did it by implication. What amounts to such an "implied statutory exception" can be seen by the wording of section 101 of the Magistrates' Courts Act 1980 which states that if a statutory provision contains an exception/proviso/excuse, then this casts the burden of proving that exception on the defendant.

Section 101[19] created a rule for summary trial but the section has been interpreted by *Edwards*[20] to be an expression of a common law rule and thus applicable also to trials on indictment. In that case, the defendant was convicted under section 160 of the Licensing Act 1964 of selling alcohol without a justices' licence. The burden of proving that he possessed a licence rested on the defendant. The conviction was upheld by the Divisional Court:

> "This exception ... is limited to offences ... which prohibit the doing of an act save in specified circumstances or by persons of specified classes or with specified qualifications or with the licence or permission of specified authorities ... (the exception's) application does not depend upon either the fact or the presumption that the defendant has peculiar knowledge."[21]

The result accords with common sense since it should be no hardship on the defendant to produce his justices' licence. However, the ratio is much broader since it does not limit this transfer of burden of proof to those cases where the defendant has "peculiar knowledge". Basing the decision on that element would have been both practical and also corresponded with principles of fairness; the statute would have been narrowly interpreted[22] and the ratio would have accorded with the principle of ease of proof.[23]

In *Hunt*[24] the accused was charged with possession of morphine. Such possession was only illegal where the preparation contained more than 0.2 per cent morphine. The defendant argued that the prosecution had not adduced any evidence as to the strength of the preparation but was still convicted on the basis that the burden on this issue lay on the defence. The House of Lords (while allowing the appeal) accepted that statutes could by implication cast the burden of proof on the accused even in indictable offences. The problem is one of statutory construction and the language of

---

[18] *e.g.* Prevention of Corruption Act 1916, s. 2 (deemed to be corrupt unless ...); Prevention of Crimes Act 1953, s. 1 (accused must show lawful excuse for carrying offensive weapon ...); Sexual Offences Act 1956, s. 30 (presumed to be living off immoral earnings unless ...); Homicide Act 1957, s. 2 (accused must prove diminished responsibility).

[19] And its predecessor, Magistrates' Courts Act 1952, s. 81.

[20] [1975] Q.B. 27.

[21] *ibid. per* Lawton L.J. at pp. 39–40.

[22] This should be the fundamental approach with any penal statute—Ashworth A., *Principles of Criminal Law* (1991), p. 67.

[23] Ashworth, *op. cit.*, p. 75.

[24] [1987] A.C. 352.

exceptions/provisos did not automatically place the burden of proof on the accused. Indeed the House placed stress on practical considerations such as the ease or difficulty that a defendant might have in discharging this burden.

The scope of *Hunt* and *Edwards* is enormous. Hundreds of statutory offences use the language of "excuse, proviso, exemption or qualification". This reversal of the burden of proof undermines the presumption of innocence expressed in *Woolmington*.[25] Such a failure to construe penal statutes in a strict fashion can only encourage legislative draftsmen routinely to place probative burdens on the defence.

6.1.3.2 EVIDENTIAL BURDEN

It is a lesser hurdle to adduce evidence to satisfy the judge to leave an issue to the jury. Clearing the hurdle does not mean that the party will therefore succeed with that issue.

- the prosecution will always have an evidential as well as a legal burden to satisfy. A failure on their part to adduce some evidence in relation to each and every element of an offence would mean that a defence submission of no case to answer would be successful.
- the defendant may have an evidential burden to satisfy if he or she wishes to raise a particular defence, for example self-defence or provocation. There would have to be enough cogent evidence of the victim's words or actions to satisfy the judge that the issue should be left to the jury. Once the defence has raised such an issue, it is for the prosecution to disprove it beyond reasonable doubt.

6.1.4 *Standard of Proof*

A court is concerned with the problem of reconstructing the past and attempting to discover the truth. These are not absolutes and our conclusions are not certainties but varying levels of likelihood. Courts need to specify the level of probability that constitutes proof and this is referred to as the standard of proof:

(a) the first stage is to overcome the evidential burden, to "pass the judge". If the judge does not believe that sufficient evidence has been adduced by the prosecution on each element of the offence so that a reasonable jury, properly directed, might convict, then he or she might direct the jury to acquit. This often happens at the end of the prosecution case on a submission by the defence of "no case to answer".[26]

    If the judge does not believe that sufficient evidence has been adduced by the defendant seeking to raise a particular defence so that a reasonable jury, properly directed, might find a reasonable doubt, then he or she can withdraw that issue from the jury

(b) the second stage is for the party with the legal burden to persuade the trier of fact of the "truth" of the assertions. There are two levels; for the

---

[25] A summary of criticisms is given in Tapper C. (ed.), *Cross on Evidence* (7th ed., 1990), p. 140 and n. 11; Zuckerman A., *Principles of Criminal Evidence* (1989), Chap. 9.
[26] On non-jury-acquittals, *supra*, para. 4.9.

prosecution, the level of persuasion is that proof must be beyond reasonable doubt; for the defence, that standard is proof on the balance of probabilities.[27]

Although formally there are only two standards of proof, Tapper[28] points out that some acts are inherently less likely than others and the consequences of some decisions are more serious than others. Thus the prosecutor in a murder case should have a higher hurdle to surmount (since people are less likely to kill and the consequences are life imprisonment) than one prosecuting on a less serious charge. However, such reasoning has not led the appellate courts to develop flexible standards and we are left with standard formulae. In *Miller v. Ministry of Pensions*,[29] Denning distinguished proof beyond reasonable doubt from certainty. Certainty was not necessary nor were remote possibilities or fancies, "reasonable" doubts. The appellate courts tend to dislike specifying a formula but "reasonable doubt" and "sure" have attained a traditional status although the Judicial Studies Board's specimen direction says; "It is for the prosecution to *establish* the defendant's guilt."

6.2 ADMISSIBILITY

Which witnesses can be heard, what questions can be asked, what documents introduced, what objects seen by the jury? Is the proposed evidence admissible? Admissibility is a key concept. The basic rule is that all relevant evidence is also admissible evidence unless there is a rule that excludes it. This is a problem for the judge who has to decide whether evidence is relevant and whether an exclusionary rule applies. If there is a dispute whether the conditions for admitting the evidence have been met, the judge will hold a hearing or trial within a trial (known as a "voire dire") with witnesses and argument. The burden is on the party seeking to admit the evidence to show that the precedent conditions exist.[30] If the burden is on the prosecution it is proof beyond reasonable doubt.[31] Where the defence is seeking to adduce evidence, then the judge merely needs to be satisfied that the conditions for its inclusion are satisfied on the balance of probabilities.

6.3 ORAL TESTIMONY AND WITNESSES

Adversarial trial relies upon oral testimony. By observing and listening to a witness, the trier of fact is believed to be able to assess the weight to be attached to the witness's evidence more effectively than by reading a written statement.[32] Furthermore, there is the principle of the right to confront your

---

[27] *Carr-Briant* [1943] K.B. 607.
[28] Tapper, *op. cit.*, p. 148.
[29] [1947] 2 All E.R. 372.
[30] *Yacoob* (1981) 72 Cr.App.R. 313.
[31] *Ewing* [1983] 2 All E.R. 645. Also where the prosecution wish to rely on the accused's confession, then they must prove beyond reasonable doubt that it was obtained in accordance with the conditions under s. 76(2) of PACE 1984.
[32] Oral testimony is often given even where there is no dispute. Formal admissions are possible under s. 10 of the Criminal Justice Act 1967 but this is significantly under-used.

accusers and to a public trial. The practice of the anonymous accusation adjudicated in secret is the hallmark of totalitarian societies.

Adversarial trial might encapsulate constitutional principle but its structure inhibits its ability to elicit reliable information:[33] the atmosphere of the court bewilders the witness; lawyers coach witnesses so that their testimony will support a particular perception of the facts; cross-examination as a technique leads the honest witness into error rather than into elucidation; tactics and surprise play a major part; there is inadequate pre-trial disclosure and insufficient acceptance of affidavit evidence on non-controversial issues.

We frequently over-estimate the quality of evidence put before juries and their ability to assess that evidence. Too much weight is placed on identification, confession or eye-witness testimony.[34] Witnesses' ability to assess the passage of time or speed or to recall colours, events or statements varies considerably. Good powers of perception and recall are not related to the coherence and demeanour with which they present their testimony which are major factors in a jury's assessment of the reliability of a witness.[35] Whether we believe or disbelieve what people tell us has as much to do with their abilities as story-tellers as with the truth of their story. Juries adopt unscientific standards to evaluate the probative quality of what is put before them.

More mundanely, the witness has to recall, without any assistance, actions which will have taken place several months ago. A statement which has been made within a few days of an incident is inevitably more accurate but if the witness is available, that statement cannot be introduced into evidence. In other European jurisdictions, that statement, taken under judicial supervision, would be put into evidence and the witness would be questioned on it. Our suspicion of statements taken by the police, unsupervised by any judicial process is a further argument for a professional magistracy.

Everyone can be compelled to attend court[36] and is competent to give evidence; everyone is under an obligation to disclose the truth. But in the eighteenth and nineteenth centuries, a range of potential witnesses was disqualified[37] because of:

(a) a fear of manufactured evidence arising from the self-interests of the witness—whether the parties themselves, their spouses or people with other interests in the outcome of the proceedings.
(b) a fear of evidence being unreliable due to the moral or other characteristics of the person giving evidence. Thus heathens, atheists, convicts, the mentally ill and children were excluded from the witness box.

Nowadays there are few restrictions on testifying. The defendants (and their spouses) have provided a longer lasting problem.

[33] Frank J., *Courts on Trial* (1949).
[34] Clifford B., "Eye-witness Testimony" in Farrington D., *et al.*, *Psychology, Law and Legal Process* (1979); Lloyd Bostock (ed.) *Evaluating Witness Evidence*.
[35] Bennet W. and Feldman M., *Reconstructing Reality in the Courtroom* (1981).
[36] Criminal Procedure (Attendance of Witnesses) Act 1865.
[37] Tapper, *op. cit.*, p. 201.

6.3.1 *The Defendant as Witness*

At common law, the accused was incompetent as a witness. Not only was there the fear of perjury but also the fear that the judiciary might compel the accused to incriminate himself or herself. Only in 1898[38] did the accused become a competent witness in all criminal proceedings, although only for the defence. The defendant cannot be compelled to testify for the prosecution[39] but once the defendant enters the witness box, he or she can be cross-examined by the prosecution notwithstanding the fact that the answers may incriminate.[40] The situations where a defendant may testify are:

(a) for the prosecution: there are cases with multiple defendants, where the accused might choose to testify for the prosecution against another defendant. This can only occur if, for some reason, the defendant has ceased being a defendant. Those situations are:

   (i) where the accused has pleaded guilty to all charges.
   (ii) where the accused has pleaded guilty to some charges and the plea of not guilty to the other charges has been accepted by the prosecution. The defendant should be sentenced after giving evidence.[41]
   (iii) where the accused has been acquitted through the prosecution offering no evidence or through the submission of a successful "no case to answer" plea at the close of the prosecution case or through a "nolle prosequi" being entered by the Attorney-General.
   (iv) where the prosecution has successfully requested severance of the indictment—although it seems to be a rule of practice that in such circumstances, accomplices should not be called to testify unless the prosecution has agreed to discontinue the case against them.[42]

Allowing co-defendants to testify against each other is fraught with risks because of the self-interest involved. The limitations above aim at situations where the co-defendant no longer has any interest. Yet this is not possible where the accomplice is seeking to underplay his or her own involvement and many miscarriages of justice have arisen from reliance on accomplice evidence.[43] The risks of such evidence will be accentuated by the abolition of the need of the corroboration

---

[38] Criminal Evidence Act, s. 1.
[39] But s. 35, Criminal Justice and Public Order Act 1994 enables the judge to call on the accused to testify with the sanction that the jury can draw adverse inferences in the event of a refusal.
[40] Criminal Evidence Act 1898, s. 1(e).
[41] *Weekes* (1982) 74 Cr.App.R. 161.
[42] In *Pipe* (1966) 51 Cr.App.R. 17, the defendant was prosecuted for theft—an accomplice, about to be tried separately for handling the stolen goods, was called to testify. Whether he should be permitted to testify is a matter of discretion.
[43] *e.g.* the Luton post-office murder—Woffinden B., *Miscarriages of Justice* (2nd ed., 1989), p. 172; Kennedy L., *Wicked Beyond Belief* (1980).

warning,[44] and even more so were the Runciman proposals for the extension of plea bargaining to become law.

(b) for the defence: the accused is competent at every stage of the proceedings, whether at committal, trial or *voire dire*. An accused should give evidence before other defence witnesses[45] although this is a matter of judicial discretion. Having elected to testify, then the accused is subject to cross-examination like any other witness.[46] Even if the accused only testifies about her or her own involvement, he or she can still be cross-examined by the prosecution about any co-defendants' involvement.[47] Further, where an accused gives evidence on his or her own behalf, he or she can be cross-examined by the co-defendant even though he or she has not given evidence adverse to that co-defendant. There is a limited right against self-incrimination and the accused can refuse to answer questions if those questions are likely to expose them to another criminal charge.[48]

Until 1994, the prosecution were not permitted to comment on the defendant's decision not to testify[49] although this was possible for a co-accused's counsel. Although the judge could comment,[50] he or she had to do so in measured terms and had to warn the jury that they must not assume guilt from the defendant's silenced.[51] Now under section 35 of the Criminal Justice and Public Order Act 1994, a failure to testify entitles the jury to draw such adverse inferences as they see fit. Silence can thus be evidence for the prosecution.

(c) for a co-accused: the accused is unlikely to give evidence for a co-accused when he has not given evidence on his own behalf, since he would open himself up to cross-examination on his own involvement. However, he might do this on *voire dire*, for example, where a co-accused is seeking a ruling on the admissibility of a piece of evidence such as a confession.

6.3.2 *The Defendant's Spouse as Witness*

There was great reluctance to allow an accused's husband or wife to give evidence against their spouse. The 1898 legislation permitted spouses to testify for the defence but whether a spouse was a competent witness for the prosecution remained obscure. At common law, the spouse was a competent witness in cases of personal violence and treason but was probably not

---

[44] Criminal Justice and Public Order Act 1994, s. 32.
[45] PACE, s. 79.
[46] There are safeguards under s. 1(f) of the Criminal Evidence Act 1898 in relation to cross-examination about the defendant's character—*infra*, para. 6.7.3.4.
[47] *Paul* [1920] 2 K.B. 183.
[48] *Blunt v. Park Lane Hotel* [1942] 2 K.B. 253.
[49] Criminal Evidence Act 1898, s. 1(b)—this provision has been repealed by the Criminal Justice and Public Order Act 1994.
[50] *Bathurst* [1968] 2 Q.B. 99; *Sparrow* [1973] 1 W.L.R. 488 although see Rupert Cross's forthright comments on "gibberish", [1973] Crim.L.R. 329 at 333.
[51] See discussion on the "right to silence" *supra*, para. 3.8.7.1.

compellable.[52] There was a range of statutes which also made the wife a competent but not a compellable witness.[53-54] But this confusion was blown away by section 80 of the Police and Criminal Evidence Act 1984 which made the spouse a competent witness in all criminal proceedings and a compellable witness in a small number of such cases:

(a) for the prosecution: the spouse is always competent but can only be compelled to testify where (i) there has been physical violence on a spouse or person under 16; (ii) where there has been sex with a person under 16 or (iii) where there has been an attempt or conspiracy at such offence.[55] This is not the most rational of provisions. Why is there a greater public interest in these offences than in others? Is the protection of children more important than the protection of other people? The changing nature of marriage has made this immunity somewhat anomalous and it is difficult to see why a spouse should be entitled to withhold information from the court, once the prosecution has been initiated.[56] Furthermore, if it is repugnant to see a wife being compelled to testify against her husband, there are other levels of relationship to which this argument would apply such as that of mother and son or unmarried couples.

(b) for the defence: the spouse is both competent and compellable on behalf of the defendant[57] although if husband and wife are jointly charged, then neither is competent nor compellable.[58] The failure of a spouse to testify cannot be made the subject of comment by the prosecution.[59]

Spouses are those who are *de iure* married to the defendant. In *Khan*[60] the woman had gone through a Moslem ceremony of marriage with an accused who was already married to another woman under English law. The marriage was bigamous and void and the witness was not a spouse for these purposes. If a person is no longer married[61] that person is competent and compellable to testify as if that person and the accused had never been married. "No longer married" would include divorce or annulment but certainly not judicial separation or just non-cohabiting.

6.3.3 *Children as Competent Witnesses*

The number of prosecutions for the sexual and physical abuse of children have led to concern about the manner in which children can give evidence.[62]

---

[52] This issue was still being argued in 1978 when it was decided by the House of Lords in *Hoskyns* [1978] 2 All E.R. 136 that, even where the husband was charged with an offence of violence against the wife, the wife was still not a compellable witness against the husband.
[53-54] The list can be seen in Keane A., *The Modern Law of Evidence* (2nd ed., 1989), p. 77.
[55] PACE, s. 80(3)(c).
[56] Zuckerman, *op. cit.*, pp. 289 ff.
[57] PACE, s. 80(3)(b).
[58] PACE, s. 80(4).
[59] *ibid.* s. 80(8). This is not affected by s. 35 Criminal Justice and Public Order Act 1994.
[60] (1986) 84 Cr.App.R. 44.
[61] PACE, s. 80(5).
[62] These concerns are thoroughly examined in Spencer J. and Flin R., *The Evidence of Children* (2nd ed., 1993).

The concerns encompass not just the question of competence but the appropriateness of children testifying in an adversarial setting,[63] the need for independent corroboration of their testimony[64] as well as the exclusion of what appears relevant and reliable evidence through the hearsay rules.[65]

Historically a child could give evidence in two ways:

(a) sworn evidence: the applicable criteria as to whether a child should take the oath were laid down in *Hayes*.[66] The judge had to consider whether the child has sufficient appreciation of the solemnity of the occasion and the responsibility to tell the truth. This is no longer a theological question and *Hayes* overturns *Brasier*[67] which held that it was a question of the child's recognition of the divine sanction behind the oath and that therefore the judge should inquire into the child's belief in God. *Hayes* also suggested as a working rule that if the child was under 14, then the judge should make some inquiries in the presence of the parties and the jury.[68]

(b) unsworn evidence: if a child did not understand the nature of the oath but understood the duty of speaking the truth, then the child could give unsworn testimony.[69] The statutory test for unsworn testimony talked of the "duty of speaking the truth". After *Hayes*, it was difficult to distinguish this from the test for giving evidence on oath.[70]

However, the problems caused by this distinction were resolved in section 52 of the Criminal Justice Act 1991 which provided that the evidence of a child under 14 should be given unsworn. It would still be necessary for the judge to inquire whether a very young child was competent and understood the duty of speaking the truth.[70a]

6.4.1 *Immunities from Testifying—Public Interest Immunity*

The obligation to disclose information to a court is central to any principle of fairness. However, there are categories of information which cannot be revealed even if the information is relevant and probative. One of these is public interest immunity (PII). The information should not be publicly

---

[63] There has been the introduction of TV links under s. 32 of the Criminal Justice Act 1988 so that the child witness does not have to confront the assailant.

[64] *infra*, para. 6.5.

[65] *Sparks* [1964] 1 All E.R. 727 but see s. 54 Criminal Justice Act 1991.

[66] [1977] 2 All E.R. 288.

[67] (1779) 1 Leach 199.

[68] To do so in the absence of the jury could lead to the conviction being quashed since the *voire dire* gave jurors a basis to assess the child's understanding—*Reynolds* [1950] 1 All E.R. 335.

[69] Children and Young Persons' Act 1933, s. 38(1).

[70] The test for giving sworn testimony in *Hayes* is also the test for those with mental handicaps—*Bellamy* (1986) 82 Cr.App.R. 222 where the victim of rape had a mental age of 10, was capable of telling the truth but was ordered to affirm after the judge had questioned her about her belief in God!

[70a] *Deakin* (1994) 4 All E.R. 769, for a recent analogous inquiry into the competence of a mentally handicapped witness.

revealed in court because it would be injurious to the public interest. If neither party to the proceedings objects, the court or another person, such as the Government, is able to do so.

Until the 1960s[71] there appeared to be a hard rule that where such public interest was claimed by the requisite certificate from a minister, then that would be accepted by the court. More recently,[72] courts have been reluctant to accept ministerial fiat and judges have assumed discretionary power to inspect documents and to decide whether the interests of the administration of justice outweigh the effects of disclosure on the State. In *Burmah Oil*,[73] Lord Scarman suggests that there is no class which is automatically excluded from inspection—"I do not accept that there are any classes of document which ... may never be disclosed". Even with regard to cabinet minutes, "... what is so important about secret government that it must be protected even at the price of injustice in our courts?" Although there is a recognised public interest in relation to governmental and administrative matters and a presumption in favour of a minister's judgement, there is a conflicting presumption in favour of disclosure[74] which is necessary for the proper administration of justice. The conclusion is that the court can always question a claim to withhold disclosure, inspect the relevant documents and balance the different public interests involved. That balance of interests will normally be exercised in favour of the accused in a criminal trial,[75] unless the documents are of extreme sensitivity.

PII is very significant in the rules concerning the disclosure of material by the prosecution. One long-standing rule has been that no question may be asked which would reveal the identity of a person who has given information for the detection of crime.[76] In *Rankine*[77] the police refused to answer questions as to the location of their observation post since the owner of the house might be at risk of reprisals. Cases such as *Davis*[78] and *Keane*[79] have developed a procedure for placing sensitive material before the court for a ruling on disclosure without compromising its confidentiality.[80]

Away from the trial, PII has been important where plaintiffs have launched civil actions against the police and have sought to rely on documents which have been created during complaints investigations under section 49 of the

---

[71] *Duncan v. Cammell Laird* [1942] A.C. 624; *Asiatic Petroleum v. Anglo-Persian Oil* [1916] 1 K.B. 822.

[72] *Conway v. Rimmer* [1968] A.C. 910.

[73] *Burmah Oil v. Bank of England* [1980] A.C. 1090; see also *Air Canada v. Secretary of State for Trade (No. 2)* [1983] 2 A.C. 394.

[74] *Campbell v. Tameside Council* [1982] Q.B. 1065.

[75] See the Matrix Churchill affair—*Report of Scott Inquiry* (forthcoming 1995); *ex p. Osman* [1992] 1 W.L.R. 281.

[76] *Marks v. Beyfus* [1890] 25 Q.B.D. 494; *D. v. NSPCC* [1978] A.C. 171; *Slowcombe* [1991] Crim.L.R. 198.

[77] [1986] Q.B. 861.

[78] [1993] 1 W.L.R. 613.

[79] [1994] 2 All E.R. 478.

[80] *supra*, para. 5.3.3.1.

Police Act 1964.[81] Inquiry reports have been held to be privileged in *Neilson v. Laugharne*[82] and *Makanjuola v. Commissioner of Police*,[83] which have held that the statutory purposes of maintaining an upright police force would be frustrated were informants aware that their statements were available to be used for other purposes.[84] However this blanket approach has now been eschewed in *ex parte Wiley*.[84a]

6.4.2 *Immunities from Testifying—Legal Professional Privilege*

There is a privilege not to disclose information within the lawyer/client relationship although this privilege does not extend to any other confidential professional relationship.[85] The objective is to encourage candour between the lawyer and the client so as to enable the lawyer to represent the client effectively. It is a privilege of the client and once the privilege has been waived, the lawyer cannot refuse to disclose the information. Confidential communications passing between a client and his legal adviser need not be given in evidence by the client nor can they be given in evidence by the client's legal adviser without the client's consent as long as:

(a) the communication was made in order to enable the client to obtain and the adviser to give legal advice, or
(b) the communication was made with reference to litigation that is actually taking place or was in the contemplation of the client.[86]

This is a privilege about communications and not facts. A defendant can avoid disclosure of any instructions to the lawyer and any advice received. But the defendant cannot hand over pre-existing documents which would be open to seizure by the police if they remained in his own hands to a solicitor for safekeeping. Yet if the communications are privileged, they are also immune from search and seizure.[87] There are two exceptions to this:

---

[81] As amended by PACE; *supra*, para. 2.6.7.
[82] [1981] 1 All E.R. 829.
[83] [1992] 3 All E.R. 617.
[84] However this was distinguished in *Peach* [1986] 2 All E.R. 129 where a similar inquiry was launched after the violent death of a demonstrator—the predominant purpose was to discover the cause of death and not simply to inquire into police misconduct; see also *ex p. Coventry Newspapers* [1993] 1 All E.R. 86.
[84a] (1994) 3 All E.R. 420.
[85] At an earlier stage such communications might be protected from seizure by the police—PACE 1984, ss. 8–14. Under s. 10 of the Contempt of Court Act 1981 journalists need only disclose sources if "necessary" for interests of justice, national security or prevention of crime—see *Secretary of State for Defence v. Guardian Newspapers* [1985] A.C. 339; *Insider Dealing Inquiry under Company Securities Act* [1988] A.C. 660 and *Maxwell v. Pressdram* [1987] 1 All E.R. 656.
[86] In *Waugh v. British Rail* (1981), the widow of an employee killed in an accident sought internal reports on the accident—the House of Lords held that the dominant purpose was not litigation but to inform BR about the cause of the accident in order to prevent recurrence. Thus the reports were not privileged.
[87] PACE, ss. 8–10.

(a) communications before a crime are not privileged if their purpose was to guide the commission of a crime.[88]
(b) secondly, the privilege is overridden where the information is required by an accused person to prove his innocence—in *Ataou*,[89] the accused and a co-defendant, H, shared the same solicitor. H made a statement to the solicitor that the accused was not involved but later changed his mind, pleaded guilty and gave prosecution evidence implicating the defendant. Could the defendant cross-examine H on this inconsistent statement? At trial, the judge held that the statement was privileged. The Court of Appeal held that it was for the defendant to show on the balance of probabilities that the defendant's interest in seeking to breach the privilege outweighed that of the client in seeking to maintain it. Since H here no longer had any interest, the line of questioning should have been allowed. Accordingly the accused's conviction was quashed.

6.5 CORROBORATION OF WITNESSES

One weakness of common law is that the testimony of a single witness is sufficient for a conviction. Traditionally there have been some situations where corroboration has been required either because of the nature of the witness (where there is a motive for lying or the court distrusts the witness's intellectual faculties) or the nature of the evidence (such as identification evidence) or the gravity of the complaint.

What is corroborative evidence? Corroborative evidence must be relevant, admissible, credible. It must be independent and emanate from a source other than the original witness. The common law has never required that such evidence should confirm the whole of the original witness's account but it must verify a material part of that evidence and implicate the defendant. In *Baskerville*,[90] Lord Reading said that corroborative evidence is evidence "... which confirms in some material particulars not only the evidence that the crime has been committed but also that the prisoner committed it." Corroboration need not only come from a single source but can be cumulative.[91]

The corroboration requirements have been criticised as being highly technical and resulting in complexity and rigidity. Can it derive from the accused?[92] Are lies corroborative?[93] Can such lies be outside or inside the court? Is silence corroborative if outside the court?[94] Such subtleties in a summing up could tax the most assiduous juror. However, the scope and impact of these rules has now been greatly reduced.

[88] *ibid.* s. 10(2); *Francis & Francis* [1988] 3 All E.R. 775 gives this a wide interpretation going beyond the common law of *Cox and Railton* [1884] 14 Q.B.D. 153.
[89] [1988] Q.B. 798; also *Barton* [1972] 2 All E.R. 1192.
[90] [1916] 2 K.B. 658.
[91] *Hills* (1988) 86 Cr.App.R. 26.
[92] *Dossi* (1918) 13 Cr.App.R. 158—the accused was charged with indecent assault. While giving evidence, he admitted some "innocent" fondling and this could be treated as some corroboration of the child's testimony.
[93] *Lucas* [1981] Q.B. 720.
[94] *Cramp* (1880) 14 Cox C.C. 390 the accused was charged with inducing a miscarriage and was silent when taxed by the woman's father about certain pills.

6.5.1 Corroboration as a Matter of Law

There are a few cases, all statutory, where the jury *must* find corroboration in the form of independent evidence. This is required as a matter of law and if there is no such corroboration, they must not convict. These are:

(i) Road Traffic Regulation Act 1984, s. 89(2)—you cannot be convicted of speeding solely on the evidence of a single witness's opinion, although observation and the reading of a speedometer is sufficient.[95] The opinion of an expert witness who bases his opinion of speed on the indications at the scene of the accident does not require corroboration under section 89.[96]

(ii) Under section 1 of the Treason Act 1795 and section 168(5) of the Representation of the People Act 1983, there is a requirement of a minimum of two witnesses.

(iii) Under section 13 of the Perjury Act 1911, you cannot be convicted of perjury on the evidence of a single witness and the evidence must corroborate the falsity of the statement.

For many years, the unsworn evidence of children[97] required corroboration as a matter of law but this was dispensed with by section 34(1) Criminal Justice Act 1988.[98] Also under sections 2, 3, 4, 22 and 23 of the Sexual Offences Act 1956 (procuring women for sex in various ways), corroborative evidence was required until 1994.[99]

6.5.2 Corroboration Warnings

The greatest criticism[1] of corroboration rules centred on the warnings that had to be given to the jury in cases of accomplices and sexual complainants. The warning was to make the jury aware of the dangers of convicting on uncorroborated evidence. They could still convict if, after consideration, they felt sure of the accused's guilt. However, if the judge has failed to warn the jury of such dangers, then any conviction will almost inevitably be quashed:

(a) accomplice evidence: until 1994, if a witness admitted to being an accomplice, the judge warned the jury that, although they may convict the defendant on the basis of the accomplice's evidence, they should recognise that it is dangerous to do so unless that evidence is corroborated. If no warning is given, then the conviction will be quashed.[2] The rationale behind the rule is that accomplice evidence is highly suspect since the witness has every reason to dissociate himself even, as in *Davies*, after his acquittal. The common law rule was very restrictive and failed to encompass a range of witnesses who have self-interests which might distort their evidence; the *agent*

---

[95] *Nicholas v. Penny* [1950] 2 K.B. 466.
[96] *Crossland v. D.P.P.* [1988] 3 All E.R. 712.
[97] Children and Young Persons Act 1933, s. 38(1).
[98] Spencer and Flin, *op. cit.*, Chap. 4.
[99] This requirement was dispensed with by s. 33 Criminal Justice and Public Order Act 1994.
[1] Law Commission, *Corroboration of Evidence in Criminal Trials* (Working Paper No. 115).
[2] *Davies* [1954] 1 All E.R. 507.

provocateur, the under-age girl in a unlawful intercourse case or the prostitute where the pimp is charged with living off immoral earnings. Yet, in other ways, it may be argued that the rule was too wide—an accomplice who incriminates himself at the same time as incriminating the defendant is presumably more to be trusted. The substantive question that the court should be asking is about the witness's motives in giving evidence and whether those motives are such as to make the testimony unreliable and in need of corroborative evidence.

(b) sexual offences: until 1994, the judge was obliged to warn the jury of the dangers of convicting on the uncorroborated evidence of a sexual complainant. The rationale here is less justified than with accomplices. There were two assumptions; first, that there was a strong risk of false accusation and secondly, that, especially with child victims, the jury would be strongly prejudiced against the accused. Yet there is never any justification in assuming that rape victims are more prone to lie than victims of other crimes nor that juries convict more in such cases than in other cases.[3]

The mandatory warning has now been abolished in both these cases.[4] The only other mandatory warnings were the old common law rules relating to children's evidence which again rested on unfounded assumptions about a child's suggestibility, the powers of observation and memory, the predilections towards fantasy, the egocentricity and children's evil nature.[5] The need for corroboration was removed in 1988 in the cases of both unsworn testimony[6] and sworn testimony.[7]

6.5.3 Corroboration Warnings as a Matter of Practice

These reforms do not affect the judge's discretion to warn the jury about the dangers of convicting on uncorroborated evidence of suspect witnesses. If the judge chooses not to do so, the conviction may be quashed but not inevitably. An example where such a warning is desirable would be where an accomplice gave evidence in own defence which implicated a co-accused.[8] In *Kilbourne*,[9] Lord Hailsham said that a judge would be wise to warn about any principal witness where that witness has some purpose of his or her own to serve. Witnesses' motives can vary considerably and discretionary warnings should not be a question of closed categories. However, in *Spencer*,[10] the defendants were charged under section 126 of the Mental Health Act 1959 with assaulting the witness-patients who were detained in Rampton, suffering from mental disorders and having committed some

[3] Temkin J., *Rape and the Legal Process* (1987), p. 133.
[4] Criminal Justice and Public Order Act 1994, s. 32 (though this has still to be implemented).
[5] The criticisms of the old law are forcefully put in Spencer and Flin, *op. cit.*, Chap. 8.
[6] Criminal Justice Act 1988, s. 34(1).
[7] *ibid.* s. 34(2), but only in trials on indictment—magistrates still need to warn themselves of the dangers of convicting on the uncorroborated but sworn evidence of a child.
[8] *Knowlden* (1983) 77 Cr.App.R. 94.
[9] [1973] A.C. 729.
[10] [1986] 2 All E.R. 928.

crime. The House of Lords held that where there was a situation which was analogous to the two established categories for corroboration warnings (accomplices and sexual offences), then the judge should give a full warning of the dangers of convicting on uncorroborated evidence.

6.5.4 *Warnings and Identification Evidence*

When a prosecution is founded wholly or mainly on the identification testimony of a single witness, then the jury should be warned, as a matter of law, of the dangers of convicting but the warning is not couched in terms of corroborative evidence.[11]

6.5.5 *The Future of Corroboration*

The abrogation of rules requiring mandatory warnings were to enable judges to tailor any warning more flexibly to the particular circumstances of any case. However, it is predictable that fewer warnings will be given with the consequent risk of more unjustified convictions. The criticisms of the old corroboration rules have obscured the primary question of whether convictions should ever rest wholly or mainly on evidence from a single source. Our experience of identifications, of confessions and of the reliability of eye-witness evidence and even of expert scientific testimony leads to the answer that the trier of fact should not just be warned of the danger of convicting on uncorroborated evidence but should not convict without supporting evidence. What is needed is the development of more appropriate forms of supporting evidence. Scottish law has a general rule that guilt cannot be established by the evidence of a single witness but then accepts a broad and flexible definition as to what can amount to additional evidence.[12]

The Runciman Commission considered whether supportive evidence should be required before a confession became admissible. Were a significant number of defendants to be acquitted as the result of such a requirement, it was felt that this would have an adverse effect on the public perception of the criminal justice system. The Commission's research[13] suggested there was supportive evidence in most cases which rested on confessions. However, perhaps 5 per cent[14] of current confession cases might end in an acquittal because of the lack of supporting evidence of any kind.

The Commission's majority recommendation[15] was that there should be a judicial warning, on analogy with identification cases, so that jurors should be aware of the dangers of convicting where the prosecution is based wholly or mainly on confession evidence. However, in law, the jury would not be

---

[11] *Turnbull* [1977] Q.B. 224; *supra*, para. 3.9. For a discussion of confessions and corroboration *supra*, para. 3.8.7.

[12] *Meredith and Lees* (1992) SCCR 459; Choo A., "Confessions and Corroboration" [1991] Crim.L.R. 867 at 872.

[13] McConville M., *Corroboration and Confessions* (Royal Commission on Criminal Justice Research Study No. 13) (1993).

[14] This figure might be less since the police would devote more resources to uncovering additional evidence than they do at the moment.

[15] Royal Commission on Criminal Justice, *op. cit.*, para. 4.76.

prevented from convicting in such cases. The jury would be told to look out for "supporting evidence" which would not be equivalent to corroborative evidence in the *Baskerville* sense. Instead it would be evidence, the effect of which is to make the jury sure that the contents of the confession are true and as such is similar to the Scottish "special knowledge" provisions.[16]

Mandatory requirements for corroboration are disappearing rapidly and being replaced by discretionary warnings. The old tests on what constitutes corroboration are being discarded, and broader, more flexible notions of "supporting evidence" introduced. In this "off with the old and on with the new" world, the principles of fairness embodied in the standard of "proof beyond reasonable doubt" requires:

(a) clearer recognition that conviction on the word of a single witness or on a single item of evidence is inherently dangerous.
(b) that there must be proper criteria for "supporting evidence", broader than the old corroboration rules but which ensure that the evidence possesses substance and is not simply circumstantial.

6.6 EXAMINATION OF WITNESSES

The parties decide what witnesses to call and what evidence to present. Prosecution and defence have the opportunity to call and examine witnesses favourable to his or her case. This is known as examination-in-chief. The parties also have the opportunity to test the strength of the other side's evidence by examining their witnesses and this is known as cross-examination. At the close of the defence case, the judge does have discretion to allow the prosecution to call further evidence. Although the prosecution cannot seek to remedy defects in its own case after the close of the defence, if a line of defence has emerged that could not have reasonably been foreseen, then rebuttal is permitted.[17] In *Milliken*,[18] the defence was that the police had fabricated evidence. The judge allowed the prosecution to call evidence in rebuttal and this was upheld by the Court of Appeal.

6.6.1 *Leading Questions*

One of the myths of oral testimony is that the testimony of a physically-present witness, recollecting the relevant events is the most reliable form of evidence. Thus the first "rule" for examining-in-chief is that counsel must not ask questions which prompt the witness by suggesting the answer. These are known as "leading questions". This is not a cast-iron rule and it is possible to lead the witness on formal and introductory matters and on those where there is no dispute between the parties.

The myth rests on the fact that the witness will have given a statement to whichever party is calling him or her. Counsel will be aware of the contents of the statement and there is great temptation to ensure that all the necessary facts emerge rather than allowing the witness to recollect them freely. This archaic rule could be easily avoided and trials speeded up by allowing the

[16] *Manuel* (1958) J.C. 41; Choo, *op. cit.*, at p. 873.
[17] *Hutchinson* (1985) 82 Cr.App.R. 51.
[18] (1969) 53 Cr.App.R. 330.

witness's statement to be admitted into evidence, copies to be supplied to the jury and examination being mainly confined to the opposing party.

6.6.2 *Refreshing the Memory*

This insistence on oral testimony can reduce a trial to a test of memory and counsel are recommended to show their witnesses their statements before they go into court in order to avoid this.[19] Once in the witness box, there is still one means for witnesses to remind themselves of the events to which they will be testifying. This is known as "refreshing the memory".

This practice is commonly seen with police officers who, once sworn, produce and proceed to read from their notebooks. The problem here is that notebooks and other such documents are hearsay evidence[20] and not admissible. Police witnesses are permitted to do this, not because they are constables, but because they have written up the notebook at the time of the incident. As a result of this "contemporaneous recording", the witness can review the document in order to jog the memory. The witness then testifies and it is this oral testimony which is evidence and not the notebook.

This bizarre process is an avoidance of the consequences of the hearsay rule more than an aid to recollection. In *Maugham v. Hubbard*,[21] the issue was whether the witness had received money. The witness had no recollection whatsoever of the transaction but was shown his written acknowledgement of receipt and swore that it must be accurate and that he had received the money.

The chief condition, before a witness can "refresh the memory", is contemporaneity. The document must have been made by the witness (or at least verified by him or her) at the time of the incident or soon after. Thus the police officer who observes an incident and later writes up the observations in a notebook can refer to that notebook. The document does not have to be written by the witness. If a witness dictates a car number plate to a police constable who writes this down and repeats it back to the witness, the witness can look at the notebook to refresh his memory, even though he did not look at it at the time.[22] Nor does it matter that the note is a result of collaboration. In *Bass*,[23] the constables wrote a joint note and both could refresh their memory from it. The requirement of contemporaneity is not strict and days if not weeks can pass between the incident and its recording in a document.

The documents used for these purposes must be produced for the other party and for the jury to inspect. The opposition is allowed to cross-examine the witness on the relevant parts of the document, without making the document part of the evidence but if counsel chooses to examine on other parts of the document, then the document can be admitted into evidence. However, the document is merely evidence of the credibility of the witness. In *Virgo*,[24] the witness in a police corruption trial was Humphries, a man whose business interests involved Soho sex shops. He was permitted to use his

[19] Murphy P., *Evidence and Advocacy* (4th ed., 1994).
[20] *infra*, para. 6.7.1.
[21] (1828) 8 B. & C. 14.
[22] *Kelsey* (1982) 74 Cr.App.R. 213.
[23] [1953] 1 Q.B. 680.
[24] (1978) 67 Cr.App.R. 323.

diaries to "refresh his memory" as to dates of payments made to Virgo and was cross-examined extensively by the defence on other aspects of his diaries which were admitted into evidence. Humphries was an accomplice to the corruption whose evidence at that time required corroboration. The diaries could not be used for that purpose and could only go towards Humphries' credibility as a witness.

Even if a witness looks at a document outside the courtroom, then if the prosecution is aware of that, then they must inform the defence and allow the defence to see the document. In *Richardson*,[25] the witness made a deposition to the police a few weeks after the burglary. This statement could not have been used as a "refresher" in the trial but was shown to the witness before the trial. The defence appealed on the grounds that the witness's evidence was thus tainted and inadmissible. The Court of Appeal held that any such rule preventing witnesses from reviewing their statements would be unenforceable but that the prosecution had a duty to disclose this fact.

There are now provisions under sections 23 and 24 of the Criminal Justice Act 1988 which permit a prior statement by a witness to be admitted under certain conditions.[26]

6.6.3 *Previous Consistent Statements*

A party cannot ask his or her own witness about earlier oral or written statements made by the witness which are consistent with current testimony. In *Roberts*,[27] the defendant was charged with murder. In his evidence, he wished to testify that it had been an accident and that, two days after the killing, he told his father that it had been an accident. He was not entitled to retail his statement to his father. At first this appears to be another illustration of the impact of the rule against hearsay. Yet, as we shall see, hearsay statements are not admitted as evidence of the facts contained within them. Here the witness wished to relate the prior statement, not as evidence of the facts, but as evidence of consistency and credibility. Despite this, such statements are still excluded. The rationale for such an exclusion takes various forms:

(a) there is a danger of manufactured evidence to bolster the credibility of a witness.
(b) such statements add little weight to a witness's testimony and are superfluous.
(c) there is a danger of irrelevant side issues as to whether this prior consistent statement was actually made.

There are several exceptions to this rule:

(a) the prior consistent statement may be used to rebut an allegation of "recent fabrication". This does not permit a witness to retail previous occasions on which the same story was told just because the witness has been attacked on cross-examination, but only where counsel has

[25] [1971] 2 Q.B. 484.
[26] For discussion, see *infra*, para. 6.7.1.7.
[27] [1942] 1 All E.R. 187.

accused the witness of recently inventing the story. In *Oyesiku*,[28] it was put to the defendant's wife that she had colluded with the defendant, charged with assault on a police officer, in making up the story that the police officer was the aggressor. The conviction was quashed after the judge did not allow the defence to show that the wife had made such a statement to the solicitor before she had even visited the defendant at the police station.

(b) complaints made by the victim of a sexual assault soon after the attack are admissible in support of the victim's testimony.[29] Perhaps this exception is a relic from the rule that a woman should raise the hue and cry directly after an attack as a preliminary to an appeal of rape. It applies to all sexual offences, including indecent assault on a male.[30] The details of the complaint can be given in evidence although those details are not evidence of the facts or corroboration of the victim's testimony but merely reinforce the victim's credibility.[31] The complaint must be voluntary and not in response to a leading question. In *Osborne*,[32] it was accepted that questions such as "What's the matter?", "Why are you crying?" or "Why didn't you wait for us?" were acceptable but not "Did X assault you?". The complaint must be made at the first opportunity that reasonably presents itself.

(c) crucially, statements which are made on accusation or on discovery of incriminating articles are admissible. Normally these are statements made by an accused to a police officer. Often it is an admission of some kind and is admissible as evidence of the facts it contains (although procedurally it must conform with the provisions of PACE).[33] This exception does not just apply to incriminating statements. Everything said to the police is admissible evidence.[34] This includes not only inculpatory statements but also exculpatory or self-serving statements. In *Duncan*,[35] the defendant told the police that he had lost his temper when the victim teased him. There was thereby both an admission and some evidence of lack of intent. The admission is treated as evidence of the facts contained. Is the self-serving statement to be treated in the same way or merely as supportive of the accused's credibility? The trial judge said that this was not evidence of facts but this was disapproved of by the Court of Appeal. This approach was supported by the House of Lords in *Sharpe*[36] so that a mixed statement to the police is admissible as evidence of the facts it contains whether the statement is an admission or is self-serving.

---

[28] (1971) 56 Cr.App.R. 240.

[29] Temkin, *op. cit.*, p. 144.

[30] *Camelleri* [1922] 2 K.B. 122.

[31] *Wallwork* (1958) 42 Cr.App.R. 153—a five year old was assaulted by the father and complained to her granny. The victim could not give evidence—could the granny testify as to the complaint? The testimony cannot be used as evidence of the facts contained but only to bolster the credit given to the testimony of the victim—since there was no such testimony, the granny's evidence was wrongly admitted.

[32] [1905] 1 K.B. 551.

[33] *supra*, para. 3.8.7.

[34] *Pearce* (1979) 69 Cr.App.R. 365.

[35] (1981) 73 Cr.App.R. 359.

[36] [1988] 1 All E.R. 65.

(d) identification evidence is often treated exceptionally. When a witness identifies an accused, evidence of a previous identification is admissible. This is not simply to add weight to the witness's consistency but the evidence of the previous identification is evidence in its own right. In *Osbourne*,[37] the witness could not identify the defendant or remember that she had identified him previously at a parade. The police officer who had been in charge of the parade was permitted to testify to the fact of the identification. This was admitted despite a strong argument that such testimony was hearsay.

(e) also admissible are statements which are made as part of the *res gestae*.[38] Everything which comprises the event itself can be rehearsed in court. In *Fowkes*[39] the accused was charged with murder. The son of the dead man was sitting in the room with his father and a policeman when a face appeared at a window and the fatal shot was fired. The son testified that he thought that the face was that of the accused but also that on seeing the face at the window, he shouted "There's Butcher". The policeman also testified as to what was said.

6.6.4 *The Hostile Witness*

A prosecution or defence witness may not give the expected testimony; it may be actively hostile or just less favourable than was hoped for. The general rule is that counsel cannot question their own witness's character or credibility, or produce prior statements which are inconsistent with the witness's testimony. However, it is possible to impeach your own witness:

(a) at common law, the judge has discretion if the attitude and demeanour of the witness is hostile, to allow leading questions and to permit prior inconsistent statements to be put to the witness.

(b) by statute under section 3 of the Criminal Procedure Act 1865, if (in the opinion of the judge) the witness's "present testimony" should prove adverse, then counsel can contradict by proving prior inconsistent statements, providing that those have been put to the witness.

The statute does not nullify the common law which gives latitude to the judge over the issue of mode of examination. In *Thompson*,[40] the defendant was accused of incest with his daughter. She refused to answer questions. The judge gave permission for her to be treated as a hostile witness and for previous statements to be put to her. Eventually she agreed that these statements were true. It was argued on appeal that, since she had stayed silent, then there was no "present testimony" and section 3 could not apply. The Court of Appeal held, regardless of section 3, that the common law gave the judge discretion as to what questions could be put to the witness.[41]

What happens if, although confronted with the earlier statements, the

[37] [1973] Q.B. 678; *Christie* [1914] A.C. 545; *McCay* [1991] 1 All E.R. 232.
[38] *infra*, para. 6.7.1.6.
[39] *The Times*, March 8, 1856.
[40] (1976) 64 Cr.App.R. 96.
[41] Had the witness denied making these earlier statements, they certainly could be proved under s. 3. But it is a moot question whether they could have been proved at common law.

witness still adheres to the initial testimony? In *White*,[42] a witness gave a statement to the police implicating the accused but gave different testimony in court. Confronted with the prior statement, the witness insisted the sworn evidence was the correct version. The judge told the jury that they had to decide which story to believe. The conviction was quashed since the prior statement could only be introduced as casting doubt on the witness's credibility. It was not evidence of the accused's guilt.

6.6.5 Cross-Examination

Cross-examination is the questioning of any witness by the opposing party. The underlying purpose is to detract from the value of the testimony given by the witness by seeking to suggest contradictions, to undermine confidence and to cast doubt upon the witness's credibility and veracity. A failure to cross-examine any witness on any part of the testimony can be taken as an acceptance of that evidence.[43]

Witnesses can be cross-examined on any relevant matter which either goes to the issue in front of the court or to the credibility of the witness. Prior statements which are inconsistent with the testimony in chief can be put to the witness.[44] Questions are not restricted to matters raised by direct examination although a witness cannot be asked about inadmissible matters. In *Treacey*,[45] the accused's confession was ruled inadmissible but when the accused testified, prosecution counsel sought to cross-examine him on that confession. The Court of Appeal held that the defendant could not be questioned on it as a prior inconsistent statement. This rule does not apply to co-defendants and in *Rowson*[46] an accused was permitted to cross-examine a co-accused on the latter's inadmissible confession in order to contradict his sworn evidence. The judge must warn the jury that the confession is not evidence of the co-accused's guilt. The relevance is to test the credibility of the co-accused who is giving evidence.

6.6.5.1 FINALITY OF ANSWERS TO COLLATERAL ISSUES

Witnesses can be cross-examined on their credibility. This includes not just prior inconsistent statements but also prejudices, evidence of a criminal record and physical and mental disabilities. There is a distinction between cross-examining on the facts relevant to issues which need to be decided in the case, and cross-examining on facts that merely go to the witness's credit.

This distinction becomes important when counsel wants to introduce evidence in rebuttal of a witness's testimony. If that testimony concerns the issues which the court has to decide, then this is possible. However, if it concerns a collateral issue, such as the credit of a witness, then counsel is bound by the answer given by the witness and cannot call independent evidence in rebuttal.

[42] (1922) 17 Cr.App.R. 59; see also *Golder* (1960) 1 W.L.R. 1169.
[43] *Bircham* [1972] Crim.L.R. 430.
[44] Criminal Procedure Act 1865, ss. 4–5.
[45] [1944] 2 All E.R. 229.
[46] [1986] Q.B. 174; *Lui Mei Lin v. R.* (1989) A.C. 288.

In *Hitchcock*,[47] the defendant was charged with unlawful use of a cistern. A witness testified that the cistern had been used. In cross-examination, the witness was asked (and denied) whether he had been paid to testify. Was the witness bribed? Although this seems a central question, the defence was not permitted to contradict his denial by other independent evidence. Zuckerman argues[48] that this distinction between issue and credit is unfounded. If the witness testifies to seeing a car number plate at 30 metres and then denies that he has poor eyesight, *Hitchcock* makes it impossible to call the witness's optician in rebuttal. Yet the weight of the witness's testimony and its probative force depends completely on the quality of his eyesight as was the case in *Hitchcock* where the value of the witness's testimony relied upon whether he had been bribed to give evidence or not.

Particular problems arise within rape cases.[49] The common law rule was that the victim might be asked about sexual relationships with other men but that once an answer has been given, then counsel have to accept it.[50] The problem arises because the issue in rape cases is frequently not just the consent of the victim but the accused's belief in that consent.[51] As soon as the legal issue is defined in that way, the accused's beliefs about the victim's prior sexual history does have bearing. In *Bashir*,[52] the defence was that the victim was a prostitute. If the defendant knew this, there was a greater possibility that he believed that the victim was consenting.

Such questioning is at the very least a humiliating experience for the victim and is now regulated by section 2 of the Sexual Offences Act 1976. This permits such cross-examination only with the leave of the judge and he should allow this where it would otherwise be "unfair" on the defendant. In *Viola*,[53] the judge refused leave to cross-examine about incidents shortly before and after the alleged rape. The Court of Appeal held that the judge should consider whether the cross-examination was relevant to the defendant's case and, if it was, then whether it was probable that it would lead the jury to take a different view of the victim's evidence. However, the impact of *Morgan* means that relevance is only too easy to establish.[54]

The experience of the rape victim in the witness box is extreme but reflects the bullying and intimidation that many witnesses face when testifying. Although the court has the power to restrain such tactics,[55] it often fails to intervene.[56] Yet there is a public interest in encouraging people to report offences and to testify. Victims and witnesses have a right to the protection of their own personal dignity and privacy. This has been recognised to some

---

[47] (1847) 1 Exch. 91.
[48] Zuckerman, *op. cit.*, p. 94.
[49] Temkin J., *op. cit.*, p. 119; Temkin J., "Sexual History Evidence—the Ravishment of Section 2" [1993] Crim.L.R. 3.
[50] *Holmes* [1871] L.R. 1 C.C.R. 334.
[51] *Morgan* [1976] A.C. 182.
[52] [1969] 1 W.L.R. 1303.
[53] [1982] 3 All E.R. 73.
[54] Temkin J. (1993) *op. cit.*
[55] *Sweet-Escott* (1971) 55 Cr.App.R. 316.
[56] Royal Commission on Criminal Justice, *op. cit.*, para. 8.12.

extent with child witnesses following the introduction of TV links[57] so that
the witness does not have to confront the assailant. For children as well there
can be video-recordings of interviews[58] played in lieu of direct examination.[59]
Yet the adversarial quality of trial gives overwhelming priority to the right of
the accused to make a full defence that these other, equally compelling, public
interests are overlooked.[60]

6.6.5.2 EXCEPTIONS TO THE FINALITY RULE

Evidence in rebuttal can be brought even on matters of credit when:

(a) a witness denies making a prior inconsistent statement. These can be
proved under sections 4 and 5 of the Criminal Procedure Act 1865.

(b) a witness denies previous convictions. These can be proved under
section 6 of the Criminal Procedure Act 1865 (although it must always
be remembered that defendants who attack a prosecution witness in
this way, put their own character at risk under section 1(f)(ii) of the
Criminal Evidence Act 1898, should they choose to testify).

(c) a defendant denies bias. In *Mendy*[61] the wife was charged with assault
and the husband was due to give evidence on her behalf. He got a man
to take notes of other testimony before he himself went into the box.
He denied this but the prosecution were permitted to rebut this. In
Busby[62] a constable denied threatening a witness. When the witness
was called, the defence were not allowed to ask whether he had been
threatened by the police officer as the judge said this only went to the
officer's credit. The Court of Appeal quashed the conviction since it
indicated that the policeman was prepared to cheat to secure a
conviction.

(d) a witness is suffering from a mental or physical disability. In *Toohey*,[63]
the accusation was assault with intent to rob. The defendants argued
that the victim had been drinking and that they were trying to get him
home when he became hysterical, alleging the accused were attacking
him. A doctor examined the victim soon afterwards but although
allowed to testify whether he was drunk or hysterical, was not allowed
to give evidence as to whether drink would exacerbate hysteria or
whether the victim was more prone than normal to hysteria. The
House of Lords held that this had been wrongly excluded.[64]

(e) a witness has a reputation for untruthfulness.[65]

---

[57] Criminal Justice Act 1988, s. 32.
[58] Criminal Justice Act 1991, s. 54.
[59] Following the recommendations of the Pigot Committee: *Report of the Advisory Group on Video-Recorded Evidence* (1989).
[60] *e.g.* the short and discursive treatment of such issues by the Royal Commission on Criminal Justice, *op. cit.*, para. 8.36.
[61] (1976) 64 Cr.App.R. 4.
[62] (1982) 75 Cr.App.R. 79.
[63] [1965] A.C. 595.
[64] But this might be compared with *MacKenny* (1981) 72 Cr.App.R. 78 where the defence were prevented from leading evidence from medical experts who had watched the chief prosecution witness and had formed the opinion that he was a psychopath who was very likely to be lying.
[65] *Richardson* [1969] 1 Q.B. 299.

6.7 EXCLUSIONARY RULES

Even when there is a competent, compellable witness in the witness box, there may be some questions which are prohibited because of an "exclusionary rule". The most significant of these rules is that against hearsay but there is also a ban on witnesses expressing their opinions and on the prosecution advancing evidence about the accused's bad character, especially any previous convictions or crimes that might have been committed in the past.

6.7.1 *Hearsay*

Witnesses are expected to testify as to the evidence of their own perceptions (sight, hearing, taste, smell, touch). A witness cannot testify about another's perceptions. This means that witnesses cannot testify to out-of-court statements if the purpose of the testimony is to rely on the truth of the contents of that statement. "My husband told me he saw the defendant at the scene" is not admissible evidence. If the prosecution wishes to prove the fact that the defendant was at the scene, they have to call the husband to testify that he saw the accused there.

This applies not just to repeating other people's statements. Witnesses cannot testify as to what they themselves said. "I told my wife that I saw the defendants at the scene" is not admissible as evidence that the defendant was there. The fact that the witness told his wife does not prove anything about the defendant's whereabouts. If the witness has already testified that he saw the accused at the place, then it does show the witness's consistency but as we saw above,[66] it is a prior consistent statement and thus not admissible for this purpose either. All out-of-court statements are excluded: whether they were sworn or unsworn; whether the person making the statement is a witness or not; whether the statement is oral or in writing or by conduct. Furthermore, it is hearsay when the statement does not expressly state another's perceptions but does so by implication.[67]

The rule against hearsay is broad,[68] its boundaries are indefinite[69] and there are a range of common law and statutory exceptions. However, it is a rule and the judge has no discretion to admit a hearsay statement simply on the grounds that, as evidence, it is relevant, reliable and probative. The classic statement of the rule was formulated by Cross; "a statement other than one made by a person while giving oral evidence in the proceedings is inadmissible as evidence of any fact stated therein."[70] The critical aspect of the rule is that the statement is only inadmissible as evidence of any fact or opinion contained in it. If the statement is introduced for a separate and different purpose, then it may be admissible. For example, where a witness's truthfulness has been doubted, a prior consistent statement may be introduced, not as evidence of the facts but as evidence that the witness is

---

[66] *supra*, para. 6.6.3.
[67] *infra*, para. 6.7.1.4.
[68] *Kearley* [1992] 2 All E.R. 345. The rule's significance is now largely limited to criminal trials as a result of the Civil Evidence Act 1968.
[69] *Woodhouse v. Hall* (1981) 72 Cr.App.R. 39.
[70] Tapper, *op. cit.*, p. 509.

consistent and therefore more credible.[71] Another example of this can be seen where the witness testifies that the defendant had stated that there were pink elephants in the road. Although the witness is repeating another's words, such a statement is not hearsay because it is introduced, not as evidence that the elephants existed but that the defendant was drunk or mad.[72]

6.7.1.1 JUSTIFICATIONS

The hearsay rule reduces the length of trials by preventing the admission of evidence of limited probative value and by stopping courts going down the blind alleys of collateral issues as to "who said what to whom". Defendants should not be confronted with evidence that, because of the repetition involved, is inherently less likely to be relevant and reliable. Yet even where the evidence can be shown to be reliable and even when that evidence is necessary for the defence,[73] it is still excluded. It is a rule that can produce results that are wholly contrary to common sense. In *Sparks*,[74] a young child was indecently assaulted. She told her mother that the assailant was coloured. The defendant was white but the child was too young to testify and the mother was not permitted to say what the child had said.

The conviction in *Sparks* was overturned on other grounds but what can justify a rule of evidence that produces such palpable injustice? A traditional plank for the rule's proponents is the unreliability of hearsay. The probative value of a hearsay statement is evidentially inferior as it is not the "best evidence".[75] There are potentially four flaws[76]:

(a) the person making the statement might have perceived the event wrongly.
(b) the memory of the person making the statement might have been faulty when they made the statement.
(c) the person making the statement might have been lying or deliberately distorting the facts.
(d) the witness reporting the statement might have misunderstood the meaning of the statement.

The first three flaws are also present when the person making the statement is in fact in court. It is the absence from court and the inability of the opposing party to cross-examine that constitutes a major problem. However, if there is no reason to doubt the statement's reliability, that absence should not be a reason to exclude. The rule is wider than its rationale requires and should be framed, not as a rule, but in terms of discretion.

A more defensible rationale is that hearsay is unsatisfactory, not simply because the jury is prevented from properly assessing the probative weight of the evidence, but because it is an abuse of due process. One of the hallmarks

---

[71] *Oyesiku* (1971) 56 Cr.App.R. 240.
[72] *Ratten* [1972] A.C. 378.
[73] *Harry* (1988) 86 Cr.App.R. 105.
[74] [1964] 1 All E.R. 727.
[75] Often the best evidence is excluded because of the hearsay rule—if a witness to a traffic accident repeats a car number to a constable, then that constable cannot prove that number if the witness did not inspect it at the time—*Jones v. Metcalfe* [1967] 3 All E.R. 205.
[76] Zuckerman, *op. cit.*, p. 180.

of totalitarian societies is the anonymous accusation based on rumour. While medieval England might be content to hang a man who is a "notorious thief", modern legal values require specificity both as to the act of theft and as to those who witnessed it. The latter must be identified and be confronted publicly with their accusation. It is this notion of fairness which lies behind the hearsay rule.

This fairness argument requires that the prosecution be restrained by the hearsay rule—concern arises as a result of the rigid application of the rule to defendants. This includes admissions by third parties to a crime as in *Blastland*[77] where the defendant was accused of sexual assault and murder. Part of his defence was that although he had sex with the victim, he had left him unharmed and that another person had later killed him. That person had made a statement containing information indicating that the declarant knew of the killing before the body was found. Yet if that third party does not testify, the statement by itself is not admissible. The "due process" argument carries less weight because there is less need for the prosecution to "confront" witnesses.

6.7.1.2 OUT-OF-COURT STATEMENTS

The oral statement is the most common example of hearsay. However, the rule also covers written statements. The classic case here is *Myers*[78] where the defendant bought wrecked cars for their registration certificates. He would then steal a similar car and alter it to fit the details in the document. The prosecution sought to show that the cars and registration documents did not match up by reference to the engine numbers. They introduced microfilm evidence, showing that this engine number did not belong in a car of this registration date or other details. Yet the microfilm was prepared from cards which were themselves prepared by workers on the assembly line. The House of Lords held that the microfilm was inadmissible despite their unchallenged reliability since it contained the out-of-court assertions by unidentified workers. The House of Lords recognised the absurdity of *their* position but felt strongly that it was for the legislature to reform the law and create new exceptions.[79]

Statements do not need language but information can be conveyed by conduct and by actions. In *Chandrasekera*,[80] the victim had her throat cut. At the trial, evidence was admitted that she had indicated by signs that it was the defendant who had committed the act. This was inadmissible.

6.7.1.3 ORIGINAL EVIDENCE

The most important distinction is between the hearsay statement, tendered as evidence of the truth of what that statement contains, and non-hearsay

---

[77] [1985] 2 All E.R. 1095: see also *Turner* (1975) 61 Cr.App.R. 67.
[78] [1964] 2 All E.R. 881.
[79] As we shall see, Parliament did this with the Criminal Evidence Act 1965 which created an exception for trade and business records. This was later extended by s. 68 PACE and by the Criminal Justice Act 1988, ss. 23–24. Subject to that legislation, *Myers* remains good law.
[80] [1937] A.C. 220.

statements (often called direct or original evidence), tendered for purposes other than proving the truth of what it contains. We might consider two categories:

(a) statements tendered as proof of a fact in issue: facts in issue might be such matters as the false representation in deception cases, the words of agreement in conspiracy or statements indicating intent. The important point is whether the statements were made and not their truth or falsity of their contents. In *Chapman*,[81] the defendant was charged under the Road Safety Act 1967 with drunk driving. Section 2(2) provided that a hospital patient should not provide a breath specimen if the doctor objected. The constable gave evidence that the doctor had said "I do not object". This was not a hearsay statement since the issue was whether any objection to a breath test had been made. The constable testified that there had been no objection and whether that statement was true or false was immaterial. In *Subramaniam*,[82] the defendant was accused of being in unlawful possession of ammunition. The defence was duress and the defendant sought to testify that he had been threatened by terrorists—the trial judge excluded the evidence but the conviction was quashed on appeal. The issue before the court was whether the defendant believed that he would be killed if he refused to carry out the terrorists' orders. To establish the defence of duress there must be evidence that threatening words were spoken. The statement by the terrorists, true or not, was relevant to that issue.

In neither *Chapman* or *Subramaniam* is the court interested in perceptions of the doctor or of the terrorists. Whether an objection or a threat was made is within the perceptions of the witness in the court. Thus, the statements are original evidence. A more complex case is *Woodhouse v. Hall*[83] where the defendant was charged with managing a brothel. Plainclothes officers went to the building for a massage and alleged that they had been offered masturbation. Could the officers testify that the offers had been made? The justices excluded the evidence as hearsay but the Divisional Court held these statements were operative words. Why?—the prosecution had to prove that the premises were in fact a brothel and the officers clearly could not have testified that the attendants had told them "This is a brothel". Yet a brothel is a place where offers of sexual services are made and accepted. Just as with any other contract, words of offer and acceptance are facts in issue which may be proved and are original evidence and not hearsay.

(b) statements tendered as proof of facts relevant to a fact in issue: if a statement is tendered for the purpose of the truth of the facts that it contains, it is inadmissible. However, if it is for another purpose, it is admissible. In *Ratten*,[84] the defendant was accused of shooting his wife. His defence was that he was cleaning his gun and it went off

[81] [1969] 2 Q.B. 436.
[82] [1956] 1 W.L.R. 965.
[83] *Woodhouse v. Hall* (1981) 72 Cr.App.R. 39.
[84] [1972] A.C. 378.

accidentally. The fact in issue needing to be proved is the non-accidental nature of the shooting and the state of mind of the wife immediately prior to the shooting is relevant to this. The prosecution sought to introduce evidence that immediately before the shooting, the wife had made a telephone call and that the telephonist at the local exchange had taken a call from that number and from a woman whose voice had sounded hysterical and that the caller had said, "Get me the police, please." The evidence was admitted—the telephonist could testify that a call had been made from that number and that the wife was apparently very upset. It is not the truth of the statement that is relevant but its demonstration of the wife's state of mind.

6.7.1.4 IMPLIED ASSERTIONS

This fine line between hearsay and original evidence is further complicated when there are assertions of fact that are not expressly or intentionally made by the declarant. In *Wright v. Tatham*,[85] one party sought to show that the testator was sane when he made his will. The evidence was letters written to the testator by certain people and the inference that could be drawn from reading the letters was that the letter writers regarded the testator as in full possession of his mental faculties. The letters were excluded as hearsay. Thus the old common law embodied a strict rule of exclusion. Parke B. gave the example of the ship's captain who is seen to examine a ship thoroughly before embarking on it with his family and setting off on a voyage. The ship disappears, presumably sunk. Was the captain's conduct a statement that in his opinion the ship was seaworthy? Obviously this was the case and it was the more reliable because it was unintentional and unlikely to be manufactured. Yet Parke B. still treated it as hearsay, perhaps because the captain could never be cross-examined on the basis of his opinion.

Cases such as *Ratten* and *Woodhouse v. Hall* suggested that a more relaxed attitude was emerging since in both cases, witnesses were permitted to testify as to what another person had said, relying not on the direct meaning of the words ("Get me the police" or "Would you like hand relief") but on the very clear implications ("I am in fear of my husband" or "This is a brothel"). There was also strong academic support: Cross[86] argued that the rationale for hearsay only covered the intentional direct assertion of fact and that there was neither doctrinal nor policy reasons to include the implied assertion. There was support also from other jurisdictions, especially the United States where the Federal Rules of Evidence excluded implied assertions from the scope of the hearsay rule.

However, the rigidity of the old common law was reasserted by the House of Lords' decision in *Kearley*[87]—the police raided a flat on a drugs warrant. While there they answered the phone and encountered visitors all requesting drugs. Since the actual amount of drugs and money discovered in the flat were not enough to raise an irresistible presumption that the accused was in possession "with intent to supply", the prosecution sought to rely on the

[85] (1838) 7 E.R. 559.
[86] Tapper, *op. cit.*, p. 516.
[87] *Kearley* [1992] 2 All E.R. 345—see also *Harry* (1988) 86 Cr.App.R. 105.

testimony of police officers who had heard these requests. The appeal raised two issues. The first of these was whether a telephone caller's belief that the accused was a drug supplier was at all relevant to proving an intent to supply and secondly, if it was relevant, was it excluded by the hearsay rule? The majority regarded the evidence as irrelevant and excluded. However, it is difficult to follow this reasoning; if I testify to my belief, based on my own experience of you, that you possess a particular characteristic, it becomes more likely that you do. A single person's belief might have little probative weight but there is some. When many witnesses are willing to testify that you possess that characteristic, not only is such testimony relevant but it has much more weight. The minority in the House were more willing to accept this argument, pointing out that the existence of a queue would be relevant in that it indicated that there was a market for the goods or services alleged to be on offer.

However, even if the belief is accepted as relevant, it remains an out-of-court assertion by a person not called as a witness, and subject to the hearsay rule, unless that rule itself is restricted to express and intentional assertions. The majority in *Kearley* adopted the *Wright v. Tatham*[88] position. The hearsay rule excludes a police officer testifying that a phone caller had said "Hey, that Kearley's dealing drugs again". Logically it must also exclude implied assertions to the same effect.

6.7.1.5 MECHANICAL DEVICES

Statements produced by mechanical devices are normally direct evidence. The video which records an event is evidence of that incident. A computer's analysis of the composition of a compound is evidence of what that compound is.[89] In *Castle v. Cross*,[90] the defendant breathed several times into an Intoximeter, a machine for measuring the alcohol level in blood. It produced a printout which stated that the machine had not received a sufficient sample in order to carry out an analysis. It was held by the Divisional Court that this printout was evidence against the accused on a charge of failing to supply a breath specimen. Similarly, a computer-generated, itemised list of telephone calls from a particular number, or a list of products and prices produced by scanning bar codes at a supermarket checkout would be admissible. The defence is limited to checking that the computer was in proper working order and was being properly used.[91]

The information in such examples is generated by the machine. This must be distinguished from information originally coming from a person but being stored in the machine. The printout from a word-processing programme remains hearsay as do statements on audio-tape. Only if such statements are otherwise admissible (for example, a record of an admission or a police interview) is the tape-recording admissible. For example, in *Kearley*, if the phone calls had been tape-recorded, this would make no difference to their admissibility.

[88] *op. cit.*
[89] *Wood* (1983) 76 Cr.App.R. 23.
[90] [1985] 1 All E.R. 87.
[91] PACE, s. 69.

6.7.1.6 COMMON LAW EXCEPTIONS AND *RES GESTAE*

There are many common law exceptions to hearsay although the list has recently been significantly amended by statute.[92] The standard rationale for these is that the evidence in these categories is more reliable and probative than other types of hearsay statement. Since reliability has not been the core test for the exclusion of hearsay, pragmatism is a more convincing explanation for the piecemeal nature of these exceptions.

The major exception at common law was the rule relating to confessions and admissions; a statement made by a defendant, adverse to his or her own case, is admissible as evidence of the truth of what it contains.[93] Other common law exceptions involve statements in public documents and statements by deceased persons.[94]

A further exception at common law is that which glories in the name of *res gestae*. If a statement is made spontaneously as an intrinsic part of the action or event, that statement is admissible as evidence of the truth of what it contains. All acts and statements which are part of the whole event are admissible and this exception overrides all other exclusionary rules.[95] The critical question is what is "part of the action" as opposed to statements preceding, or subsequent to, the event?

The normal *res gestae* situations are the statements by participants or observers at events.[96] When a participant makes an uncalculated outburst in the heat of the moment, this is felt to be more reliable and less likely to be an invention. The critical elements are that the statement was spontaneous and contemporaneous with the events. In early cases, these elements were often seen as technical rules. *Bedingfield*[97] was a case where the defendant was charged with murder by cutting the victims's throat. There was evidence that the accused was in a room with the victim who emerged with her throat cut and said, "Oh dear, Aunt, see what Bedingfield has done to me!" The evidence of that statement was held inadmissible because it occurred after the throat cutting and the *res* had been completed. Such a strict approach to contemporaneity has long since disappeared.

In *Ratten*,[98] the phone call by a sobbing woman was made at 13:15 and the wife was dead by 13:20. If we interpret her statement "Get me the police" as containing an inference, namely "My husband is attacking me", that implied assertion is hearsay. The Privy Council held that, even if this was the correct interpretation, the statement itself was part of the *res gestae*, was made under the overwhelming pressure of the situation and was thus admissible as an exception to hearsay. Lord Wilberforce said that the approach was not purely

---

[92] Admissions and confessions in criminal law are now governed by s. 76 PACE. Criminal Justice Act 1988, ss. 23 and 24 have also made substantial inroads into the scope of the hearsay rule.
[93] This issue is discussed *supra*, para. 3.8.7.
[94] Only where these were against interest, in the course of a duty, as to pedigree or as to public rights or in the settled and hopeless expectation of death. Statements by murder victims before death are not automatically admissible.
[95] *Ellis* (1826) 6 B. & C. 145.
[96] Cross discusses statements accompanying relevant acts, statements concerning physical sensation and statements concerning the maker's state of mind—Tapper, *op. cit.*, p. 657.
[97] (1879) 14 Cox C.C. 341.
[98] [1972] A.C. 378—see *supra*, p. 211.

technical in the sense of lapse of time or change of venue—these were factors but were not decisive. The judge must be satisfied that the statement was made in circumstances of spontaneity or of involvement so that the possibility of concoction could be disregarded:

"... if the drama, leading up to the climax, has commenced and assumed such intensity and pressure that the utterance can be safely regarded as a true reflection of what was unrolling or actually happening, it ought to be received."

This approach was accepted by the House of Lords in *Andrews*[99] where the victim was attacked and stabbed in his own flat, made his way a few minutes later to the flat below and made statements to an extent identifying the defendant. Although factually similar to *Bedingfield*, the evidence was admitted. Lord Ackner said that the judge should be satisfied that the event was so unusual or startling that the victim's utterance would be an instinctive, spontaneous reaction without opportunity for reasoned reflection, and that the possibility of concoction could be disregarded.

6.7.1.7 STATUTORY EXCEPTIONS TO HEARSAY

The major statutory exceptions to the hearsay rule, apart from confessions, come under the provisions of the Criminal Justice Act 1988 admitting certain categories of documentary hearsay.

The first steps towards the current position were tentative; the effect of *Myers*[1] was to exclude all business documents. The Criminal Evidence Act 1965 went a little way towards overturning this so that records compiled within a trade or a business were admissible, so long as they were based on information supplied by people with direct knowledge and those people were unavailable or could not be expected to give evidence. However, this was restrictively interpreted; a car's registration document was not evidence of the engine number[2] nor was a Home Office record evidence of legal immigrant status.[3] These provisions were broadened through section 68[4] of PACE in 1984. Although it removed the "business or trade" limitation, section 68 still only applied to records, the limits of which can be seen in *Cunningham*[5] where the accused was charged with smuggling drugs from Swaziland. He sought to rely on statements taken from witnesses in Swaziland who were unable to attend trial. Yet such proofs were only admissible under section 68 if they formed part of a record and so the conviction was upheld. Section 68 has itself been repealed by the Criminal Justice Act 1988.

A complementary provision in PACE, section 69, applies to documents generated by computers so that these are only admissible where there is a certificate that the computer was properly used, in proper working order and the original supplier of the information is not available to give evidence. There must be evidence from a senior member of the staff that the machine

---

[99] [1987] 1 All E.R. 513.
[1] [1965] A.C. 1001.
[2] *Sealby* [1965] 1 All E.R. 701.
[3] *Patel* [1981] 3 All E.R. 94.
[4] This followed recommendations in the 11th Report of the Criminal Law Revision Committee (Cmnd. 499) (1972).
[5] (1989) 4 Crim.L.R. 435; *Iqbal* [1990] 3 All E.R. 787.

had been working properly at the time.[6] This section applies to both direct and hearsay evidence contained in computer records.[7] In relation to hearsay documents, section 69 is not a self-enclosed code of admissibility but provides additional conditions for documents which already are admissible under some exception to hearsay. Nowadays this is under Sections 23 and 24 of the Criminal Justice Act 1988.

6.7.1.7.1 CRIMINAL JUSTICE ACT 1988, SECTION 23

For the first time, this provides a general exception to the hearsay rule in criminal proceedings for first-hand documentary hearsay:

> "... a statement made by a person in a document shall be admissible in criminal proceedings as evidence of any fact of which direct oral evidence by him would be admissible ...."

There are conditions under which such statements are admissible—these are alternatives: either that the maker of the statement is unavailable in one of the ways specified in section 23(2) or that the statement was made in the course of investigating criminal offences and the witness is in fear or being kept out of the way.

A statement is any representation of fact whether made in words or otherwise. The statement must be made by a person. This does not mean that the maker writes it down but that it must be checked or accepted by the person.[8] It must be a statement of fact and not an expression of opinion. This exception is also limited to "direct" hearsay; that is, where a witness has directly perceived some fact and recorded this in writing.[9]

The statement must be made in a document. There is no restriction here (unlike previous legislation) about documents created in the course of a trade or business and thus can encompass not just trade records, business letters but all forms of maps, plans, discs, tapes, films, diaries, indeed shopping lists.

This provision only cures the vice of hearsay. The statement is admissible as evidence of any fact of which direct oral evidence would be admissible. Thus the incompetent witness statement does not become admissible because it is written down and signed[10]—nor would evidence about the accused's character or evidence in breach of the public policy provisions. Equally under section 28(1)(a), section 23 does not prejudice the admissibility of hearsay statements that might be admissible under the common law or other statutory

---

[6] *Cochrane* [1993] Crim.L.R. 48.

[7] In *Spiby* (1990) 91 Cr.App.R. 186, the court suggested that since the itemised telephone bill was original evidence, s. 69 did not apply. This was corrected in *Shepherd* [1993] 1 All E.R. 225.

[8] This would seem to exclude the client's statement to the solicitor in *Re D* (1986) 2 F.L.R. 189 where the lawyer made notes and did not show them to the client. As a result the statement was inadmissible under s. 2 of the Civil Evidence Act and this would also be the case under s. 23, Criminal Justice Act 1988.

[9] Professor Birch has suggested that the section allows any statement to be admitted if the person creating or verifying the document could have testified as to the contents of that statement—this would go beyond "direct hearsay" since this might include the witness recording a statement made by third parties which would have been admissible under another exception to hearsay (*res gestae*, for example)—see [1989] Crim.L.R. 603.

[10] *H v. H* [1989] 3 W.L.R. 933—a five year old would not be competent to testify and her statements to a social worker, written down, do not become admissible as a result of s. 23.

exceptions. In other words, if a confession is admissible under section 76 of PACE, or expert testimony under section 30 of Criminal Justice Act 1988, it does not have to satisfy section 23 conditions as well.

Those conditions are to be found in section 23(2). The document is only admissible where the maker of the statement is unavailable—there are three situations:

(a) where the maker is dead or mentally or physically unfit, or[11]
(b) where the maker is outside the U.K. and it is not reasonably practicable to secure his attendance, or[12]
(c) reasonable steps have been taken but the maker of the statement cannot be found.

However, even where the maker of the statement is available, section 23(3) creates a more controversial situation where a document can be used. This is where the statement is made to a person charged with investigating offences and where the maker of the statement is in fear or because he or she is being kept out of the way. This has to be compared with section 13(3) of the Criminal Justice Act 1925 which provided that a deposition might be admissible where the witness was being "kept out of the way by means of the procurement of the accused". This was restrictively interpreted in *O'Loughlin*[13] where two witnesses failed to turn up out of fear and the prosecution argued unsuccessfully that their depositions should be admitted. Yet section 23 is more widely drawn and has attracted both criticism[14] and a desire to see the term "fear" interpreted widely, especially in the context of domestic violence where the section might be used to protect victims from direct court confrontation with their attackers.[15] Although the primary witness is not available for cross-examination, this can be seen as the defendant's own fault.

6.7.1.7.2 CRIMINAL JUSTICE ACT 1988, SECTION 24

Section 24 is the successor to section 68 and applies where the hearsay is indirect hearsay. However, section 24 extends the scope of this exception. It provides:

s. 24(1) (i) the document was created or received by a person in the course of a trade, business, profession or other occupation, or as a holder of a paid or unpaid office and,
(ii) the information ... was supplied by a person (whether or not the maker of the statement) who had, or may reasonably be supposed to have had, personal knowledge of the matters dealt with.

[11] *Cole* [1990] 2 All E.R. 108.
[12] *Iqbal* [1990] 3 All E.R. 787; *Bray* [1988] Crim.L.R. 829—the prosecution cannot make such a claim where they only realise at the date of trial that the witness is abroad when he has been away seven months.
[13] (1987) 85 Cr.App.R. 157.
[14] Wolchover D., "Keeping Witnesses Out of the Way" (1988) New L.J. 461.
[15] Edwards S., "What shall we do with a frightened witness?" (1989) New L.J. 1740; McEwan J., "Documentary Hearsay Evidence—Refuge for the Vulnerable Witness" [1989] Crim.L.R. 629 at 637; *Renshaw* [1989] Crim.L.R. 811.

s. 24(2) (iii) Subsection (1) above applies whether the information ... was supplied directly or indirectly but if it was supplied indirectly, only if each person through whom it was supplied received it;
  (a) in the course of a trade, business, etc., or
  (b) as the holder of a paid or unpaid office.

Under section 24(4) there is no requirement that the maker of the statement be unable to testify unless the statement was made for the specific purpose of a criminal investigation or criminal proceedings. If this is the case, the conditions in section 23(2) or section 23(3) apply. However there is an additional possibility—that the person who made the statement cannot reasonably be expected to have any recollection of the matters dealt with in the statement. In *Farrand v. Galland*,[16] the charge was supplying a car with a false odometer reading. The evidence consisted of record cards of a previous owner, a car hire firm. The person who compiled the record was available but not called and the justices threw out the case. However, the provisions have to be read disjunctively so that as long as one condition applies, then that is sufficient. Here it would be unreasonable to expect the person who filled out the card to have any recollection of the mileage.

6.7.1.7.3 OTHER PROVISIONS

Under section 25(1), the court has the power to exclude evidence which would be admissible under sections 23 and 24 if, in the interests of justice, it ought not to be admitted. Under section 25(2), while not detracting from the generality of section 25(1), directs the court to look at the nature and source of the document, to the extent to which other evidence on the issue is available, to the relevance of the evidence or to the risk of unfairness.[17] Under paragraph 3 of Schedule 2, the court must have regard to all the circumstances in estimating weight.

Under section 26, a party seeking to introduce a document admissible under sections 23 or 24 requires the leave of the court[18] and under paragraph 1 of Schedule 2, you can attack the credibility of the maker of the statement admitted under sections 23 or 24.

6.7.1.7.4 CRIMINAL JUSTICE ACT 1991, SECTION 54

The recognition of the distress caused to child victims by testifying in cases involving physical or sexual abuse has led to one inroad into the hearsay rule and into the primacy of the adversarial trial. Under section 54, a video-recording of an interview with the child can stand as the evidence-in-chief in such cases.[19] Although the child must be available for cross-examination, this can be through a live television link.[20]

---

[16] (1989) Crim.L.R. 573—although decided under PACE, it is relevant to s. 24.
[17] *Price* [1991] Crim.L.R. 707; *Cole* [1990] 2 All E.R. 108.
[18] *Cole* [1990] 2 All E.R. 108.
[19] The offences are those provided for in s. 32 of the Criminal Justice Act 1988.
[20] As provided for in s. 32 of the Criminal Justice Act 1988.

6.7.2 *Opinion Evidence*

Witnesses give evidence of what they have seen, heard, smelt, felt or touched—direct evidence of their own perceptions. A witness's opinions, beliefs or inferences are not their perceptions but conclusions drawn from those perceptions and are not admissible to prove the truth of what is believed or inferred. Opinions are seen as having little probative weight and as usurping the function of the finder of fact whose task it is to draw the necessary inferences from the evidence unless:

(i) the matter calls for special skill or knowledge which a judge or jury does not possess in which case an expert witness will be allowed to express an opinion. In *Mason*,[21] the defence to a charge of murder was that the victim had committed suicide and the issue was whether the doctor could be asked whether the injuries could have been self-inflicted. The Court of Appeal held the answer admissible. Even experts are not permitted to give their opinion on the ultimate issue or issues that are within the competence of the ordinary juror.

(ii) the perceptions and statements of "fact" are conclusions in themselves or mixtures of inference and facts. Witnesses are allowed to express their opinion on issues which do not call for specialist knowledge and where it would be impossible to separate observed fact from inference, such as the speed of a car. Even in such cases, the non-expert is not permitted to testify as to the ultimate issue that has to be decided or as to those issues which are within the competence of the trier of fact.

6.7.2.1 EXPERT EVIDENCE

The common law always has accepted expert evidence[22] in matters scientific, architectural, engineering, of ballistics, blood, foreign law,[23] literary merit, handwriting, fingerprints, DNA,[24] voice identification,[25] ESDA,[26] market value etc.

The expert witness must establish his or her credentials which may be practical experience or professional qualification. The opposing party might inquire into these. If there are some credentials, then the evidence is likely to be admitted and the rest would be a matter of weight.[27]

The facts on which an expert may form an opinion should be proved by admissible evidence. This is normally on the basis of his or her own perceptions: the pathologist who performs a post-mortem may give an

---

[21] (1911) 7 Cr.App.R. 67.

[22] In *Folkes v. Chadd* [1782] 3 Doug.K.B. 157, the opinion of an engineer was admitted on the issue of whether an embankment had caused the silting up of a harbour.

[23] *Bumper Development v. Metropolitan Police Commissioner* [1991] 4 All E.R. 638.

[24] Farington D., "Unacceptable Evidence" (1993) New L.J., p. 806 and p. 857.

[25] *Robb* (1991) 93 Cr.App.R. 161.

[26] *Wellington* [1991] Crim.L.R. 543.

[27] *Silverlock* [1894] 2 Q.B. 766, a solicitor was accepted as an expert on handwriting although his experience had been picked up as an amateur. See *Robb* (1991) 93 Cr.App.R. 161 where the evidence was still accepted though there was doubt as to the techniques of voice identification used.

opinion as to the cause of death. However, it can also be on the basis of facts supplied by others: the pathologist might be asked whether, given certain marks on the body, what might be the likely cause of death. In such cases the expert should state the assumed facts on which the opinion is based so that the trier of fact can assess the weight of the opinion. However, the expert witness may rely on facts of which he or she has no first-hand knowledge and which would be hearsay. In *Abadom*[28] the charge was robbery. The accused had some glass splinters in his shoe. Did they come from the scene of the robbery? The expert witness measured the glass's refractive index and the referred to Home Office statistics as to how common this kind of glass was. It occurred in only 4 per cent of glass samples investigated and the presence of such glass in the accused's shoe was, at the very least, a coincidence. The expert witness was relying on inadmissible hearsay contained in the Home Office statistics but was entitled to rely on such material in forming his expert opinion.[29]

The courts have always sought to prevent the expert witness from expressing an opinion on the very point that the jury has to decide, the ultimate issue in the case. The rule is often evaded so that the expert witness is allowed to express an opinion on the final issue, so long as he uses different language to that employed by the court.[30] The rationale here is that the finder of fact might be unduly influenced by an expert but in many trials, any expert evidence for one party is likely to be countered by expert evidence from the other side, not surprisingly coming to diametrically opposed conclusions favouring the party by whom they are retained. The weight given by juries to expert testimony will inevitably vary: while juries should not be directed to accept inevitably the evidence of an expert witness, neither should they be invited to disregard it in favour of unaided lay opinion.

Nor should witnesses express opinions on matters within the competence of the jury although courts draw fine distinctions. In *ABC Chewing Gum*[31] the issue was whether the "battle cards" sold with the gum might deprave and corrupt children contrary to the Obscene Publications Act 1959. Lord Parker C.J. suggested, although expert psychiatric evidence in general was admissible, that it would be wrong to ask whether the cards would "deprave and corrupt". This was not the case in *Stamford*[32] where the issue was whether an indecent or obscene article had been sent through the post. The Court of Appeal held that this was a matter for the judge and jury and that the judge was right in preventing the accused from calling evidence on current moral standards.

This causes problems especially in the area of psychiatric and psychological testimony. This can be raised not merely with specific defences such as insanity, diminished responsibility and provocation but generally with *mens rea* issues. In *Chard*,[33] the defendant was accused of murder. The defence was

---

[28] [1983] 1 All E.R. 364.
[29] See also *Bradshaw* (1985) 82 Cr.App.R. 79.
[30] In *Rich v. Pierpoint* (1862) 3 F. & F. 35, the issue was medical negligence—a doctor who had been present in court throughout the proceedings could not be asked whether the defendant was guilty of any want of skill but might be asked whether anything he heard suggested improper conduct on the defendant's part.
[31] [1968] 1 Q.B. 159.
[32] [1972] 2 Q.B. 391.
[33] (1971) 56 Cr.App.R. 268.

neither diminished responsibility nor insanity but the defendant sought to introduce the testimony of a psychiatrist as to his mental state at the time of the killing. The Court of Appeal upheld the trial judge's rejection of this since the issue of intent was a matter within the ordinary experience of the jury. A similar conclusion was reached in *Turner*[34] where the accused raised the defence of provocation and wished to call evidence of a psychiatrist as to how he would have reacted when confronted with his girlfriend's confession of infidelity. Since no issue of mental illness was involved, the court held that the jury did not need experts to inform them how ordinary people reacted to the stresses and strains of life. Lord Lawton said:

> "If on the proven facts a judge or jury can form their own conclusions without help, then the opinion of an expert is unnecessary. In such a case if it is given dressed up in scientific jargon it may make judgement more difficulty. The facts that an expert witness has impressive qualifications does not by that fact alone make his opinion on matters of human nature and behaviour within the limits of normality any more helpful than that of the jurors themselves; but there is a danger that they may think it does."

Zuckerman defends this approach:

> "A judge deciding whether expert opinion should be accepted as an arbiter of a certain matter has to consider the state of public opinion on the point. If the community has come to defer to professional standards on the matters in question, the courts will normally follow suit. Medical evidence is admissible on matters of health because we accept the authority of the medical profession in this regard. Psychiatry has not yet obtained a like acceptance. Psychiatric evidence is admissible on the issue of insanity but not ... on the mental state of a normal person. It is argued that the distinction is irrational; for to understand abnormality, psychiatry has first to master the normal mental processes. However, as long as the community does not defer to psychiatry on matters such as intention and credibility, the scope for expert evidence on such matters must remain limited. ... Only when public opinion is clear one way or another can we demand consistency from the courts.[35]

Turner was followed in *Roberts*[36] where the defendant was profoundly and pre-lingually deaf. The court refused to permit psychiatric evidence as to the likely effect of physical abuse by the father of the accused. *Chard* was followed in *Reynolds*[37] where evidence was excluded that the defendant was emotionally disturbed and living in a fantasy world. There has been one exception to *Turner* in *Lowery*[38] where the Privy Council came to a different conclusion when faced with two defendants charged with a sadistic murder. One of the accused wished to call a psychiatrist to testify that the other was more predisposed to the crime. In the circumstances of the case, the jury might be seen to need assistance in relation to the relative aggression of the two accused.

---

[34] [1975] 1 All E.R. 70.
[35] Zuckerman, *op. cit.*, p. 67.
[36] [1990] Crim.L.R. 122.
[37] [1989] Crim.L.R. 220; *Masih* [1986] Crim.L.R. 395 where on a charge of rape, the accused had an IQ of 72—expert evidence was inadmissible on issue of consent although it would have been admissible if the defendant had been a mental defective with an IQ of less than 69; *Wood* [1990] Crim.L.R. 264; *Toner* (1991) 93 Cr.App.R. 382.
[38] [1974] A.C. 85.

Thus expert evidence:

(a) is admissible if it concerns an issue outside the knowledge and experience of the jury.
(b) is inadmissible if it concerns an issue of human nature and behaviour within the bounds of normality.
(c) is inadmissible if it concerns the personality of a witness/accused.

Such restrictions on the accused's ability to mount a full defence seem unjustified. If there is professional opinion to go before a jury, there is little reason to reject it. The common sense of the jury has led to many wrongful convictions in cases involving identification evidence and confessions. Similarly, with issues of responsibility there is no clear division between the normal and abnormal.[39] People's reactions and behaviour are often counter-intuitive, especially in the areas of provocation and criminal intent. There might be a strong case for departure from the *Turner* approach.

6.7.2.2 NON-EXPERT OPINION

The non-expert can give an opinion in relation to those matters where it is almost impossible to separate out the inferences from the perceived facts on which the inferences were based—age, speed, weather, handwriting, identity might all be given as examples. The condition of objects or indeed general value might also come in. In *Davies (No. 2)*[40] there was a court martial where the charge was driving a vehicle while unfit through drink. The witness testified that the accused had been drinking and was in no condition to handle the car. While the first part of this was admissible (a non-expert can testify as to whether somebody has been drinking), the latter part was not (only an expert could testify as to whether the accused was fit to drive).

6.7.3 *The Accused's Character*

The character of the defendant, whether churchgoer or sinner, at first sight seems irrelevant and thus inadmissible as evidence as to whether he or she committed an offence. After sentence prior convictions can be relevant to the issue of sentence.[40a] Yet even during the trial, it has not been feasible to treat the biography of the accused as a blank sheet. Evidence relating to the accused's character can be admitted in several contexts:

(a) good character as evidence for the defence that the accused is not the sort of person likely to commit such an offence.
(b) bad character which needs to be proved by the prosecution as an element of the offence.
(c) prior offences which the prosecution alleges are evidence that the accused has committed the offence charged. Although the principle is

---

[39] Mackay R. D. and Colman A., "Excluding Expert Evidence; A Tale of Ordinary Folk and Common Experience" [1991] Crim.L.R. 800; Sheldon D. and MacLeod M., "From Normative to Positive Data: Expert Psychological Evidence Re-examined" [1991] Crim.L.R. 811.
[40] [1962] 1 W.L.R. 1111.
[40a] *infra*, para. 7.5.

that a person should only be tried for the crime charged, if a person has acted in a dramatically similar way previously, it can be argued that this tends to make it more likely that they have acted in the same manner this time. This is known as the "similar facts" rule. The prejudice aroused when a jury hears of previous crimes is considerable and there is a difficult juggling act for the judge who must decide whether the probative weight of the previous actions exceeds the prejudicial effect.

(d) if the accused decides to testify, the problem of previous discreditable acts arises again. A normal witness can be cross-examined as to credit. However, this would be very prejudicial for the defendant. When the defendant was made a competent witness on his or her own behalf by the Criminal Evidence Act 1898, section 1(f) provided a shield which protected the accused from such questions. There are situations when that shield can be lost such as where the accused alleges good character, gives evidence against a fellow defendant or attacks the character of prosecution witnesses.

6.7.3.1 THE ACCUSED'S GOOD CHARACTER

A defendant can adduce evidence of his own good character, either by testifying himself or through witnesses. In *Rowton*,[41] the defendant was charged with indecent assault and was permitted to introduce such evidence of good reputation. This evidence was confined to general reputation and could not extend to detailing specific creditable acts nor could a witness be asked about the accused's disposition, *i.e.* whether he would be likely to commit the acts with which he was charged.[42]

The accused is entitled to a direction on evidence of good character.[43] The purpose of such testimony appears primarily to go to the credibility of the accused who has testified, giving his or her denials more weight.[44] However, whether or not the defendant has testified, he or she is entitled to a direction that good character is an indicator of innocence.[45] One final problem is where there are co-accused, one with good character and the other with bad character. The accused with good character is entitled to a direction that good character is relevant to both credibility and to innocence. However, the judge should either not mention the other defendant's character or direct the jury not to speculate about it.

6.7.3.2 BAD CHARACTER AS AN ELEMENT OF THE OFFENCE

Bad character, in the shape of a previous conviction, can be an element of another offence. In such circumstances, this can be proved (driving while disqualified; section 21 of the Firearms Act 1968 ... person sentenced to three

---

[41] (1865) Le. & Ca. 520.
[42] See also *Redgrave* (1982) 74 Cr.App.R. 10.
[43] *Berrada* (1989) 91 Cr.App.R. 131.
[44] In medieval England the accused could escape liability by such means through compurgation—producing sufficient neighbours to swear to your honesty and credibility.
[45] *Vye* [1993] Crim.L.R. 602.

years or more shall not possess . . .). In pleas of autrefois convict, a defence by which the accused alleges that he or she has already been tried and convicted of this very offence, it may be the defendant who pleads the prior conviction.

6.7.3.3 BAD CHARACTER AND SIMILAR FACT EVIDENCE

At common law there is a general rule that the prosecution is not allowed to adduce evidence-in-chief of the defendant's bad character or to cross-examine defence witnesses with a view to eliciting such evidence. If it is inadvertently referred to, then the jury may be discharged and a new trial ordered. In terms of cross-examining the accused, the major exception is under the Criminal Evidence Act 1898 but there are also two common law exceptions:

(a) where the defendant puts his own character into issue, then the prosecution can cross-examine and put evidence in rebuttal.
(b) where the prosecution is allowed to advance evidence of previous acts which are so similar to the offences charged that they are seen as having probative force. This is the similar fact rule.

6.7.3.3.1 REBUTTAL OF "GOOD CHARACTER"

In *Rowton*, after the accused had put his own character into issue, the prosecution were able to call witnesses as to his reputation (who testified that he was a man capable of the grossest indecency and the most flagrant immorality!). Such evidence is restricted to reputation and not to specific discreditable acts. This only applies where the accused puts his or her character into issue by advancing evidence of that good character. In *Butterwasser*,[46] the accused cross-examined the prosecution witnesses on their bad character. The prosecution sought to counter this by calling a police officer to testify as to the accused's prior convictions. Although these convictions could have been put to him if he had testified,[47] he did not do so and there is no common law rule which permits the prosecution to counter defence imputations against prosecution witnesses by advancing evidence of the defendant's bad character.

Once the accused's character is in issue, everything is in. In *Winfield*,[48] the charge was indecent assault and the accused led evidence of his sexual propriety. However, the prosecution were permitted to counter this by advancing evidence of convictions for dishonesty.

6.7.3.3.2 SIMILAR FACT EVIDENCE

As a general rule the prosecution are prohibited (at common law) from introducing evidence of the defendant's bad character or reputation and (by statute) from cross-examining the defendant about his or her character. It is regarded as an unwarranted inference that because the accused was a thief on a previous occasion, therefore he or she is also a thief on this occasion. This

---

[46] [1948] 1 K.B. 4.
[47] Criminal Evidence Act 1898, s. 1(f)(ii).
[48] [1939] 4 All E.R. 164.

prohibition is modified since the consistencies and patterns in people's behaviour mean that we are justified in treating previous conduct as a factor in deciding whether a person has committed an act. Previous conduct can have probative weight. At the same time, such testimony about an accused's previous offences is highly prejudicial. The prejudice exists because the proof of the previous conviction detracts attention from the proof of guilt of this offence and tends to undermine the standard of proof required. The court must balance the prejudice against the relevance and probative weight of such evidence.

In *Makin*,[49] the defendants accepted children from their mothers, alleging that they would adopt them on payment of a small sum of money. A baby's body was found buried in the garden and the accused were charged with the murder. The prosecution sought to adduce evidence that other such bodies have been found in gardens of other houses occupied by the defendants in order to rebut any possible defence of accident. Lord Herschell said:

> "It is undoubtedly not competent for the prosecution to adduce evidence tending to show that the accused has been guilty of criminal acts other than those covered by the indictment for the purpose of leading to the conclusion that the accused is a person likely from his criminal conduct or character to have committed the offence for which he is being tried. On the other hand, the mere fact that the evidence adduced tends to show the commission of other crimes does not render it inadmissible if it be relevant to an issue before the jury and it may be so relevant if it bears upon the question whether the acts alleged to constitute the crimes charged in the indictment were designed or accidental or to rebut a defence which would have been otherwise open to the accused."

There are two legs to the *Makin* principle, the first of which reiterates the inadmissible character of evidence of disposition: in *Brown*,[50] the defendants were charged with shopbreaking and the prosecution sought to show that one of the accused had broken into a shop five days previously, during the lunch hour and using a skeleton key. All of these were characteristics of the alleged offence but the evidence was excluded.

However, the second leg of *Makin* allows evidence of disposition to be introduced where it is relevant to an issue before the jury. One of these issues might be to rebut a defence. In *Makin* itself, evidence of other bodies tend to rebut any defence of accident or natural causes. Similarly in *Smith*,[51] the defendant was charged with the murder of his third wife by drowning her in the bath. The prosecution were allowed to advance evidence that the first and second wives had died in identical circumstances.

Although the logic of *Makin* is powerful, the courts have used the banner of similar facts to allow deeply prejudicial testimony especially in cases involving what the courts regarded as sexual deviancy. In *Thompson*,[52] the defendant was accused of indecent assault on two boys. They had taken the police to the place where the defendant had made a second assignation. The defendant was arrested without any further offence taking place. Could the police use evidence that the accused had two powder puffs on him

[49] [1894] A.C. 57.
[50] (1963) 47 Cr.App.R. 205.
[51] (1915) 11 Cr.App.R. 229.
[52] [1918] A.C. 221.

and that he had indecent photographs of his flat? The House of Lords held that they could; although the accused's sexuality could be seen as confirming the boys' identification of him, the probative aspect of this must have been overwhelmed by the prejudice created in the minds of the jury. The failure of the appeal courts to recognise this is seen in *Sims*,[53] where the accused was charged on counts of buggery and indecent assault against several men. He applied for severance of the trials but this was refused since the evidence relating to one complaint was admissible on the other charges. Sodomy, according to the Court of Appeal, was an especial category and the Court cited Lord Sumner in *Thompson*;

> "Persons ... who commit the offences now under consideration seek the habitual gratification of a particular perverted lust which not only takes them out of the class of ordinary men gone wrong but stamps them with a hallmark of a special and extraordinary class as much as if they carried on their bodies some physical peculiarity."

Homophobia of this nature illustrates the problems of inarticulated generalisations that can distort the process of proof.

Historically the quality of Lord Herschell's logic was diminished as the relevance of *Makin* was reduced into a list of formal categories:

(a) where the previous acts showed proof of a system, as in *Straffen*,[54] where the accused, just discharged from Broadmoor, was on trial for strangling a little girl. Evidence was permitted that he had strangled two other girls in identical circumstances.

(b) where disposition supports evidence of identity.[55]

(c) where the evidence would rebut a defence of accident.[56]

(d) where the evidence would rebut a defence of innocent association. In *Ball*,[57] the accused were brother and sister charged with incest. The House of Lords held that evidence that the sister had had a child by the brother before the passage of the Incest Act was admissible.

Underlying *Makin* was the rationale that if the relevance/probative force outweighed the prejudicial effect, the evidence of disposition should be admitted. However, artificiality was introduced by treating that relevance as a technical matter. Did it conform to an artificial category? *Boardman*[58] did not conform to the earlier category approach and seemed to herald a return to a simpler approach, based on judicial discretion on the balance between the prejudicial and probative effects of the evidence. The accused was the headmaster of a boarding school for boys, and was charged with sexual offences against two pupils on separate occasions. The similarities in the accounts by the two pupils were striking but the defence was that the boys were lying and that the incidents never occurred. Were the accounts given by each boy admissible on the charge relating to the other boy? The House of

[53] [1946] K.B. 531.
[54] [1952] 2 Q.B. 911.
[55] *Thompson* [1918] A.C. 221.
[56] *Smith* (1915) 11 Cr.App.R. 229.
[57] [1911] A.C. 47.
[58] [1975] A.C. 421.

Lords upheld the trial judge's decision to admit the evidence. Evidence of a similar-fact nature may be admitted if the judge views its probative force in relation to an issue in the trial as outweighing its prejudicial effect. The strength of the probative force lies in its striking similarity where that similarity is inexplicable on the basis of coincidence or concoction.

A common theme from the *Boardman* judgments was that the previous conduct should possess a "unique or striking similarity" to the offence charged. However, pragmatically that approach proved less than easy to apply[59] and, in addition, the courts became fixated by "striking similarity" and failed to see it simply as an illustration of the need to balance probative weight and prejudicial effect. The House of Lords issued a corrective to this in *P*[60] where the defendant was accused of incest with, and rape of, his two daughters. Was the testimony of one daughter admissible evidence on charges involving the other daughter (and vice versa)? The House held that the test of admissibility was whether the evidence was relevant and had probative value which outweighed its prejudicial effect. It was not necessary to single out "striking similarity" as an essential element, although in some cases where identity was in issue a "signature" might be looked for.

This reflects the principles propounded by Lord Wilberforce in *Boardman*. The accusers' stories must derive from a common cause, collusion, coincidence or from the fact that they are all telling the truth. The degree of probative weight required is that which rules out collusion or coincidence. This can be seen in *Roy*,[61] where a doctor was accused of indecent assault on a number of patients. There was nothing "striking" about the accounts with no bizarre elements but yet, aggregated, the stories had considerable probative weight, rebutting any suggestion that these assaults might have been bona fide medical examinations.

However, although the cases lay down a valid principle, there are no criteria for determining the probative weight, let alone the prejudicial effect, of evidence of previous criminal conduct. As long as the trial judge addresses his or her mind to the balance between proof and prejudice, the appellate court will not interfere with any conclusion. Without guiding criteria, it becomes a lottery and abrogates the principle that it is unfair that an accused should be answerable at a trial for anything other than the offence charged. It also infringes the concept of treating like cases alike because an accused with a criminal record will be treated differently from an accused without a record. The need is for the courts to take a less relaxed attitude to identifying and combating prejudice.

6.7.3.4 CROSS-EXAMINING THE ACCUSED

Under the Criminal Evidence Act 1898, for the first time the defendant became a competent witness. The evidence-in-chief posed no problems but what constraints were to be imposed on the prosecution in cross-examination?

The structure decided upon was that the prosecution, under section 1(e),

---

[59] *Novac* (1976) 65 Cr.App.R. 107; *Johannsen* (1977) 65 Cr.App.R. 101; *Tricoglus* (1976) 65 Cr.App.R. 16; *Barrington* [1981] 1 W.L.R. 419.
[60] [1991] 3 All E.R. 337.
[61] [1992] Crim.L.R. 185; *Laidman and Agnew* [1992] Crim.L.R. 428.

was able to ask the defendant questions notwithstanding the fact that the answers might incriminate the accused as to the offence charged:

> "A person charged and being a witness ... may be asked any question in cross-examination notwithstanding that it would tend to criminate him as to the offence charged."

However, they could not attack the defendant's credibility, as they might other defence witnesses, by asking questions about prior convictions. This was achieved by section 1(f):

> "A person charged and called as a witness ... shall not be asked ... any question tending to show that he has committed or been convicted of or been charged with any offence other than that wherewith he is then charged or is of bad character ..."

Section 1(f) enabled the accused to testify about the offence while keeping secret any murky past. Only under certain circumstances would the prosecution be entitled to inquire into that past. Yet what is the relationship between section 1(e) and section 1(f)? The sections can be mutually contradictory since a question on a previous conviction can tend to incriminate, (thus within section 1(e)), while at the same time showing that the accused has committed another offence (thus outside section 1(f)).

In *Jones*,[62] the accused was charged with murder and rape of a young girl guide. Previously he had been convicted of the rape of another young girl. At his trial for murder, he gave an account of his movements which corresponded almost word for word with the account he had given in the previous trial. Could he be questioned about this with a view to showing that the account was false? It could be argued that section 1(e) permitted the question since it tended to show that his account was false but that section 1(f) prohibited the question since it revealed a previous conviction. However, the defendant had also testified in chief that he had "been in trouble with the police". The majority in the House of Lords held that section 1(f) prohibited any question "... tending to show that he has committed...". This meant "reveal such offences". Since the defendant had mentioned "being in trouble with the police", the prosecution were not "revealing" prior offences and thus their questions were permissible. This approach subordinated section 1(e) to section 1(f) and construed section 1(e) narrowly to permit questioning only on those facts which directly link the accused with the offence. Yet this interpretation of section 1(f) was in itself highly technical and the protection afforded to the accused easily avoided. The defendant had not revealed any specific prior offence and yet the seriousness of the previous incident must have been apparent to the jury. Lords Denning and Devlin took a broader view that the line of questioning was permissible under section 1(e) because it tended to persuade the jury that the alibi was false and thus incriminated the defendant. This interpretation has logical weight but diminished the protection afforded by section 1(f). Any shield for the accused was secondary to probative value.

This approach was mirrored in *Anderson*,[63] in which the defendant was

---

[62] [1962] A.C. 635.
[63] [1988] 2 W.L.R. 1017.

charged with conspiracy to cause explosions. She had been arrested at a flat, with others, where there were considerable amounts of incriminating evidence. She testified that she knew nothing of any conspiracy but had come over from Northern Ireland to smuggle escapees from the Maze prison through Scotland to Denmark. She was to play the innocent female escort to hoodwink immigration. At trial, the prosecution obtained permission to question her on the fact that she was wanted by the Northern Ireland police. The prosecution did not elicit the reason why she was wanted but they had been "ambushed" by the direction the defence had taken and wished to show that it was unlikely that the accused would be chosen as an "innocent" escort. However, this line of questioning showed that the accused had committed another criminal offence. It could be argued that section 1(e) permitted the question and section 1(f) prohibited it. Following *Jones*, since the accused had testified to offences she had committed (assisting escapees), the prosecution were entitled to reveal that she was wanted by the police.

Common law authority such as *Makin*[64] permits any question which is relevant and probative (whether directly or indirectly). That common law position is expressed in section 1(e). All section 1(f) aims to do is to prevent the questioning of the defendant as to credit. The mere fact that evidence tends to show other crimes does not make it inadmissible if it is relevant to a matter before jury. The prosecution should be entitled advance evidence-in-chief as long as the probative weight is sufficient to outweigh any prejudicial effect.[65] It is difficult to argue that the defence in *Jones* should be permitted to advance a complicated exculpatory story without the jury being made aware that the same story had been used before.

The argument against is that the accused is at a considerable disadvantage by having leading questions (such as "It's true, isn't it, that the police in Northern Ireland wish to interview you?") advanced in cross-examination, without prior argument and without foundation being laid by the prosecution. Procedurally, it would be better if the prosecution advanced their own witnesses who could then be cross-examined by the defence.[66] Although this would disadvantage the prosecution since they would be unable to cross-examine the defendant on the issue, the relevant facts could still be laid before the jury.

6.7.3.4.1 DROPPING THE SHIELD

The defendant who chooses to testify can be questioned about any matter that is probative and relevant.[67] However, section 1(f) protects the defendant from being questioned about extraneous matters of character that go solely to credit. The accused can throw away this shield under the exceptions to section 1(f). Whether the shield is lost at any time is a matter for the judge:

    (a) the first exception contained in section 1(f)(i) is not an illustration of the accused throwing away the shield, but losing it: the accused can be

---

[64] [1894] A.C. 57.
[65] *P* [1991] 3 All E.R. 337.
[66] In *Cokar* [1960] 2 Q.B. 207 the prosecution were not allowed to advance similar fact evidence in cross-examination—a proper foundation had to be laid.
[67] Subject to the judicial discretion to disallow any line of questioning that is more prejudicial than probative.

asked questions about other offences where such evidence would be admissible at common law or statute. This refers to "similar fact" evidence discussed above. However, if the broad interpretation of section 1(e) advanced above is correct, this paragraph is redundant.

(b) Under section 1(f)(ii), the shield is thrown away either by the defendant seeking to establish his or her own good character, or by the defence casting imputations on the character of the prosecution witnesses.

The first part merely extends the common law to cross-examination. In *Samuel*,[68] the accused testified as to the occasions on which he had returned lost property and was then properly cross-examined on his theft convictions. However, a simple assertion of innocence is not putting your character into issue.

If the nature or character of the defence is to impute the character of the prosecution witnesses, then the defendant's shield is lost and there can be cross-examination about character and previous convictions. Again mere denials are not enough. In *Jones*,[69] Lord Hewart said that it was one thing for the defendant to deny making a confession but another matter to allege that it was a deliberate and elaborate concoction. Such a borderline is very difficult.[70] In *Britzman*,[71] the Court of Appeal said that if there was denial of a short interview, the presumption was in favour of the defendant. Yet if the accused denied a long conversation, made wild allegations or used unrestrained language and the judge was sure that there was no possibility of mistake or confusion, cross-examination under section 1(f)(ii) was permissible. Judges should not rely on section 1(f)(ii) where the other evidence was overwhelming.

The defence loses the shield even where the imputation is a necessary part of the defence. In *Selvey*,[72] the accused was charged with buggery and his defence was that the complainant had already committed buggery with another man on the same day, had offered himself to the accused and when the defendant refused, he had planted indecent photographs on him. The trial judge allowed the prosecution to question the accused on previous convictions for soliciting for a lewd and immoral purpose. The House of Lords held that section 1(f)(ii) was applicable even where the "... casting of such imputations is necessary to establish the defence ...".

This is well illustrated in *Bishop*,[73] where the accused was charged with burglary. His fingerprints were found on the premises and his explanation was that he had had a homosexual affair with the occupant of the premises, who was called for the prosecution. The prosecution were entitled to cross-examine about his previous convictions. The conviction was upheld since it was not material that the imputation had been made, not to blacken the name of the witness, but to explain the accused's presence there.

---

[68] (1956) 40 Cr.App.R. 8.
[69] (1923) 17 Cr.App.R. 117.
[70] *Tanner* (1977) 66 Cr.App.R. 56; *Nelson* (1978) 68 Cr.App.R. 12.
[71] [1983] 1 W.L.R. 350.
[72] [1970] A.C. 304.
[73] [1975] Q.B. 274.

Had the occupant been a woman and the allegation one of a heterosexual affair, would the result have been different? The logic of *Selvey* and *Bishop* would seem to apply to rape. Where the defence is that the victim consented, this should theoretically mean that the accused opens himself to cross-examination on his own record. Yet the House of Lords in *Selvey* held that the accused in rape cases can allege consent without risking such cross-examination, either because rape is *sui generis* or on the ground that the issue is one raised by the prosecution. Such decisions have magnified the problems surrounding the use of the victim's sexual history.[74]

The cross-examination goes to the credibility of the accused.[75] Where the accused's previous convictions bear a close resemblance to the offence charged, it is possible that the judge will disallow the examination.[76] In *Watts*,[77] the charge was indecent assault and the accused alleged that the admission had been fabricated. The prosecution were allowed to cross-examine on previous convictions for indecent assault on young girls. The conviction was quashed since the risk of prejudice was too great. This depends on the discretion of the judge.[78]

(c) Under section 1(f)(iii), the shield is lost where the accused has given evidence against any other person charged in the same proceedings.[79] It does not matter whether the evidence is given in chief or on cross-examination and the issue is the effect on the jury. It does not require hostile intent. It encompasses more than mere denial of something said by the co-accused and requires support of the prosecution case.

In *Bruce*,[80] the two accused were charged with robbery. The first admitted the plan to rob but denied taking part in its execution. The second denied any plan to rob at all. The first defendant cross-examined the second on his previous convictions. The second defendant's conviction was quashed. Although he had contradicted his co-defendant's evidence, he had not given evidence against him.

6.8 ESTOPPEL

The general principle is that a party to an action is not allowed to assert or to contradict certain facts which are either a matter of record, of deed or of conduct. This is largely a matter of civil law but in criminal cases, there are the special pleas of *autrefois acquit* and *autrefois convict* which are based on the double jeopardy rule that a person should not be prosecuted twice for the same offence. The "same offence" means one for which the defendant could have lawfully been convicted at the original hearing. Thus if the

---

[74] *supra*, para. 6.6.5.1.
[75] *France* [1979] Crim.L.R. 48.
[76] *Maxwell v. D.P.P.* [1935] A.C. 309.
[77] [1983] 3 All E.R. 101.
[78] *Powell* [1986] 1 All E.R. 193.
[79] *Murdoch v. Taylor* [1965] A.C. 574.
[80] [1975] 1 W.L.R. 1252.

accused is convicted of GBH, there is no bar to a homicide prosecution if the victim dies subsequent to the conviction.

In *Sambasivam*,[81] the defendant was charged with both possession of ammunition and carrying firearms. At the first trial he was acquitted on the first charge and a new trial was ordered on the second charge. At that trial, the defendant was convicted but the prosecution relied on a confession admitting both charges. The conviction was quashed since the court should have been told that the prosecution were bound by the acquittal and that made the confession less reliable.

There are situations where the outcome of the previous proceedings are relevant. In *Ollis*,[82] the accused was acquitted of an offence involving passing a dud cheque. Subsequently, he was charged with a similar offence and the prosecution adduced evidence of the earlier acquittal, arguing that it did not re-open that issue but that it showed the defendant's knowledge about the state of his bank account.

In civil law, once parties have fought and decided an issue, they are bound by that result. However, issue estoppel appears to have no place in criminal proceedings. In *Humphrys*,[83] the defendant was acquitted of driving while disqualified in July 1972. Although a police officer gave evidence of identification, the defendant testified that he had not driven anything in 1972. He was later charged with perjury in relation to that statement—the prosecution had other witnesses as to his driving at that time but also sought to reintroduce the officer to give the same evidence. The House of Lords upheld the conviction—there is no such thing as issue estoppel in criminal law largely because of the difficulty of defining the issues in criminal cases in the absence of pleadings and a reasoned decision, because it would operate unfairly in the defendant's favour because of the burden of proof and, if it operated on behalf of the prosecution, this might be equally unfair on the defendant. Thus in *Hogan*,[84] the defendant was convicted of GBH but then the victim died and he was charged with murder. The trial judge refused to allow the defendant to argue lack of intent and self-defence since these issues had been determined at the original trial. *Hogan* is overruled in *Humphrys*.

6.9 PRIOR CONVICTIONS AS EVIDENCE OF THEIR FACTS

To what extent can the prosecution use previous convictions as evidence of the facts on which they were based? The old common law rule was in *Hollington v. Hewthorn*.[85] This was a negligence action between two drivers where the Court of Appeal held that the plaintiff was not entitled to use the prior conviction of the defendant for careless driving as evidence of the defendant's negligence. This would mean that the prosecution would need to prove the facts anew even in related trials. In *Spinks*,[86] the principal offender stabbed the victim and was convicted of GBH. The defendant was tried as an

---

[81] [1950] A.C. 458.
[82] [1900] 2 Q.B. 758 but see *G v. Coltart* [1967] 1 Q.B. 432.
[83] [1977] A.C. 1.
[84] [1974] Q.B. 398.
[85] [1943] K.B. 587.
[86] [1982] 1 All E.R. 587; *Hassan* [1970] 1 Q.B. 423.

accomplice and it was held that the prosecution could not use the principal's conviction as evidence that the offence had been convicted.

This position was changed by section 74 of PACE so that a conviction is admissible where it is relevant to an issue in the case. The problem is that of relevance to an "issue". In *Robertson and Golder*,[87] the charge involved in one case was conspiracy to burgle, and evidence of convictions for burglaries carried out by Robertson's alleged co-conspirators was permitted; in the other case, Golder was charged with robbery and the convictions of his alleged partners were given in evidence against him. The burden of proving the convictions wrong would normally rest on the defence.

The prejudicial effect of proving convictions is obvious and the problem is one of fairness. Even where the conviction is admissible under section 74, it may be excluded under section 78 since it would have an adverse effect on the fairness of the proceedings.[88] In *Mattison*,[89] the accused was charged with indecency with another person who was similarly charged with indecency with the accused. The other person pleaded guilty but the defendant pleaded not guilty. The conviction was quashed after the other person's conviction was admitted into evidence.

---

[87] [1987] 3 All E.R. 231.
[88] *O'Connor* (1987) 85 Cr.App.R. 298.
[89] [1990] Crim.L.R. 117; see also *Turner* [1991] Crim.L.R. 57.

CHAPTER SEVEN

The Sentencing Decision and Non-Custodial Penalties

7.1 INTRODUCTION

In 1993, 1.43 million people, having pleaded guilty, or having been found guilty, were sentenced by the courts. The courts have available a range of sentencing options, custodial and non-custodial. For each disposal, there are levels of severity in terms of financial penalty, periods of supervision or incarceration.

Table 7.1 Types of Sentence 1988 and 1993[1]

Type of Sentence	1988	1993
Absolute discharge	19,000	25,900
Conditional discharge	77,600	111,600
Fine	1,248,300	1,091,500

[1] *Criminal Statistics 1993* Cm. 2680, Table 7A, p. 141.

Table 7.1—*cont.*

Type of Sentence	1988	1993
Probation order	43,600	43,800
Supervision order*	7,400	7,300
Community Service Order	35,300	48,000
Attendance Sentence Order*	8,500	6,800
Care Order*	500	n/a
Combination Order	n/a	8,900
Young Offender Institution*	24,100	15,200
Fully suspended imprisonment	30,900	3,800
Partly suspended imprisonment	2,800	n/a
Immediate imprisonment	45,200	43,200
Otherwise dealt with	12,300	19,100
ALL SENTENCES	1,555,400	1,425,000
Immediate custody	72,100	58,400
Community sentences	94,700	114,800

* Applicable to children and young persons.

In the public's eyes, the sentence is the test as to whether justice has been done, both to the victim and to the defendant. Any sentence, by any court, involves doing harm to the defendant in some way: it might be as limited as the humiliation and stigma associated with a court appearance followed by an absolute discharge; it might involve financial penalties; it might be a partial curtailment of personal liberty through weekend working on a community service order; it might involve extreme restriction on liberty of movement and major interference with personal, social and economic relationships through an immediate custodial sentence.

For the public, justice in sentencing involves the harm being meted out to the defendant having an equivalence to that suffered by the victim; the punishment is proportional to the seriousness of the offence. Fairness exists in the act of balancing. It is easily stated. Although it is one of our key indicators of justice, the sentencing decision is almost invariably unsatisfactory in terms of its objectives, its effectiveness and its internal coherence and consistency.

7.2 OBJECTIVES OF SENTENCING[2]

The judge has broad discretion in choosing which sanction to impose and at what level of severity. Sentencers are guided in this by their own penal philosophy,[3] be it incapacitation of the offender, protection of society, belief in the reformative qualities of punishment, general or individual deterrence, compensation to the victim or some interpretation of retribution and just deserts. This freedom is inevitably a source of disparity because judges pursuing different objectives will treat similar cases differently. The judge pursuing the objective of deterrence, for example, would consider a different type and severity of sentence than the retributively-minded judge. Such disparity is a plain breach of equal treatment principles of due process.

Should we permit judges this latitude, subject to their expressing in advance in open court what their criteria and objectives are? All the rationales of punishment possess some importance and that importance will vary according to the exact nature of the case that is before the court. Yet to allow such free choice for the sentencer is a negation of equal treatment. Constitutionally, penal policy should be a matter for government and legislature and not for the judiciary.[3a] Furthermore, although the objectives might all possess some importance, it is far from saying that they all possess equal importance or validity. Although much is claimed empirically for, say, the deterrent effect of exemplary sentences, there are different ethical values which attach to different philosophies of punishment and we need to make social choices between these. Such choices that cannot be left to the individual sentencer.

The alternative approach to judicial discretion is to define a principal objective through legislation (although shackling the judiciary is not the easiest task). The 1991 Criminal Justice Act provided an authoritative primary rationale, focusing on retribution and just deserts.[4] Secondary considerations (in certain circumstances) can be incapacitation, in order to protect the public from risk of serious harm or reform, since under the legislation the court must decide which of various non-custodial options is most suitable for the offender.

Despite this modern concentration on a single aim, we will explore briefly the traditional objectives of punishment, considering two different levels, not simply the purpose being pursued but also its justification. The overall social purpose is normally utilitarian, with either the aim of reducing crime through reform, deterrence or incapacitation or perhaps the object of diverting of private vengeance. Whether a purpose is successful is an empirical question: is there less crime? This does not answer the question of whether the punishment is justified which is not an empirical, but an ethical, issue. We

---

[2] There is an immense literature on this—for a recent anthology, see von Hirsch A. and Ashworth A., *Principled Sentencing* (1992).
[3] Hogarth J., *Sentencing as a Human Process* (1971).
[3a] See Lord Rustill in *Doody* (1993) 3 All E.R. 92, pp. 104–105.
[4] Criminal Justice Act 1991, s. 1; *cf.* California Penal Code s. 1170(a)(i).

might reduce crime by general deterrent punishments but are we justified in doing so if this involves punishing the innocent or the merely negligent?[5]

7.2.1 *Incapacitation and Protection of Society*

With offenders such as serial killers or multiple rapists, the fundamental purpose is to incapacitate them until the risk of repetition of the offence has passed. Normally the offence will be an offence of homicide or serious assault, posing a threat to the community at large, and is of such a character as to enable the sentencer to pass a long term of imprisonment. This comes comfortably within the provisions of the Criminal Justice Act 1991 regarding the imposition of custody and the necessary length of sentence.[6]

But this same language of "protection of society" is used for lesser offenders. With phrases like "Society needs a rest from your activities", judges have given longer sentences than merited by the instant offence, and have been willing to pull the inadequate petty recidivist into this net. From the eighteenth century, writers such as Beccaria and Bentham have stressed the importance of proportionality of punishment. The quality and quantity of punishment must now match that of the offence. Under sections 1 and 2 of the Criminal Justice Act 1991, judges must use the seriousness of the immediate offence as the primary criterion, removing the possibility of increasing the punishment every time a defendant appears before a court.[7] Although the persistent offender is more to blame because he has lost all mitigation and knows what to expect, this does not justify a disproportionate sentence.

Protection comes a close second to retribution as a purpose of punishment. Over the past decade, we have sent fewer people to prison but for longer periods: in 1985, 83,300 were sentenced to immediate custody but by 1993, that figure was 58,400; the proportionate use of custody has declined so that 19 per cent of adults convicted of indictable offences were imprisoned in 1987 whereas 16 per cent were imprisoned in 1993[8]; the average length of sentence for the adult male in Crown Court was 16.6 months in 1982 but 21.8 months in 1993. This has been referred to as a policy of bifurcation: "ordinary" offenders are dealt with presumptively by fines, punishment in the community or relatively short sentences; more serious offenders are given long sentences.

Protection is of course a valid purpose for any society. We are morally justified in protecting ourselves from even a low level of risk of serious harms. There is less justification in protecting ourselves by incapacitating an offender who presents a high level of risk but of less serious harms. There are two issues:

(a) the first is pragmatic: although it is easy to accept the abstract notion of incapacitation[9] of the "dangerous" offender, by what criteria are we to

[5] Although Bentham argued that punishing the innocent would be dysfunctional, since it would be seen as unjust, reducing our faith in the legal system and thus not maximising utility.
[6] Criminal Justice Act 1991, s. 1(2) and s. 2(2)—see below, para. 7.5.
[7] But see discussion on the changes to s. 29 by the 1993 Criminal Justice Act—*infra*, para. 7.5.
[8] *Criminal Statistics 1993, op. cit.*, para. 7.31, p. 150.
[9] Floud J. and Young W., *Dangerousness and Criminal Justice* (1981); Ashworth A., *Sentencing and Criminal Justice* (1992), p. 64.

distinguish the "dangerous" from the "not-so-dangerous"? Reliable prediction is virtually impossible.[10] Those identified as dangerous are no more likely to commit "dangerous" offences within five years of release from prison than those not so identified. Judicial discretion was advocated in the Floud Report but the lesson of the history of punishment has always been the need to control judicial discretion.

(b) the second issue is ethical: through using the idea of a "dangerous" offender, even were we to agree on the criteria, we would be imposing a heavy sentence, not merely (or sometimes not at all) on the basis of past conduct, but on the likelihood of the offender committing future offences. Is it "just" to impose sentences for crimes that have not yet been committed? If we see the "wrong" to the individual measured alongside the potentially serious harm to unidentified victims in the community, this can be seen as redistribution of risk. So long as there was some past action on which to base the prediction, this might be seen as "just".[11]

7.2.2 *Rehabilitation of the Offender*

Incapacitation looks to the future in the sense that it involves an assessment of the risk posed by an individual to others and the imposition of a sentence which reduces that risk. Reform also looks to the future in the belief that the defendant can be led towards conformity, not through fear of sanctions, but by more ambiguous ways, through inner motivation or re-establishing links to community norms of behaviour. Sentencing for reform necessarily involves an assessment of the defendant's needs and problems which led to the offence, and the imposition of a "sanction" which addresses these. The sentencing court is in the diagnostics business and individualising the sentence. Although some jurisdictions have explored this route, notably the Scottish Family Panels for juveniles and the Californian Adult Authority, it has never commended itself here. Although some judges have extended sentences to allow for a full programme of treatment, this has rarely been accepted by the Court of Appeal. In *Ford*,[12] an alcoholic on dishonesty charges was given a longer sentence than his co-accused, to allow for a cure.

Nor have there been genuine "reform" options for sentencers. Perhaps the sole historical example would have been the Borstal system for young offenders. This was created in 1908 and, selecting its inmates carefully, operated a rehabilitative regime based on education and training. It was highly successful when judged by recidivist rates. In the 1960s, the selectivity principle was abandoned and they became, in essence, juvenile prisons. The "success" rate plummeted. Nowadays, after other changes, they are known as Young Offender Institutions.

Other new penal measures have used the language of "reform". Suspended sentences and parole were introduced in 1967 with claims for their

[10] Brody S. and Tarling R., *Taking Offenders Out of Circulation* (Home Office Research Study No. 64) (1981).
[11] Von Hirsch A., *Past or Future Crimes* (1986).
[12] [1969] 3 All E.R. 782.

reformative potential. Their underlying aims were more concerned with reducing the prison population. Apart from probation, the most likely contender would be the community service orders, involving unpaid service to the community, but even these have a chameleon quality to them and nowadays the number of hours of community service to which an offender is sentenced has more to do with the seriousness of the offence than the rehabilitative quality of the work to be undertaken.

Reform as a primary rationale for sentencing is largely discredited.[13] Bottoms[14] has argued that as an objective, rehabilitation suffers from three problems:

(a) it is theoretically faulty as it rests on an assumption that crime is a matter of individual pathology and that offending has its roots in the deficiencies of individuals. Crime is as much related to the overall organisation of society.
(b) it is systematically discriminatory since it leads to more severe intervention from those seen as coming from "unsatisfactory" backgrounds. Those who are already poor and disadvantaged are more likely to get "reformative sentences" than those from more privileged backgrounds.
(c) it is inconsistent with any justice model since punishments are inflicted on impressionistic evidence, in the name of "casework" that is difficult to challenge, and offenders are sentenced on their background and circumstances rather than on the offence committed.

Does reform ever work? Even if it was a practical possibility, are we justified morally in reshaping another to some conception of "a good and useful life"? Such a phrase raises questions as to "whose good?", "what utility?". Carlen[15] quotes one offender; "Why do you object to people being drunk? . . . and then make them pay?" Is it a denial of human autonomy to be "reformed"? Bentham has a phrase that to be punished for the purposes of reform is to be treated like a dog.

Despite reform's unhappy history, it resurfaces in the Criminal Justice Act 1991. Although this legislation has just deserts as its primary rationale, a secondary consideration can be reform since the court must decide which of various non-custodial community sentences is most suitable for the offender.[16]

Within the prison, regimes should be facilitative in enabling inmates to develop, be it their muscles, their morals or their minds. Prison Rule I talks of teaching the prisoner to lead "a good and useful life". Reform has been the official ideology of the prison since the development of the penitentiary in the nineteenth century, in which the reform of the offender was approached by

---

[13] Von Hirsch A., *Doing Justice* (1976).
[14] Bottoms A., "An Introduction to the 'Coming Crisis' " in Bottoms A. and Preston R., *The Coming Penal Crisis* (1980), pp. 1–3.
[15] Carlen P., "Remedial Routines for the Maintenance of Control in Magistrates' Courts" 1 Brit. J. Law and Soc. (1974), p. 101.
[16] Criminal Justice Act 1991, s. 6(2)(a), although s. 6(2)(b) orders the court to ensure that the restrictions on liberty are also commensurate with the seriousness of the offence.

the inculcation of work habits through labour and of proper moral precepts through the reading of the Bible. Reformative ideals still motivate many who work in modern prisons and the Prison Service's mission statement talks of "helping (prisoners) to lead law-abiding and useful lives". This is often an incidental consequence rather than a *raison d'etre* of an institution's regime. Overall, prisons do not operate on any overall rehabilitative model but there are many, often excellent but discrete, programmes to be found in individual prisons: tackling the staggering illiteracy rate amongst prisoners (or enabling them to get degrees); coping with alcohol and other drug abuse; seeking to develop vocational skills; dealing with psychiatric problems.

When such programmes are generalised into compulsory regimes, there are further problems. Well-planned, well-resourced rehabilitative programmes in California were no more "effective" in terms of recidivism than other penal measures.[17] The rehabilitative ideal can encourage the most grotesque interference with the dignity and privacy of offenders,[18] even extending to electrode implants in the brain. Although such excesses have not occurred here, some units have tried experimental medical programmes; in Wormwood Scrubs, in the 1970s, these involved hormone and drug treatment for sex offenders. Although nominally voluntary, the failure to participate in such schemes were perceived as lessening chances of parole.[19]

Such false starts have not dimmed the optimism of those who see reform as a central aspect of any prison regime, not least because it builds upon the best rather than the worst of people. There are those that argue that facilitative, voluntary programmes have never been given a fair trial[20] and that there remain sound reasons to continue to experiment with such approaches.

7.2.3 *Deterrence*

Deterrence has forward-looking and utilitarian aims. A punishment is inflicted which is sufficiently harmful to discourage the offender and other people from committing offences in the future. This is a time-honoured justification for punishment and involves the classic utilitarian calculus by which we balance the benefits to be gained from the crime, against the pains and costs of the punishment. It is a justification which has to be reassessed in the light of the Criminal Justice Act 1991, under the provisions of which a sentence longer than that justified by the seriousness of the instant offence but justified in terms of deterrence would probably be struck down by the Court of Appeal.[21]

There are two forms of deterrence. The first of these is individual deterrence whereby the punishment is fixed at a sufficient level so as to discourage the offender from re-offending. A core characteristic is the escalation of penalties for persistent offenders. If, after one conviction, a person commits a similar offence, a more severe sentence will be imposed.

---

[17] Von Hirsch (1976), *op. cit.*
[18] Mitford J., *The American Prison Business* (1973), Chap. 7.
[19] Radical Alternatives to Prison, *Newsletter*, Vol. 2, No. 11 (Christian Action, November 1973).
[20] Hudson B., *Justice Through Punishment* (1987), p. 170.
[21] But see Taylor L.C.J.'s comments in *Cunningham* [1993] 2 All E.R. 15 at 17e–18c.

This was a common aspect of pre-1991 sentencing whereby sentences were based on the offender's record as much as on the seriousness of the offence.

Low detection rates dilute the deterrent effect on individuals who calculate that the offence is unlikely to be detected. Further the effect becomes weaker with each conviction; the chances of those with five or more convictions re-offending are very high, no matter what sentence they are given. Those with fewer convictions are less likely to re-offend when fined or put on probation rather than imprisoned.[22] If at all the deterrence value may be maximised at an early stage by a "short, sharp shock", a relatively long sentence for the offender at an early stage. There is little support for this and although this approach was tried with detention centres orders under the Criminal Justice Act 1982, it was soon abolished.[23] Furthermore, even if such sentences were effective, are we ethically justified in imposing such a sentence which is not merited by the offence?

That is also the key issue with the general deterrence. The level of punishment is set not to discourage the offender but to deter the rest of the community from committing such crimes. It works on the thesis that it is the threat of punishment that makes people conform. This has two aspects:

(a) there is a general level of punishment visibly and continuously in operation to keep the threat of punishment alive and thus the overall crime rate down. An example of this threat breaking down was in occupied Denmark during the Second World War when all the Danish police were arrested in September 1944. Despite increases in punishment, the risk of being caught declined and the number of property offences soared.[24] The converse of this can be seen with saturation policing, where large numbers of officers are drafted into a particular area when the number of burglaries, thefts and public order offences decline but not offences against the person, such as homicides or assaults.[25]

(b) as well as this there is the exemplary sentence. When specific crimes are on the increase, very high sentences are imposed. Mugging,[26] baby snatching, football hooligans are all recent examples of attempts to impose this policy. Andenaes gives an example from Norway where drink-driving invariably attracts a short prison sentence and suggests not only that there are many fewer drink related accidents but also people grow to see the act as "wrong".[27]

Is general deterrence effective? The crucial assumption is that people do not commit crime because of the threat of punishment. Even if the empirical

---

[22] Walker N., Farrington D. and Tucker G., "Reconviction Rates of Adult Males after Different Sentences" (1981) 21 Brit.J.Criminol. 357.

[23] Criminal Justice Act 1988, s. 123—discussed in Emmins C. and Scanlan G., *Criminal Justice Act 1988* (1988), p. 101 but see new proposals for "boot camps"—*The Times*, February 6, 1995, p. 1.

[24] Andenaes J., "The General Preventive Effects of Punishment" (1966) 114 U.Pa.L.Rev. 949.

[25] Sellin T., "The Law and Some Aspects of Criminal Conduct" in Sellin T. (ed.), *Aims and Methods of Legal Research* (1955).

[26] *Storey* (1973) 57 Cr.App.R. 840.

[27] Andenaes, *op. cit.*

evidence were to be conclusive, we would still need to ask whether we were morally justified in punishing one offender more severely than the actual offence requires in order to deter another? This question has been overtaken by the impact of the 1991 legislation especially sections 1(2)(a) and 2(2)(a) which suggest that courts must look to the seriousness of the offence, implicitly excluding any reference to deterrent effect. In *Cunningham*, the court said that "... what section 2(2)(a) does prohibit is adding any extra length to the sentence ... simply to make a special example of the defendant".[28] However, Lord Taylor C.J. also said, "... 'commensurate with the seriousness of the offence' must mean commensurate with the punishment and deterrence which the seriousness of the offence requires".

7.2.4 *Punishment and Just Deserts*

The word "retribution" can surface in many different guises; vengeance, denunciation, atonement or just deserts:

(a) the language of vengeance implies an instinctive human need to strike back either on behalf of the victim or because of a public need for revenge. Punishment based on vengeance, on simple hatred of the criminal, would have no moral boundaries (such as proportionality) and it has been suggested that punishment based on vengeance represents a breakdown of human intelligence and the ugliest phase of our human nature.[29] Any state system of punishment should demonstrate moral imperatives to a community through the constraints that we ourselves impose upon the barbarities and humiliations imposed upon offenders. Equally, penal sanctions must reflect the victim's needs, especially the need for "satisfaction" and the sense that an affair is closed.

(b) denunciation evokes the idea of the expression of social abhorrence. Criminal courts have a dramatic impact and there is a symbolic, expressive and educative quality about them. They demonstrate moral imperatives to a community. Durkheim discussed it in terms of drawing the moral boundaries of a society. Feinberg[30] talks of the act of "disavowing": through the punishment, we deny collective responsibility for the acts of this individual. Thus the sentence must be of sufficient weight to achieve this: probation for the armed robber carries the wrong message.

(c) expiation and atonement have overtones of religious penitence for sin. The more mundane phrase is "paying for your crime". You are accepted back into the community because you are seen as having paid the price.[31]

(d) in the 1970s, the critique of reform and deterrence theories led theorists[32] to develop the principle of "just deserts". The criminal sanction is imposing a harm for harm, a crime for a crime which may be

[28] *supra*, at 18b–c.
[29] Cohen M., "Moral Aspects of Criminal Law" (1940) 49 Yale L.J. 1025.
[30] Feinberg J., "The Expressive Function of Punishment" (1965) 49 *The Monist* 397.
[31] *Williams* [1974] Crim.L.R. 558.
[32] Von Hirsh, *op. cit.*, (1976).

as limited as the humiliation of a court appearance, or as extreme as a prison sentence.

What is the purpose in this second, state-inflicted crime? There is no intent to look forward and to reduce crime by incapacitating, deterring or reforming the offender although this might be an incidental effect. It is not designed to restore the status quo in the manner that compensation does in civil matters. Instead, the sentence looks backward and is based on matching the harm inflicted on the offender with that suffered by the victim. The fact that the harm being meted out to the defendant has an equivalence to that suffered by the victim, that the punishment is proportional to the seriousness of the offence, is central for the public perception of justice. Fairness is seen in that act of balancing wrongs.

The punishment is not just fair but is also deserved. Von Hirsch uses Kant's notion of "deserved punishment"; that individuals have to be seen as exercising a free choice with an obligation to limit their behaviour so as not to interfere with the freedom of others. By infringing another's rights, a person gains an unfair advantage and the punishment, by imposing a counterbalancing disadvantage, restores the equilibrium. Culturally, we accept that the person who contributes positively to society in some way earns or deserves reward. Similarly, we believe that bad behaviour merits punishment; "He deserved all he got!". Usually, informal social sanctions through the family, school, workplace or community suffice but there are situations when the strength of disapproval requires that justice is done through formal state intervention.

The unfair advantage is balanced by inflicting an equal and proportional harm through which social equilibrium is restored. The key is proportionality. Although critics of desert theory have attacked it at various points,[33] its highwater mark is indubitably the Criminal Justice Act 1991 by which sentencing is based on the seriousness of the offence. There is less concern with what might be achieved by punishment, but more with punishment for its own sake. There are fewer pragmatic problems since it has no objectives and "success" cannot be measured. There can be difficulties in assessing the degree of harm that needs to be paid for. Ethically, just deserts is more defensible than the utilitarian aspects of deterrence or reform. Furthermore, if it is accepted that people "deserve" reward or punishment, it is a policy that can be justified positively.

7.3 WHO ARE THE SENTENCERS?

The sentencers consist of about 1,400 circuit and High Court judges and over 30,000 magistrates. On conviction or a guilty plea, they exercise a wide discretion: for all offences created by statute, the maximum penalty will be expressly stated whereas the minimum will be implied as an absolute discharge; for common law offences, the maximum is life imprisonment.[34]

---

[33] Hudson, *op. cit.*; Lacey N., *State Punishment* (1988); Mathieson T., *Prisons on Trial* (1990)—see Ashworth (1992), *op. cit.*, at 67.
[34] Even for minor offences such as cheating—Smith J. and Hogan B., *Criminal Law* (7th ed., 1992), *op. cit.*, p. 581.

This discretion exists for all offences except for murder where the sentence is a mandatory life sentence.

Other jurisdictions do not grant such latitude to the judge. Many United States states employ "indeterminate" sentencing by which a conviction automatically means a sentence of, say, one to five years imprisonment and the exact length of the sentence will depend on the prison authorities. In England, it is taken for granted that the courts are responsible for sentence. Historically this was not the case[35]: the development of "broad band" criminal offences, such as theft replacing large numbers of more specific crimes, led to wide discretionary sentencing powers and this has been coupled with the development of a jurisprudence of sentencing by the Court of Appeal.[36] Recently, control over sentencing has been identified as one of the hallmarks of judicial independence.[37] Legislative reform and proposals for sentencing councils have been greeted as interference with the judiciary's proper constitutional sphere of action. However, there is little constitutional basis for judicial control over sentencing policy whereas there is legitimate Parliamentary concern over sentencing policies and practices.[38] An attempt to achieve legislative dominance is the Criminal Justice Act 1991 which lays down a very detailed sentencing framework for the courts. A sceptic might suggest that historically any attempts to control the judiciary by legislation are usually doomed to failure.[39]

Although the role of Parliament is unchallenged, the relationship between the judiciary and the executive is not. Friction between judicial sentencing policy and executive penal policy might arise in two ways: first, through the executive's attempts to influence sentencing, for example, to encourage more non-custodial sentences at a time of prison overcrowding. However, there has been judicial resentment at Home Office interference. Co-operation and co-ordination between the executive and judiciary to find answers to the problems in the criminal justice system have been rare.[40] Recently there have been genuflections towards greater dialogue especially with the development of the national and local elements of the Criminal Justice Consultative Council.[41]

The second site of potential discord is executive control over prisons. Judges sentence for specific reasons, with the nature of the offence, offender and the prison regime in mind. Once the prisoner is inside, the executive have considerable power over the conditions and over the time served. The objectives of the penal system are not necessarily those of a sentencing body. Moreover, the managerial responsibilities of a prison department invariably diverge from those of the judge, let alone from the political concerns of a Home Secretary. Again there are some gestures towards integration: trial judges must be consulted before the release of life sentence prisoners; other judges sit on the Parole Board.

---

[35] Radzinowicz, Sir L. and Hood R., *The Emergence of Penal Policy in Victorian and Edwardian England* (1986), Chaps. 22 and 23.
[36] Thomas D. A., *The Principles of Sentencing* (2nd ed., 1979).
[37] Ashworth (1992), *op. cit.*, Chap. 2.
[38] Ashworth (1992), *op. cit.*, p. 43.
[39] *e.g.* the introduction of parole in 1967 led to a sharp increase in the average length of sentences.
[40] Ashworth (1992), *op. cit.*, p. 44.
[41] This was established following a recommendation of the Woolf Inquiry (*Report of an Inquiry*

Are the interests of victims or defendants served by such a system? Barbara Wootton[42] castigated the amateurism of our sentencing system, amateur in the sense that judges, while well-qualified legally, possess few if any penological qualifications. Even legally, although the Court of Appeal have developed guidelines on sentencing significantly in some areas,[43] there is little or no guidance for lesser offences such as burglary, theft and deception. These are crucial offences where the borderline between custodial and non-custodial penalties cries out for definition, but in *Mussel*,[44] Lane L.C.J. declined the opportunity to lay down guidelines for domestic burglary on the ground that there was too great a variety of possible situations.

Reformers have argued for change at two levels; first, at the point of the individual sentence, with less power for the sentencing judge and with sentencing tribunals with a membership drawn from the local community, reflecting a broader range of social, professional, ethnic backgrounds, an approach which has been taken up in the Scottish system which employs Family Panels for the sentencing of young offenders[45]; secondly, there has been concern about a central policy vacuum. In 1990, the Government's policy was that the new legislation, guidance from the Court of Appeal and the Attorney-General's new power to refer over-lenient sentences would contribute to the development of coherent sentencing practice which would be disseminated to the courts by the Judicial Studies Board.[46] Others feel that a more proactive approach is required, with proposals for the creation of a Sentencing Council with membership including senior judges but also a circuit judge and lay and stipendiary magistrates, a prison governor and probation officer as well as an academic lawyer and criminologist.[47] The task of such a council would be to formulate and keep under review guidance for the courts on sentencing matters.[48]

The training of sentencers remains desultory in comparison with countries with a professional judiciary. Most of our judges come from barristers whose professional training does not include sentencing or penological issues. For Crown Court judges, there is a Judicial Studies Board within the Lord Chancellor's department. This was set up in 1979 as a result of the Bridge Report.[49] Its functions[50] include sentencing seminars which seek to reduce inconsistencies in sentencing in the Crown Court. There are programmes of

---

into Prison Disturbances, April 1990 Cm. 1456)—for the membership of the council, [1992] Crim.L.R. 141.

[42] Wootton B., *Crime and the Criminal Law* (1963).

[43] *Billam* (1986) 82 Cr.App.R. 347 (rape); *Bilinksi* (1988) 86 Cr.App.R. 146 (drug offences); *Attorney-General's Reference (No. 1 of 1989)* (1989) 11 Cr.App.R.(S.) 409 (incest); *Boswell* [1984] 1 W.L.R. 1047 (causing death by reckless driving).

[44] (1990) 12 Cr.App.R.(S.) 607—for criticisms, see Ashworth (1992), *op. cit.*, pp. 229–230.

[45] On the other hand, in 1976 California, the forerunner of the rehabilitation movement, abolished its "Adult Authority" in which experts imposed the sentence most appropriate for the reform of the offender.

[46] White Paper, *Crime, Justice and Protecting the Public* Cm. 965 (1990).

[47] Ashworth A., *Custody Reconsidered* (Centre for Policy Studies 1989); Ashworth (1992), *op. cit.*, p. 321.

[48] In the Netherlands, this is a task undertaken by the prosecutors: Downes D., *Contrasts in Tolerance* (1988), p. 14.

[49] Bridge, Lord, *Report of Working Party on Judicial Studies and Information* (1978).

[50] Glidewell, Lord Justice, "The Judicial Studies Board" in Wasik M. and Munro C. (eds.), *Sentencing, Judicial Discretion and Judicial Training* (1992).

courses for newly appointed judges and refresher courses for more experienced judges. It now publishes a regular Bulletin summarising recent legislation, sentencing decisions, research findings and comparative developments.

From 1985, the Board took on the training of stipendiary magistrates as well as advising the Lord Chancellor on the training for J.P.s (for whom there had been a compulsory training programme since 1966).[51] In practice, the training is in the hands of local justices' clerks who exercise considerable autonomy under the general supervision of the Lord Chancellor's Department.[52] There are other influences: the Magistrates' Association issue a "Sentencing Guide for Criminal Offences" to its members,[53] (while very influential although such a publication has no legal effect) all local benches will have a liaison judge who might speak at training meetings and conferences, giving, for example, detailed guidance on mode-of-trial decisions.[54]

7.4 INFORMATION FOR SENTENCERS

In exercising their discretion as to the nature and length of the sentence, magistrates and judges will take into account a range of information:

(a) facts[55] about the offence itself will emerge during the course of the trial (if contested) or by narration by the prosecutor (if there is a guilty plea). There can be ambiguities about the precise factual basis of a jury verdict and in such cases judges are expected to form their own view on the evidence heard at the trial.[56] There can be similar problems with a guilty plea; where there is a conflict between defence and prosecution versions of a particular act, there has to be a *"Newton*[57] hearing" whereby the judge has to hear evidence[58] before passing sentence. This is a major step forward in procedural justice in sentencing.

The interpretation of the facts is all important. The extent to which the sentencer regards the offence as grave or as venal can be the central issue in deciding between a custodial and non-custodial sentence and under section 1 of the Criminal Justice Act 1991, the sentencer must have regard to the "seriousness" of the offence.[59] Sentencers can display unconscious bias; Hood found that the age of the magistrate was related to the view taken of the seriousness of driving offences by younger drivers as opposed to older drivers.[60] Class, occupation, race, gender, religion can all affect the sentencer's view as well as other, often inarticulated, beliefs about crime and punishment and the aims

---

[51] Baldwin J., "The Compulsory Training of Magistrates" [1975] Crim.L.R. 634.
[52] Ashworth (1992), *op. cit.*, p. 53.
[53] Wasik M. and Turner A., "Sentencing Guidelines for Magistrates' Courts" [1993] Crim.L.R. 345.
[54] Riley D. and Vennard J., *Triable Either Way Cases* (Home Office Research Study No. 98) (1988).
[55] It is not common in this country to have a "victim impact" statement nor is the victim necessarily present in court nor will he or she be represented.
[56] *McGlade* (1990) 12 Cr.App.R.(S.) 105.
[57] (1982) 4 Cr.App.R.(S.) 388.
[58] Wasik M., "Rules of Evidence at the Sentencing Stage" (1985) *Current Legal Problems* 187.
[59] Ashworth (1992), *op. cit.*, Chap. 5.
[60] Hood R., *Sentencing the Motoring Offender* (1972), p. 140.

of the criminal justice system.[61] These beliefs often represent a shared tradition among particular benches, a tradition that can often explain sentencing practices.[62]

(b) although the fact that the defendant has committed other similar offences cannot be mentioned during the course of trial, in sentencing however, the defendant can ask for other offences to be taken into consideration. The defendant will be treated as admitting to those offences and can be sentenced on that basis.[63] Although the defendant might receive a heavier sentence for the immediate offence (although not more than the maximum for such an offence), on release, he or she cannot be prosecuted for those other offences and it represents an effective means of disposing of a number of minor offences.[64]

(c) information about the offender can come in various ways:

    (i) a police antecedent statement should refer to the basic facts of the defendant's life (age, education, employment, marital status) as well as the record of any previous convictions. The quality of such information can vary.[65] Since 1985, this record has also included those occasions on which the accused has been cautioned. A suspect has to admit an offence before he or she can be cautioned for it but when the alternative is prosecution, that admission might be treated sceptically.

    (ii) either personally or through counsel, the accused is entitled to make a plea in mitigation. Defence counsel can emphasise the contributory reasons for the offence such as provocation, can address the issue of the seriousness of the offence, can outline the defendant's personal circumstances and can also make known the defendant's attitude to the offence such as feelings of remorse and willingness to make some form of recompense to the victim.[66] The most effective speeches are those which are realistic in recognising the seriousness of the offence, in which there is supporting evidence of assertions and where there is a sound knowledge of the various alternatives that face the court.[67]

    (iii) there may be a medical report on the physical or mental health of the accused.[68] The defendant may be remanded in custody for such a report.

(d) after conviction, the prosecution's job is over and there is no involvement in the disposition of the offender. It is still the case that CPS do not make any recommendation as to type or length of sentence although this can be affected indirectly by the decision on the nature of

[61] Hogarth J., *Sentencing as a Human Process* (1971).

[62] Tarling R., *Sentencing Practice in Magistrates Courts* (Home Office Research Study No. 56) (1979).

[63] *Anderson v. D.P.P.* (1978) 67 Cr.App.R. 185.

[64] Although it has been used, less legitimately, by the police as a means of improving the clear-up rate.

[65] Shapland J., *Between Conviction and Sentence* (1981).

[66] Shapland, *op. cit.*

[67] Ashworth A., *et al.*, *Sentencing in the Crown Court: Report of an Exploratory Study* (Oxford University Centre for Criminological Research Occasional Paper No. 10 1984).

[68] *e.g.* under s. 4(1) Criminal Justice Act 1991, if the offender is or appears to be mentally disordered, the court shall obtain and consider a medical report before passing a custodial sentence.

the charge and acceptance of plea. There have been proposals for reform in this area.[69] Recently, the Court of Appeal have placed certain responsibilities on prosecuting counsel in ensuring that the court's attention is drawn to any guideline cases.[70] The new powers of the Attorney-General[71] to refer unduly lenient sentences to the Court of Appeal means that the prosecution will need to be more familiar with sentencing policy and practice. Although this practice is common in other jurisdictions,[72] reform of this nature would place the CPS under considerable media and political pressure. The current anorexic Code[73] would require considerable development towards a framework of the ethical and public interest factors to be taken account of in sentencing.

7.4.1 *Pre-Sentence Reports*

The probation service was founded in 1908[74] and has always prepared reports on offenders for the court, initially just on candidates for probation but later on a broader basis. By the 1960s, there was a need to improve the quantity and quality of information coming before the court. The Streatfield Committee[75] encouraged greater use of social inquiry reports (SIRs) and nowadays reports will contain:

- an assessment of the accused's personality, character, family and social background.
- information about the accused and his or her surroundings which may be relevant to the way in which a criminal career might be checked.
- information on employment or prospects of employment and attitudes to it.
- information about financial circumstances and an opinion as to the likely effect of any sentence.
- the majority (80 per cent) outline the options available to the court and will contain a recommendation as to the most suitable sentence.

The absence of a recommendation is often regarded as an implied recommendation for a custodial sentence. In recommending a sentence, the probation officer, a trained social worker who thus should regard the accused as a client, should be concerned with the client's needs and the prevention of further offending behaviour. At the same time probation officers have to be aware of what is a feasible sentence in the eyes of the court which must

---

[69] Zellick G., "The Role of Prosecuting Counsel in Sentencing" [1979] Crim.L.R. 493; Ashworth A., "Prosecution and Procedure in Criminal Justice" [1979] Crim.L.R. 480.
[70] *Panayioutou* (1989) 11 Cr.App.R.(S.) 535.
[71] Criminal Justice Act 1988, ss. 35–36.
[72] Downes, *op. cit.*, p. 14.
[73] *Code for Crown Prosecutors* (CPS June 1994); Ashworth A. and Fianda J., "The New Code for Crown Prosecutors: Prosecution Accountability and the Public Interest" [1994] Crim.L.R. 894.
[74] Probation of Offenders Act 1907.
[75] *Report of the Interdepartmental Committee on the Business of the Criminal Courts* Cmnd. 1289 (1961).

also consider the nature of the offence and the public interest. Any recommendation outside that range is likely to be disregarded by the court and this would be to the detriment of the client. The extent to which courts follow SIR recommendations is uncertain and research studies have produced varied results.[76] Any result will be difficult to interpret since it may not show that the probation officer is successful in influencing the court but merely that any recommendation is tailored to suit a particular judge.[77]

The quality of the contents of SIRs was frequently criticised,[78] not least for discrimination against black defendants. Such criticisms were that probation officers failed more often to prepare SIRs for black defendants, did not recommend the same range of sentences for black offenders as for white offenders and were less successful in getting their recommendations accepted by the court.[79] Other research suggests that blacks are less likely to be recommended for probation.[80]

The Criminal Justice Act 1991 renames SIRs as "pre-sentence reports" (PSR).[81] These are mandatory[82] when the accused is facing a custodial sentence[83] or various community sentences.[84] These two categories cover a majority of cases (excluding those involving discharges and fines) and PSRs will have a central role in sentencing, although even prior to 1991, some 250,000 SIRs were prepared each year, taking up around 25 per cent of a probation officer's time.

7.5 THE DEVELOPMENT OF A STATUTORY SENTENCING FRAMEWORK

Prior to 1991, the sentencing of adults involved an awareness of the statutory maximum for the offence and recognition of certain limited statutory restrictions and exhortations.[85] For the judge it also involved a

[76] Thorpe J., *Social Inquiry Reports* (Home Office Research Study No. 49) (1979) concluded that they were followed in circa 66 per cent of cases but Moxon D., *Sentencing Practice in the Crown Court* (Home Office Research Study No. 103) (1988) found that only one-third were in line with the eventual sentence.

[77] Roberts C., "The Probation Officer's Dilemma: Preparing Social Inquiry Reports" in Pennington D. and Lloyd-Bostock S. (eds.), *The Psychology of Sentencing* (Centre for Socio-Legal Studies, Oxford 1987).

[78] Thorpe, *op. cit.*

[79] Voakes R. and Fowler Q., *Sentencing, Races and Social Enquiry Reports* (West Yorkshire Probation Service 1989).

[80] Moxon (1988), *op. cit.*

[81] Following the recommendations of the White Paper *Crime, Justice and Protecting the Public*, *op cit.*

[82] Prior to 1991, SIRs were mandatory when the accused was facing a first term of imprisonment (s. 20 Powers of Criminal Courts Act 1973); custody for the under-21s (s. 2 Criminal Justice Act 1982); community service (s. 14 Powers of Criminal Courts Act 1973); probation (s. 2 Powers of Criminal Courts Act 1973). They were recommended for all offenders under 21; for older offenders if there has been no prison sentence since 17; for females; for those recently in touch with the probation service; for anyone remanded for psychiatric reports.

[83] Criminal Justice Act 1991, s. 3(1), except where one of the offences is triable only on indictment and the court considers a PSR unnecessary.

[84] *ibid.* s. 7(3).

[85] I refer to well-meaning statutes which encouraged courts to obtain SIRs and not to imprison unless absolutely necessary.

cautious glance over the shoulder at Court of Appeal sentencing decisions, although such guidance was conspicuous by its absence on primary decisions of whether to impose a custodial or non-custodial sentence in basic third-tier Crown Court work on burglary or deception.[86] From 1991, this changed entirely. The objectives of the 1991 Criminal Justice Act itself and the preceding White Paper[87] were to centre the court's attention on the seriousness of the offence and just deserts for the offender. Rehabilitation or deterrence would play little part in future sentencing. If the punishment is proportional and equivalent to the offence, both victim and public will perceive of it as just.[88] In the House of Lords, Lord Windlesham suggested three principles underlying the legislation:

(a) punishment for an offence should be related directly to the gravity of the offence.
(b) imprisonment should be used only where it it strictly necessary to protect the public from serious harm or where the offence is so serious that only a custodial sentence can be justified.
(c) an objective is to reduce crime as well as to punish and that, for less serious offences, prison is not necessarily the most effective sanction.

These principles have led to a new sentencing framework which must be followed by the court. The basic decision is between categories of disposition which are:

(a) custodial sentences
(b) community sentence
(c) fines
(d) discharges, binding-over orders or other disposals

The 1991 Criminal Justice Act laid down a framework for the first three of these.[89] The framework is a pyramid where the base is the fine which is the presumptive penalty in most cases.[90] If the court is to move up the pyramid, it has to clear certain thresholds: if the court wishes to move from a fine to a community sentence, it has to be satisfied that the offence is sufficiently serious to warrant this[91]; if the court is to take the next step and move from a community sentence to a custodial sentence, it must be satisfied that the offence (or a combination of the offence and others associated with it)[92] is so serious that only a custodial sentence can be justified.[93] The secondary

---

[86] *Mussel* (1990) 12 Cr.App.R.(S.) 607.
[87] *Crime, Justice and Protecting the Public, op. cit.*
[88] *ibid.* para. 2.4.
[89] This has been amended by the Criminal Justice Act 1993 and in the case of fines, wholly jettisoned.
[90] Ashworth (1992), *op. cit.*, p. 290.
[91] Criminal Justice Act 1991, s. 6(1).
[92] Under the 1991 Act, the rule was that the court could only decide on the seriousness of an offence based on the offence and one other associated with it. This has now been altered by s. 66(1) of the Criminal Justice Act 1993 which allows a court to consider any number of associated offences.
[93] Criminal Justice Act 1991, s. 1(2).

decision is that of the tariff: the length of prison sentence, the content of the community sentence or the amount of a fine. Under the framework, this has also to be "commensurate with the seriousness of the offence".[94]

There is another principle of social protection. Where the offence is sexual or violent (even if not that serious in itself), a custodial sentence of a particular length may be imposed if only such a sentence would be adequate to protect the public from serious harm from the offender.[95] For example, in *Hewson*,[96] a sentence of nine years was upheld for indecency with an eight-year-old boy. The record disclosed previous similar offences and there was medical evidence of a deep-rooted personality disorder.

There are certain key concepts embedded in the sentencing framework:

(a) the foremost principle is that of proportionality and seriousness. Despite other factors,[97] the twin pillars of the new sentencing framework are:
  (i) that neither a custodial nor a community sentence should be imposed unless the offence is so serious that the imposition of the lower band of sentence could not be justified.[98]
  (ii) that the length of the custodial sentence or the nature of the community sentence should be proportional to the seriousness of the offence.[99]

This is mandatory for the court which must address the question of seriousness. However, seriousness is not defined: in *Cox*,[1] the defendant, aged 18, pleaded guilty to theft of some tools and reckless driving. He was sentenced to four months detention. The Court of Appeal relied on Lawton L.J. in *Bradbourne*[2] where he had indicated that the term meant:

"... the kind of offence which when committed by a young person would make right-thinking members of the public, knowing all the facts, feel that justice had not been done by the passing of any sentence other than a custodial one ..."

The court felt that hurdle had been overcome in this case. Finding that an offence is sufficiently serious does not oblige a court to impose a custodial sentence. The court must subsequently take into account all information about the offence (including aggravating and mitigating circumstances) as is available to it.[3]

---

[94] *ibid.* s. 2(2)(a), s. 6(2)(b) and s. 18(2) (this latter is the amended section introduced by s. 65 of the Criminal Justice Act 1993).
[95] *ibid.*, s. 1(2)(b) and s. 2(2)(b).
[96] (1986) 8 Cr.App.R.(S.) 338.
[97] Such as protection of society and the impact of multiple offences and past convictions.
[98] Criminal Justice Act 1991, s. 1(2)(a) and s. 6(1).
[99] *ibid.* s. 2(2)(a) and s. 6(2).
[1] [1993] Crim.L.R. 152.
[2] (1985) 7 Cr.App.R.(S.) 180 (interpreting similar provisions in s. 1(4A)(a) Criminal Justice Act 1982).
[3] s. 3(3)(a) and s. 7(1)—in addition there is a fifth wheel on this coach since s. 28(1) permits the court to mitigate the sentence by reference to any matters that the court feels are relevant to sentence.

The focus on the seriousness of the offence should have outlawed considerations of general deterrence, prevalence of the offence or incapacitation. However, in *Cunningham*,[4] a robbery case, Taylor L.C.J. made it clear that seriousness could not be interpreted in a vacuum. The prevalence of the offence was a legitimate factor: whereas one violent sexual attack on a woman gravely harmed the victim, a series of attacks put women into fear and limited their freedom of movement and accordingly such an attack might be viewed even more seriously. Seriousness is not an abstraction but is a factor rooted in the material circumstances of the community.

Lord Taylor also felt that deterrence could enter into the determination of the length of a sentence. The aims of a custodial sentence are to punish and deter and the phrase "commensurate with the seriousness of the offence" must mean commensurate with the punishment and deterrence that the offence required. However, section 2(2)(a) did prohibit the "exemplary" sentence by which extra length is added to a sentence to make a special example of the offender.

The case law seriousness will inevitably build on the established sentencing jurisprudence of the Court of Appeal. Certain classes of offence have always been regarded as so serious that a prison sentence is inevitable[5]: attempted murder, serious wounding, rape,[6] drug trafficking or violent robbery.[7] Manslaughter presents specific difficulties because it can vary from a killing close to murder to events akin to accident. This is due to the operation of the "unlawful act" doctrine.[8]

A consensus exists of the "seriousness" of certain crimes where imprisonment is almost inevitable. There are other offences where there is less agreement. Seventy-nine per cent of residential burglaries attract a custodial sentence.[9] A few years ago this was in direct contrast to cases of causing death by reckless driving where only one in five offenders were imprisoned.[10] Similarly the courts are content to regard shoplifting as so serious that "only a custodial sentence could be justified".[11] The prisons are filled with property offenders who are neither violent nor frightening. In these marginal areas, the paucity of appellate guidelines is particularly felt.

The quality of the Court of Appeal's supervision over sentencing is

---

[4] [1993] 2 All E.R. 15.
[5] Ashworth (1992), *op. cit.*, p. 95 for a discussion of the relative seriousness of various offences.
[6] *Billam* (1986) 82 Cr.App.R. 347 established that the starting point was five years or eight years if any of the following factors were present—more than one attacker, entering the victim's home, attacker in position of trust or abduction of victim.
[7] Moxon, *op. cit.*, p. 21—he found that 80 per cent of robbers received custodial sentences with 45 months being the average length of sentence.
[8] *Church* [1966] 1 Q.B. 59.
[9] Moxon, *op. cit.*, p. 34.
[10] However, the Attorney-General's power to refer unduly lenient sentences to the Court of Appeal has led to non-custodial sentences being replaced by custodial ones—*Attorney-General's Reference No. 3 of 1989* (1989) 11 Cr.App.R.(S.) 486.
[11] *Goldrick* (1988) 10 Cr.App.R.(S.) 346.

most open to criticism at this level. Their decisions are often contradictory and of little help to the first instance court, especially in considering what weight to give to mitigating or aggravating factors.[12] Such factors might include the damage caused, the nature of the victim (especially if they are vulnerable or public officials), the numbers involved, the motive (attacks prompted by racialism will be treated more severely), any additional violence especially where weapons are involved, the planning (or lack of it), whether the offender was in a position of trust, the length of time over which the offence took place. Most of these can be in different guises as aggravating or, conversely, mitigating factors.

One aggravating factor that the court must take into account is whether the offence was committed while the offender was on bail on another charge.[13] The principle is that if a burglar on bail commits further burglaries before the initial trial, there should be at least a loss of any mitigation that might be called on. However, critics have pointed out that the wording of the statute contains no reference to the need for any logical link between the offences. Further, this legislation was introduced despite unpublished Home Office research which suggested that there had been no rise in the number of offences committed on bail over the past decade.[14]

One further aggravating factor may be a failure to respond to previous non-custodial penalties. In 1991, the view was that the central principle in sentencing should be the seriousness of the immediate offence and not the offender's previous record. This was reversed in 1993[15] and the court is now allowed, in deciding on the seriousness of an offence, to take into account any failure of the defendant to respond to sentences for previous offences. The logical connection between the seriousness of the instant offence and the defendant's past behaviour is far from obvious.[16]

(b) a second key area is when a defendant is convicted of multiple offences. The court has the option of making the sentences on different offences concurrent or consecutive.[17] Where the offences are broadly of the same type and at the same time, the sentences will be concurrent. However, there are exceptions so that charges involving a firearms offence,[18] an assault on a police officer[19] or perverting the course of justice[20] will often be sentenced consecutively regardless of whether they took place at the same time as other offences.

This is affected by the "totality" principle,[21] stated by Lawton L.J.:

---

[12] Ashworth (1992), *op. cit.*, Chap. 5.
[13] Introduced by s. 66(6) of the Criminal Justice Act 1993, substituting a new s. 29 in the Criminal Justice Act 1991.
[14] *The Guardian*, July 4, 1994, p. 1.
[15] Criminal Justice Act 1993, s. 66(6).
[16] Ashworth *et al.* (1994) *op. cit.*, p. 105.
[17] For further discussion, see Thomas (1979) *op. cit.*, p. 55; Ashworth (1992), *op. cit.*, p. 190.
[18] *Faulkner* (1972) 56 Cr.App.R. 594.
[19] *Kastercum* (1972) 56 Cr.App.R. 298.
[20] *Attorney-General's Reference No. 1 of 1990* (1990) 12 Cr.App.R.(S.) 245.
[21] Thomas (1979), *op. cit.*, p. 59.

"When cases of multiplicity of offences come before the court, the court must not content itself by doing the arithmetic and passing the sentence that the arithmetic produces. It must look at the totality of the criminal behaviour and ask itself what is the appropriate sentence for all the offences"[22]

Problems emerge; the logic of this would produce what Ashworth has called "a discount for bulk offending" and yet sentencing a multiple burglar to the same term as a rapist offends a moral sense. The sentencer is forced into pragmatic compromises so that the final sentence should bear a recognisable relationship to the sentence that would have been passed for the single most serious offence, and that no defendant should be faced with a crushing weight of sentence simply as a result of arithmetic.

The totality rule is endorsed by section 28(2) of the Criminal Justice Act 1991 which states that nothing in the Act should prevent a court "in the case of an offender who is convicted of one or more other offences, from mitigating his sentence by applying any rule of law as to the totality of offences".

The issue of sentencing multiple offenders is affected by the requirement to assess the seriousness of an offence under the provisions of the Criminal Justice Act 1991. Under similar legislation for young offenders in 1982, the Court of Appeal held that where there were multiple offences, these could not be aggregated to increase the seriousness of any single incident and thus warrant a custodial sentence.[23] In *Choudhary*,[24] the defendant used a stolen credit card in a series of small offences but overall obtained some £3,000. In that case, the detention order was quashed by the Court of Appeal.

This 1982 principle, focusing solely on the seriousness of the specific offence, was modified in 1991 so that the court, in assessing the seriousness of an offence, could consider that offence and one other associated with it. This applied not only in assessing seriousness in relation to custodial sentences but to community sentences also.[25] Despite the limited retreat, the prohibition on aggregating offences so as to increase overall seriousness still held. But this has now been altered by section 66(1) of the Criminal Justice Act 1993 which allows a court, in assessing seriousness, to take into account "... the offence, or the combination of the offence and one or more other offences associated with it ...". This reverses the previous policy and allows courts to aggregate offences, none of which would in themselves have been serious enough to warrant a custodial sentence, in order that a prison sentence can be imposed. It is doubtful whether the court in *Choudhary* would now reach the same result.

(c) multiple offenders are frequently petty recidivist offenders. How

---

[22] Quoted by Thomas (1979), *op. cit.*, p. 56.
[23] *Davison* (1989) 11 Cr.App.R.(S.) 570.
[24] (1992) 13 Cr.App.R.(S.) 290.
[25] Criminal Justice Act 1991, s. 1(2)(a), s. 2(2)(a) and s. 6(1).

should the courts treat the previous convictions of the defendant?[26] This has been a tortuous episode.[27] In 1991, under section 29(1) of the Criminal Justice Act, previous convictions were no longer to be taken into account in assessing the "seriousness" of an offence. This was qualified by section 29(2) so that if the circumstances of those other offences disclosed an aggravating feature[28] of the current offence, then that could be taken into account by the court in forming an opinion about the seriousness of that offence. Taylor L.C.J., in *Bexley*,[29] said that section 29(1) embodied a common law principle, but section 66(6) of the Criminal Justice Act 1993 reverses this[30] so that previous convictions and responses to earlier sentences can now be taken into account. Ashworth and Gibson comment that ". . . prisons may once again fill with people who have been sentenced on their record than for a serious offence".[31] The reinstatement of the cumulative principle inevitably means that we imprison more persistent petty offenders[32] and that prisons are used as dustbins for the inadequate, the nuisances and the difficult, rather than the dangerous.

(d) at last recognising the imperatives of natural justice, a court is obliged under section 1(4) to give reasons, in ordinary language, for its view that a custodial sentence is necessary. It remains to be seen whether judges[33] will ritually mouth the statutory formula or become more specific in their views on the "seriousness" criterion. Furthermore, will they reveal their calculations by identifying the base sentence and explaining what might have been added or subtracted for any mitigating or aggravating factors?

7.5.1 *The Decision to Imprison—An Outline Process*

After conviction or a guilty plea, if the court is considering imposing a custodial or community sentence, before making up its mind, the court must:

(a) obtain a pre-sentence report[34] and take it into account before making up its mind about whether a custodial sentence is justified, what the length of such a custodial sentence should be, whether a community sentence is justified and whether the offender is suitable for such a sentence.

---

[26] The problems of dealing with persistent offenders are well discussed in Ashworth (1992), *op. cit.*, Chap. 6.

[27] Radzinowicz and Hood, *op. cit.*, Parts 4 and 9.

[28] Examples might be where the circumstances of a previous burglary led to the conclusion that the immediate offence was a professional and calculated crime rather than an opportunistic one or where previous racially motivated offences mean that an attack on a black person is aggravated for that reason. See Gibson B. (ed.), *Criminal Justice Act 1991: Legal Points* (1992).

[29] (1993) 14 Cr.App.R.(S.) 462.

[30] Ashworth A. and Gibson B., "The Criminal Justice Act 1993—Altering the Sentencing Framework" [1994] Crim.L.R. 101.

[31] Ashworth *et al.* (1994), *op. cit.*, at p. 106.

[32] Fairhead S., *Persistent Petty Offenders* (Home Office Research Study No. 66) (1981).

[33] Spreutels J., "Giving Reasons for Sentence in the Crown Courts" [1980] Crim.L.R. 486.

[34] Criminal Justice Act 1991, s. 3(1) and s. 7(3).

(b) obtain information about the circumstances of the offence.[35]
(c) take into account any information about the offender which is before it. In deciding on a custodial sentence, this information is not relevant to the seriousness of the offence but is relevant to whether the offender presents a serious risk of harm to the public.[36] It is also relevant to whether the defendant is suitable for community sentence.[37]

Having obtained and taken into account this information, the court must then ask itself the following:

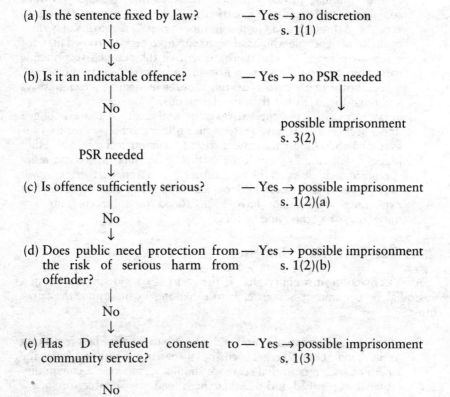

(a) Is the sentence fixed by law?   — Yes → no discretion
       | s. 1(1)
      No
       ↓

(b) Is it an indictable offence?   — Yes → no PSR needed
       | ↓
      No
       | possible imprisonment
       | s. 3(2)
   PSR needed
       ↓

(c) Is offence sufficiently serious?   — Yes → possible imprisonment
       | s. 1(2)(a)
      No
       ↓

(d) Does public need protection from — Yes → possible imprisonment
      the risk of serious harm from   s. 1(2)(b)
      offender?
       |
      No
       ↓

(e) Has D refused consent to — Yes → possible imprisonment
      community service?   s. 1(3)
       |
      No
       ↓

If the answer is "no" to all these questions, then the court must consider a non-custodial sentence: a discharge, fine or community sentence under s. 6

If the answer is "yes" to any of these questions, the court may choose to imprison and if it does, it must explain to the offender in open court and in ordinary language why it is passing a custodial sentence.[38]

---

[35] Criminal Justice Act 1991, s. 3(3)(a) and s. 7(1).
[36] *ibid.* s. 3(3)(b).
[37] *ibid.* s. 7(2).
[38] *ibid.* s. 1(4).

The length of sentence must be:

either: (a) commensurate with seriousness of offence (or a combination of the offence and other offences associated with it).[39]

or: (b) necessary to protect public from serious harm from the defendant.[40] Where such a term is longer than that commensurate with the seriousness of the offence, then the court must state its reasons why this section applies and explain to the offender in open court and in plain language why the sentence is for this term.[41]

7.5.1.1 SUSPENDED SENTENCES

Courts possess the power[42] to suspend a sentence of imprisonment of two years or less. The period during which it is suspended is between one and two years. If the offender re-offends during that period, the suspended sentence is activated unless the court feels that it would be unjust to do so.

Suspended sentences were introduced, along with parole, by the Criminal Justice Act 1967[43] against a background of a sharply rising prison population.[44] The pragmatic aim of the Government was to reduce prison population. This proved short-sighted. In 1968 there was an immediate drop of 20 per cent in the prison population as sentencers used suspended, as opposed to immediate, prison sentences. The population then rose again. This was due to a combination of factors: first, the suspended sentence was not being used purely as an alternative to imprisonment but was also employed in place of fines and probation orders; secondly, the courts gave longer suspended sentences than they would had custody been immediate. The effect was that the number of persons given either suspended or immediate sentences of imprisonment rose and when they re-offended, their suspended sentences were automatically activated. More people were imprisoned and for longer periods, mainly because of the psychology of the sentencers who felt that suspended imprisonment gave them more deterrence at no cost.

Although automatic activation was quickly removed, criticisms persisted that the suspended sentence was still used inappropriately since it was not always used as an alternative to imprisonment. It was also disproportionately employed in favour of middle-class offenders.[45] More significantly for modern policy-makers, the suspended sentence, if completed successfully, lacked any element of punishment apart from the stigma of the court appearance. Following the recommendations of the White Paper,[46] the

---

[39] *ibid.* s. 2(2)(a) (as amended).
[40] *ibid.* s. 2(2)(b).
[41] *ibid.* s. 2(3).
[42] Powers of Criminal Courts Act 1973, s. 22.
[43] Partially suspended sentences were introduced by s. 47 Criminal Law Act 1977. This was repealed by s. 5(2)(b) Criminal Justice Act 1991.
[44] Bottoms A., "The Suspended Sentence in England 1967–78" (1981) 21 Brit.J.Criminol. 1.
[45] Moxon, *op. cit.*, p. 35—especially for such offenders convicted in cases involving breach of trust.
[46] *Crime, Justice and Protecting the Public, op. cit.*, para. 3.20.

Criminal Justice Act 1991 restricted the conditions for suspending imprisonment: under section 5, the offence has to be one which is punishable by imprisonment and the suspension has to be justified by the exceptional circumstances of the case.[47] *Okinikan*[48] indicates that they should be exceptional and that good character, youth and an early plea are not exceptional by themselves or in combination. The impact of section 5 has to be considered in the context of the 1991 restrictions on the use of custody generally but in 1991 10 per cent of adult offenders sentenced for indictable offences received a suspended sentence. For the first three-quarters of 1992 the figure was 9 per cent but, by the final quarter of 1992, that was reduced to 3 per cent.[49]

Table 7.2 Types of Sentence (Nos. and Percentages) for adult males sentenced for indictable offences 1983, 1988 and 1993[50]

Type of Sentence	1983	1988	1993
Absolute or conditional discharge	18,400 (9%)	20,500 (10%)	33,000 (18%)
Fine	100,800 (47%)	86,600 (42%)	69,300 (38%)
Probation order	13,300 (6%)	16,000 (8%)	17,500 (10%)
Community Service Order	14,300 (7%)	14,200 (7%)	20,700 (11%)
Combination Order	n/a	n/a	3,500 (2%)
Fully suspended imprisonment	24,600 (11%)	24,700 (12%)	2,300 (1%)
Partly suspended imprisonment	3,500 (2%)	2,400 (1%)	n/a
Immediate imprisonment	38,100 (18%)	39,400 (19%)	32,100 (18%)
Otherwise dealt with	3,100 (1%)	3,600 (2%)	4,700 (3%)

[47] It can be combined with fines or compensation orders.
[48] [1993] 2 All E.R. 5.
[49] *Criminal Statistics 1992, op. cit.,* Table 7B, p. 139. This remained the case in 1993—*Criminal Statistics 1993, op. cit.,* Table 7A, p. 141.
[50] *Criminal Statistics 1993, op. cit.,* Table 7.12, p. 169.

Table 7.2—*cont.*

Type of Sentence	1983	1988	1993
ALL SENTENCES	216,200	207,400	183,100
Immediate custody	41,600 (19%)	41,900 (20%)	32,100 (18%)
Community sentences	27,600 (13%)	30,200 (15%)	41,700 (23%)

7.5.2 Non-Custodial Penalties

Throughout the 1980s,[51] the image of conservative criminal justice policy was that of strict social control: by 1990, expenditure on the criminal justice system had reached £7 billion per annum, a 77 per cent increase in real terms over 10 years and moving from 4 per cent to 6 per cent of total government spending; new offences had been introduced especially in the area of public order, football hooliganism and drugs and there had been no significant decriminalisation; police forces had been strengthened, in terms of personnel, legal powers and resources; a new, rationalised and "streamlined" prosecution process had been initiated; there had been a 25 per cent increase in the prison population and a building programme for 26 new prisons.

In the context of this policy, sentencers still remained wedded to custodial sentencing despite a broad range of non-custodial options. Those options, introduced in a piecemeal fashion, bear no obvious relationship to each other or to the sentencing process in terms of severity of punishment. Non-custodial penalties might fairly be said to be in some disarray. Yet at the start of the 1990s, the White Paper[52] and the Criminal Justice Act 1991 were concerned with reducing the prison population and developed a more coherent philosophy, not solely for imprisonment but also for non-custodial penalties. The latter were to be grouped as "community sentences" with stress on reparation and punishment in the community. The rhetoric remained that of punishment[53] with the aim of attaching a more punitive image to non-custodial sentences and making them acceptable to the public as punishment and not as a "slap-on-the-wrist". The emphasis was that probation and other community service should involve significant elements of reparation and intrusions into an offender's freedom. The White Paper[54] talked of restructuring community services to reflect the concept of graduated restrictions on liberty, consistent with the just deserts principle, from

---

[51] Brake M. and Hale C., *Public Order and Private Lives* (1992).
[52] *Crime, Justice and Protecting the Public, op. cit.*, (1990).
[53] *ibid.* para. 4.1.
[54] *ibid.* para. 4.7.

probation to community service to curfew orders. Despite this, the 1991 legislation did not introduce any radically new measures.

7.5.2.1 COMMUNITY SENTENCES

The 1991 legislation identified community sentences as a half-way house between fines and discharges on one hand and custodial sentences on the other. Such community orders are[55]:

(a) probation
(b) community service order
(c) combination order
(d) curfew order
(e) supervision order (for young offenders)
(f) attendance centre order (for young offenders)

The stages of sentencing are comparable to those for custodial sentencing:

(a) the community sentence can only be imposed where the "seriousness" threshold, has been crossed and the court believes that the offence was serious enough to warrant such a sentence.[56] Otherwise the court should content itself with financial or other penalties. The seriousness of the immediate offence is the focus for the sentencing decision and deterrence should no longer be a factor in sentencing. Increasing penalties for repeat convictions should, in theory, be a thing of the past.
(b) the community order should be one most suitable for the offender.[57] The court must obtain a PSR before forming an opinion about the suitability of the offender for probation, community service, a combination order or a supervision order.[58] The court must also take into account any other information about the offender that is before it.[59]
(c) the restrictions on liberty imposed by the order (*i.e.* the type and length) must be commensurate with the seriousness of the offence.[60]

The court is thus expected to balance the needs of the offender with denunciation marking the seriousness of the offence. Through the type and length of order, the court is expected to impose a punitive calculus tempered by some attention to the needs of the defendant. It must take all information about the circumstances of the offence (including mitigating and aggravating factors) into account[61] before forming an opinion about how serious the offence is or what restrictions on liberty would be appropriate.

The 1991 Act[62] brings together existing provisions for enforcement of community orders so that generally breach of the requirements can lead to a

---

[55] Criminal Justice Act 1991, s. 6(4).
[56] *ibid.* s. 6(1).
[57] *ibid.* s. 6(2)(a).
[58] *ibid.* s. 7(3).
[59] *ibid.* s. 7(2).
[60] *ibid.* s. 6(2)(b).
[61] *ibid.* s. 7(1).
[62] Schedule 2.

fine, a community service order of not more than 60 hours, an attendance centre order (for breach of a probation order) or the original community order can be revoked and the court can pass any sentence which it could have passed for the original offence. Wilful breach of conditions can be seen as refusal of consent to the order and that refusal of consent enables a court to impose a custodial sentence.[63] A further offence does not mean automatic revocation of the order although it may lead to this.

7.5.2.2 PROBATION

Probation orders were first introduced for adults in 1908 and have a tradition rooted in reform of the offender and social work. The modern probation service adopts a less treatment-oriented approach with greater stress on the offender confronting his or her behaviour, on self-reliance and self-discipline which some commentators[64] see as compatible with the individuality and autonomy of the offender.[65]

Prior to 1991, probation orders were only available for those over 17 but the court can now make an order for offenders aged over 16. They can be for a minimum of six months and a maximum of three years. It must be with the consent of the offender and the court must be of the opinion that probation will lead to the rehabilitation or the offender, or will protect the public from harm from him, or prevent the commission by him of further offences.[66] It is now a sentence of the court.[67] The offender will be under the supervision of a probation officer. Eleven per cent breached the order in 1993, 37 per cent of whom were sentenced to immediate custody.[68] However, since about one third of offenders on probation have already served a custodial sentence, the fact that over 80 per cent of probationers complete an average of two years on probation successfully is a considerable achievement.

There can be conditions attached to the order[69] which can be used both to provide the punitive restrictions on liberty as well as ensuring that the order is tailored to the needs of the individual:

(a) to undergo psychiatric treatment.[70]
(b) to live in a particular place (including probation hostels).
(c) to attend a day training centre,[71] now renamed "probation centre". Such centres have regimes which combine skills, learning, discussion, counselling and therapy sessions with the objectives of confronting offenders with their offending and making them tackle their problems.

[63] Criminal Justice Act 1991, s. 1(3).
[64] McWilliams W. and Pease K., "Probation Practice and an End to Punishment" (1990) 29 Howard J. Crim. Just. 14.
[65] For a discussion for these changes, Ashworth (1992), *op. cit.*, p. 260.
[66] Powers of Criminal Courts Act 1973, s. 2(1), as amended by s. 8 Criminal Justice Act 1991.
[67] s. 8 Criminal Justice Act 1991—previously it was an order made instead of sentencing. The significance of this is that the court can combine probation with a fine or another community order.
[68] *Criminal Statistics 1993*, *op. cit.*, Table 7.28, p. 187.
[69] Powers of Criminal Courts Act 1973, s. 3, as amended by s. 9 Criminal Justice Act 1991.
[70] Ashworth A. and Gostin L., "Mentally Disordered Offenders and the Sentencing Process" [1984] Crim.L.R. 195.
[71] Created by the Criminal Justice Act 1972 after recommendations in the Wootton Report—

(d) to undertake "specified activities" for no more than 60 days so that the offender takes part in schemes and activities organised by the probation service.

(e) to participate in drug or alcohol rehabilitation schemes.

(f) negatively not to undertake particular activities at particular times.

7.5.2.3 COMMUNITY SERVICE ORDERS

Community service orders were introduced by the Criminal Justice Act 1972 after recommendations in the Wootton Report.[72] These are available only for offenders aged 16 and over and require the offender to undertake unpaid work in the community usually organised by the probation service. After an initial assessment period, offenders will spend weekends painting and decorating old people's houses, helping in youth clubs, cleaning out canals. Some of the work must be manual. The work will normally be supervised by people employed by the probation service. The minimum number of hours is 40 and the maximum 240.[73] The court must be satisfied on the general criteria for making a community sentence and that the offender is a suitable person for such work. The offender must consent to the making of the order. It can be combined with a fine.[74]

The structure of CSOs was left unchanged in 1991 but there was a move away from any rehabilitative ethic and towards punishment so that the seriousness of the offence was matched by the number of hours of volunteer work. The 1991 Act also established that CSOs are community sentences in their own right, representing considerable restrictions on liberty. No longer are they presented as an alternative to custody. They are also recognised as the high tariff end of non-custodial measures.[75]

That punitive aspect was stressed in the 1989 National Standards.[76] Enforcement was to be more effective and procedures for offenders to keep in touch with supervisors were to be tightened up. Three unexplained absences would lead to the offender being returned to court. As number on CSOs have risen,[77] more orders have been breached: 24 per cent in 1993 as opposed to 16 per cent in 1983, but only 18 per cent of those were sentenced to immediate custody as opposed to 37 per cent in 1983.[78] The courts were thus adjudicating on more cases of breached CSOs but still not sentencing any more, in absolute numbers, to imprisonment.

7.5.2.4 COMBINATION ORDERS

The 1991 Act allows the court to impose one or more community orders[79] (a curfew order linked with community service, for example). However,

---

Advisory Council on the Penal System: *Non-Custodial and Semi-Custodial Penalties* (1970); Mair G., *Probation Day Centres* (Home Office Research Study No. 100) (1988).

[72] Advisory Council on the Penal System, *op. cit.*

[73] It was raised to 240 for 16-year-olds by s. 10(2) of the Criminal Justice Act 1991.

[74] Criminal Justice Act 1991, s. 10(1).

[75] Moxon, *op. cit.*, p. 45.

[76] The standards are laid down in Home Office Circular 18/1989.

[77] See *supra*, Table 7.2.

[78] *Criminal Statistics 1993, op. cit.*, Table 7.28, p. 187.

[79] Criminal Justice Act 1991, s. 6(1).

section 11 provides a new sentencing measure, the combination order, with elements of community service and probation. This is aimed at offenders whom the courts believe should make reparation through community service but who also need supervision to tackle their problems. The minimum period is 12 months rather than the usual probation minimum of six months and the maximum number of CSO hours are 100 as opposed to 240. It must be with the consent of the offender and the court must be of the opinion that the order will lead to the rehabilitation of the offender, or will protect the public from harm from him, or prevent the commission by him of further offences.[80]

7.5.2.5 CURFEW ORDERS

Curfew orders were introduced in 1991[81] and require the offender to remain at a specified place[82] for a specified time of between two and twelve hours per day. They may be imposed on their own or with the requirement of electronic monitoring.[83] There is flexibility to specify different lengths of time for different days and places. The overall maximum length is for six months with a maximum daily period twelve hours, either as a block or in sets of shorter periods totalling no more than twelve hours. The minimum period is two hours in one day. The court must avoid conflict with religious observance, the requirements of any other community sentence and employment or educational obligations. A person must be made responsible for monitoring the offender's whereabouts and the court must obtain information about the place where the offender will be placed under curfew and the attitude of those likely to be affected by the enforced presence of the offender.

The curfew order is only practical if there is effective enforcement and the only realistic way that has been suggested has been through electronic tagging. This raises issues as whether such a system is ethical since it involves a significant intrusion into the offender's dignity and privacy.[84] The other issue is more practical; do electronic tags work and does the capital cost involved make them worthwhile? Research has raised several question marks about the failure rate of the equipment and the feasibility of creating a nationwide structure.[85]

7.5.3 *Other Non-custodial penalties*

Once custody and community sentences have been considered and rejected, the court has a range of other penalties:

---

[80] *ibid.* s. 11(2).

[81] *ibid.* s. 12.

[82] Under s. 12(6) of the Criminal Justice Act 1991 the court must consider the attitude of other people who will be affected by the offenders' enforced presence, presumably at home! The court must also avoid impact on religious beliefs, work, school and the performance of other community orders.

[83] Criminal Justice Act 1991, s. 13.

[84] Von Hirsch A. "The Ethics of Community Sanctions" (1990) 36 *Crime and Delinquency* 162.

[85] Mair G. and Nee C., *Electronic Monitoring* (Home Office Research Study No. 120).

7.5.3.1 DISCHARGES

Discharges can be of two types, either absolute or conditional. An absolute discharge is the least severe of all disposals and does not even count as a conviction. It is used where the court considers that no penalty is required reflecting the triviality of the offence, the circumstances in which it came to be prosecuted or factors relating to the offender.[86]

A conditional discharge also imposes no immediate penalty on the offender who, however, remains liable to punishment for the offence if convicted of another offence within a set period, not exceeding three years. This re-sentencing is not automatic. In 1993, there were nearly 112,000 conditional discharges, being used in 5 per cent of Crown Court cases and 19 per cent of Magistrates' Courts cases. Of these, only 9 per cent were brought back to court for breach of the order.[87]

7.5.3.2 BINDING OVER ORDERS

Under the Justices of the Peace Act 1361, any person (whether charged with an offence or not) can be bound over to keep the peace. The person enters into a recognisance for a certain sum of money to be of good behaviour. It is a sort of conditional fine which is liable to be forfeited if there is a breach of the order. The person need not have been convicted of any offence to be bound over: in *Lansbury v. Riley*,[88] George Lansbury was making speeches on behalf of Women's Social and Political Union, advocating militant action. The binding-over order effectively prevented him from speaking. The lack of clear boundaries and the inconsistency with which it is applied has led to calls for the abolition of this order.[89]

7.5.3.3 DEFERMENT OF SENTENCE

A court can of course postpone sentencing for reports to be prepared. It also has the power to defer sentencing for up to six months.[90] This was introduced by section 22 of the Criminal Justice Act 1972,[91] again as a result of recommendations in the Wootton Report. The purpose is to allow the court to have regard to the offender's conduct after conviction, especially to changes in circumstances, for example, where the offender is starting a new job. In the guideline judgment in *George*,[92] it was made clear that there should be no other way of dealing with the offender and that the court should be specific, preferably in writing, about its expectations as to the offender's conduct over the six month period of deferment.

---

[86] Wasik M., "The Grant of an Absolute Discharge" (1985) 5 *Oxford Jour. Legal Studies* 211.
[87] *Criminal Statistics 1993, op. cit.*, Table 7.28, p. 187.
[88] [1914] 3 K.B. 229.
[89] Morgan N., "Binding Over: the Law Commission Working Paper" [1988] Crim.L.R. 355.
[90] Corden J. and Nott D., "The Power to Defer Sentence" 20 Brit.J.Criminol. 358 (1980).
[91] Now Powers of Criminal Courts Act 1973, s. 1.
[92] (1984) 6 Cr.App.R.(S.) 211.

7.5.3.4 FINES

This is the most common form of sentences in magistrates' courts: 91 per cent of motoring offences, 85 per cent of other summary offences and 41 per cent of indictable offences were disposed of by magistrates' fines in 1993. In Crown Courts in 1993, the relative figures were 23 per cent, 19 per cent and 5 per cent. For all courts, 78 per cent of all offenders were fined.[93] However, there has been a steep decline in the proportional use of the fine for indictable offences from 50.6 per cent in 1978 to 34 per cent in 1993.[94]

A fine is a possible sentence in any case where sentence is not fixed by statute. At common law, the maximum is unlimited although magistrates have a normal ceiling of £5000. With statutory crimes, the maximum will be specified by the legislation. Over the last 20 years, a system of fine levels (1–5) has been introduced with each offence allocated to a particular level and a maximum amount laid down for each level.

The great advantage of the fine is its flexibility. It can be related to the seriousness of the offence. The problem comes with the offenders' means to pay. Prior to 1991, a court could mitigate the amount for offenders of limited means (*Fairbairn*[95]) but not increase it. In 1991, following a number of other jurisdictions which had introduced "day fines",[96] the Criminal Justice Act created a new system of "unit fines" in magistrates' courts.[97] The impact was a rise in the proportionate use of the fine, most apparent among the unemployed. Although the average fine remained the same, this masked a rise in the level of fines for the employed and a decline for fines for the unemployed.[98] However, there was public criticism[99] and although the Magistrates' Association, among others, felt that such complaints confirmed a need for fine-tuning the system and not abolishing it, the entire commendable reform was swept away in 1993[1] and fining returned to its previous diversity.[2]

Now the magistrates must ensure that the amount of the fine reflects the seriousness of the offence.[3] The Magistrates' Association's guidelines suggest certain "entry points" (*e.g.* £180 for careless driving), after which the court should consider mitigating and aggravating factors. After that, the court is

---

[93] *Criminal Statistics 1993, op. cit.*, Table 7.1, p. 153.
[94] *Criminal Statistics 1993, op. cit.*, Table 7.3, p. 157.
[95] (1980) 2 Cr.App.R.(S.) 315.
[96] Grebing G., *The Fine in Comparative Law* (1982).
[97] There were maximum units for each level of offence (two for level 1 and 50 for level 5) and the offender would be sentenced to a set number of units. The amount was assessed by multiplying units by the offender's weekly disposable income.
[98] Home Office Statistical Bulletin, "Monitoring of the Criminal Justice Act 1991" (Issue 25/93).
[99] If offenders did not reveal their means, there was an assumption that they possessed the maximum disposable income—this led to some notorious cases of very large fines for dropping crisp packets! There was a case for increasing the court's discretion.
[1] 1993, s. 65 Criminal Justice Act.
[2] For criticism, see Ashworth (1994), *op. cit.*, at p. 106.
[3] Criminal Justice Act 1991, s. 18(2) (as amended by Criminal Justice Act 1993).

obligated to inquire into the offender's financial circumstances and take account of these in fixing the amount of the fine.[4]

These financial circumstances can have the effect of reducing and increasing the fine[5] and this is an important change to the pre-1991 law.[6]

The Crown Court was never covered by the unit fine system but has power to increase or to reduce the level of fine by taking into account offender's means. Such fines can be very high.[7]

Courts do have the power to allow time to pay fines,[8] with the ultimate resort being imprisonment. Although periods in prison are quite short, fine defaulters place a significant burden on prison service resources:

Table 7.3 Population and Reception of Fine Defaulters 1982–1992[9]

Year	Average daily population	Annual receptions	Average time served (men)
1982	909	24,492	14.1 days
1987	626	18,723	10.9 days
1992	382	19,826	7.3 days

Since there was a link between default, unemployment and committal to prison,[10] the unit fine system should have seen a further decline. Ethically, this seemed correct since if a person is unable to pay a fine, it is unjust that a term of imprisonment should be served for an offence which was not serious enough for custody. Pragmatically, the prison processing of fine defaulters places considerable unnecessary pressure on prison resources. It seems an extraordinary and short-sighted decision to sweep away a system which had only just been inaugurated with the consequent risk of injustice to the poor and of increasing the prison population.

Fines have always been seen as effective since there is a lower number of re-convictions than with other disposals. This face-value analysis has been doubted[11] since the courts tend to select those offenders for fining whose

---

[4] *ibid.* s. 18(1) and (3).
[5] *ibid.* s. 18(5).
[6] *Fairbairn, supra.*
[7] *Ronson* [1991] Crim.L.R. 794 where a fine of £5m was imposed.
[8] Morgan R. and Bowles R., "Fines: Where does Sentencing End and Enforcement Begin?" [1983] Crim.L.R. 203; Morris A. and Gelsthorpe A., "Not Paying for Crime: Issues in Fine Enforcement" [1990] Crim.L.R. 839.
[9] *Prison Statistics 1992*, Cm. 2581. Table 7.1, p. 114.
[10] NACRO: Fines and Fine Default (Briefing No. 72) (1990).
[11] Bottoms A., "The Efficacy of the Fine: the Case for Agnosticism" [1973] Crim.L.R. 543.

other characteristics in terms of employment, community and family ties would indicate stability in their lives and little chance of re-offending.

7.5.3.5 COMPENSATION ORDERS

Compensation orders are available where an offence has caused loss or damage. The offender may be required to pay compensation. It may be the only sentence or it may be in addition to another sentence. If the offender is under 16, the parent must pay. If the offender is over 16, the court may order the parent to pay. In determining the amount of compensation, the court should have regard to the offender's (or the parents') means.[12] In 1993, 96,500 offenders were ordered to pay compensation orders, 14 per cent of all offenders sentenced, though it was the sole or main penalty for under 1 per cent. In magistrates' courts, the average compensation was £173 while in Crown Courts, it was £1,175.[13]

---

[12] Guidance on assessment of compensation is to be found in Home Office Circular 85/1988.
[13] *Criminal Statistics 1993, op. cit.* Table 7.24, p. 182.

CHAPTER EIGHT

The Prison System of England and Wales

8.1 INTRODUCTION

We are accustomed to imprisonment as the primary technique of state punishment. The "mission statement" of the prison department, well-publicised in all prison establishments, reads:

> "Her Majesty's Prison Service serves the public by keeping in custody those committed by the courts. Our duty is to look after them with humanity and to help them lead law-abiding and useful lives in custody and after release."[1]

There is a chameleon quality about prisons; they are expected to be the visible manifestation of the punishment, to protect the public by incapacitation and to provide humane and constructive containment. Many people would also expect them to operate regimes which were severe enough to act as a deterrent. It is an uneasy balancing act especially as different government

---

[1] This has been criticised for failing to mention an obligation to treat prisoners with justice—*Prison Disturbances April 1990, Report of an Inquiry by Lord Justice Woolf*. Cm. 1456, (1991) (henceforth Woolf) para. 10.4; Richardson G., *Law, Process and Custody: Prisoner and Patients* (1993), p. 72.

reports adopt different focuses: after the Mountbatten Report,[2] the emphasis was on security and control; the May Committee[3] encouraged the ideas of "positive custody"; the Woolf Report[4] recognised the juggling act between security (prevention of escapes), control (prevention of disturbances) and justice (provision of humane and fair regime for prisoners).

The Woolf review foresaw a future for the prison service which contained:

(a) relatively small prisons with populations less than 400,[5] internally divided into units of 70–80, with much closer links to the community and to the prisoner's families. Prisoners should be entitled to a single cell and improved physical conditions, especially in relation to integral sanitation.

(b) prison management where the governors exercise greater authority and act in a contractual relationship with the central prison department, consequently with clearer expectations and obligations.

(c) regimes that are more purposeful with improved facilities for physical exercise, employment and pay as well as education. The opportunities for bitterness should be removed: improved standards in terms of clothing and food, better opportunities for visits and home leave, as well as family visits for long-termers; better access to telephones and a reduction in censorship. By ensuring that prisoners were treated with fairness inside, Woolf felt that prisoners were less likely to leave embittered and disaffected with the consequent hope that they were less likely to re-offend.

(d) the appointment of a prison ombudsman and an improved system for the redress of grievances would remove the inmate's sense of impotence when faced with adverse decisions.

(e) the sense of purpose should be addressed by more and better sentence planning and the introduction of personal officers for all prisoners.

In significant ways, this programme is being carried into effect. However, the underlying assumptions in the Woolf Report are opposed to those of an administration whose policy is to concentrate on containment of an increasing population in even more austere conditions.

8.2 A BRIEF HISTORY OF PUNISHMENT

The British use prison considerably and yet this emphasis on imprisonment is far from universal: on one hand, many cultures still employ savage capital and corporal punishments; on the other, there are nations which imprison much less than ourselves. The Netherlands[6] have a prison population of less than a half (per head of population) than that in the United Kingdom. The United States has a prison population of about 1 million, much higher than any European country.

Historically,[7] imprisonment was never seen as a "solution" to wrongs. In

---

[2] *Report of the Inquiry into Prison Escapes and Security* Cmnd. 3175 (1966).
[3] *Report of the Inquiry into the United Kingdom Prison Services* (1981) Cmnd. 7673.
[4] Woolf, *op. cit.*
[5] There are currently over 30 establishments well in excess of this target figure.
[6] See Table 8.7 *infra*.
[7] Harding C., *et al.*, *Imprisonment in England and Wales, A Concise History* (1985); McConville S., *The History of Prison Administration* (1981).

early Germanic and Anglo-Saxon communities, wrongs were regarded as private matters to be dealt with by the wrongdoer (and his family) and the victim. Retribution was a matter of compensation and there were graduated lists of the "damages" payable for different harms to different victims. Imprisonment was seen as a method of inducing the offender to pay up but not as a punishment in itself.

State involvement was minimal and appears to have remained so until at least the twelfth century and it is difficult to make out a "criminal" justice system or state-regulated punishment before that time. The development of that regulation correlates with the development of the functions and role of king. Punishment is used not just as a mechanism of controlling the king's enemies but also as representing royal power and authority.

8.2.1 *Capital and Corporal Punishment*

The ability to impose your will on the body of another—to detain, dictate movements, maim or even kill—is one way in which individuals seek to demonstrate their power. It can occur within families, factories, schools as well as through the sanctions of the criminal court. The ability to use other peoples' bodies as objects is a powerful symbol. It is not simple force. Foucault suggests that we know about ourselves and our society through such representations of power:

> "... there is no power relation without the correlative constitution of a field of knowledge, nor any knowledge that does not presuppose and constitute at the same time power relations."[8]

The "right" of the husband to batter the wife or the slave-owner to chain the slave emphasises not only individual relationships but also embodies social relationships, whether of class, gender or race. Punishment is also significant in political terms. The right to use and abuse the bodies of others is a symbol of absolute power and an affirmation of sovereignty. The emergence of state punishment correlates with the changing conception of kingship. No longer the *primus inter pares* that was common among Saxon tribes, the Angevin monarchs were moving towards a new idea of sovereignty.[9] This was manifested in religious terms as the king was "God's anointed", in terms of blood relationships and primogeniture, in his position as the supreme landholder in feudal tenure and as the fount of justice. The monopoly over executions, in particular, was symbolic of that supremacy and only as a matter of royal favour would feudal lords be allowed to hang thieves.

To what extent did the Angevin monarchs develop a "New Punishment" which used the body as an object of expression? In the Anglo-Saxon period, the laws of the kings might stipulate capital punishment for a wrong and many crimes could be paid for with death.[10] In Alfred's reign, lords are holding court and hanging thieves.[11] Alfred's laws, though, permit

---

[8] Foucault M., *Discipline and Punish* (1977), p. 127.
[9] Barlow F., "The Holy Crown" in Barlow F. (ed.), *The Norman Conquest and Beyond* (1983), p. 3.
[10] Pollock and Maitland, *History of English Law* (2nd ed., 1898), Vol. II, p. 452.
[11] Cam H., "The Evolution of the Medieval English Franchise" in *Speculum*, Vol. 32, (1958) p. 427 at 430.

redemption through fine except for treason to one's lord which is unatonable. Clearly the king had influence over the nature of the penalties inflicted; Aethelred was against capital punishment and Wihtrehd instituted selling malefactors into slavery beyond the seas as an alternative to death. Discretion was vested in the king as to the nature of the punishment.[12] Still composition might be made: even at the time of Cnut for whom secret killing was unatonable, the killer was handed over to the kindred of the victim.

After 1066, little seems to change. Despite his reputation for severity, William I, in several cases, substituted mutilation for the death penalty; castration was introduced for rapists.[13] Although conspiring against the king was punishable by death, various Norman rebels were not put to death[14] and the gallows were spoken of as an "English institution". Henry I also has a reputation for severity, legislating on theft and restoring capital punishment in 1108.[15] This reputation rests on certain acts of mutilation, castrating and chopping off the right hands of minters[16] and blinding three captive rebels. In 1125, there is the story of royal justice, Ralph Bassett, hanging 44 thieves at Huntingdon in a single day.

There is an obscurity about the history of punishment, until the mid-twelfth century, which reflects the long tradition of dealing with wrongs as a private affair. Formalised state violence, and the royal monopoly to inflict that violence, gradually emerges. In Henry II's reign, corporal punishments were stiffened under the Assize of Northampton in 1176, execution supplanted the *wite*[16a] and composition became more difficult. Glanvil suggested that agreements with malefactors were no longer possible and certainly a composition with a thief in itself became a crime. Killings remained a different matter: many never proceeded beyond the local level since the prosecutor discontinued the suit, presumably having been bought off by the defendant. Appeals of rape were also brought to encourage the proposal of marriage.[17] Throughout the thirteenth century, there was considerable latitude permitted (if not official encouragement)[18] in the buying off of prosecutions. The major exception to this policy seems to have been in the area of theft and robbery since the prosecutor that brought a suit could recover his property but if he sought to make an agreement with the thief, he could himself be prosecuted.

Given's[19] study of thirteenth century killings reveals that, although there was formal royal control, it is an illusion that all criminals would face the death penalty. Relatively few were executed and composition in cases of violence was common. Given's sample[20] comprised 3,492 identified killings

---

[12] Pollock and Maitland, *op. cit.*, Vol. II, p. 461.

[13] Laws c. 5, 9, 10.

[14] Pollock and Maitland, *op. cit.*, Vol. I, p. 74, n. 3.

[15] *ibid.* p. 96.

[16] Warren Hollister, "Royal Acts of Mutilation" in *Albion* (1978), Vol. 10, pp. 330–340—the culprits had attacked a central symbol of sovereignty, the control of the coinage. At a time when communications were rudimentary, the king's head on the coin embodied royal authority throughout the kingdom. False coining was treason and political authority was at stake.

[16a] In essence, a fine to the King.

[17] Kaye J. M., "Survey of the History of the Criminal Law up to 1500" [1977] Crim.L.R., p. 1.

[18] Both Glanvil and Bracton, good public servants, suggest that compensation is not a possibility.

[19] Given J., *Society and Homicide* (1977).

[20] *ibid.* Chap. 5.

in some sort of court proceeding of which only 247 (7.1 per cent) were found to have been executed, mainly at general eyres and gaol deliveries. Interestingly 20 were hanged at courts held by local lords but such communal/seigniorial executions were seen as usurpations of the king's power, and the courtholder was amerced.[21]

Hanawalt's study[22] of the first half of the fourteenth century bears out this pattern over a broader range of crimes. Prerogatives of local courts such as "infangthef" (the right to hang thieves caught in the act) were being discouraged. It was royal justice but the "royal" justices on gaol delivery were themselves often the local landowners. Once convicted and sentenced to death, there was little time for reflection or appeal since 99 per cent of executions were carried out within two days of sentence. Overall, there is little evidence of mutilations or excessive hangings. Even after the Black Death, the drastic reforms that were instituted to reduce mobility of labour and wage-bargaining merely relied on short periods of imprisonment, or the stocks, as deterrents.[23]

It is the sixteenth century which sees a dramatic increase in the severity of punishment.[24] The vagrants shall be:

> "... had to the next market town, or other place where they (the constables) shall think most convenient, and there to be tied to the end of a cart naked, and to be beaten with whips throughout the same market town or other place, till his body be bloody by reason of such whipping."[25]

Mutilation and branding of vagrants followed and, under Elizabeth, vagabonds were strung up in rows, "as many as three or four hundred at a time".[26] It is the disintegration of feudal society in the sixteenth century that coincides with an enormous increase in capital punishment. The gallows dominate the face of punishment for several centuries. Nor is it necessarily a simple hanging and there was a whole technology bound up with the form of execution.[27] In 1819, the anti-capital punishment campaigner, Buxton, suggested that there were 223 offences punishable by death in England and there were wide variations in how that sentence might be carried out: being dragged to the scaffold at the end of a horse's tail; being strangled, mutilated and disembowelled; being burnt alive.

Punishment could not rest simply on its quality of terror. It had to be seen as part of the rule of law[28] and in the eighteenth century executions occur less and less frequently. The power to commute the sentence of death through pardons and to substitute imprisonment or transportation was an important aspect of the ideology of the law. It also constituted power relationships within society, no longer symbolising the authority of the king as an individual but of the state and of the class that administered it.

---

[21] *ibid*. p. 94.

[22] Hanawalt B., *Crime and Conflict 1300–1348* (1979).

[23] Chambliss W., "The Law of Vagrancy" in Chambliss W. (ed.), *Crime and Legal Process* (1969), p. 51.

[24] *ibid*. p. 56.

[25] 22 Henry VIII c. 12 (1530).

[26] Rusche G. and Kircheimer O., *Punishment and Social Structure* (1939), p. 19.

[27] Foucault, *op. cit.*, pp. 1–3 for a description of the execution of the regicide, Damiens.

[28] Hay D., "Property, Authority and the Criminal Law" in Hay D., *et al.* (eds), *Albion's Fatal Tree* (1975).

8.2.2 *From Gallows to Penitentiary*

In the nineteenth century came the gradual metamorphosis of punishment. The spectacle of the gallows and the birch gave way to the penitentiary and the cell. Retribution was now to take the form of hidden administrative correction through deprivation of liberty. It was no longer the body, but the soul and the personality that was the object of punishment.

Prisons had existed in medieval England but not as a punishment, as a holding system. The early judges were given commissions by the king of "*oyer et terminer*" (to hear and decide) and of "gaol delivery" (emptying the gaols). The real punishments were corporal and capital. But from the seventeenth century, judges were commuting death penalties on the condition that the person sailed beyond the seas. Transportation to the colonies had begun and, in 1767, judges were statutorily empowered to order this.[29] However, the American War of Independence started in 1776 and although the penal colonies were switched to Australia, those colonies were soon objecting to the practice. Transportation formally ended in 1867 but well before then, the convict transportation ships were moored along the Thames estuary, providing accommodation for convicts who emerged during the day to labour on public work projects.

Confinement as punishment rather than just as a holding system had some earlier roots. In the sixteenth century, under Edward VI, there was the emergence of the bridewells (named after the palace donated by the king in 1553) for the reformation of vagrants. By 1576, all J.P.s were ordered to provide such houses of correction, with work at proper rates of pay, religious instruction and discipline. The model was the Rasphuis in Amsterdam. Yet these became indistinguishable from the prisons and the penal labour became the uppermost motive although the two systems remained formally separate until 1866.

Early prisons were farmed out on a franchise, profit-making basis. In the eighteenth century, 50 per cent of the prisons were privately owned. The duty of the gaoler was to deliver the prisoner to the court in whatever condition. There was little differentiation on grounds of age or sex and there was little food except that brought in by relatives and friends. In 1729, a Parliamentary Commission found 350 prisoners starving to death in Marshalsea prison. Prisons were also insanitary; gaol fever was a recognised disease and at the Black Assize in Oxford in 1577, 500 people died. Each prison had its own tap and the owners of the prisons made their profits from sale of alcohol although they might also sell better quarters or easement of irons.

The prison reform movement, if not prison reform, started in the eighteenth century,[30] spearheaded by religious non-conformists and utilitarian social reformers. John Howard published *State of the Prisons* in 1777, a damning indictment of the system. A Penitentiary Act was passed but little constructive happened. The Napoleonic Wars and economic depression pushed prison reform way down any list of priorities. Any improvement was the result of individual efforts such as Elizabeth Fry's re-organisation of the women's side at Newgate.

---

[29] Hibbert C., *The Roots of Evil* (1978), pp. 161–172.
[30] For an account of this period, Ignatieff M., *A Just Measure of Pain* (1978).

By the start of the nineteenth century, the situation can be summarised as follows:

(a) there was capital and corporal punishment.
(b) there were "convict" prisons administered by central government and consisting of the hulks and the penitentiary at Millbank, built in 1813.
(c) there were the local gaols and bridewells (now scarcely distinguishable) administered by the J.P.s.

However, across the Atlantic, the prison cell was the real alternative to execution. The Quakers in Pennsylvania instituted their prisons on the "solitary system" in which the prisoner was confined to his cell, unable to see out, taking exercise alone, working alone, reading the bible and meditating on his sins. Even the church service would be in the cell with the face of the chaplain hidden behind a black cloth. The New Yorkers evolved a more economic alternative to this known as the "silent system"; prisoners were allowed to work in association but in strict silence, discipline was rigorously enforced, eyes kept down and faces turned to the wall if a guard or visitor passed by, good behaviour was rewarded with tobacco, letters, visits and possibly commutation of sentence.[31]

In England, the early nineteenth century saw great changes to the criminal justice system, including abolition of many capital punishment offences. It also saw prison reform. In 1823, Peel introduced his Gaol Act in an effort to bring some semblance of order: secure and sanitary accommodation; making gaolers into salaried officials accountable to local government; visiting justices with statutory duties to inspect. In 1835, a group of prison inspectors was created and, in 1842, the first penitentiary was built at Pentonville. The brave new world was still some way off since prisoners walked around with hoods over their faces, undertook meaningless and degrading labour and had a mental illness rate of grotesque proportions. In the central prisons, there were some moves towards progressive stages and, although an inmate might start in solitary confinement, he would move on to labour in association and finally to release through the "ticket of leave" system. The Penal Servitude Act 1853 encouraged this as well as classifying prisoners into "star" (on first offender) and the rest. Overall, it was a punitive and deterrent regime, characterised by hard and monotonous labour, the tone of which was set by the Carnarvon Committee, set up in 1863, in the wake of the garrotting panic; reform and imprisonment were contradictions and its watchcry was "hard labour, hard fare and a hard bed".

In the middle of the century, responsibility for prisons was still split between the central prisons under the Home Office and 193[32] local prisons under the control of local authorities. Statutes in 1865 and 1877 swept away the powers exercised by local authorities and all prisons were placed under the Prison Commissioners who were responsible to the Home Secretary and Parliament. Du Cane became the head of the Commissioners and introduced a regime of unparalleled severity which lasted until the end of the century. In

---

[31] Ignatieff, *op. cit.*, pp. 194–195.
[32] 80 were closed prior to 1877 and a further 38 were closed when they came under direct Home Office control in 1878.

its first edition in the 1890s, the *Law Quarterly Review* described the prison system as a "manufactory of lunatics and criminals". In 1895, the Gladstone Committee was set up and its Report was essentially a crushing indictment of the Du Cane regime, criticising the failure to pay regard to the "moral as well as the legal responsibilities of the prison authorities". It recommended productive labour, proper treatment of juveniles, training for prison officers and better medical facilities. The 1898 Prison Act followed many of the Report's recommendations. The detailed administration of the prison service was taken away from Parliament and placed under the Home Secretary. The Act introduced classification of prisoners and allowed the sentencing court to decide in which of three divisions a prisoner should serve his sentence. It abolished hard labour of the first class, and limited situations where corporal punishment could be used.[33] It introduced remission of sentences for good conduct.

Ruggles-Brise became the new chairman of the Prison Commissioners. More forward looking than Du Cane, he was associated with the development of probation, Borstal training and preventive detention. Conditions improved in the areas of education, visits, diet and letters. Yet there was little fundamental change. Ruggles-Brise resigned in 1921 after prison conditions had been subject to scrutiny again as a result of the imprisonment of conscientious objectors:

> "Self respect is systematically destroyed and self-expression prevented in every phase of prison existence . . . . The labour is mostly mechanical and largely wasteful and every indication of craftsmanship or creative ability is suppressed. The meals are distributed through momentarily open doors as though the prisoners were caged animals. The sanitary arrangements are degrading and filthy and the dress is hideous, slovenly and humiliating."[34]

The inter-war period was dominated by Alexander Paterson, a Commissioner, but never Chairman. With a social work background, he used his influence to improve prison conditions, to develop open prisons and Borstal regimes as well as after-care for prisoners. This period had been called;

> "... the essential period of penological "optimism" when imprisonment as an institution of social reform was at its most viable and some of the ideals of the Gladstone Committee came closest to realisation."[35]

The post-war developments are discussed throughout this chapter but the following broad picture has emerged:

(a) the management of the service was removed from the Prison Commissioners to the Prison Department in the Home Office in 1963. Although criticised for inertia and as monolithic and secretive, the 1990s saw the service being given agency status, with a businessman appointed as Director-General, contracts[36] between the centre and establishments, the privatisation of some escort services and remand

[33] It was only finally abolished in 1967.
[34] Hobhouse S. and Brockway F. (eds), *English Prisons Today* (1922).
[35] Harding, *et al.* (1985), *op. cit.*, p. 194.
[36] These are specific as to unlocking time, hours at work or education, visits, specialist groups to tackle offending behaviour, resettlement units, etc.—in the contract (if not in practice) these are a vast improvement.

prisons[37] as well as limited financial and operational decentralisation to prison governors.

(b) the system has undergone a period of renovation and expansion with an extensive prison building and refurbishment programme.

(c) the independent Inspectorate of Prisons set up in the 1980s has published detailed and critical reports which have contributed to greater accountability.

(d) the prison population climbed steadily to a peak of around 50,000 in the early 1990s. Home Office predictions do not foresee any sharp decline. This figure conceals several contradictory trends:

    (i) a smaller proportion of convicted persons are being imprisoned; 16 per cent of adults convicted of indictable offences were imprisoned in 1992,[38] half the figure 40 years ago. This century has seen the development of a range of non-custodial sentences, particularly probation (1907), suspended sentences (1967), community service orders (1972), combination orders and curfew orders (1991).

    (ii) there is an increase in the average length of sentence of those who are being imprisoned; the average length of sentence for the adult male in Crown Court was 16.6 months in 1982 but 21.1 months in 1992.

    (iii) although Parliament has sought to reduce numbers of remand prisoners (through the Bail Act 1976) and fine-defaulters (by allowing time and flexible methods for payment of fines) the numbers, especially of remand prisoners, remain high.

    (iv) the twentieth century has seen the prohibition of imprisonment for children (in 1908) and the segregation of children into separate institutions with community homes and young offender institutions. The 1980s saw a dramatic decrease in the use of custody for those under 17, declining from 6,544 receptions of boys in 1982 to 1,479 in 1992[39] with a similar picture for young offenders under 21.

    (v) 1967 saw the introduction of parole (now "early release") which gave considerable power to the executive to control prison population.

(e) there has been improvement of conditions within adult prisons with more education and work opportunities, greater contact with the outside and less censorship. But many establishments are very old, conditions are cramped and the diet and sanitation would still be recognised by nineteenth-century prisoners. There are few exciting regimes and priority is still given to security and control.

(f) there is little uniformity between establishments. Prisons vary in terms of security, specialist functions and regime.

(g) for the prisoner, the nature and length of sentence to be served is in the hands of the executive and not in the hands of the courts.

---

[37] The Wolds on Humberside was the first privately-managed prison in 1992—for adult remand prisoners.
[38] *Criminal Statistics 1993* Cm. 2680, para. 7.31, p. 150.
[39] *Prison Statistics 1992* Cm. 2581, Table 3.11, p. 66.

8.3 MODERN PRISONS—ADMINISTRATION AND ACCOUNTABILITY

The basic statutory framework remains the Prison Act 1952.[40] The Home Secretary has a direct ministerial responsibility to Parliament for the working of the prison service but, to a considerable extent, the service operates autonomously in creating internal policy. There is little Parliamentary involvement. This autonomy will be increased by the change to "agency status". Until 1963, the prison system was administered by the (nominally) independent Prison Commissioners but since that date, prisons have come under the Prison Department of the Home Office, headed by a Director-General. Since 1992 the service has operated as an executive agency.[41] The agency is headed by the Prisons Board, chaired by the Director-General with two non-executive and six executive directors. These six are responsible for inmate administration, inmate programmes, custody, health care, personnel and services and finance and planning. The Board has no statutory authority and is in essence an advisory and co-ordinating body.

Regionally there are approximately 160 establishments organised into 15 areas. Area managers will be responsible for the application of national policy within the establishments, for the proper functioning and funding of those establishments and specialist tasks such as allocation of prisoners to particular prisons and dealing with prisoners' complaints.

External accountability is provided by three means:

(a) there is an independent Inspectorate of Prisons.[42] This was originally set up under section 5 of the Prison Act 1952. The reports remained confidential and a change was recommended in the May Report.[43] This came about in 1982.[44] The Inspectorate has produced a lively series of reports on individual establishments, incidents or aspects of prison life as well as producing annual reports.[45] Rarely bland, these reports[46] have been detailed, often praising individual prison regimes but have been consistently critical of certain aspects of prison life, especially catering, sanitation, the lack of education, recreation and employment opportunities and the medical service. Many of its concerns such as time out of cell, personal officers and sentence planning are reflected in the Woolf Report.[47]

(b) each establishment has its own Board of Visitors (BoV),[48] appointed by the Home Office and including local J.P.s and worthy citizens. Under

---

[40] Amended in 1991 by the Criminal Justice Act to take account of private sector involvement.
[41] Richardson, *op. cit.*, p. 75 for a more detailed discussion of the implications and the relationship between the agency and the Home Secretary.
[42] This is currently headed by Judge Stephen Tumim—for a brief review of the inspectorate, see Richardson, *op. cit.*, p. 138.
[43] *Report of the Inquiry into the United Kingdom Prison Services, op. cit.*, p. 92.
[44] Criminal Justice Act 1982, s. 57.
[45] *Report of HM Chief Inspector of Prisons 1992/93*, Cm. 2128.
[46] Useful summaries are provided by NACRO, *Criminal Justice Digest* and in the *AMBOV Quarterly*.
[47] Woolf, *op. cit.*, esp. Part II which was authored by Judge Tumim.
[48] Maguire M. and Vagg J., *The Watchdog Roles of Boards of Visitors*; Richardson, *op. cit.*, p. 132.

the Prison Act 1964, they have the right of access to every part of the prison and to every prisoner and have the power to inquire into the state of the premises and treatment of prisoners and even to suspend officers. Boards produce annual reports[49] of variable quality although little notice seems to be taken of these. Until 1992, they also acted as a disciplinary body, hearing charges against prisoners. These powers were taken away[50] and such charges are now heard either by the governor or the courts.[51]

(c) grievance procedures: within the intimate, hierarchical, strictly controlled atmosphere of the prison, at once disturbed and disturbing and yet deeply boring, friction and grievances are normal. Woolf records that in 1988 it was estimated that some 290,000 applications were made. In their induction pack, prisoners are informed of the levels at which applications can be made[52]:
   (i) informally talking to a personal officer
   (ii) making a formal but oral application to the wing officer or governor
   (iii) making written requests to the governor, BoV, area manager or Headquarters.

There can be confidential access using a sealed envelope to write to the governor, Chair of the BoV or Area Manager. Reasons for decisions should be given although the extent to which this is done may be doubted, especially on "administrative" decisions such as the moving of prisoners from one establishment to another at short notice (known as "ghosting") or moving inmates from open to closed visits.[53] Woolf recommended an independent element in the arbitration of grievances[54] and the Prison Ombudsman became operational in October 1994.

Prisons are also accountable to law for their treatment of prisoners. The old concept of "civil death" has no place and a prisoner retains his or her civil rights which cannot be taken away unless expressly or by necessary implication.[55] The prisoner can bring civil proceedings for torts although not to obtain damages for breaches of the Prison Rules. There can be judicial review of an adverse decision.[56] The prisoner also has access to the European Court of Human Rights, can approach the Ombudsman through his or her M.P., the new Independent Complaints Adjudicator or indeed petition the Queen.[57]

---

[49] Useful summaries are provided by NACRO, *Criminal Justice Digest*.
[50] Woolf, *op. cit.*, para. 12.169; Appleton J., *Boards of Visitors Post Woolf* (NACRO 1992).
[51] *infra*, para. 8.5.4.
[52] Woolf, *op. cit.*, para. 14.309. A new system of dealing with prisoners' applications and complaints was introduced in September 1990—it is discussed in Richardson, *op. cit.*, p. 127.
[53] Often prisons are reluctant to reveal the source of information on which the decision was based or indeed the information itself (which would tend to reveal the source).
[54] Woolf, *op. cit.*, para. 14.342.
[55] *R. v. The Board of Visitors of Hull Prison, ex p. St Germain* [1979] Q.B. 425 at 454; *Raymond v. Honey* [1983] 1 A.C. 1 at 10; Richardson, *op. cit.*, p. 135.
[56] *infra*, para. 8.5.4.
[57] In 1988, there were 14,500 petitions to the Secretary of State—Woolf, *op. cit.*, para. 14.317. This procedure has now been abandoned.

8.3.1 *Staffing and Costs*

Each establishment is headed by a governor who with his or her deputies are responsible for the day-to-day running of the establishment. In April 1993, staffing consisted of 500 at governor rank, with around 24,000 uniformed officers,[58] 11,600 administrative, professional staff or industrial civil servants in establishments and 2,050 outside establishments. The total is of 37,650, increasing by 33 per cent from the 1987 figure of 28,200.[59] This is extraordinary, occurring at a time when there has been a decrease in the annual receptions into prison and during a period characterised by cutbacks in the public sector resources.

Table 8.1 The costs of the system[60]

Year	Cash Cost (Real Cost)
1979	£206m
1987/88	£920m (£1,255m)
1991/92	£1,632m (£1,688m)
1992/93	£1,660m (£1,660m)

Table 8.2 Weekly Operating Costs per prisoner[61]

Year	Open Prison	Dispersal[62]	Average
1988/89	£199	£541	£288
1991/92	£316	£807	£442
1992/93	£331	£816	£494

These increases in cost reflect the opening of new prisons and the resulting staff costs. The key target for 1993/94 for the Prison Service is to ensure that the average annual cost per prisoner does not exceed £23,561. These figures can be compared with the costs in 1990/91 for non-custodial alternatives[63]:

- £1,070 per year for supervising an offender on a probation order.
- £6,881 is the annual cost to the Home Office for a place in an approved bail/probation hostel (20 per cent of the cost is provided by local authorities).

---

[58] This amounts to one officer to every two prisoners (not allowing for shift systems).
[59] Prison Service, *Annual Report 1992/93* Cm. 2385, Vol. 1, para. 204.
[60] Prison Service, *op. cit.*, Vol. 1, para. 203.
[61] Prison Service, *op. cit.*, Vol. 2, Table D, p. 2; Prison Service: *Annual Report 1991/92* Cm. 2087, Table D, p. 80.
[62] This is the term used for a high security establishment.
[63] NACRO, *The Cost of Penal Measures* (Briefing No. 23), (July 1992).

- £920 per year for supervising a community service order.
- £171 is the average annual cost of an attendance centre order.

Fines cost nothing but the total income from fines, fees and fixed penalties collected by magistrates' courts in 1990/91 was £269,088,000.

8.4 THE SENTENCE OF IMPRISONMENT AND TYPES OF PRISON

Throughout the nineteenth and twentieth centuries there have been varieties of prison sentence, differentiated not merely by length but by the supposed nature of the regime: nineteenth century prison sentences with differing forms of hard labour; more recently corrective training or preventive detention; extended sentences were introduced by the 1967 Criminal Justice Act enabling the court to disregard statutory maxima in certain circumstances.[64] Such differentiation has now disappeared and for adults there is a single generic prison sentence. We do distinguish between different types of establishment: by sex, by age and by function.

Table 8.3 Prison Service Estate in England and Wales[65]

Type	No. Male	No. Female
Local	34	6
Closed training	54	4
Open training	12	3
Remand centres	17	0
Closed Young Offender Institutions	20	3
Open YOIs	6	2

If we include three contracted-out prisons,[66] 164 establishments are listed providing a "certified normal accommodation" (CNA) of 46,574.[67] Precision on the numbers is difficult. There are approximately 130 prison centres, several of which have dual functions.[68] In addition, functions change regularly with prison closures[69] and new prisons opening.[70]

[64] The nature of the sentence did not change, only its length. It was rarely employed, less than 100 times per annum. The philosophy behind the sentence, that of deterrence, was at variance with the aims of the 1991 Criminal Justice Act which repealed it in s. 5(2)(a).
[65] Derived from *Report on the Work of the Prison Service 1992/93* Cm. 2385, Vol. II, Appendix 1, p. 27.
[66] Blakenhurst and Doncaster (local prisons for males) and the Wolds (adult remands).
[67] Above, Table F, p. 4.
[68] *e.g.* Durham operates both as a male local prison and as a female closed training prison.
[69] *e.g.* Oxford closed as a local prison in February 1993.
[70] Four establishments were opened in 1992/93. A new privatised local prison opened in Doncaster in 1994.

The current administration has actively pursued a prison building and refurbishment programme. One estimate[71] suggests that the building programme will mean a total of 24 new prisons at a current cost of £1.355 billion since 1979. These will provide a total of 21,000 new places and almost inevitably new facilities will mean a rise in the prison population.[72] The Home Office projection is of a prison population of 57,500 by the year 2000.[73] The exact timing of the construction of the new prisons depends on availability of resources[74] and changing estimates of the prison population. Many of these new prisons still provide for double cells, although this is contrary to the European Prison Rules. None of these new prisons are for woman although Holloway has recently had a major facelift and two other male establishments have been refurbished and changed over to female prisons.

From 1991, the Government has actively pursued a policy of privatisation especially of escort services and remand and local prisons. The Wolds opened in 1992, Blakenhurst in 1993 and Doncaster in 1994. All new prisons will be open to competitive tender and there will be market-testing for existing establishments.[75] Privatisation raises serious questions as to whether it is legitimate for the government to delegate their responsibilities for punishment[76] which is an issue that can also be posed in terms of a minister's constitutional accountability to Parliament for the operation of such prisons.[77]

8.4.1 *Remand Centres*

There are 17 such institutions, often attached to other establishments. In 1993 they held, on average, 2,778 adults and young offenders awaiting trial which was 90 per cent CNA.[78] Unlike local prisons which hold the bulk of the remand population, such centres are able to separate unconvicted prisoners from sentenced inmates. However, regimes are even more limited than local prisons. For example, the HMCIP Report on Feltham in 1993 still regarded the basic lifestyle for the young prisoners as unsatisfactory, with too much time in cells and too little stimulation. There were too few training courses, poor medical services, high levels of bullying and inmates were often a long distance from family ties.[79]

---

[71] NACRO Briefing 9 (June 1990).
[72] Fitzgerald M. and Sim J., *British Prisons* (2nd ed., 1982), p. 33.
[73] Home Office Statistical Bulletin (10/92), *Projections of Long Term Trends in the Prison Population to the Year 2000* although such projections must be treated sceptically—a year later, the figure was revised to 51,500 (Home Office Statistical Bulletin 6/93).
[74] A further six prisons, built with private money, were announced in the budget statement on November 30, 1993.
[75] An in-house team were successful in tendering for the rebuilt Strangeways—Prison Service 1992/93, *op. cit.*, Vol. I, para. 219.
[76] Palley C., *The United Kingdom and Human Rights* (1991), pp. 173–174.
[77] Richardson, *op. cit.*, p. 77.
[78] These and similar statistics following are derived from Prison Service 1992/93, *op. cit.*, Vol. II, Appendix 1, p. 27.
[79] The Report is available from the Home Office Library—it is summarised in NACRO *Criminal Justice Digest* No. 79 (Jan. 1994), p. 9.

8.4.2 *Young Offender Institutions*[80] *(YOI)*

Under section 123 of the Criminal Justice Act 1988, a sentence of "detention in a young offender institution" replaced detention centre orders[81] and youth custody orders[82] for offenders under 21. Courts can pass the same term of imprisonment on a juvenile as on an adult. There are a range of differing YOIs, from short stay, open institutions to relatively secure establishments. Many have secure juvenile units attached to them. There are 31 such institutions and in 1993 they held, on average, 4,475 young prisoners, 75 per cent of the CNA. Open YOIs operate at only 54 per cent of capacity.

8.4.2.1 *Secure Training Centres*

Section 5 of the Criminal Justice and Public Order Act 1994 provides for secure training centres to hold children over 12 who are the subject of a secure training order. Five centres are planned, four of which will be contracted out.

8.4.3 *Adult Prisons—Local Prisons*

Adult prisons are categorised into two types: the local prison and the training prison. The term "local" comes from the time when such prisons were under local authority control but nowadays neither "local" nor "training" has any technical meaning. The types are to be distinguished by their different functions. The local prison has three such functions:

(a) holding those on remand, either awaiting trial or sentence.
(b) acting as an observation and classification centre prior to the allocation of prisoners to other establishments.
(c) housing inmates under sentence, normally those serving short sentences of six months or under but also some long or medium termers especially when they are coming to the end of their sentence in a resettlement wing.

The local prison's primary function could be described as serving the courts, holding prisoners awaiting trial or sentence and escorting them to and from the courts.[83] Because of this role, the typical local prison was inner city, closed

---

[80] These are discussed further in Chap. 9.

[81] Detention centres orders were introduced by the 1948 Criminal Justice Act for young offenders along the lines of the military detention centre or "glass house". They were for short sentences, usually three months and never more than six. Remission was half of the sentence and so average length of time served was around eight weeks. The regime was punitive in the sense that little attention was paid to reformation, education or training. There was a lot of physical activity, hard work and "the highest possible standards of discipline and achievement, behaviour and manners are insisted upon".

[82] Youth Custody Centres were introduced in the Criminal Justice Act 1982, replacing the old Borstals, themselves the product of the Gladstone Report 1895 and introduced in 1908. Borstals were intended as reformative with an indeterminate regime for young offenders and for many decades were highly successful, probably because they were very selective in their intake. That selectivity was abandoned in 1961 and the reconviction rate climbed. In 1982, the Criminal Justice Act created Youth Custody Centres and a court could pass a YCC order on males between 15 and 21.

[83] These services are becoming increasingly privatised under s. 80 of the Criminal Justice Act 1991.

and of Victorian construction. New ones have been built such as Belmarsh[84] in south-east London and Elmley on the Isle of Sheppey in Kent. Some have specialist functions: vulnerable prisoner units,[85] immigration detainees[86] or pre-release employment schemes. Woolf envisages a change in function to "community prisons" which contain a cross-section of the prison population and are genuinely "local" in the sense of serving a local community.[87]

8.4.3.1 LOCAL PRISONS—OVERCROWDING

Although the Secretary of State specifies the maximum capacity of the system,[88] he can and does condone grotesque overcrowding. This peaked in July 1987 when there were 5,091 inmates sharing three to a cell and 13,892 sharing two to a cell.[89] This problem is concentrated in local prisons which have the worst overcrowding in the system. In 1992/93, the CNA of local prisons for adult males was 12,666 but the average daily population (ADP) was 14,504 which was 115 per cent of capacity. This was during a period when the system as a whole was operating below capacity. Even these figures conceal enormous differences between establishments; Wormwood Scrubs was 72 per cent overcrowded while Belmarsh was operating at 84 per cent of capacity.[90]

1992 represented a low point in prison overcrowding, benefiting from the impact of the 1991 Criminal Justice Act. By March 1993, overcrowding had been reduced to 108 sharing three to a cell and 6,872 sharing two to a cell. By 1994, the changes to the early release system by that statute and the passage of the 1993 Criminal Justice Act (with sentencers taking more account of previous convictions and a tougher stance on bail) had led to an increase in prison population,[91] which will probably rise to 52,000 by 1995.

The Prison Service is reopening closed prisons,[92] there are significant numbers of prisoners in police cells[93] and more prisoners will once again find themselves sharing cells which are designed for single occupancy. Overcrowding had been overcome and reversing this trend will mean that the work of the Prison Service will again be distorted by overcrowding, the removal of which "is an indispensable pre-condition of sustained and universal improvement in prison conditions."[94]

8.4.3.2 LOCAL PRISONS—REGIMES

The rise in prison numbers will mainly and adversely affect local prisons. Training prisons do not accept inmates unless there is space. Facilities such as

---

[84] This has a separate unit for high security remand prisoners.
[85] These house offenders at risk from other inmates, especially sex offenders. They can be put in solitary confinement under Rule 43 for their own protection, but specialist units are a better solution.
[86] Haslar in Hampshire.
[87] Woolf, *op. cit.*, para. 11.50.
[88] Richardson, *op. cit.*, p. 103.
[89] Prison Service, *Annual Report 1987/88* Cm. 516.
[90] Prison Service, *Annual Report 1992/93* Cm. 2385, Vol. I, para. 57, p. 10.
[91] Prison Reform Trust, *Prison Overcrowding: A Crisis Waiting in the Wings* (1993).
[92] *e.g.* Oxford.
[93] 146 on May 27, 1994—144 New L.J. (1994) 747; Woolf, *op. cit.*, para. 11.152.
[94] This was the view of the Director General of the Prison Service in evidence to Woolf, *op. cit.*, para. 11.135.

sanitation and catering tend to be worse in local prisons.[95] Local prisons have very limited facilities for work, education or recreation. Prisoners can remain locked up for substantial periods of the day. The Chelmsford BoV reported that there was little structured activity and no training courses or useful work available. There was a complete absence of evening activity and "very unsatisfactory" provisions for education.[96] In such situations, regardless of the time unlocked, all prisoners can do is to waste time on their beds, on the landings, in the yard, watching TV or, if lucky, playing pool. Such conditions frustrate the argument that, legally and morally, unconvicted prisoners should possess a different status, and also undermine the special provisions that are made for remand prisoners; they should be kept separate from convicted prisoners,[97] have access to outside doctors,[98] wear their own clothing,[99] cannot be compelled to work[1] and are allowed more letters,[2] visits and personal property.[3]

There are 40 local prisons, 34 for males and six for females. Despite a prison rebuilding programme which includes extra local prisons to absorb some of the present overcrowding, the old Victorian prisons will last well into the twenty-first century. In theory, the new training prisons and remand centres will also take some of the pressure off local prisons, by absorbing short sentence prisoners and remand prisoners. This process will also be helped by overall demographic shifts which should have meant a reduction in the prison population over the next decade but legislative changes and sentencing practices seem to ensure that the prison population will remain high in the foreseeable future.

There are observation, classification and allocation units in all local prisons and if a prisoner is serving a sentence of more than three months, he or she will come under the scrutiny of such a unit. For men or women serving four years or more, there are regional units while the classification and allocation of those who are serving life sentences are dealt with at Headquarters. The function is to ascertain background information on the prisoner, including any special needs and the background circumstances to the offence. The primary issue to be decided is that of security classification. The final decision is a recommendation as to where the sentence will be served.

8.4.4 *Adult Prisons—Training Prisons*

The training prison is to hold those serving sentences of imprisonment, usually medium or long term. Thus they are places where there are greater opportunities for work, vocational training, education and leisure. They tend to be purpose built (although some may be based on ex-military camps), relatively modern and are not overcrowded.

---

[95] There have been many refurbishments with integral sanitation and new kitchens.
[96] NACRO *Criminal Justice Digest* No. 80, p. 7 (April 1994).
[97] Prison Rules, Rule 3(2).
[98] *ibid*. Rule 17(4).
[99] *ibid*. Rule 20(1).
[1] *ibid*. Rule 28(5).
[2] *ibid*. Rule 34(1).
[3] *ibid*. Rule 41(1).

Table 8.4 Training Prisons—Population 1992/93[4]

Type of Institution (Nos.)	Certified Normal Accommodation (CNA)	Average Daily Population (ADP) (% operating capacity)
Closed, male (54)	19,001	17,294 (91%)
Open, male (12)	3,581	3,157 (88%)
Closed, female (4)	366	374 (102%)
Open, female (3)	416	317 (76%)

The normal prison is closed and there are 54 male and 4 female.[5] Many of the establishments are specialist either in whole or in part; vulnerable prisoner units,[6] life sentence prisoners only,[7] pre-release units, industrial units,[8] psychiatric centre,[9] surgical centres. Drug abuse is so widespread that individual establishments have their own policies and teams to tackle the problems rather than relying on specialist establishments. There are now three special units for long-term prisoners who pose special control problems, being persistently too disruptive for normal prison conditions.[10] These are at Hull, Parkhurst (taking prisoners with psychiatric disturbances) and Woodhill, although only Parkhurst is a training prison.[11] These are resource-intensive—Hull has 20 cells, integral sanitation with a broad range of training and recreational facilities, arts and crafts, gym, library and TV rooms.

The central distinction between training prisons is their level of security. Earl Mountbatten headed a six-week inquiry on prison security in 1966, following the abolition of the death penalty, the rise of spectacular crimes (the Great Train Robbery), and several notorious escapes, notably that of George Blake, a Russian spy and two Train Robbers, Wilson and Biggs. Mountbatten recommended the introduction of a classification system[12] which would divide prisoners into four main categories, dependent upon the level of security risk, nowadays still the predominant consideration:

[4] Prison Service 1992/93, *op. cit.*, Vol. II, Appendix 1, p. 27.
[5] Durham (a special security wing for 20 women), Styal, Cookham Wood and Bullwood Park. Holloway has facilities for sentenced prisoners requiring psychiatric treatment and a mother and baby unit.
[6] There were 1,494 inmates segregated under rule 43 in 1988—in 1993, the figure was 1,180 with a further 1,605 in vulnerable prisoner units. 20 closed male training prisons had such units. The Home Office are liable for the safety of prisoners—*Egerton v. Home Office* [1978] Crim.L.R. 494.
[7] Kingston is unique in this regard.
[8] Coldingley is the only example.
[9] Grendon Underwood is again the only example—its therapy programme has a reconviction rate of about 33% compared with 45% nationally.
[10] For discussion of transfer policy in relation to these, see Richardson, *op. cit.*, pp. 89 and 117.
[11] Walmsley R., *Managing Difficult Prisoners: The Parkhurst Special Unit* (Home Office Research Study No. 122) (1991).
[12] *Report of the Inquiry into Prison Escapes and Security, op. cit.*

(a) *Category A*: those prisoners whose escape would be highly dangerous to the public, to the police or to the security of the State. Such prisoners are identified early and are held in special cells from first remand. There are annual reviews of the categorisation.[13] Mountbatten suggested that there should be a single high security fortress-like prison on the Isle of Wight. This concentration policy found little favour with the Home Office who commissioned a report from the Advisory Council on the Penal System, chaired by Leon Radzinowicz. This Report[14] recommended the dispersal of high risk prisoners throughout a number of secure prisons in a regime which would be shared with category B prisoners. There are currently six[15] dispersal prisons: Frankland (Durham), Full Sutton (York), Gartree (Leicester), Long Lartin (Worcester), Wakefield and Whitemoor (Cambridge). Such security is expensive: Frankland cost £15 million in 1982 for 339 places; Full Sutton cost £29 million in 1987 for 494 places. The dispersal system has a capacity of 2,694. In 1992/93, these six prisons had an ADP of 2,436 or 90 per cent of capacity. Of those inmates, under 500 are Category A. The rest of the places are taken up by Category B prisioners who must live under Category A regimes.

That regime involves strict perimeter security, floodlights, CCTV, detection devices, dogs. There will be the vetting of all visitors by the police and usually visits are limited to immediate family. Prisoners will have all their movements logged, their letters and parcels examined with some care and might need to leave clothes outside their cells at night. In the early days, there were serious riots in all dispersal prisons. More control has led to the stripping away of a civilised regime.[16] In 1992, the HMCIP Report on Long Lartin talked of a pervasive drug culture and intimidation of staff and inmates by "influential, ruthless men". Workshops and work training courses had been closed.[16a]

In all establishments, control and security remain high on the Home Office agenda. The options are to achieve this through architecture and technology on one hand or through proper management and purposive regimes on the other. The Control Review Committee[17] questioned the continuance of the dispersal system but there still exists an official belief in American-style "new generation" prison architecture. Woolf argues[18] that, while physical conditions are important, they are neither a necessary nor sufficient excuse for a poorly-run prison. His prescription for establishments is that they should be relatively small (under 400) with self-contained (and thus more easily controlled) accommodation units of no more than 60–70 with single cells and no

---

[13] The prisoner is entitled to reasons for the classification—*ex p. Duggan* (1993) *The Guardian* December 13, 1993.

[14] Advisory Council on the Penal System, *The Regime for Long Term Prisoners in Conditions of Maximum Security* (1968).

[15] Albany was taken out of the system during 1992.

[16] Stern V., *Bricks of Shame* (2nd ed., 1989), p. 214.

[16a] Further problems were encountered in late 1994 with escape attempts and explosive finds at Whitemoor.

[17] *Managing the Long Term Prison System: Report of the Control Review Committee* (Home Office 1984); the possibility of a single "Alcatraz" for Category A prisoners is under review—*The Guardian*, December 21st, 1994, p. 2.

[18] Woolf, *op. cit.*, section 11, p. 265.

dormitories.[19] There is also considerable agreement with the conclusions of the Prior Committee[20] that the three central elements for control are the quality of relationships between staff and inmates, a full and purposeful programme of activities and, finally, fairness in dealings with prisoners.

(b) *Category B*: these are prisoners for whom the very highest conditions of security are not necessary but for whom escape must be made very difficult indeed. Perhaps up to 25 per cent of sentenced prisoners, they are often held in dispersal prisons and suffer many of the deprivations of Category A inmates. There were eleven Category B prisons in 1992. With a capacity of 3,968, they had an ADP of 3,686, 93 per cent of capacity.[21]

(c) *Category C*: these prisoners cannot be trusted in open conditions but lack the ability or resources to make a determined escape attempt. These will form a majority of sentenced prisoners. The shorter sentence prisoners will be held in local prison or in Category C prisons. There were 33 of these in 1992. With a capacity of 12,063, these had an ADP of 11,132 or 92 per cent of capacity.

(d) *Category D*: these inmates can reasonably be trusted in open conditions and are often held in open prisons, although this categorisation is also important for being allocated to resettlement wings and to pre-release employment schemes in closed prisons.

Table 8.5 Open Institutions—Population 1992/93[22]

Type of institution	CNA	ADP	% occupancy
Training prisons for males (12)	3,581	3,157	88%
Training prisons for females (3)	416	317	76%
YOIs for males (6)	1,196	650	54%
YOIs for females (2)	53	24	45%
TOTAL (23)	5,246	4,148	79%

[19] The report on the Wymott riots in 1993 criticised this aspect—it had led to staff being scarcely in control of the prison, especially at night.

[20] *Report of the Committee on the Prison Disciplinary System* Cmnd. 9641 (1985).

[21] These figures (and those for Category C) are taken from Prison Service 1992/93, *op. cit.*, Vol. II, Table F, p. 4 but the figures given vary considerably from those contained in Appendix 1, p. 27.

[22] *ibid*. Vol. II, Appendix 1, p. 27.

Open institutions house about 15 per cent of the prison population. The inmates have much greater freedom of movement and escaping is much easier.[23] In 1992/93, there were 9 escapes, 1,276 absconding and 1 escape from escort by males held in open conditions, representing an attempt by nearly 31 per cent of the average population. This can be compared to 230 escapes, 547 absconding and 142 escapes from escorts from closed prisons, representing an attempt by only 2 per cent.

The open prison will have no perimeter security, little censorship. Costs are low. There have been undertakings to local authorities that no offenders with records of sex or violence will be allowed in such prisons. Only at Leyhill has no such undertaking been given. It is the one section of the prison system that operates significantly below capacity.

8.5 DAILY LIFE

The need for positive and purposeful regimes in prison has been stressed by Woolf[24] and by countless reports of H.M. Chief Inspector of Prisons. To an extent, the early 1990s has seen a change. A decade ago, prisoners would spend large amounts of time locked up in the cell, especially in local prisons where inmates might be unlocked for as little as one to two hours a day. The work provided was limited and monotonous: sewing mailbags still happened regularly. There was rigid censorship, little contact with the outside world and poor visiting facilities. Although there was the refurbishment of the old prisons and the building of new,[25] the pace of the change has been accelerated, first, by the riot at Strangeways and the subsequent Woolf scrutiny and secondly, through privatisation.

An unexpected incident of privatisation has been the drawing up of contracts that lay out in detail the standards which are expected, far above those in the state sector: the Wolds have cells with duvets, curtains, wardrobes, hot and cold running water; inmates have keys so that they may come and go as they please for most of the day; six hours of education and six hours in the gym are required. Direct comparison with state prisons is not possible, not least because the financial components of the contracts are secret. But the extent of change can be seen in the Prison Service Reports which now set targets for "purposive activity", its key ones being that 34 per cent of prisoners will be unlocked for at least 12 hours every weekday and that prisoners spend 24.9 hours per week on "purposive activity". The current average hours are 25.45[26] but that conceals a much lower figure of 18.61 in local prisons. When that latter figure is broken down, it reveals that work for prisoners on remand, or serving sentences in local prisons, is still domestic and kitchen work with few workshops, little education or vocational training. There is less opportunity even for physical education than in other sectors of the prison service.

---

[23] It is necessary to distinguish "escaping" from "absconding"—the latter is walking out of an open institution or when a prisoner on home leave or work release fails to return.
[24] *op. cit.*, section 14 *passim*; Stern, *op. cit.*, *passim*.
[25] A new local/Cat. C prison such as Elmley in Kent has a much broader range of workshops, educational and sports facilities than a cramped Victorian urban local prison such as its neighbour at Canterbury.
[26] Prison Service 1992/93, *op. cit.*, Vol. II, p. 19.

8.5.1 *Work*

In the nineteenth century, crime was seen as a symptom of the crisis in the labour market disciplines, and re-establishing work habits was part of the penitentiary regime. Although Prison Rule 28(1) states that a convicted prisoner shall be required to do useful work for not more than 10 hours a day, inculcating work discipline is no longer seen as central but as a palliative to alleviate tension and boredom. However, it is an offence to refuse to work. The European Prison Rules[27] lay down that sufficient work of a useful nature or other purposeful activity should be provided to keep prisoners actively employed for a normal working day. The European Convention on Human Rights talks of the benefits of work but emphasises that the interests of the prisoner must not be subordinated to profit.

Prison Service Industries and Farms (PSIF) provides work opportunities for prisoners. In 1992/93, there were 16,000 employment places producing 13.3 million hours of inmate occupation. The net cost was £17 million at an average cost per hour of £1.32. Of those places, 11,000 were in 250 industrial workshops, with a product range including metal and wooden furniture, security grills, weaving, workwear, footwear, printing, brushmaking, injection moulding, concrete moulding, road signs and laundry. In addition, some 2,500 work on a sub-contract basis for private industry. PSIF also employ some 3,500 in farms and gardens. There are 5,800 hectares for crops and lifestock, providing most milk and eggs and significant amounts of vegetables. These are profitable (£32.8 million sales at a net profit of £2.2 million in 1989/90) but restricted to open prisons.[28] On a daily average, 65 per cent of PSIF employment places are filled. In addition to PSIF, there were some 2,500 employment places found in the catering services and an average of 3,800 prisoners were employed on building maintenance.

Although the Prison Service Report is undoubtedly optimistic about employment for prisoners,[29] generalisations are very misleading. Woolf talks of the depression among the Inquiry members, engendered by seeing intelligent prisoners knotting string into nets.[30] The Woolf proposals include normalising the working day (at present made abnormal by a prison's extraordinary meal times) and providing a greater range of arrangements for work and type of work with greater linkages to education and vocational opportunities. The possibilities of involving the private sector have been shown in Germany where major companies had set up prison workshops. One major Woolf proposal is to reduce PSIF involvement and make the governor responsible for the work and training within the establishment.

One central problem is that earnings are very low: in 1983, they varied between £1.16 and £3.30; by NACRO's review of prison work[31] in 1990, this had only gone up to a minimum of £1.75 for whom no work was available, with a normal average of around £2.95 and a maximum for those on a modified piecework scheme of £5.75. These rates meet with almost universal criticism, not least from the Prison Governors' Association and Woolf,[32]

[27] Rule 71(3).
[28] Most prison farms have a rare breeds unit!
[29] Prison Service 1992/93, *op. cit.*, Vol. I, p. 20.
[30] Woolf, *op. cit.*, para. 14.135.
[31] NACRO, *Work in Prisons* (Briefing No. 21 June 1990).
[32] *op. cit.*, para. 14.149.

whose recommendation was to move to an average of about £8 per week in the short term but more radically to pay prisoners realistically for their work, expect them to take more direct responsibility to support their families and, more controversially, to allow prisoners to build up to pay levels which would then be taken into account in assessing release date.[33] There are now examples of realistic wages: at Latchmere House, a resettlement prison[33a] in Surrey, prisoners earn over £100 per week on assembly work and at East Sutton Park, a women's open prison in Kent, the inmates earn £3 per hour making mozzarella. Other non-financial incentives involve linking eligibility for home leave to productivity.[34]

Such opportunities rarely exist for remand prisoners.[35] Not only are there few facilities, the prisons are often overcrowded and prison officers are frequently engaged shuttling prisoners to and from court so that staffing levels do not permit the opening of workshops and other facilities. The transient nature of the population also means that training prisoners for tasks can be regarded as wasted when the inmate moves on. The work opportunities in local and training prisons have deteriorated markedly over the past 20 years.[36]

8.5.2 *Education*

The education system is one of the few positive aspects of an otherwise depressing scene. Even in small, Victorian, provincial local prisons, there are good quality courses, provided by a skilled and well-motivated staff. It is relatively cheap, popular with prisoners, very flexible in adjusting to inmate needs, ranging from university[37] to vocational and illiteracy courses, and there is some evidence from other jurisdictions that it contributes to rehabilitation.[38] Although there is official support, "Every prisoner able to profit from the educational facilities at a prison shall be encouraged to do so",[39] there is a financial disincentive through loss of wages to undertaking full-time education.

Until 1993, education was provided by inviting Local Education Authorities to supply teaching staff. In 1992/93, there was provision for 7.57 million student hours, around £3.57 per inmate hour. Nearly 20 per cent of inmates are in full time education[40] and there are significant numbers of evening classes. The system changed in 1993 and there is now direct competitive tendering for providing prison education services. This produced chaos[41] and some commentators believe that it will take several years for the

---

[33] *op. cit.*, paras. 14.173–14.175.

[33a] Many prisons have resettlement wings with inmates working in the community and returning to prison at night. 1994 saw restrictions on such temporary release schemes and on home leave—IG70/1994.

[34] Prison Service 1992/93, *op. cit.*, Vol. I, paras. 116–118, p. 20.

[35] NACRO, *Criminal Justice Digest* No. 80 April 1994 carries reports by HMCIP on Chelmsford and Pentonville and BoV reports on Bristol, Chelmsford and Hull, all mentioning the lack of structured work.

[36] NACRO, *Criminal Justice Digest* No. 59 November 1989, p. 12; also Stern, *op. cit.*, p. 152.

[37] In 1992, 336 prisoners completed a year's Open University course—224 passed.

[38] Prison Reform Trust, *The Future of the Prison Education Service* (1993).

[39] Prison Rule 29(1).

[40] It is voluntary for all inmates over 16.

[41] Including legal action by existing suppliers for judicial review of the process—these were settled out of court.

service to recover.[42] Woolf has argued for more priority for the education service and greater integration of an inmate's educational needs with work and training opportunities. This should be linked into overall sentence planning and tied into the education that an inmate can receive in the community on release.[43]

8.5.3 *Contact with the outside world*

One of the most distressing aspects of imprisonment is the disruption to the family. Prison Standing Order 5 requires that the Prison Service ensures that the harmful effects of imprisonment are minimised as far as possible and that the inmate's contacts, especially those with family and friends, are maintained. The Woolf Report noted the significance which inmates attached to such communication and the limits on visits, letters, telephones and home leave. The Woolf agenda for reform was substantial[44]:

(a) Visits: legally the minimum visit for convicted adults is two per month for thirty minutes duration[45] while for remanded inmates, it is three, one hour, visits per week. The practice varies considerably. 90 per cent of prisons allowed more than the minimum prior to the changes in 1992 and the duration can be very flexible. Some prisons have introduced afternoon and evening as well as Sunday visiting. Many have open plan visitors' centres with creche facilities. The lower security prison allows greater flexibility. Dependents on income support can claim the cost of a visit every four weeks.[46]

Other jurisdictions adopt different customs, especially in the area of "family visits". In Swedish open prisons, prisoners have cell keys and entertain visitors in their cells. Canadian Federal prisons have PortaKabins where the prisoner can spend 48 hours with his family. Woolf recommended that the Prison Service should make provision for family visits, especially for those high security prisoners who would not be eligible for home leave in the course of a long sentence.[47]

(b) Home leave: this was seen as a process of re-adjustment to normal life before the end of a sentence. Inmates in Category C and D establishments, serving a sentence of 18 months or more[48] are eligible for a long home leave (5 consecutive days) in the four months before the earliest date of release. Short home leave is of two clear days, available to inmates in Category B establishments (as well as those in Category C and D) serving sentences of three years or more. This can be applied for after a prisoner has become eligible for parole.

Such temporary release is not uncommon: between April and June 1991, there were 8,276 such releases.[49] Other European countries have much broader programmes: Swedish prisoners become eligible after

---

[42] Prison Reform Trust, *op. cit.*
[43] Woolf, *op. cit.*, para. 14.84.
[44] Woolf, *op. cit.*, paras. 14.220–14.288.
[45] Until 1992, this was only one but see Prison (Amendment) Rules 1992 (S.I. 1992 No. 514)—in the Netherlands, prisoners are allowed a minimum weekly one hour visit.
[46] This is run, not by the DSS, but by the Prison Service's Assisted Prison Visits Scheme.
[47] Woolf, *op. cit.*, para. 14.246.
[48] Including lifers with a provisional release date.
[49] NACRO, *Criminal Justice Digest* No. 77 July, 1993, p. 23.

six months with the first leave for 48 hours and then additional home leaves every two months for up to 72 hours; in Denmark an eight hour leave is allowed to prisoners in open prisons every three weeks and it can be accumulated to last a weekend, although weekend leaves have to be requested by families or friends; in the Netherlands, prisoners in closed prisons may be allowed up to six periods of leave a year, with prisoners in semi-open establishments having automatic leave once a week. This latter system is now the norm for open prisoners in the United Kingdom.

Woolf's recommendation was an extension of these schemes as well as more flexible "day leave" arrangements. The Criminal Justice Act 1991 brought in a new scheme for early release and that included[50] a power for the Home Secretary to release prisoners on licence. The new rules now provide for prisoners to apply for home leave based on their own security category and on an assessment of individual risk, not on that of the establishment.

(c) Letters: there is an entitlement of one per week and any extra stamps have to be paid for. All letters may be censored—in open prisons this was abolished in 1986 and was reduced to a random 5 per cent in Category C establishments from 1988. Remand prisoners and those in Categories A and B still had correspondence opened and read until the Home Office accepted the recommendation in the Woolf Report,[51] and now only the mail of those prisoners in dispersal prisons will be read.

(d) Telephones: special phonecards were introduced into open prisons 1986 and, by 1992, all establishments had cardphones available for prisoners' use. All calls can be monitored by staff.

(e) Legal advice: for many years, the Home Office restricted the inmate's access to legal advice.[52] The inmate had to petition the Home Secretary and any complaint regarding treatment by prison authorities had to be first made through the formal channels (the "prior ventilation" rule). Petitioning was declared in breach of the European Convention on Human Rights in *Golder v. United Kingdom*[53] and the "prior ventilation" rule was seen as ultra vires in *ex p. Anderson*.[54]

Proper management in prisons is not only about communication with the outside world. There also needs to be greater involvement of prisoners in the day-to-day running of the prisons. Techniques such as prisoners' committees are beginning to be explored to improve communication between governor and inmates.[55]

8.5.4 Discipline[56]

The statutory basis is section 47 of the Prison Act 1952 which empowers the Home Secretary to make rules for the discipline and control of prisoners

---

[50] s. 36.
[51] *op. cit.*, para. 14.263.
[52] Richardson, *op. cit.*, p. 96.
[53] (1975) 1 E.H.R.R. 524; see also *Silver v. United Kingdom* (1980) 3 E.H.R.R. 475 [Comm]; (1983) 5 E.H.R.R. 347 [Crt].
[54] [1984] Q.B. 778.
[55] Woolf, *op. cit.*, para. 14.275.
[56] Richardson, *op. cit.*, Chap. 7.

as well as rules to ensure that any inmate shall have a proper opportunity of presenting his or her case. There were 85,648 offences against prison discipline punished in 1991. These are dealt with by prison governors whose powers include cellular confinement in a segregation unit, forfeiture of privileges[57] (such as tobacco), stoppage or reduction of earnings, cautions, exclusion from work, additional days[58] and removals from wing or living unit. Only the most serious cases will be dealt with by an outside criminal court. Offences often relate to abusive language or disrespect for officers and refusal to carry out orders but also involve violence. There were 4,473 incidents of violence to staff or other inmates in 1992/93,[59] with local prisons and young offender institutions being the establishments with the greatest likelihood of violence.

The lack of natural justice requirements in such proceedings has been the subject of scrutiny. Prior to 1992, the BoV were also involved in hearing disciplinary charges and there were many criticisms since neither the governor nor BoV members were qualified nor "ostensibly independent". However in 1978 in *R. v. The Board of Visitors of Hull Prison, ex p. St Germain*,[60] the Court of Appeal held that the rules of natural justice did apply to BoV disciplinary hearings in prisons. The English courts have also decided that there was a discretion to allow legal representation,[61] while the European Court on Human Rights concluded that Article 6 of the European Convention guaranteeing a fair hearing also applied to all such disciplinary tribunals.[62]

With that background, the Prior Committee[63] made proposals for procedural reform. These, and those of the muted White Paper[64] that followed, were turned down. Yet in *Leech*,[65] the courts intervened again, treating governors' adjudications in the same manner as BoV hearings and open to judicial review. However, neither common law nor the European Convention established a right to legal representation.[66]

Up to 1990, the leading players were undoubtedly the courts. The Woolf Report developed the theme with an insistence that inmates had to be treated with justice.[67] Woolf was amazed at the regularity with which remission[68] was forfeited: the estimate was that it added 600–700 to the daily prison population. Such penalties required the safeguards of the criminal law. Thus, there should be a distinction between disciplinary proceedings (defined as

---

[57] The use of the term "privileges" by the Prison Service was attacked by Woolf (para. 14.32)—these are facilities which should only be withdrawn for good and clear reasons. See also Richardson, *op. cit.*, pp. 92–94.

[58] Prior to 1991 this was forfeiture of remission but the Criminal Justice Act abolished remission and s. 42 provided for additional days to be awarded instead.

[59] Prison Service Report 1992/93, *op. cit.*, Vol. II, p. 14.

[60] [1979] Q.B. 425.

[61] *R. v. Home Secretary, ex p. Tarrant* [1985] 1 Q.B. 251.

[62] *Campbell and Fell v. United Kingdom* (1983) 5 E.H.R.R. 207.

[63] *Report of the Committee on the Prison Disciplinary System, op. cit.*

[64] *The Prison Disciplinary System* Cmnd. 9920.

[65] *Leech v. Deputy Governor of Parkhurst* [1988] A.C. 533.

[66] *R. v. Board of Visitors of Maze Prison, ex p. Hone* [1988] A.C. 379.

[67] Woolf, *op. cit.*, para. 14.363.

[68] Remission no longer exists and instead of "losing" remission, a prisoner can be sentenced to "extra days".

those with the limited aim of maintaining order in a prison) and criminal proceedings. These changes were introduced in 1992 and the maximum "additional days" that can be awarded by a governor is now 28. If higher penalties are required, the case must be referred to the magistrates' court. At the same time, the BoV role came to an end. They should now monitor the governor's adjudications, a proper function for a watchdog. There is still the lack of true independence of the governor/adjudicator and of proper representation. Crucially, the power to deprive a person of liberty without the safeguards of the court still exists.

As well as "additional days", the next most severe sanction is cellular confinement in a segregation unit which can be ordered under Rule 43 for the purposes of "good order and discipline" within the prison.[69] It can be for up to 28 days but this has to be authorised by a member of the BoV although the member need not interview the prisoner, nor need there be reasons given for continuance of the segregation.[70] Both aspects illustrate the lack of "justice" with which the inmate can be treated that concerned Woolf.[71]

Another administrative sanction is that of transfer to another prison by which difficult prisoners are often moved, at very short notice, to another establishment. This process is known as "ghosting" and the disruption is bitterly resented by prisoners who have no opportunity to challenge the decision, either internally or through the courts. It is also resented by BoVs, who are robbed of jurisdiction and often find that when an incident arises, the inmate (and sometimes witnesses) has been transferred.

The validity of segregation and transfers is considered in *Hague v. Governor of Pentonville*[72] where Taylor L.C.J. held that the court had the jurisdiction to review the legality of the governor's decision directly. As such, the court has gone further than it was prepared to do in considering segregation in control units[73] or transfer to other institutions.[74] The court is prepared to consider judicial review not only in pure disciplinary cases[75] but also in managerial decisions in relation to the confinement and allocation of prisoners.

8.5.5 *Medical Services*

There is a statutory requirement that each establishment have a qualified medical officer.[76] The Prison Medical Service was reorganised in 1992 as the Health Care Service for Prisoners, with the intention of taking a more co-ordinated and multi-disciplinary approach. The service is formally distinct from the NHS and has attracted criticism for the quality of medical provision,[77] the abuse of sedative drugs and its capacity to deal with the depressed and the mentally ill. Forty-three inmates committed suicide in

---

[69] This must be distinguished from segregation under Rule 43 for the prisoner's own protection.
[70] Richardson, *op. cit.*, pp. 83 and 111.
[71] Woolf, *op. cit.*, para. 12.272.
[72] [1990] 3 All E.R. 687; affirmed [1991] 3 All E.R. 733; this issue is discussed in Richardson, *op. cit.*, p. 118 and Woolf, *op. cit.*, para. 12.240.
[73] *Williams v. Home Office (No. 2)* [1981] 2 All E.R. 1211.
[74] *R. v. Home Secretary, ex p. McAvoy* [1984] 3 All E.R. 417.
[75] *Leech v. Deputy Governor of Parkhurst* [1988] A.C. 533.
[76] Prison Act 1952, s. 7.
[77] This is not helped by decisions such as *Knight v. Home Office* [1990] 3 All E.R. 237 that NHS standards cannot be expected within prisons.

1992/93, including seven young offenders.[78] Recent reports no longer give figures for attempts but in 1988/89, there were 323 attempted suicides and 1,211 self-mutilations. The response to this has been improvement of cell design and living conditions, new guidelines to improve identifying and helping those at risk as well as the involvement of the Samaritans and the introduction of "listener" schemes at several prisons.[79]

There are many problems, not least drug abuse. In 1992, there were 3,150 drugs offenders in prison. Many who are not drugs offenders are users and drugs are easily available. Although the figure known to be HIV positive was only 57 in March 1989, it is undoubtedly higher as a result of sharing needles or sexual activity.

8.6 THE PRISON POPULATION (ADP)

The average daily population in 1992/93 was 44,628, a decline on the previous year's figure of 45,817.[80] This figure has risen steadily over 20 years, from the 1969 figure of approximately 35,000 to a 1988 high of nearly 50,000. It declined through the next few years, especially as a result of the 1991 Criminal Justice Act but from 1994 is rising again, principally because of the impact of the 1993 Criminal Justice Act:

Table 8.6 Annual Receptions and Average Daily Population 1982–93[81]

Year	Receptions	Average Daily Population
1982	162,360	43,754
1983	157,148	43,772
1984	158,315	43,349
1985	164,179	46,278
1986	153,813	46,889
1987	159,459	48,963
1988	152,267	49,949
1989	148,281	48,610

[78] Prison Service 1992/93, *op. cit.*, Vol. II, p. 22.
[79] On suicides, see Richardson, *op. cit.*, p. 101; NACRO, *Suicide in Prison* (Briefing No. 103, November 1990).
[80] Prison Service, *Annual Report 1991–92* Cm. 2087, p. 5; *1992–93*, *op. cit.*, p. 3. The figures include those held in police cells, on average 715 in 1992–93, a reduction on 1,098 in the calendar year 1992.
[81] *Prison Statistics 1992* Cm. 2581, Table 1.6, p. 25 and Table 1.14, p. 38.

Table 8.6—*cont.*

Year	Receptions	Average Daily Population
1990	136,448	45,636
1991	142,585	45,897
1992	137,150	45,817
1993	n/a	44,628[82]

If we compare this to other European countries, the United Kingdom consistently imprisons more people per head of population than most other countries[83]:

Table 8.7 Comparative Imprisonment in Western Europe

Country	Prison population on 1/2/90	Prisoners per 100,000 of population
United Kingdom[84]	53,182	93.3
Luxembourg	347	92.6
Portugal	8,730	85.0
West Germany	51,972	83.8
Austria	6,294	83.0
Turkey	46,357	82.1
France	46,798	81.2
Spain	31,711	80.0
Switzerland	5,074	76.9
Finland	3,537	71.1
Belgium	7,001	71.0
Denmark	3,551	61.0
Sweden	5,046	60.0

[82] Taken from Prison Service 1992–93, *op. cit.* at p. 3—these figures do not necessarily tally with those in the Prison Statistics.
[83] NACRO Briefing Paper 25 (January 1993).
[84] These figures break down into: England and Wales 46,628 (92.5); Scotland 4,777 (94.8); Northern Ireland 1,777 (112.3).

Table 8.7—cont.

Country	Prison population on 1/2/90	Prisoners per 100,000 of population
Norway	2,260	56.5
Ireland	2,104	56.0
Italy	31,234	55.1
Greece	4,747	48.7
Netherlands	6,405	44.2
Iceland	101	39.8

Not only do we imprison more, both absolutely and proportionally, than any other Member State of the European Union, we also imprison more young people under 21 than other countries except for Ireland: 20.7 per cent of the prison population in 1990 was under 21 whereas for France only 11.1 per cent were under 21.

Does the rate of imprisonment reflect higher crime rates? Using victim surveys, the International Crime Survey[85] found that while autotheft and burglary in England and Wales were above the European average, assault, sexual assault and robbery were below it. The same survey discovered that the English were more in favour of imprisonment than their European counterparts: 37.7 per cent would imprison a recidivist, 21-year-old burglar compared with 12.8 per cent of the French or 25.8 per cent of the Dutch.

Why we imprison so many is an imponderable. The public are not put at risk even when prison populations are cut: in Germany, the decline started in 1984, especially among remand prisoners, the young and as a result of the development of non-custodial alternatives[86] without adverse effects on public safety. As we have seen in Table 8.6, England and Wales have seen a similar decline in total population since the mid-1980s but that encompasses different and contradictory trends:

Table 8.8 Changes in the Prison ADP 1982–1992[87]

Type of Custody	1982	1987	1992
Untried	5,409	9,611	8,076
Unsentenced	2,023	1,551	2,014

[85] Mayhew P., *Findings from the International Crime Survey* (Home Office Research and Statistics Department: Research Findings No. 8 April 1994).
[86] Feest J., *Reducing the Prison Population: Lessons from the West German Experience* (NACRO 1988); Graham J., "The Declining Prison Population in the Federal Republic of Germany" (1987) HORPU *Research Bulletin* No. 24, p. 47.
[87] *Prison Statistics 1992, op. cit.*, Table 1.5, p. 24.

Table 8.8—*cont.*

Type of Custody	1982	1987	1992
Police cells	70	537	1,098
Young offenders under sentence	10,365	8,762	5,469
Adults under sentence	25,563	28,769	29,951
Non-criminal	394	270	308
TOTAL	43,754	48,963	45,817

What is obvious from this table is that while there is a decline among the young offender population (falling in absolute numbers, and proportionally, from 29 per cent of the sentenced population in 1982 to 15 per cent in 1992), there is a rise in the remand population (again in absolute numbers and as a proportion of the ADP from 17 per cent in 1982 to 22 per cent in 1992). If this is analysed in terms of annual receptions (Table 8.9), the dramatic fall in young offenders is again apparent. However, while the proportion of remands in 1992 to all prison receptions is nearly 50 per cent, the absolute numbers in 1992 are very similar to those in 1982. The fact that the ADP of remand prisoners has risen must mean that people are spending longer on remand in 1992 than they did in 1982. In other words, there is a problem of court efficiency in the time taken to process cases as well as an over-eagerness to remand into custody.

Table 8.9 Changes in Annual Receptions 1982–1992[88]

Type of custody	1982	1987	1992
Untried	48,474	59,210	49,869
Unsentenced	23,268	18,335	21,250
Young offenders under sentence	33,781	28,384	17,456
Adults under sentence	60,596	57,974	52,376
Non-criminal	4,715	3,399	3,109
TOTAL	170,834	167,302	144,060

[88] *ibid.* Table 1.14, p. 38.

Comparison of Tables 8.8 and 8.9 also shows us that, although fewer adults are received under sentence, the daily population of adults under sentence has risen by 18 per cent in the decade. The profile of that population has changed considerably:

Table 8.10 Changes in Adult Sentenced Population (ADP) 1982–1992[89]

Type of sentence	1982	1987	1992
Adult population under sentence	25,490	29,747	29,992
Less than 18 months	12,282 (48%)	10,518 (35%)	8,079 (27%)
18 mths–4 yrs	7,826 (31%)	10,286 (35%)	9,556 (32%)
4 yrs +	5,382 (21%)	8,943 (30%)	12,357 (41%)

In absolute numbers and as proportions of the population, short-term prisoners have decreased and long-termers have increased. This presents a problem for policies aimed at reducing overall prison numbers. While it is possible to divert short-termers and young offenders in increasing numbers, to develop new policies for fine defaulters[90] and to improve bail policies to reduce the numbers of those held on remand,[91] the long-term population will just continue to grow. The issue is that of over-sentencing and a need to recognise that longer sentences are no more effective than shorter ones, just more expensive and less humane.

The sentencing framework introduced by the 1991 Criminal Justice Act had a short-term effect by reducing reliance on custody, decreasing the number of short-term prisoners and cutting sentence length. In the medium term, that effect will be countered by the early release provisions. But the 1991 reforms were severely undermined by the 1993 Criminal Justice Act, the provisions of which will increase remand population, reduce the use of non-custodial penalties, swell the numbers of short-term prisoners as well as increase sentence length.

An interesting comparison is that of the Netherlands, whose immediate post-war imprisonment rates exceeded those in Britain. As we have seen, the situation has been transformed, not just because of the role of the prosecution service in waiving prosecutions, harmonising and recommending levels of sentence but also because of sentencing attitudes: the Dutch use imprisonment frequently but the average length of sentence is much shorter than in this country.[92] This is the single most important factor in reducing a prison population.

[89] *ibid.* Table 1.9, p. 29.
[90] *supra*, para. 7.5.3.4.
[91] *supra*, para. 5.3.1.
[92] Downes D., *Contrasts in Tolerance* (1988), Table 2.1, p. 38.

The number of life sentence prisoners has risen from 1,788 in 1982 to 3,000 in 1992. This exceeded the combined number of life sentences in all other Western European countries. One problem has always been the mandatory life sentence for murder so that the mercy killing of a terminally-ill patient would, in theory,[93] attract the same sentence as the contract or serial killer. There have been regular parliamentary recommendations for the mandatory life sentence for murder to be abolished,[94] as indeed should be the judicial power to recommend minimum terms for life sentences.[95] Lifers are not just murderers and there are also discretionary life sentences for those who have committed serious offences, have a history of offending and mental disturbance and a prognosis of further offending.[96] In 1992 there were 620 people serving discretionary life sentences, including 186 for manslaughter, 132 for other homicides or violence against the person, 198 for rape or other sexual offences and 72 for arson.[97]

Table 8.11 ADP by Offence Type 1982–1992[98]

Offence Category	1982	1987	1992
Violence	6,572	8,239	7,077
Rape	562	887	1,584
Other sexual	832	1,442	1,572
Burglary	10,937	8,954	5,400
Robbery	2,554	3,847	4,230
Theft/Fraud	8,315	7,161	3,953
Drugs	995	3,456	3,158
Other	2,465	3,820	3,615
Not recorded	1,825	828	4,593
Courts martial	34	43	n/a
TOTAL	35,091	38,677	35,182

[93] "In theory" because in practice, even though the killing is technically murder, it would by some means be re-classified as manslaughter.
[94] *Report of the Select Committee on Murder and Life Imprisonment* (HL Papers 1989/90 78–1).
[95] Abolition of Death Penalty Act 1965, s. 1(2).
[96] Ashworth A., *Sentencing and Criminal Justice* (1992), p. 167.
[97] *Prison Statistics 1992, op. cit.*, Table 8.1, p. 126.
[98] *Prison Statistics 1992, op. cit.*, Table 1.8, p. 28—refers to offenders with immediate custodial sentences and not fine defaulters. There are some problems with 1992 figures for particular offences because of the high number of "not recorded".

The offence profile of the prison population has also changed. Whereas in 1982, the typical inmate would have been convicted of burglary (31 per cent of ADP), in 1992 the burglar represents only 15 per cent of the population. This is, at least partly, a result of the decline in imprisonment of young offenders. There is a similar decline in the proportion of property offenders: from 24 per cent in 1982 to 11 per cent in 1992.[99] The rises are in those offences (sex offences from 4 per cent to 9 per cent, robbery from 7 per cent to 12 per cent and drugs from 3 per cent to 9 per cent) which have been targeted as ones from which the public need protection through longer sentences.

The major factor in the size of the prison population is not necessarily the numbers imprisoned but the length of sentence. While fewer are being imprisoned, the profile of the prison population has changed because of the increase in that average length of sentence. From 1950–80, there was a 60 per cent increase in the length of sentences handed down by the courts.[1] The May Report suggested that this increase was the product of a perception that crime was on the increase but it was also a reaction to reforms such as suspended sentences and parole, introduced by the 1967 Criminal Justice Act.

Over the past decade, although there has been a decrease in the average length of sentences in magistrates' courts, there has been a significant increase in Crown courts.

Table 8.12 Adult Males Sentenced to Imprisonment for Indictable Offences by Numbers and Average Length of Sentence 1983–93[2]

Court	1983	1988	1993
Crown Court Numbers	26,300	32,000	24,600
Crown Court Average sentence	16.6 mths	19.0 mths	21.8 mths
Mags. Court Numbers	15,300	9,800	7,600
Mags. Court Average Sentence	3.0 mths	2.9 mths	3.2 mths

For all courts, the average length of sentence in 1993 was 15.4 months in comparison with 11.1 months in 1984. One reason may be that fewer defendants are being processed by the courts; 622,000 were proceeded against in 1982 for indictable offences and only 562,000 in 1993.[3] Pre-trial

---

[99] For women this represents the normal offence for which they are imprisoned (21%). 16% are imprisoned for violence against the person and 22% for drugs offences.
[1] *Report of the Inquiry into the United Kingdom Prison Services, op. cit.*, para. 3.8.
[2] *Criminal Statistics 1993* Cm. 2680, Tables 7.17 and 7.18, pp. 175–176.
[3] *Criminal Statistics 1993, op. cit.*, Table 1.1, p. 22.

selection and more cautioning mean that only the more serious cases, likely to attract longer sentences, are taken to court.

Courts themselves are more selective about custodial sentencing: there has been a large decrease in the proportion of those convicted of indictable offences and sentenced to immediate imprisonment. Among adult males, this has declined from 9 per cent to 6 per cent in magistrates' courts from 1983–93, and from 52 per cent to 51 per cent in Crown courts.[4] Looking at all courts, whereas in 1957 33 per cent of males convicted of indictable offences went to prison, by 1976 only 17 per cent of the cohort went to prison. By 1993 it has decreased further to 14.3 per cent.[5]

As Table 8.13 reveals, although the Crown Courts are imprisoning a smaller proportion of non-violent property offenders, the average length of sentence for, say, a burglar remains the same in 1992 as it did in 1982. On the other hand, the courts in 1992 are imprisoning similar proportions of violent, sexual and drug-related offenders as they did in 1982 but the average length of sentence has increased markedly, not lease with rape where the average length has gone up by 30 per cent.

Table 8.13 Males Convicted of Indictable Offences at Crown Court by Offence, Proportion Sentenced to Custody and Average Length of Sentence 1982–92[6]

Offence	1982	1992
Total	(52%) 16.6 mths	(47%) 21.1 mths
Violence	(46%) 16.9 mths	(46%) 21.0 mths
Sexual Offences	(64%) 29.5 mths	(66%) 38.2 mths
Burglary	(66%) 15.9 mths	(55%) 16.0 mths
Robbery	(89%) 41.5 mths	(88%) 47.9 mths
Theft	(42%) 10.0 mths	(34%) 10.5 mths
Fraud	(42%) 14.8 mths	(40%) 15.9 mths
Criminal damage	(42%) 20.0 mths	(34%) 22.7 mths
Drugs	(57%) 23.5 mths	(55%) 31.0 mths

One conclusion is that we have a bifurcated prison system:

(a) There are still large numbers of prisoners who are serving relatively short sentences (especially fine defaulters), or indeed no sentences at all

[4] The decline is especially marked in non-violent property offences—burglary, theft, criminal damage—*Criminal Statistics 1993, op. cit.*, Tables 7.17 and 7.18, pp. 175–176.
[5] 44,129 from 308,000—*Criminal Statistics 1993, op. cit.*, Tables 1.1, p. 22 and Table 7.16, p. 174.
[6] *Criminal Statistics 1992* Cm. 2410, Tables 7.17 and 7.18, pp. 170–171.

such as remand prisoners. It is this population that has been the object of executive intervention through early release, or attempts to influence sentencing and remand practices, as well as attempts to divert from prison by the development of non-custodial alternatives.

(b) There is a growing number of long-term prisoners, forming a high proportion of the prison population, often regarded as the dangerous element, requiring higher security. On June 30, 1992, 14,463 prisoners were serving sentences for violence, sexual offences or robbery which constitutes 32 per cent of a population that day of 45,817.

8.7 EARLY RELEASE

Getting out before the end of the sentence has been a regular concern, not just for prisoners, but also for the legislature. Remission was introduced in 1898[7] and parole in 1967. The Carlisle Report[8] recommended the abolition of the joint system of remission and parole. This has been done under the new framework for early release under the Criminal Justice Act 1991.[9] In summary, remission was abolished and any prisoner serving less than four years is automatically released after serving one half of the sentence. Those serving more than four years would be eligible for parole after one half of the sentence but would be automatically released after two thirds of the sentence. All of this would be subject to good behaviour.

Before considering that, there are various other methods of temporary release from a prison sentence before the end of that sentence:

(a) leave granted at the discretion of the governor for compassionate reasons: marital problems or family deaths. A prisoner might be allowed leave shortly before release to make arrangements for housing or employment.[10] There are some prisons which operate pre-release resettlement schemes, which allow prisoners to work in the community during the latter stages of a long sentence.

(b) the Home Secretary is able to order early release of prisoners (within six months of the date that their release was due) in order to make effective use of prison places.[11]

(c) the Home Secretary is allowed to release a prisoner on compassionate grounds, though he must consult the Parole Board in long term/life cases.[12]

8.7.1 *An Introduction to Parole*

Parole is a system which allows prisoners serving a fixed term sentence to apply, after a proportion of that term, to be released. If parole were granted, it

---

[7] Under the old Prison Rules, a prisoner may have been released after two-thirds of his sentence "on the grounds of his industry and good conduct". This was authorised by the 1898 Prison Act and remained at a quarter until the Second World War when it was increased to a third to reduce the prison population. Half remission for short sentence prisoners was introduced in 1987. The minimum a prisoner had to serve before entitlement to remission was 31 days but this was reduced to five days in 1981, again in order to reduce the prison population.

[8] *The Parole System in England and Wales* Cm. 532 (1988).

[9] Part II; Richardson, *op. cit.*, Chap. 8.

[10] See home leave *supra*, para. 8.5.3.

[11] Criminal Justice Act 1982, s. 32.

[12] Criminal Justice Act 1991, s. 36.

would be normal that the prisoner would be released under supervision from a probation officer and, if he misbehaved in some serious fashion, would be liable to recall to prison to serve the remainder of the sentence.

The modern attitude to parole emerged in the United States in the nineteenth century where release on licence was seen as part of the rehabilitative ideals behind prisons. Having responded to "treatment" in prison, release could be geared to the inmate's behaviour, desire to reform and capacity to adapt to the outside world. It was linked with the American idea of the indeterminate sentence which provided the prison executive with considerable control over the exact length and nature of the sentence.

This rehabilitative function of parole (the "half-way house"), was echoed in the 1965 White Paper[13] which talked of "prisoners reaching a recognisable peak in their training at which they may respond to generous treatment". The ideological impetus was apparent but prison overcrowding had become an issue in the years before parole was introduced in 1967.[14] The reform was against the wishes of governors and the Prison Officers' Association who opposed greater indeterminacy in the length of sentences, regarding it as a cause of tension within prisoners.

There was certainly an ambiguity in the motivation behind the introduction of parole.[15] Economic motives (reduction of public spending) played little part and, although the pragmatic motive of the reduction of the prison population was present, initially at least, parole was used so cautiously that the reforms had no effect on the overcrowding, concentrated as it was in the local prisons. The real impetus was the political context of the 1960s when there was a strong liberal consensus about penal reform supported by a socially conscious Labour government.

8.7.2 The Old Structure of Parole[16]

The process started in the prison itself which would have a Local Review Committee (LRC), consisting of five members. There were approximately 75 LRCs, each with the governor, a member of the BoV, a probation officer and two members of the public. The Chair rotates among the members, although the governor cannot be chairperson.

All prisoners serving a determinate sentence[17] were eligible, although they did not have to be considered if they did not wish to be. About 15 weeks before the date at which the prisoner would become eligible for parole, (*i.e.* at one third of sentence), one member of the committee would read the prisoner's file: the nature of the offence, police antecedents, staff observations, disciplinary record, release plan relating to home circumstances and employment, prisoner's application, any other available reports (medical, SIRs, etc.). The member would visit the prisoner and put to the LRC any oral or written representations that the prisoner wished to make. If they decide not to recommend, that was the end of the matter as there was

---

[13] *The Adult Offender* Cmnd. 2852 (1965).
[14] Criminal Justice Act 1967, ss. 59–62.
[15] Morgan N., "The Shaping of Parole in England and Wales" [1983] Crim.L.R. 137.
[16] This will continue to apply for certain long-term prisoners sentenced prior to the implementation of the new provisions.
[17] Since the prisoner had to have served at least six months, this meant that the sentence had to be at least ten-and-a-half months.

no system of appeal,[18] although the prisoner would automatically be reconsidered a year later. In *Payne*,[19] the Court of Appeal held that neither the LRC nor the Parole Board had to explain the reasons for the decision.

Any recommendation would be sent to the Home Office Parole Unit who would check on its legality and timing, ensure that all the relevant paperwork was present, including information about any accomplices involved in the same offence. If necessary the unit would make a statistical assessment of reconviction risk and consider whether this is a case where the Secretary of State might wish to exercise his veto.

There were certain categories of cases[20] where the LRC was expected to recommend parole unless there is evidence that the prisoner is a "bad parole risk". These recommendations went to the Home Office who released them without consideration by the Parole Board. In all other categories, the papers were passed on to the Parole Board. This is a national committee which must include a judge, a psychiatrist, a criminologist and a person experienced in after-care.[21] The Board consists of some 50 people, although it divides itself into small panels of five to consider applications. The workload is relatively heavy, dossiers may be 50 pages, and some 25 per fortnight may have to be studied. The Board had to decide whether to accept the recommendation of the LRC and, if it did, what date of release and what conditions to impose. These duties continue under the new structure.

8.7.3 *The New Structure of Early Release*[22]

The Carlisle recommendations[23] included:

- the phasing out of the LRCs—these do not appear in the new structure.
- the phasing out of the Home Secretary's role so that the Parole Board became solely responsible for early release—this did not happen.
- statutory criteria for parole—this has been ignored[24] so that decisions appear to rely on intuition rather than on other rationales such as the statistical risk of reconviction or concepts of desert.
- a more open system with representatives or lawyers making the representations on behalf of the prisoner—this may still be provided for in the procedural rules.[25]
- a statutory right to reasons for an adverse decision. The 1991 legislation only provides this in cases of recall of long-term or life prisoners in breach of parole conditions.[26] This is not surprising in light of the Home Secretary's response to the Carlisle Report that these recommendations;

---

[18] The Home Office Parole Unit monitored rejection rates between institutions, looking at reconviction prediction scores, to ensure parity of treatment.
[19] *Payne v. Lord Harris* [1981] 1 W.L.R. 754.
[20] Richardson, *op. cit.*, p. 176.
[21] Its existence continues under s. 32 and Schedule 5 to the Criminal Justice Act 1991.
[22] Wasik M., "The Arrangements for Early Release" [1992] Crim.L.R. 252.
[23] *The Parole System in England and Wales, op. cit.*
[24] Except that s. 32(6) talks blandly of having regard to the protection of the public and the desirability of securing the offender's rehabilitation.
[25] To be made under s. 32(5) Criminal Justice Act 1991.
[26] Criminal Justice Act 1991, s. 39(3)(b).

"... raise difficult questions in the context of the Government's policies for ensuring that the public is adequately protected and that offenders who commit serious crimes are adequately punished."

The Carlisle review was the context for the repeal of the 1967 legislation and its replacement by[27] the new provisions introduced in October 1992:

(a) the Secretary of State is under a duty[28] to release any short-term prisoner serving less than four years after one half of the sentence has been served.
   (i) this is unconditional and there will be no supervision for those serving less than 12 months.[29]
   (ii) for those serving over 12 months, the release will be on licence. The supervision would continue until three quarters of the original sentence has been completed.[30] All of this would be subject to good behaviour and if the prisoner breaches the conditions of the licence, then this is made a summary offence and a magistrates' court can suspend the licence.[31]
(b) the Secretary of State has the power to release those serving more than four years after they have served one half of their sentence if recommended to do so by the Parole Board.[32] If parole is not granted, the Secretary of State is under a duty[33] to release any such prisoner after two thirds of the sentence. Again supervision would last until three quarters of the original sentence has been completed.[34] All of this would be subject to good behaviour and the licence can be revoked, either on recommendation of the Parole Board, or by the Secretary of State on the grounds of public interest.[35]
(c) the Secretary of State has a broad power to release on compassionate grounds which does not require the involvement of the Parole Board.[36]

The impact of these changes is hard to gauge at this moment. The Parole Board's workload will be reduced from around 24,000 to 4,500 applications per year. Local review committees will become obsolete once the transitional arrangements are completed although there are likely to be "parole assessors" in prisons as local agents of the Parole Board. Their role is as yet unclear. The inmate's rights remain very limited: the Board "may" interview the prisoner[37] although this is not a legal right; there is no right to representation before the Board; there is no right of appeal; nor is there any right to be given reasons for an adverse decision[38]

The Board is at root an advisory body and its relationship with the Home

---

[27] ss. 32–51 Criminal Justice Act 1991.
[28] *ibid.* s. 33(1).
[29] *ibid.* s. 33(1)(a).
[30] *ibid.* s. 37.
[31] *ibid.* s. 38—also a conviction within the currency of the original sentence can give the court power to return the prisoner to prison—s. 40.
[32] *ibid.* s. 35(1).
[33] *ibid.* s. 33(2).
[34] *ibid.* s. 37.
[35] *ibid.* s. 39—also a conviction within the currency of the original sentence can give the court power to return the prisoner to prison under s. 40.
[36] *ibid.* s. 36.
[37] *ibid.* s. 32(3).
[38] *Payne, supra.*

Secretary remains uneasy: the Minister cannot release a prisoner without a recommendation from the Board; equally the Minister has the power to veto any recommendation for parole and this has been used increasingly in recent years.[39] Under section 50, the Home Secretary can reduce his own role in relation to long term prisoners and has chosen to leave the final decision with regard to prisoners serving less than seven years to the Board. He has retained the final decision on prisoners serving longer sentences than this.[40]

The power of the Home Secretary over the parole system was seen in 1983 when the then Home Secretary, Leon Brittan, announced that he was not going to grant parole to those serving more than five years for offences involving drugs or violence nor would he release on licence certain categories or murderer (killers of policemen, terrorists and sexual murders of children) until they had served at least 20 years.[41] The 1991 legislation reinforces this power and enables the government to pursue the policy of alleviating the worst overcrowding while maintaining high sentencing tariffs.[42]

8.7.4 *Life Sentence Prisoners*[43]

Life prisoners did not come under the 1967 parole provisions but were looked at separately.[44] This remains the case.[45] The 1967 legislation empowered the Home Secretary to release lifers on licence. From 1973 there was a joint committee of the Parole Board and the Home Office which considered all lifers after 3 years of their sentence to recommend a date for first review by the Parole Board. It would be the LRC that eventually reviewed the case and any recommendations for release from the LRC would be considered by the committee who themselves would make a recommendation for an actual release date which would come before the Home Secretary to make the final decision.

But in October 1983, Leon Brittan altered the procedure so that the Home Secretary decided the date for first review by the LRC after consultation with the Lord Chief Justice and the trial judge[46] had been undertaken to decide the appropriate period to satisfy the demands for general deterrence and retribution. Any recommendations for release by the LRC went to a special panel of the Parole Board and thence to the Home Secretary who decided what additional period needed to be served in "the public interest".[47] This procedure was criticised by the European Court of Human Rights[48] which held that "discretionary" life sentence prisoners were entitled to have their sentences reviewed once the requirements of deterrence and retribution had

[39] Wasik M. and Pease K., "The Parole Veto and Party Politics" [1986] Crim.L.R. 379.
[40] See S.I. 1992 No. 1829.
[41] This was challenged unsuccessfully in *Re Findlay, supra.*
[42] Wasik (1992), *op. cit.*, at p. 254.
[43] Windlesham, Lord, "Life Sentences: law, practice and release decisions 1989–93" [1993] Crim.L.R. 644.
[44] Criminal Justice Act 1967, s. 61.
[45] Criminal Justice Act 1991, ss. 34 and 35.
[46] Under s. 1(2) Murder (Abolition of Death Penalty) Act 1965, the trial judge was given the power to recommend a minimum period that a life sentence prisoner should serve before release on licence. This practice had diminished in the 1970s but has increased recently.
[47] This chronology is discussed by Lord Mustill in *Doody* [1993] 3 All E.R. 92 at 99 ff.
[48] *Thynne, Wilson and Gunnell* (1991) 13 E.H.R.R. 135.

been satisfied. The Parole Board was not sufficiently judicial to undertake this.

The 1991 legislation now draws a distinction between discretionary lifers (where sentence is not fixed by law) and others (mandatory sentence or where more than one discretionary life sentence has been imposed.[49] Under section 34, the discretionary life sentence is one imposed for a violent or sexual offence and where the trial court makes an order that, after a period specified by the trial court, that the case must be referred to the Board.[50] The panel of the Board (the Discretionary Lifer Panel—DLP) must be chaired by a judicial member and the prisoner is entitled to appear and be legally represented. The Board shall only order release if it is satisfied that it is no longer necessary in the public interest for the prisoner to be confined.[51] If the Board recommends release, then there is a duty on the minister to release on licence. The duration of that licence is until death and the offender remains subject to recall. In 1993, the DLP heard 265 cases and directed release in 54 cases.

With non-discretionary cases, the old system applies[52] although significantly amended by the House of Lords decision in *Doody*.[53] A life sentence contains a fixed period of years for the penal element, punishment for the offence itself, but also a further period, a risk period, which reflects wider public policy concerns:

- the Home Secretary is not bound by the judicial view of the risk period (overruling *Handscombe*[54]).
- the prisoner is not at the mercy of the Home Secretary but is entitled to know the minimum period of their imprisonment.[55]
- a prisoner is entitled to put reasons to the Secretary of State for fixing a lower rather than a higher penal term.
- a prisoner is entitled to know the criteria which the Secretary of State would take into account in fixing the penal part of the sentence.
- a prisoner is entitled to know the reasons of the Secretary of State in departing from any judicial recommendation as to the penal part of the sentence[56] and also to be given information regarding the substance of that judicial advice.[57]

The tariff period is then set by the Home Secretary and the date of first review by the Parole Board is fixed by reference to that period. Only then can the Board review the case and, if it wishes, recommend release though the Home

---

[49] Criminal Justice Act 1991, s. 34(7)(a).
[50] A trial court may decide not to make such an order.
[51] *supra*, s. 34(4)(b).
[52] Now in statute—*supra*, s. 35.
[53] *supra*.
[54] *ex parte Handscombe* (1987) 86 Cr.App.R. 59.
[55] In December 1994 mandatory lifers were told of their minimum sentence—a group of around 20 (including Brady and Hindley, the Moors murderers) were told that the minimum period was their natural life.
[56] Cases such as *R. v. Parole Board, ex p. Wilson* [1992] 2 All E.R. 576 gives a right to see any material suggesting that the person is a danger to the public.
[57] In December 1992, the Home Secretary announced that mandatory life sentence prisoners would be given access to their parole dossiers and would be given reasons for adverse decisions by the Board or by the Home Secretary.

Secretary retains the final power of decision. In 1993, the Parole Board considered 415 cases of mandatory life sentences, recommending 88 prisoners as suitable for release.

However, the European Court has already expressed its concern about the role of the Secretary of State in these decisions.[58] The European Commission on Human Rights has now referred to the Court the issue of the release of young offenders detained at Her Majesty's pleasure under section 53 of the Children and Young Persons Act 1933. The commission considers that to have such decisions taken by politicians rather than judicially infringes the European Convention on Human Rights which requires the lawfulness of detention to be determined by a court.[59]

8.7.5 Revocation

On parole, a prisoner must report to the local probation service and he is subject to supervision until the time when he would have been released anyway. There is a power to revoke the licence for breach of conditions or misbehaviour. In 1993, 773 parolees on determinate sentences, and 12 lifers,[60] had their licence revoked. Of the determinate prisoners, 386 had committed further offences, 283 were revoked for being out of touch and 104 were revoked for other reasons.[61] Most revocations (696) are by the Board with 74 by the Home Secretary and three by the courts. Since there were 14,336 recommendations for parole in 1992, this appears to be a very low rate of revocation. Research[62] suggests that there is a substantially lower reoffending rate amongst parolees—from 1968–88, 130,000 prisoners have been released and 90 per cent have not reoffended during period of licence. If your licence is revoked, then there is a statutory right to written reasons for the revocation.

Although in the early years very small numbers of those eligible were in fact granted parole (perhaps under 10 per cent), by the late 1970s, this figure had moved to 50 per cent and this remained the broad picture until recently. In 1990, 23,937 cases were dealt with and 56 per cent of those were finally recommended for parole. The effect of the Criminal Justice Act 1991 can be seen in the 1993 figures when the Parole Board dealt with half that number of cases (11,766) although 48.5 per cent of these were finally recommended for parole.[63] The average length of time, an inmate might be on parole has also increased. In the 1970s this might be a matter of a few weeks but by 1988 the average length was around 177 days and in 1993 it was 284 days.[64]

---

[58] *Thynne, supra.*
[59] See *The Guardian*, December 17, 1994—this could affect Thompson and Venables, the killers of James Bulger, since the trial judge recommended a minimum of 10 years but the tariff fixed by the Home Secretary was 15 years.
[60] *Report of the Parole Board 1993* (HCP 1993/94 450) Appendix D, p. 42.
[61] *ibid., op. cit.,* Table 4, p. 38.
[62] Ward D., *The Validity of Reconviction Prediction Scores,* Home Office Research Study No. 94 (1987).
[63] *Report of the Parole Board 1993* (HCP 1993/94 450) Appendix C, Table 1, p. 33.
[64] *ibid.* Table 10, p. 40.

CHAPTER NINE

Justice for Juveniles and Young Adults

9.1 A BRIEF HISTORY OF JUVENILE JUSTICE

In the modern youth court, the predominant philosophy of criminal justice (based on individual responsibility for actions leading to punishment) confronts the social work ideology of the welfare of the child (based on diagnosis and treatment). But in the eighteenth century and nineteenth centuries, there was little or no distinction made between the adult and the juvenile offender, either procedurally or in terms of punishments—the child was punished physically,[1] transported, or sent to prison or the hulks, under the same conditions as adults.[2] The glimmerings of differentiation came not in the court process but in the systems of punishment. In 1838 Parkhurst was opened as a special prison for boys between 10 and 18 and there was some effort at classification between older and younger boys, with a probationary ward for newcomers as well as a punishment ward. But it was still run along traditional lines with leg irons and whipping and was closed as a juvenile institution in 1864.[3] There were other initiatives such as the Youthful Offenders Act, passed in 1854, the result of the work of reformer, Mary Carpenter. It gave the courts power to send children to "reformatory schools" which were run by voluntary agencies as an alternative to sending them to adult prisons. The Government contributed towards the running costs. This system was further developed in 1857 by the Industrial Schools Act which provided some rudimentary education for the children.[4] Again they were managed by voluntary agencies and by the 1880s there were more than 200 of these reformatory and industrial schools. There were also many thousands of children in adult prisons.

The Gladstone Committee was set up in 1895 to look into the prison

---

[1] 90 per cent of those hanged in 1785 were under 21 and in 1816 the reformer, Samuel Romilly, said in a Parliamentary debate that there was a boy of 10 in prison in Newgate under sentence of death.
[2] Berlins M. and Wansell G., *Caught in the Act* (1974), Chap. 1.
[3] Later in its life Parkhurst (on the Isle of Wight) was to become a high security prison for adult males.
[4] Musgrove F., *Youth and the Social Order* (1964), Chap. 3.

system as a whole including the special schools for juveniles. Its report recognised that public attitudes towards juvenile offenders had changed, with less emphasis on their moral responsibility, and seeing them more as victims of society. It was not until 1908 that the Liberal Government passed the Children Act which abolished prison as a punishment for children under 14 and set up special juvenile courts.[5] The new juvenile court was still the magistrates' court but sat at separate times from the adult courts. It also gained certain powers over neglected children (whose parents were drunks or criminals or who were found begging or destitute).

The distinction was made between the neglected and the delinquent child. It was not until 1927 that it was officially recognised that such a distinction was not tenable. A Home Office Departmental Committee Report on *The Treatment of Young Offenders* in 1927[6] concluded that the two were inseparable and that it was the court's job to look after the welfare of children and not to punish them. In 1933, this philosophy was enshrined in the Children and Young Persons Act:

> "Every court in dealing with a child or young person who is brought before it, either as being in need of care or protection of as an offender or otherwise, shall have regard to the welfare of the child or young person and shall in a proper case take steps for removing him from undesirable surroundings and for securing that proper provision is made for his education and training."[7]

The juvenile justice system has always been haunted by a contradiction in aims, between welfare and punishment. Despite the destructive effects of the crime/responsibility/punishment model and its inapplicability in dealing with youngsters, courts have continued to treat juveniles as rational beings in assessing liability. It is only in the disposition stage that treatment and training principles come more to the fore. England and Wales suffer from having one body combining these functions of both adjudication and disposition, whereas Scotland divide the fact-finding process from that of disposition which is left to a Family Panel.[7a]

The 1933 legislation abolished the distinction between the reformatory and the industrial school, both of which became known as "approved schools"[8] (the "approval" being that of the Home Office). The quality of juvenile court itself was improved. There was special selection of magistrates as well as provisions allowing for the segregation of juveniles at the police station, at court or on remand. The court hearings themselves were to be held in camera and there were restrictions on what the press could report.

The reforms set in train by this legislation were rudely interrupted by war. The Labour Government of 1945 did little to alleviate the bifurcation of aims: the Children Act 1948 provided powers for local government to take neglected children into care, but at the same time the Criminal Justice Act 1948 increased the punitive element in the system, introducing remand

---

[5] There had been some movement to separate out the trial of juveniles from the trial of adults. Legislation in 1847 and in 1879 meant that children would be dealt with summarily in magistrates courts rather than in Assizes or Quarter Sessions.
[6] The Home Office Children's Department was set up by the Children Act in 1908.
[7] Children and Young Persons Act 1933, s. 44.
[7a] Children's hearings were developed by the Social Work (Scotland) Act 1968.
[8] Taylor I., "Approved School: How Does It Feel?" 101 *Anarchy* 124 (1969).

centres, the custodial, short-stay detention centres[9] (along the lines of army disciplinary centres) and semi-custodial attendance centres.

In the early 1960s the Ingleby Report[9a] pointed out the deepening dilemma of the juvenile courts, arguing for a rise in the age of criminal responsibility and a change in the role of the juvenile court. Legislation in 1963 did little to implement the recommendations. But the new Labour administration was imbued by the Fabian philosophy which argued that "depraved" children were often deprived children. That family courts should replace the current structure and that welfare concerns should be dominant was the keynote both of the Longford Report[10] and of the 1965 White Paper.[11] Criticisms of these proposals led to a new White Paper[12] which formed the basis of the 1969 Children and Young Persons Act. This Act dealt with children in need, as well as juvenile offenders. Unlike Scotland,[13] it was a compromise, since the juvenile court itself was retained. Yet there were several radical elements, though many were never implemented:

- the age of criminal responsibility was to be raised to 14 (never implemented) by section 4 which would have ensured that all children under 14 would be dealt with in non-criminal proceedings.
- children would never have been prosecuted just on the decision of the police. There had to be liaison between relevant agencies under section 5. This was never implemented.
- the old approved schools were abolished and it was also intended to phase out borstals and detention centres for the under-17s.[14]
- the juvenile court's sentencing powers were *de facto* reduced so that the substance of the treatment would be decided by social services departments under whose care or supervision the young offender would (normally) be placed. The normal orders would have been to remit the child to the social services under a supervision order or a care order. The former was non-custodial but the latter gave the social services the power to take the child into some form of custody. However, the substance of both these orders was a matter for the social services and not the court. The magistracy constantly fought against this restriction.[15]

Key aspects of the overall scheme were never implemented and the social services were never given the necessary resources for those which were. From 1979, there has been a retreat from these principles, especially in placing an emphasis on offending rather than on the offender. Ironically, the new

[9] Cohen S., "Notes on Detention Centres" 101 *Anarchy* 124 (1969).
[9a] Report of the Committee on Children and Young Persons, Cmnd. 1191 (1960).
[10] *Crime—A Challenge to Us All* (1964).
[11] *The Child, The Family and the Young Offender* Cmnd. 2742 (1965).
[12] *Children in Trouble* Cmnd. 3601 (1968).
[13] There had been a report (Cmnd. 2306 (1964)) on the Scottish situation chaired by Lord Kilbrandon which had been implemented by the Social Work (Scotland) Act 1968. This was a much more innovative approach than the eventual English legislation.
[14] This finally occurred with the Criminal Justice Acts of 1982 and 1988.
[15] By the Criminal Justice Act 1982, they acquired more control through residential care orders, curfew orders and the power to impose conditions on supervision orders.

statutory framework for sentencing juveniles, linked to the diversion of young offenders from the courts through cautioning schemes, has led to a dramatic decline in the young offender population in custody.

It was the Criminal Justice Act 1982, following the Younger Report,[16] that introduced a sentencing framework for the juvenile court[17] as well as reorganising the system of custody for young people. Borstals disappeared to become "youth custody centres". Youth custody centres did not last long as they were amalgamated with detention centres by the Criminal Justice Act 1988 and renamed "young offenders' institutions" (YOI).

The care order was abolished by the Childrens Act 1989 and the court's power to detain children under 14 was not reinstated until the creation of "secure training units" in 1994.

The Criminal Justice Act 1991 renamed[18] the juvenile court the "Youth Court", and changes in its jurisdiction mean that it now deals with offenders aged under 18. Parents or guardians of children under 16 must attend court at all stages of the proceedings[19] and the court has the power to require the parents of older children to attend.

There is a special group of magistrates who sit as a youth court, operating on its own procedures. Only magistrates who have been selected by their peers are eligible to sit on the youth court bench. Benches must not be single sex and the age limit is 65. The courtroom should be one not used for normal hearings and cases are not open to the public. There are also restrictions on press reporting—for example, they are not permitted to identify the juvenile. However, in many ways the youth court remains a carbon copy of a magistrates' court and there remains the tension between differing philosophies in dealing with offenders.

There is greater legalism in the youth court today. Whereas in 1969, only three per cent of juveniles would have legal representation, today that figure is over 30 per cent. Representation is mandatory[20] in situations where the court was considering a custodial sentence of some kind. A child's legal representative has his or her own problems:

> "Should he (the lawyer) protect the child's legal rights or try to promote his welfare? Should he try to get the child off or get appropriate treatment for him? Should he sacrifice the child's legal rights if the child's general welfare seems to require it? Should he look to the child's a legal rights and his welfare?"[21]

9.2 AGE RANGES AND CRIMINAL JUSTICE

(a) a child under 10 is incapable of criminal intent—although they can be brought before the youth court, it can only be under care proceedings under the Children and Young Persons Act 1969.[22]

(b) a child under 14 can be convicted of a criminal offence. Previously there was a presumption of *doli incapax* so that the prosecution had to

[16] Advisory Council on the Penal System: *Young Adult Offenders* (Home Office 1974).
[17] *infra*, para. 9.6.
[18] Criminal Justice Act 1991, s. 70.
[19] *ibid.* s. 56.
[20] Criminal Justice Act 1982, ss. 3 and 24.
[21] Morris A. and Giller (eds.), *Providing Criminal Justice For Children*, (1983) p. 125.
[22] Children and Young Persons Act 1969, s. 1.

prove that the defendant knew the difference between right and wrong. This presumption no longer exists.[23] Children under 14 must be tried in the Youth Court unless they are charged with homicide or jointly charged with an adult. The court can make one of the following disposals[24]:

   (i) absolute or conditional discharge.

   (ii) fine or compensation order (payable by the parent).

   (iii) supervision order.

   (iv) attendance centre order.

   (v) the Crown Court can impose a determinate sentence under section 53 CYPA 1933.[25]

   (vi) secure training order.[26]

(c) arrested offenders aged 12 or over can be held in police custody if transfer to local accommodation is impracticable or where there is no local authority secure accommodation and other local authority accommodation would not be adequate to protect the public from serious harm.[27]

(d) offenders aged 15 or over can be remanded into prison custody[28] if it is necessary to protect the public from serious harm from them[29] although remands to local authorities with a 'security requirement' are more likely. Such remands are available for all offenders aged over 12.[30]

(e) offenders aged 15 or over still stand trial at Youth Court unless they are charged with homicide or jointly charged with an adult. Similar disposals apply as in the case of those under 15 (with the exception of the secure training order). In addition the court can make the following orders:

   (i) the offender aged over 15 is eligible for the sentence of detention in a young offender institution up to a maximum of 24 months.[31]

   (ii) the offender aged over 16 is also eligible for community service orders, probation orders, attendance centre orders (with a higher maximum), combination orders and curfew orders.

(f) defendants aged 17 and over are subject to the same rules as adults in regard to conditions in police custody, bail and remand but are still dealt with by the Youth Court.[32]

(g) offenders aged 18 and over[33] are no longer dealt with in the Youth Court, but in an adult court and are subject to the same procedures. In

[23] *C v. DPP* [1994] Crim.L.R. 523.

[24] For more details of these, see *infra*, paras. 9.7–9.9.

[25] As amended by s. 16 Criminal Justice and Public Order Act 1994.

[26] *ibid.* ss. 1–15.

[27] s. 59 Criminal Justice Act 1991 amending s. 38(6) PACE; the age limit was reduced by s. 24 Criminal Justice and Public Order Act 1994.

[28] *infra*, para. 9.5.

[29] When s. 60 Criminal Justice Act 1991 is implemented, it will not be possible to remand defendants aged under 17 to prison.

[30] Criminal Justice Act 1991, s. 60 as amended by Criminal Justice and Public Order Act 1994, s. 20.

[31] Extended from 12 months by Criminal Justice and Public Order Act 1994, s. 17.

[32] This reform was brought in by s. 68 Criminal Justice Act 1991.

[33] In relation to sentencing powers, the determining fact is the defendant's age when convicted.

West Germany, it is discretionary whether to use the youth or adult court[34] and a similar approach was considered by the Government[35] in 1988 but was not implemented in the 1991 legislation. They are no longer eligible for supervision orders nor can they be dealt with under section 53 Children and Young Persons Act 1933 but they can be sentenced to a term of detention in a young offenders' institution up to the same maximum as the maximum term of imprisonment available for an adult convicted of the same offence.

(h) offenders over 21 can be sentenced to imprisonment and are no longer eligible for sentences in young offenders' institutions.

9.3 THE POLICE AND CODES OF PRACTICE

As has been seen, pre-trial process in England revolves around the police. The vulnerability of juveniles requires that the police meet higher standards in the investigation and prosecution of juveniles. On the street, where the decisions are of low visibility with little control over the individual officer, there is a problem of discrimination on grounds of race, colour and class. The black, working class youth is more likely to be the subject of police attention that his white middle class counterpart.[36]

Police conduct is regulated by the PACE Codes of Practice. Code A deals with police powers to stop and search people on the streets. There is no special provision made for juveniles.[37] Neither Code B (involving the searching of premises and the seizure of property), nor Code D (identification procedures) has special relevance for juveniles.

However, Code C is most important since it deals with the detention, treatment and questioning of persons in the police station. Considerable attention is paid to the position of juveniles. They should not be arrested or interviewed at school.[38] When brought to the police station, they should not be held in a police cell.[39] The key element is that the police should do nothing except in the presence of an "appropriate adult". This might be a parent, social worker or, failing these, another responsible adult.[40] The adult is not "appropriate" if involved in the offence, of low intelligence[41] or is hostile to the juvenile. A solicitor acting in a professional capacity does not qualify.

But if defendant attains the age of 18 during the proceedings, the court can choose to sentence as if the defendant is still under 18—s. 29 Children and Young Person's Act 1963 and Sched. 8 Criminal Justice Act 1991. Where a defendant attains 21 during proceedings, the court should treat him or her as under 21 for the purposes of sentencing—*Danga* [1992] 2 W.L.R. 277.

[34] Graham J., "The Declining Prison Population in the Federal Republic of Germany" (1987) HORPU *Research Bulletin* No. 24, p. 47.

[35] Green Paper *Punishment, Custody and the Community* (HMSO 1988) para. 3.41.

[36] McConville M., *et al.*, *The Case for the Prosecution* (1991) Chap. 2.

[37] s. 1 PACE provides powers for an involuntary search. The officer can always search with the suspect's consent and the Code's only mention of juveniles is that they may not give adequate informed consent.

[38] Code C para. 11.15 and n.11C.

[39] *ibid.* para. 8.8 unless no other secure accommodation is available (which is unlikely). The child must be kept apart from detained adults.

[40] Code C para. 1.7 and nn.1C, 1D.

[41] *Morse* [1991] Crim.L.R. 195.

The police are under an obligation to discover the person responsible for the juvenile's welfare as quickly as possible and to inform that person of the fact of arrest, the reason for it and the place where the juvenile is being held.[42] Juveniles often do not wish their parents to be present, or parents choose not to attend, in which case the police must find another adult. The juvenile must be made aware of the adult's presence. The adult's role is to ensure that the child is aware of the right to legal advice and not to be held incommunicado. The adult should also be present at the various stages of cautioning,[43] identification processes (under Code D) or intimate searches.[44] The crucial stage is the interview and officers are warned of the problems of the reliability of juveniles' statements and the need for special care when interviewing. The appropriate adult must be present at all times and told that his or her role is not just that of observer but as adviser to the juvenile, ensuring that the interview is conducted properly and facilitating communication between the juvenile and the interviewer.[45] Some adults are so overawed that they are of little value as advisers and may even side with the interviewer.[46]

How effective has the promulgation of the Codes been? In *Fogah*[47] the court excluded evidence of a confession where the juvenile was interviewed on the street after a handbag snatch without an adult being present. However, the overall picture of protection suggests that, except for the presence of an adult, who may be as confused and unsure of the procedure as the child, there is little recognition that a juvenile can be very vulnerable and suggestible and requires particular and professional protection.[48]

9.4 CAUTIONING AND DIVERSION[49]

As with adults, the police act as the focal point in deciding the action to take against a juvenile. Because they decide whether to prosecute, they have the discretion to warn or caution[50] the juvenile as to his or her future conduct. The police have used this power to divert more and more children, in the last 10 years, from the youth courts.

Juvenile crime, committed by those aged between 10–16,[51] is predominantly property crime. Over the last decade, it has been falling, especially among young boys. Crime among young people between 17–21 reflects the general rise in crime levels over this period.[52]

---

[42] Code C para. 3.7.
[43] *ibid.* para. 10.6.
[44] *ibid.* Annex A, para. 4.
[45] *ibid.* paras. 11.14–11.16 and n. 11B.
[46] Brown D., Ellis T. and Larcombe K., *Changing the Code: Police Detention under the Revised PACE Codes of Practice* (Home Office Research Study No. 129) (HMSO 1992) p. 72.
[47] [1989] Crim.L.R. 141; *Weekes* [1993] Crim.L.R. 211.
[48] Miscarriage of justice cases reinforce this point—see *Lattimore* (1976) Cr.App.R. 53.
[49] For a recent survey, see NACRO Young Offenders Committee: *Diverting Young Offenders From Prosecution* (Policy Paper No. 2) (1992).
[50] We might distinguish between the informal warning, given on the spot or in the station after inquiries, from the formal caution administered by a uniformed officer and recorded.
[51] NACRO Briefing *Some Facts About Juvenile Crime* (Youth Crime Section) (Nov. 1992).
[52] NACRO Briefing *Some Facts About Young Adult Crime* (Youth Crime Section) (May 1993).

Table 9.1 Young Offenders convicted of or cautioned for indictable offences per 100,000 of age group: 1983–93[53]

Category	1983	1993
Male under 14	2,926	1,686
Male under 18	7,536	6,406
Male under 21	6,744	7,739
Female under 14	941	621
Female under 18	1,513	1,885
Female under 21	920	1,376

What is particularly remarkable is the expansion of the use of cautioning as opposed to prosecution especially among young adults.

Table 9.2 Young offenders cautioned as a percentage of those convicted of or cautioned for indictable offences: 1983–93[54]

Category	1983	1993
Male under 14	73%	90%
Male under 18	32%	62%
Male under 21	3%	32%
Female under 14	90%	97%
Female under 18	58%	83%
Female under 21	5%	52%

Although the increase in the use of cautions is across the board, the figures vary with age (the younger the child, the more likely he or she is to be cautioned) and locally: Kent, for example, has consistently used cautions, whereas Durham has been more reluctant to do so.

In many forces, there are "caution plus" schemes by which the juvenile is not merely cautioned but is required to participate in an offender group over a period of months with the aim of helping the person to overcome personal

[53] *Criminal Statistics 1993*, Cm. 2680, Table 5.24, p. 122.
[54] *ibid.*

difficulties, be they at home, at school or work, health or emotional problems. Magistrates and others have expressed concern that the police adopt a quasi-judicial role which goes beyond waiver of prosecution and involves sanctioning. Home Office guidelines make it clear that a caution should not be conditional on attendance at such groups.

In some areas, decisions over prosecutions and cautioning has been taken over by multi-agency panels[55] which can be very successful in the context of a local strategy agreed on by social services, education and youth services as well as the police. Local authorities have also been given the responsibility by the Children Act 1989 to take reasonable steps to encourage children within their area not to commit crime, and a growing commitment to issues of youth crime appears to be developing[56] which should encourage less resort to formal prosecution and more diversion schemes.

The power and practice of cautioning and diversion has expanded across Europe[57] over the past 20 years. Although many jurisdictions have the tradition of expediency (allowing prosecutors to waive prosecution) as in the Netherlands, others, such as Germany, operated on a stricter principle of legality which required prosecution. In such countries, such strict principles were still modified either in practice (on the basis that there was not sufficient evidence) or through changes to the law so as to permit waiver or even to impose "administrative" sanctions, as in Germany[58] or Scotland.[59]

Cautioning is a very effective and, importantly, immediate response to a young offender. There is a much lower reconviction rate of those cautioned than of those who are taken to court and receive a non-custodial sentence, let alone of those who are sentenced to custody.[60] Such statistics reinforce arguments for keeping young people out of the formal criminal justice system for as long as possible, especially away from the courts and from custody. For many years, this was the official Home Office view;

> "... delay in the entry of a young person into the formal criminal justice system may help to prevent his entry into that system altogether. The prosecution of the juvenile is not a step to be taken without the fullest consideration of whether the public interest (and the interests of the juvenile concerned) may be better served by a course of action which falls short of prosecution."[61]

While keeping children out of court is a major benefit, the caution is recorded on the criminal record and this does raise important questions about the role of the police, and the parents' ability to examine the decision and to protect

---

[55] Uglow S., Dart A., Hale C. and Bottomley A., "Multi-Agency Impotence" [1992] Crim.L.R. 632; Evans R., Evaluating Young Adult Diversion Schemes [1993] Crim.L.R. 490.
[56] For a survey of local authorities responses, see NACRO: *Youth Crime and Local Authority Action* (NACRO 1992).
[57] Tak P.J., *The Legal Scope of Non-Prosecution in Europe* HEUNI Publications No. 8 (Helsinki 1986) cited in NACRO, *supra.*
[58] Since 1976, a case can be dismissed on condition that the offender pays a fine, performs community work or pays reparation.
[59] "Fiscal fines" were introduced by s. 56 Criminal Justice (Scotland) Act 1987.
[60] Mott J., "Police Decisions for Dealing with Juvenile Offenders" (1983) Vol. 23 Brit.J.Criminol. 249; Home Office Statistical Bulletin 20/92 *Crime Histories of those Cautioned in 1985 and 1988.*
[61] Home Office Circular 14/1985, echoed in Home Office Circular 59/1990. Also youth is a significant factor for the CPS in any decision whether to discontinue a prosecution.

the child. Cautioning is regulated by national guidelines[62]—there must be evidence of the offender's guilt which would give a realistic chance of conviction if prosecuted, the offender must admit the offence and the young person (and parent, if a juvenile) must give informed consent to being prosecuted. Despite this, problems have emerged:

(a) there are inequalities of treatment: young blacks are less likely to be cautioned than young whites,[63] as well as discrepancies between areas,[64] as well as under-use for older age groups.

(b) cautioning can lead to "net-widening": in other words, young people will be cautioned and their offences recorded, who previously would have been dealt with by even less formal means.

(c) cautions are unreliable since the prospect of not facing prosecution induces a suspect to admit an offence even when he or she is not guilty.

(d) that unreliability raises problems as to whether cautions should be cited in court. This is common in youth courts in contrast to the position in magistrates' or Crown courts. Under section 29 of the Criminal Justice Act 1991[65] previous conviction, or failure to respond to previous sentences, can be taken into account in assessing the seriousness of an offence. Although it is difficult to interpret such language as applying to a caution, youth court magistrates argue that they need to have the fullest information on a defendant and that the guiding principles of a youth court are not those of strict legality.

The value of cautioning as diversion was recognised by the Runciman Report[66] which felt that the limits of cautioning had not yet been reached and that there were many more petty offenders who could be cautioned. Despite the effectiveness and economy of the cautioning system, the new national guidelines published in March 1994[67] turn their back on the lessons of the previous decade. They remove any presumption that juveniles should be cautioned rather than prosecuted. Furthermore, they discourage the use of second or third repeat cautions[68] except where there has been a lapse of time or the offences are trivial. The guidelines also effectively ban the use of cautions for serious offences, which should be used only in exceptional cases.[69] These restrictions will change the picture painted by Table 9.2 and will inevitably lead to an increase in the numbers of young people in custody.

[62] *supra.*

[63] Landau S. and Nathan G., "Selection of Delinquents for Cautioning in the London Metropolitan Area" 23 Brit.J.Criminol. (1983) 128. Ethnic monitoring in criminal justice (introduced by s. 95 Criminal Justice Act 1991) should provide more systematic and reliable data.

[64] Evans R. and Wilkinson C., *The Impact of the Home Office Circular 14/1985 on Police Cautioning Policy and Practice in England and Wales* (HORPU 1988).

[65] As amended by s. 66 of the Criminal Justice Act 1993.

[66] *Report of the Royal Commission on Criminal Justice* (1993) Cm. 2263, para. 5.57.

[67] *The Guardian*, March 16, 1994, p. 5; Home Office Circular 18/1994; Evans R., "Cautioning: Counting the Cost of Retrenchment" [1994] Crim.L.R. 566. Initial reaction from probation officers was that these would result in an additional 60,000 prosecutions a year.

[68] 8 per cent of those cautioned in 1991 had received repeat cautions although even repeat cautions can be effective.

[69] In 1992, 1,735 cautions were issued for offences triable only on indictment, including rape and attempted murder (*The Guardian, supra*).

9.5 REMANDING YOUNG PEOPLE IN CUSTODY

When a young person has been charged with an offence, then he or she has a right to bail under the Bail Act 1976. Bail can be refused for an imprisonable offence where[70]:

(a) there are grounds for believing that the offender would abscond, commit a further offence, interfere with witnesses or otherwise obstruct the course of justice.
(b) the court is satisfied that the offender should be kept in custody for his or her own protection.
(c) the defendant has been arrested for being in breach of conditions of bail.
(d) the case has been adjourned for reports which are impracticable to complete without keeping the defendant in custody.

If the offence is non-imprisonable, then bail can only be refused if (b) or (c) above apply, or if the defendant has absconded when previously granted bail. Bail can be granted subject to conditions to ensure that the defendant does not abscond, interfere with witnesses, commit an offence on bail or make himself or herself available to enable inquiries or a report to be made.

Where the police do not grant bail, the juvenile should not be held in police custody before being brought to court unless the custody officer certifies that it is impracticable to transfer the juvenile to local authority accommodation or that the juvenile is over 12, that no local authority "secure accommodation" is available and that other accommodation would not be adequate to protect the public from serious harm.[71]

The considerations for a court in deciding whether to grant bail are the nature and seriousness of the offence (and the probable sentence), the accused's character and background including any previous breaches of bail, whether there would be co-operation in preparing reports and the behaviour and proximity to witnesses. Children under 17 who are refused bail are normally remanded to local authority accommodation.[72] The authority must bear in mind[73] that the court has already determined that it is not appropriate for the juvenile to return home and also that it is the authority's responsibility to produce the child in court. To that end, they are enjoined to provide a comprehensive range of facilities for remanded juveniles ranging from remand fostering schemes to accommodation with high levels of supervision. Failure to prevent absconding or further offences might lead to juveniles being remanded further to penal establishments on unruliness certificates.

The local authority may place the juvenile in secure accommodation for up to 72 hours in any 28 day period although secure accommodation must be a

---

[70] Bail Act 1976, Sched. 1. These have been affected by ss. 25–30, Criminal Justice and Public Order Act 1994. These are considered *supra*, 5.3.1.
[71] Criminal Justice Act 1991, amending s. 38(6) PACE. The age limit was reduced to 12 by s. 24 Criminal Justice and Public Order Act 1994.
[72] Under s. 23 Children and Young Persons Act 1969 as amended by Children Act 1989 and Criminal Justice Act 1991; NACRO: *Juveniles Remanded in Custody* (NACRO Briefing No. 84) (Nov. 1993).
[73] According to *The Children Act 1989 Guidance and Regulations* Vol. 1 para. 6.37 (Dept. of Health).

last resort, and not because nowhere else is available or because the child is a nuisance and runs away.[74] Longer periods require authorisation by the court. The court can only impose a "security requirement", either if the juvenile has both a history of absconding and is likely to abscond from other accommodation and that, if he absconds, he is likely to suffer significant harm,[75] or that if he is kept in any other sort of accommodation he is likely to harm himself or another.[76]

Where the juvenile is charged with an offence carrying a maximum of 14 years or more in the case of an adult, or with an offence of violence or has previously been convicted of an offence of violence, then different criteria apply to the imposition of a "security requirement", namely the court must consider that the child is likely to abscond from non-secure accommodation or is likely to injure himself or others if kept in non-secure accommodation.[77] In such cases, the child must be legally represented or have been offered representation and refused it.[78]

Under the new provisions, local authorities will be expected to provide secure accommodation for juveniles, and the use of prisons and remand centres for those under 17 will be at an end.[79] Meanwhile, despite tragic suicides of youngsters held on remand,[80] there is still the scandalous use of prisons for certain juveniles not granted bail. In March 1994 there was a daily average of 132 juveniles held in prisons or remand centres[81] and 658 had been remanded in the six months preceding March 31.

This practice was possible for defendants over 15 but under 17, under section 23 of the Children and Young Persons Act 1969, if the defendant was "of so unruly a character that he cannot safely be committed to the care of a local authority". Section 60 of the Criminal Justice Act 1991 contains provisions which, when implemented, will end the practice of remanding juveniles to prisons which will be replaced by local authority secure accommodation. Until that point, section 62 of the Act contains transitional provisions whereby the "certificate of unruliness" procedure will be abolished but the courts can still remand to prison if the juvenile is legally represented and there has been consultation with probation or the local authority. After this the court must declare that the defendant has been charged with a violent or sexual offence, punishable, in the case of an adult, with 14 years or more imprisonment, or has a recent history of absconding while remanded to local authority accommodation and is charged with an imprisonable offence committed while he was so remanded. Finally, the court must be of the opinion that remand to prison is the only way to protect the public from serious harm from him.

Defendants aged 17 who are refused bail are remanded in custody and held in either a remand centre or prison.

---

[74] *The Children Act 1989 Guidance and Regulations* Vol. 4, para. 8.5 (Dept. of Health).
[75] Children Act 1989, s. 25(a). Harm is defined in s. 31.
[76] *ibid.* s. 25(b).
[77] Reg. 6 Children (Secure Accommodation) Regulations 1991.
[78] s. 20 Criminal Justice and Public Order Act 1994 extends the age range to those aged between 12–14.
[79] Criminal Justice Act 1991, s. 60.
[80] In July 1990, Philip Knight, 15 years old, hanged himself in Swansea Prison.
[81] NACRO, *Interim Findings from the 3rd ACOP/NACRO Survey* (Nov. 1994).

9.6 SENTENCING YOUNG OFFENDERS—THE STATUTORY FRAMEWORK

It was the 1982 Criminal Justice Act which laid down a statutory framework for sentencing young offenders.[82] The most basic principle[83] was that custodial sentences should only be imposed when no other method of dealing with the offender is appropriate because either:

(i) the offender was unable or unwilling to respond to non-custodial alternatives, or
(ii) the custodial sentence was necessary for the protection of the public, or
(iii) the offence was so serious that a non-custodial punishment could not be justified

These detailed criteria led to a decline in the use of custody for juveniles in the later 1980s.[84] The 1988 Criminal Justice Act raised the threshold for custody still further:

(i) the court, in addition to considering the three existing criteria above, had also to ask themselves whether, given all the circumstances, they would pass a custodial sentence in the case of an adult.
(ii) the criterion of "being unable or unwilling to respond to non-custodial penalties" was tightened to require a history of failure to respond, indicating a series of unsuccessful non-custodial disposals.
(iii) to the criterion of "protection from serious harm" were added the words "from him". This meant that a custodial sentence could not be justified on the grounds that it would deter other potential offenders.
(iv) the criterion of "seriousness" was amended so that it read "the offence ... was so serious that a non-custodial sentence *for it* could not be justified."
(v) the principle was introduced that on passing a custodial sentence, the court should specify on which criterion it is based and their reasons for believing the criterion to be satisfied.

Such provisions had a significant effect on the young offender population in prison service establishments which fell from 10,510 in 1982 to 5,572 in 1992.[85]

These enactments were overtaken by the Criminal Justice Act 1991 which lays down a statutory framework for custodial sentencing of both adults and young offenders. In essence, the presumptive penalty is a fine. If the court wishes to impose either a community sentence or custody, it must be satisfied that the threshold of the "seriousness of the offence" has been crossed so that either a community sentence or custody is justified. The length of a custodial sentence, the content of a community sentence or the amount of a fine must

---

[82] The broad structure is followed in the sentencing framework for adults introduced by the Criminal Justice Act 1991.
[83] Criminal Justice Act 1982, s. 1(4).
[84] Stanley C., "Making Statutory Guidelines Work" *Justice of the Peace* October 8, 1988.
[85] *Prison Statistics 1992* Cm. 2581, Table 3.4, p. 59.

also be commensurate with the seriousness of the offence. However, when considering a custodial sentence, the court can employ an additional criterion: though the offence is not serious in itself, it did involve sex and violence and that only a custodial sentence would be adequate to protect the public from serious harm from the offender.[86]

9.7 NON-CUSTODIAL PENAL MEASURES FOR YOUNG OFFENDERS

Such penalties are very similar to those imposed on adults:

(a) discharges can be of two types, either absolute or conditional. An absolute discharge is used where the court considers that no penalty is required, reflecting the triviality of the offence, the circumstances in which it came to be prosecuted or factors relating to the offender. A conditional discharge also imposes no immediate penalty on the offender who, however, remains liable to punishment for the offence if convicted of another offence within a set period, not exceeding three years.

(b) binding-over orders involve the court requiring the offender to enter into a recognisance (with or without sureties) to be of good behaviour and to keep the peace. Failure to do so means the forfeiture of the sum stipulated by the court. When the offender is under 18, the parent might be ordered to enter into such a recognisance.[87]

(c) compensation orders may be imposed where an offence has caused loss or damage for which the offender may be required to pay. It may be the only sentence or it may be in addition to another sentence. If the offender is under 16, the parent must pay. If the offender is over 16, the court may order the parent to pay. In determining the amount of compensation, the court should have regard to the offender's (or the parents') means.[88]

(d) an offender can be fined for any offence except for murder. If the offender is under 16, the parent must pay and it is his or her means that are taken into account in assessing the size of the fine. If the offender is over 16, the court may order the parent to pay the fine.[89] If the offender is in the care of the local authority, the local authority may be ordered to pay.

9.8 COMMUNITY SENTENCES[90]

The sentencing framework requires that community sentences can only be imposed where the "seriousness" threshold, (parallel with that for custodial sentences but obviously less difficult to satisfy) has been crossed,[91] otherwise

---

[86] The framework is discussed in more detail *supra*, para. 7.5.

[87] Criminal Justice Act 1991, s. 58.

[88] Guidance on assessment of compensation is to be found in Home Office Circular 85/1988. In the 4th quarter of 1992 nearly 25% of parents paid the compensation order.

[89] Criminal Justice Act 1991, s. 57. In the 4th quarter of 1992, 15% of parents paid the fines.

[90] *supra*, para. 7.5.2.1.

[91] Criminal Justice Act 1991, s. 6(1).

the court should content itself with financial or other penalties. Having crossed that threshold, the court must then perform a balancing act by which the type and length of community order must be commensurate with the seriousness of the offence and also must be most suitable for the offender.[92] Ludicrously the court is required:

(a) to take into account all information about the circumstances of the offences, including aggravating or mitigating factors.[93]
(b) to obtain a pre-sentence report for certain orders.[94]
(c) to take into account mitigating (but not aggravating) factors not related to the circumstances of the case, that would reduce the sentence.[95]
(d) to take into account any information about the defendant which it possesses.[96]

Having worked their way through this maze, the court, through the type and length of order, may be able to impose a punitive calculus tempered by some attention to the needs of the defendant.

The 1991 Act[97] brings together existing provisions for enforcement of community orders so that, generally, breach of the requirements can lead to a fine, a community service order of not more than 60 hours, an attendance centre order (for breach of a probation order) or, the original community order can be revoked and the court can impose any sentence which it could have passed for the original offence. Wilful breach of conditions can be seen as refusal of consent to the order and that refusal of consent enables a court to impose a custodial sentence.[98] A further offence does not mean automatic revocation of the order although it may lead to this.

There are six community orders:

(a) Attendance centre orders: these orders were first introduced in the Criminal Justice Act 1948. The offender is ordered to spend a fixed number of hours, usually on a Saturday afternoon, at the centre which will often be run by policemen. The timetable will consist of physical exercise of some kind, instruction on technical skills or crafts and discussion on topics such as citizenship. They are available for offenders up to 21 with a maximum number of hours of 24 for the under 16s and 36 hours for the older offenders.[99] In 1993, approximately 5,300 orders were made.
(b) Supervision orders: these were introduced by the Children and Young Persons Act 1969 and all offenders under 18 are eligible.[1] Consent is not required and the maximum period that can be spent under supervision is three years. The offender will be under the supervision of

[92] *ibid.* s. 6(2).
[93] *ibid.* s. 7(1).
[94] *ibid.* s. 7(3).
[95] *ibid.* s. 28.
[96] Criminal Justice Act 1991, s. 7(2)—pre-sentence reports are required for certain community orders under s. 7(3).
[97] Criminal Justice Act 1991, Schedule 2.
[98] *ibid.* s. 1(3).
[99] Reduced from 17 to 16 by Criminal Justice Act 1991, s. 67.
[1] Criminal Justice Act 1991, s. 66 and Sched. 7.

a local authority social worker or probation officer. There may be conditions to live at a particular address, to attend at a specified place at specified times and to take part in specified activities. These conditions may be specified by the court or the court may delegate this power to the supervisor. These activities are known as intermediate treatment and cannot involve more than 90 days during the duration of the order.

There can be more restrictive conditions: the court may require the offender to remain at home for up to 10 hours between 6 p.m. and 6 a.m. during the first three months of the order and to refrain from certain activities. If the court imposes any of these conditions, it must get the offender's consent and consult with the supervisor. There may also be a requirement to receive psychiatric treatment and to attend school. Schedule 12 of the Children Act 1989 allows the court to include a residence requirement to live in local authority accommodation. The court may also specify people with whom the offender is not to live, if the offence is serious and the offending is due to the circumstances in which he or she has been living, and if he or she was already subject to a supervision order when the offence was committed.

If the court specifies that a supervision order containing conditions to participate in certain activities was made instead of a custodial order, then the court has wider powers if the juvenile or young person fails to comply with the requirements in the order. In 1993, approximately 5,900 supervision orders were made.

(c) Probation orders: these were first introduced for adults in 1908 and, prior to 1991, they were only available for those over 17. The court can now make an order for offenders aged over 16. They can be for a maximum of three years. It must be with the consent of the offender and the court must be of the opinion that probation will lead to the rehabilitation of the offender or will protect the public from harm from him, or prevent the commission by him, of further offences.[2] It is now a sentence of the court.[3] The offender will be under the supervision of a probation officer. There can be conditions attached to the order.[4] In 1993, approximately 8,600 probation orders were made for the under-21s.

(d) Community service orders: these were introduced by the Criminal Justice Act 1972 after recommendations in the Wootton Report. These are available only for offenders aged 16 and over and require the offender to undertake unpaid work in the community usually organised by the probation service. Offenders will spend weekends painting and decorating old people's houses, helping in youth clubs, cleaning out canals,[5] but some of the work must be manual. It will be

---

[2] Powers of Criminal Courts Act 1973, s. 2(1) as amended by Criminal Justice Act 1991, s. 8.
[3] Criminal Justice Act 1991, s. 8—previously it was an order made instead of sentencing. The significance of this is that the court can combine probation with a fine or another community order.
[4] Powers of Criminal Courts Act 1973, s. 3 as amended by Criminal Justice Act 1991, s. 9—see *supra*, para. 7.5.2.2.
[5] The standards are laid down in Home Office Circular 18/1989.

supervised by people employed by the probation service or some local body. The maximum number of hours is 240.[6] The court must be satisfied that the offender is a suitable person for such work and the offender must consent to the making of the order. It can be combined with a fine.[7] There were 10,300 CSOs in 1993.

(e) Combination orders: these were created by section 11 of the Criminal Justice Act 1991 with the twin aims of reparation and rehabilitation. These combine probation for a period up to three years and community service of between forty and one hundred hours. It must be with the consent of the offender and the court must be of the opinion that the order will lead to the rehabilitation of the offender or will protect the public from harm from him, or prevent the commission by him, of further offences.[8] There were 2,300 such orders in 1993.

(f) Curfew orders: these were introduced by section 12 of the Criminal Justice Act 1991 and require the offender to remain at a specified place[9] for a specified time of between two and twelve hours per day for a period not exceeding six months. They apply to offenders aged 16 or over and require consent. The order will name a person responsible for monitoring the whereabouts of the offender. Section 13 introduced a more controversial note providing for electronic monitoring "tagging".[10]

9.9 CUSTODIAL SENTENCES

The sentencing framework for such sentences has already been discussed. The custodial orders that can be made by the youth court are:

(a) secure training orders: previously under the Children and Young Persons Act 1969, care orders gave the power to the local authority to remove a child from the home. Children might be accommodated in a variety of institutions, ranging from foster parents to accommodation with a high level of security. In 1989, the Childrens Act swept away the care order and until 1994 the court had no power to impose a sentence of detention on a child under the age of 15. Section 1 of the Criminal Justice and Public Order Act 1994 provides for the introduction of a "secure training order" for 12–14-year-old offenders. Those eligible will be offenders who have been convicted of three or more imprisonable offences and who have re-offended or been in breach of a supervision order.

Five secure training centres are planned, four of which will be

---

[6] It was raised to 240 for 16-year-olds by s. 10(2) Criminal Justice Act 1991.
[7] Criminal Justice Act 1991, s. 10(1).
[8] *ibid.* s. 11(2).
[9] Under s. 12(6) Criminal Justice Act 1991 the court must consider the attitude of other people who will be affected by the offender's enforced presence, presumably at home! The court must also avoid impact on religious beliefs, work, school and the performance of other community orders.
[10] NACRO Briefing No. 70 *Electronic Monitoring of Offenders* (May 1989) gives a brief history and outlines developments in the USA; NACRO Briefing No. 70 *Electronic Monitoring of Offenders* (September 1990) gives an account of the inconclusive (and continuing) trials in this country.

contracted out. Each centre will have 40 places with the minimum sentence being 6 months and the maximum 2 years. Half the sentence will be spent in custody and the other half on supervision.

The need for this new order has been questioned—Hagell and Newburn[11] argue that at this age crime is overwhelmingly minor in character, predominantly property-related and that section 53 powers are sufficient for the exceptional case.[12] Furthermore, the criteria are loose[13]—three convictions for shoplifting or criminal damage might be sufficient and although the "seriousness" threshold under section 1 of the Criminal Justice Act 1991 should also be met, juveniles will unnecessarily be put at risk of custody.

(b) detention in a young offender institution: this was introduced in 1988.[14] This order brought together into one custodial category the court's previous powers to sentence either to a detention centre, youth custody centre (or borstal) or prison. The minimum age for a YOI order is 15 and the maximum age 21. For those aged between 15 and 17, the maximum term is 24 months[15] while the minimum term is 2 months.

In 1987, about 64,700 boys and girls over 14 and under 18 were sentenced: about 600 were made the subject of a care order and about 8,300 were given immediate penal custody, in those days either in a detention centre or youth custody centre. In 1993, about 33,000 boys and girls of that age were sentenced: only about 3,400 were detained in a YOI.[16]

In the older age group between 18 and 21, in 1987 about 84,800 offenders were sentenced: about 16,900 were given immediate penal custody. In 1993, about 59,400 offenders were sentenced: about 9,300 were detained in a YOI.[17]

(c) under section 53(1) of the Children and Young Persons Act 1933, an offender convicted of murder who was under 18 when the offence was committed shall be sentenced to be detained "during her Majesty's pleasure". In 1993, 24 such orders were made.

(d) there is also the power under section 53(2) of the CYPA 1993 which states that where a juvenile aged 10[18] or over has been convicted in the Crown Court (but not where he or she has been committed to the Crown Court for sentence) of an offence with a maximum term of imprisonment for adults of 14 years or more, then the court may sentence the offender to a term not exceeding the maximum that an adult would receive for that offence. In 1993, 315 such orders were made, 60 for violence, 20 for sexual offences, 137 for robbery with the others for offences such as burglary, criminal damage and drugs. The sentence will be served either in a YOI, in one of the two youth

---

[11] Hagell A. and Newburn T., *Persistent Young Offenders* (PSI 1994).
[12] Such as the murder of James Bulger by two Merseyside 11-year-olds in 1993.
[13] NACRO: *Seriously Persistent Juvenile Offenders* (NACRO 1993).
[14] Criminal Justice Act 1988, s. 124.
[15] Increased by s. 17, Criminal Justice and Public Order Act 1994.
[16] *Criminal Statistics 1993*, Cm. 2680, Table 7.8, p. 165.
[17] *ibid*. Table 7.10, p. 167.
[18] Amended by s. 16, Criminal Justice and Public Order Act 1994.

treatment centres run by the Department of Health or in local authority secure accommodation.

Since the maximum term for an offender under 18 in a YOI until 1994 was 12 months, it was sometimes tempting for the courts to use this section. However the Court of Appeal has held that section 53 should only be used if the offence calls for a sentence of at least 2 years or if the offender is under 15 and not eligible for a sentence to a YOI.[19]

---

[19] *Fairhurst* (1986) 8 Cr.App.R.(S) 346. But see *Criminal Statistics 1993, supra,* Table 7.23, p. 181 which shows an increase in s. 53(2) orders from 93 in 1992 to 315 in 1993.

Bibliography

Advisory Council on the Penal System: *The Regime for Long Term Prisoners in Conditions of Maximum Security* (1968).

Advisory Council on the Penal System: *Non-Custodial and Semi-Custodial Penalties* (1970).

Advisory Council on the Penal System: *Young Adult Offenders* (1974).

Advisory Council on the Penal System: *The Length of Prison Sentences* (1977).

Advisory Council on the Penal System: *Sentences of Imprisonment: A Review of Maximum Penalties* (1978).

Alderson, J., *Policing Freedom* (1979).

An Independent Prosecution Service, Cmnd. 9074 (1983).

Andenaes, J., "The General Preventive Effects of Punishment" (1966) 114 Univ. of Penn Law Rev. 949.

Anderson, P., *Lineages of the Absolutist State* (1979).

Anderson, S. and Twining, W., *Analysis of Evidence* (1991).

Appleton, J., *Boards of Visitors Post Woolf* (1992).

Arnold, T., *Symbols of Government* (1962).

Ashworth, A., "Prosecution and Procedure in Criminal Justice" [1979] Crim.L.R. 480.

Ashworth, A., "The 'Public Interest' Element in Prosecutions" [1987] Crim.L.R. 595.

Ashworth, A., *Custody Reconsidered* (1989).

Ashworth, A., *Principles of Criminal Law* (1991).

Ashworth, A., *Sentencing and Criminal Justice* (1992).

Ashworth, A., "Pleas, Venue and Discontinuance" [1993] Crim.L.R. 830.

Ashworth, A., *The Criminal Process: An Evaluative Study* (1994).

Ashworth, A. and Fionda, J., "The New Code for Crown Prosecutors: Prosecution, Accountability and the Public Interest" [1994] Crim.L.R. 894.

Ashworth, A. and Gibson, B., "The Criminal Justice Act 1993—Altering the Sentencing Framework" [1994] Crim.L.R. 101.

Ashworth, A. and Gostin, L., "Mentally Disordered Offenders and the Sentencing Process" [1984] Crim.L.R. 195.

Ashworth, A. *et al.*, *Sentencing in the Crown Court: Report of an Exploratory Study* (Oxford University Centre for Criminological Research Occasional Paper No. 10) (1984).

Atkinson, J.M. and Drew, P., *Order in Court* (1979).

Audit Commission: *The Probation Service Promoting Value for Money* (1989).

Audit Commission: *The Management of Police Training* (Police Paper No. 4) (1989).

Audit Commission: *Reviewing the Organisation of Provincial Police Forces* (Police Paper No. 9) (1991).

Audit Commission: *Helping With Enquiries* (Police Paper No. 12) (1993).

Bailey, V., (ed.) *Policing and Punishment* (1981).

Baldwin, J., "The Compulsory Training of Magistrates" [1975] Crim.L.R. 634.

Baldwin, J., *Pre-Trial Justice* (1985).

Baldwin, J., *Preparing the Record of Taped Interview* (1992) (Royal Commission on Criminal Justice Research Study No. 2).

Baldwin, J., *The Role of Legal Representatives at the Police Station* (1992) (Royal Commission on Criminal Justice Research Study No. 3).

Baldwin, J. and McConville, M., *Negotiated Justice* (1977).

Baldwin, J. and McConville, M., "Police Interrogation and the Right to See a Solicitor" [1979] Crim.L.R. 145.

Baldwin, J. and McConville, M., "Plea Bargaining and the Court of Appeal" (1979) 6 *British Journal of Law and Society* 200.

Baldwin, J. and McConville, M., *Jury Trials* (1979).

Baldwin, J. and Mulvaney, A., "Advance Disclosure in Magistrates' Courts: How Useful are Prosecution Summaries?" [1987] Crim.L.R. 805.

Bar Council: *The Crown Court—A Guide to Good Practice*.

Barlow, F., "The Holy Crown" in Barlow F., (ed.) *The Norman Conquest and Beyond* (1983).

Barlow, F., (ed.) *The Norman Conquest and Beyond* (1983).
Becker, H., *Outsiders* (1963).
Bennet, W. and Feldman, M., *Reconstructing Reality in the Courtroom* (1981).
Berger, P. and Luckman, R., *Social Construction of Reality* (1971).
Bergman, D., *Deaths at Work: Accidents or Corporate Crime* (1991).
Berlins, M. and Wansell, G., *Caught in the Act* (1974).
Bevan, V. and Lidstone, K., *The Investigation of Crime* (1991).
Black, D., *Manners and Customs of the Police* (1980).
Block, B., Corbett, C. and Peay, J., *Ordered and Directed Acquittals in the Crown Court* (1993) (Royal Commission on Criminal Justice Research Study No. 15).
Bodkin, Sir Archibald, "The Prosecution of Offenders" (1928) 1 Police Journal 353.
Bohannan, P., *Justice and Judgment Among the Tiv* (1957).
Bottomley, A., *Decisions in the Criminal Process* (1973).
Bottomley, A. and Coleman, C., *Understanding Crime Rates* (1986).
Bottoms, A., "An Introduction to the 'Coming Crisis'" in Bottoms, A. and Preston, R., *The Coming Penal Crisis* (1980).
Bottoms, A., "The Efficacy of the Fine: the Case for Agnosticism" [1973] Crim.L.R. 543.
Bottoms, A., "The Suspended Sentence in England 1967–78" (1981) 21 Brit. Jour. Criminol. 1.
Bottoms, A. and Preston, R., *The Coming Penal Crisis* (1980).
Box, S., *Power, Crime and Mystification* (1983).
Brake, M. and Hale, C., *Public Order and Private Lives* (1992).
Bridge, Lord Justice, *Report of the Working Party on Judicial Studies and Information* (1978).
Brody, S., *The Effectiveness of Sentencing* (1975).
Brody, S. and Tarling R., *Taking Offenders Out of Circulation* (1981).
Brouwer, G., "Inquisitorial and Adversary Procedures—a Comparative Analysis" (1981) 55 *Australian Law Journal* 207.
Brown, D. *et al.*, *Changing the Code: Police Detention under the revised PACE Codes of Practice* (1992) (Home Office Research Study No. 129).
Bunyan, T., *The Political Police in Britain* (1977).
Butler-Sloss, Lord Justice, *Report of the Inquiry into Child Abuse in Cleveland* Cm. 413 (1987).
Buxton, R., "Miscarriages of Justice and the Court of Appeal" (1993) 109 LQR 66.

Cam, H., "The Evolution of the Medieval English Franchise" (1958) 32 Speculum 427.
Carlen, P., "Remedial Routines for the Maintenance of Control in Magistrates Courts" (1974) 1 Brit. Jour. of Law and Society 101.
Carlen, P., *Magistrates' Justice* (1976).
Carson, W., "Sociology of Crime" in Rock, P. and MacIntosh, M., (eds.) *Deviance and Social Control* (1974).
Chambliss, W., "The Law of Vagrancy" in Chambliss, W. (ed.) *Crime and Legal Process* 51 (1969).
Chambliss, W., (ed.) Crime and Legal Process (1969).
Chatterton, M., "Police in Social Control" in King, M., (ed.) *Control Without Custody* (1976).
Chibnall, S., *Law and Order News* (1977).
Children in Trouble, Cmnd. 3601 (1968).
Choo, A., "Confessions and Corroboration" [1991] Crim.L.R. 867.
Christian, L., *Policing By Coercion* (1983).
Clarke, R. and Hough, J., *The Effectiveness of Policing* (1980).
Clayton, R. and Tomlinson, H., *Civil Actions against the Police* (2nd ed., 1992).
Clifford, B., "The Relevance of Psychological Investigation to Legal Issues in Testimony and Identification" [1979] Crim.L.R. 153.
Clifford, B., "Eye-witness Testimony" in Farrington D., *et al. Psychology, Law and Legal Process* (1979).
Cohen, M., "Moral Aspects of Criminal Law" (1940) 49 Yale L.J. 1025.
Cohen, S., "Notes on Detention Centres" (1969) 101 Anarchy 124.
Corden, J. and Nott, D., "The Power to Defer Sentence" (1980) 20 Brit. Jour. Criminol. 358.
Cowell, D., *et al.*, (eds.) *Policing the Riots* (1982).
Cox, B., Shirley, J. and Short, M., *The Fall of Scotland Yard* (1977).
Crime, Justice and Protecting the Public, Cm. 965 (1990).
Criminal Law Revision Committee, 11th Report, Cmnd. 4991 (1972).
Critchley, T., *A History of the Police in England and Wales* (1978).
Cross, R., "A Very Wicked Animal ..." [1973] Crim.L.R. 329.

Crown Prosecution Service: *Code for Crown Prosecutors* (1994).
Crown Prosecution Service: Annual Report 1993–94 (HCP 1993/94 444) (1994).

Darbyshire, P., *The Magistrates' Clerk* (1984).
Dashwood, A., "The Jury and the Angry Brigade" 11 West. Aust.L.R. 245.
de Gama, K., "Police Process and Public Prosecutions: Winning by Appearing to Lose" (1988) 16 Int. Jour. Soc. Law.
Dell, S., *Silent in Court* (1971).
Devlin, P., *Trial By Jury* (1956).
Devlin, P., *Criminal Prosecution in England* (1960).
Devlin, P., *The Enforcement of Morals* (1965).
Devlin, P., *Report of Departmental Committee on Evidence of Identification in Criminal Cases* (HCP 1975/76 338) (1976).
Devlin, P., *The Judge* (1979).
Devons, E., "Serving as a Juryman in Britain" (1965) 28 M.L.R. 561.
Diplock Commission, *Report of the Commission to consider legal procedures to deal with terrorist activities in Northern Ireland*, Cmnd. 5185 (1972).
Ditton, J., *Part-Time Crime* (1977).
Dixon, D., *et al.*, "Safeguarding the rights of the accused ... (1990) 1 Policing and Society 115.
Downes, D., *Contrasts in Tolerance* (1988).
Dummett, M., *Southall 23 April 1979* (1989).
Durkheim, E., *The Division of Labour in Society* (1984).

East, R., "Jury Packing: A Thing of the Past?" (1985) 48 M.L.R. 418.
Edgar, D., "Bitter Harvest" (1983) New Socialist 19.
Edwards, J.L.T.J., *The Law Officers of the Crown* (1964).
Edwards, S., "What shall we do with a frightened witness?" (1989) New L.J. 1740.
Edwards, S., *Policing Domestic Violence* (1989).
Emmins, C. and Scanlan, G., *A Guide to the Criminal Justice Act 1988* (1988).
Emsley, C., *Policing and its Context* (1983).
Evans, R. and Wilkinson, C., *The Impact of the Home Office Circular 14/1985 on Police Cautioning Policy and Practice in England and Wales* (1988).
Evans, R. and Wilkinson, C., "Variations in Police Cautioning Policy and Practice in England and Wales" (1990) 29 Howard J.C.J. 155.
Evans, R., *The Conduct of Police Interviews with Juveniles* (1993) (Royal Commission on Criminal Justice Research Study No. 8).
Evans, R., "Cautioning: Counting the Cost of Retrenchment" [1994] Crim.L.R. 566.

Fairhead, S., *Persistent Petty Offenders* (1981) (Home Office Research Study No. 66).
Farrington, D., *et al.*, *Psychology, Law and Legal Process* (1979).
Farrington, D., "Unacceptable Evidence" (1993) New L.J. 806 and 857.
Feest, J., *Reducing the Prison Population: Lessons from the West German Experience* (1988).
Feinberg, J., "The Expressive Function of Punishment" (1965) 49 The Monist 397.
Fennell, P., "Diversion of Mentally Disordered Offenders from Custody" [1991] Crim.L.R. 333.
Field, S., *Trends in Crime and their Interpretation* (1990) (Home Office Research Study No. 119).
Fine, B. and Millar, R., (eds.) *Policing the Miners' Strike* (1985).
Fisher, Sir H., *The Confait Case: Report* (1977) (HCP 1977/78 90).
Fitzgerald, M. and Sim, J., *British Prisons* (2nd ed. 1982).
Floud, J. and Young, W., *Dangerousness and Criminal Justice* (1981).
Foot, P., *Who Killed Hanratty?* (1971).
Foucault, M., *Discipline and Punish* (1977).
Frank, J., *Courts on Trial* (1949).

Garfinkel, H., "The Trial as a Degradation Ceremony" (1956) 66 American Journal of Sociology 420.
Garland, D., *Punishment and Welfare* (1985).
Garland, D., *Punishment and Modern Society* (1990).
Geary, R., *Policing Industrial Disputes* (1985).
Gibbs, J., "The Kpelle Moot" (1963) 33 Africa 1.

Gibson, B., (ed.) *Criminal Justice Act 1991: Legal Points* (1992).

Giles, M., "Judicial Law-Making" [1992] Crim.L.R. 407.

Given, J., *Society and Homicide* (1977).

Glidewell, Lord Justice, "The Judicial Studies Board" in Wasik M. and Munro C., (eds.) *Sentencing, Judicial Discretion and Judicial Training* (1992).

Glynn, J., "Disclosure" [1993] Crim.L.R. 841.

Goebel, J., *Felony and Misdemeanour* (1976).

Goodhart, A.L., "Thomas v. Sawkins: A Constitutional Innovation" (1936) 6 C.L.J. 22.

Graham, J., *The Declining Prison Population in the Federal Republic of Germany* (1987) (Home Office Research and Planning Unit Research Bulletin No. 24).

Grebing, G., *The Fine in Comparative Law* (1982).

Green Paper *Punishment, Custody and the Community* (1988).

Greer, S., "Miscarriages of Justice Reconsidered" (1994) 57 M.L.R. 58.

Gudjonsson, G., *Persons at Risk During Interviews in Police Custody* (1992) (Royal Commission on Criminal Justice Research Study No. 12) (HMSO).

Gurr, T., Grabosky, P. and Hula, R., *The Politics of Crime and Conflict* (1977).

Gurr, T., "Historical Trends in Violent Crime" in *Crime and Justice: An Annual Review of Research* (1981), Vol. III, 295–353.

Gusfield, J.R., *Symbolic Crusade* (1966).

Hale, C., *Fear of Crime* (1994) (Metropolitan Police Working Party on Fear of Crime).

Hall, J., *Theft, Law and Society* (2nd ed., (1952)).

Hanawalt, B., *Crime and Conflict 1300–1348* (1979).

Harding, C., *et al.*, *Imprisonment in England and Wales. A Concise History* (1985).

Harman, H. and Griffith, J., *Justice Deserted* (1979).

Hart, H.L.A., *Law, Liberty and Morality* (1963).

Hay, D., "Property, Authority and the Criminal Law" in Hay D., *et al.*, (eds.) *Albion's Fatal Tree* (1975).

Hay, D., *et al.*, (eds.) *Albion's Fatal Tree* (1975).

Hay, D., "Controlling the English Prosecutor" (1983) 21 Osgoode Hall Law Journal 165.

Hay, D., "The Criminal Prosecution in England" (1984) 47 M.L.R. 1.

Hedderman, C. and Moxon, D., *Magistrates' Court or Crown Court? Mode of Trial Decisions and Sentencing* (1992) (Home Office Research Study No. 125).

Henham, R., "Attorney General's References and Sentencing Policy" [1994] Crim.L.R. 499.

Henry, S., *Informal Economy* (1978) (Martin Robinson).

Her Majesty's Inspectorate of Constabulary, Annual Report 1992 (HCP 1992/93 679) (1993).

Hibbert, C., *The Roots of Evil* (1978).

Hilson, C., "Discretion to Prosecute and Judicial Review" [1993] Crim.L.R. 739.

Hobhouse, S. and Brockway, F., (eds.) *English Prisons Today* (1922).

Hogarth, J., *Sentencing as a Human Process* (1971).

Holdaway, S., (ed.) *The British Police* (1979).

Holdaway, S., *Inside the British Police* (1983).

Holdsworth, W.S., *History of English Law* (1936–72).

Hollister, W., "Royal Acts of Mutilation" *Albion*, Vol. 10, 330 (1978).

Home Office: *Police Manpower, Equipment and Efficiency* (1967).

Home Office: *Managing the Long Term Prison System: Report of the Control Review Committee* (1984).

Home Office: *The Parole System in England and Wales* (1988) Cm. 532.

Home Office Circular: *Provision for Mentally Disordered Offenders* (1990) No. 66/1990.

Home Office: *Criminal Histories of those Cautioned in 1985 and 1988* Statistical Bulletin 20/92 (1992).

Home Office: *Inquiry into Police Responsibilities and Rewards* (Sheehy Report) Cm. 2280 (1993).

Home Office: *Criminal Statistics 1993* Cm. 2680 (1994).

Home Office: *Prison Statistics 1992* Cm. 2581 (1994).

Hood, R., (1972): *Sentencing the Motoring Offender* (1972).

Hough, M. and Mayhew, P., *The British Crime Survey* (1983) (Home Office Research Study No. 76).

Hough, M. and Mayhew, P., *Taking Account of Crime: Key Findings from the 1984 British Crime Survey* (1983) (Home Office Research Study No. 85).

House of Lords: *Report of the Select Committee on Murder and Life Imprisonment* (1989) (HL Papers 1989/90 78–1).

Hudson, B., *Justice Through Punishment* (1987).

Ignatieff, M., *A Just Measure of Pain* (1978).

Irving, B. and McKenzie, I., *Police Interrogation: The Effects of PACE* (1989).

Irving, B. and Dunninghan, C., *Human Factors in the Quality Control of CID Investigations* (1993) (Royal Commission on Criminal Justice Research Study No. 21).

Irving, B. and Hilgendorf, L., *Police Interrogation: The Psychological Approach* (1980).

Jackson, J., "Curtailing the Right of Silence: Lessons from Northern Ireland" [1991] Crim.L.R. 404.

Jackson, J., "The Insufficiency of Identification Evidence Based on Personal Impression" [1986] Crim.L.R. 203.

James Committee, *Report of the Committee on the Distribution of Criminal Business Between the Crown Court and the Magistrates' Court*, Cmnd. 6323 (1975).

Jefferson, T. and Grimshaw, R., *Controlling the Constable* (1984).

Jeffery, C.R., "Crime in Early English Society" (1957) 47 J.Crim.L., C. and P.S. 647.

Jeffries, J.C., "Legality, Vagueness and the Construction of Penal Statutes" (1985) 71 Virginia L.R. 189.

Jones, M. and Winkler, J., "Policing in a Riotous City" (1982) 9 Jour. Law and Soc. 103.

Jones, M., *Organisational Aspects of Police Behaviour* (1980).

Jones, P., Tarling, R. and Vennard, J., (1985): "The Effectiveness of Committal Proceedings as a Filter in the Criminal Justice System" in Moxon D. (ed.), *Managing Criminal Justice* (1985).

Kaye, J.M., "Survey of the History of the Criminal Law up to 1500" [1977] Crim.L.R. 4.

Kaye, T., *Unsafe and Unsatisfactory* (1991).

Keane, A., *The Modern Law of Evidence* (3rd ed. 1994).

Kennedy, L., *Ten Rillington Place* (1961).

Kennedy, L., *Wicked Beyond Belief* (1980).

Kettle, M., "The National Reporting Centre" in Fine B. and Millar R., (eds.) *Policing the Miners' Strike* (1985).

King, M., (ed.) *Control Without Custody* (1976).

Lacey, N., *State Punishment* (1988).

Landau, S. and Nathan, G., "Selection of Delinquents for Cautioning in the London Metropolitan Area" (1983) 23 Brit. J. Criminal. 128.

Langbein, J., *Prosecuting Crime in the Renaissance* (1974).

Langbein, J., *Torture and the Law of Proof* (1977).

Langbein, J., *Comparative Criminal Procedure: Germany* (1977).

Languier, J., *La Procedure Penale* (6th ed. 1987).

Law Commission: *Counts in an Indictment* (1992).

Law Commission: *Corroboration of Evidence in Criminal Trials* (1990) (Working Paper No. 115).

Le Clere M., *Histoire de la Police* (4th ed. 1973).

Leigh, L., *Police Powers* (2nd ed. 1985).

Leigh, L. and Zedner, L., *Report on the Administration of Criminal Justice in the Pre-Trial Phase in France and Germany* (1992) (Royal Commission on Criminal Justice: Research Study No. 1).

Leng, R., *The Right to Silence in Police Interrogation* (1993) (Royal Commission on Criminal Justice Research Study 10).

Lensing, H. and Rayar, L., "Notes on Criminal Procedure in the Netherlands" [1992] Crim.L.R. 623.

Light, R., *et al.*, *Car Theft: The Offender's Perspective* (1993) (Home Office Research Study 130).

Lloyd Bostock, S. and Clifford, B., (eds.) *Evaluating Witness Evidence* (1983).

Longford, Lord, *Crime—A Challenge to Us All* (1964).

Lord Chancellor's Department: *Magistrates' Courts—Report of a Scrutiny* (1989).

Lord Chancellor's Department: *A New Framework for Local Justice*, Cm. 1829 (1992).
Lord Chancellor's Department: *Judicial Statistics 1993*, Cm. 2623 (1994).
Loveday, B., "The New Police Authorities" (1991) 1 Policing and Society 3.
Loveday, B., "Local Accountability of Police: Future Prospects" in Reiner R. and Spencer S.,
    (eds.): *Accountable Policing* 55 (1993).
Loyn, H.R., *The Governance of Anglo-Saxon England* (1984).
Lustgarten, L., *The Governance of Police* (1986).
Lyman, J., "The Metropolitan Police Act 1829" (1964) 55 J.Crim.L., C. and P.S. 141

McBarnett, D., *Conviction* (1981).
McCabe, S., *The Jury At Work* (1972).
McCabe, S. and Purves, R., *By-passing the Jury* (1972).
McConville, M., *Corroboration and Confessions: The Impact of a Rule Requiring that no
    Conviction be sustained on the Basis of Confession Evidence Alone* (1993) (Royal
    Commission on Criminal Justice Research Study No. 13).
McConville, M. and Baldwin, J., *Prosecution, Courts and Conviction* (1981).
McConville, M. and Hodgson, J., *Custodial Legal Advice and the Right to Silence* (1993) (Royal
    Commission on Criminal Justice Research Study 16).
McConville, M., Sanders A. and Leng R., *The Case for the Prosecution* (1991).
McConville, S., *The History of Prison Administration* (1981).
McEwan, J., "Documentary Hearsay Evidence—Refuge for the Vulnerable Witness" [1989]
    Crim.L.R. 629.
McEwan, J., *Evidence and the Adversarial Process* (1991).
Mackay, R.D. and Colman, A., "Excluding Expert Evidence; A Tale of Ordinary Folk and
    Common Experience" [1991] Crim.L.R. 800.
McKenzie, I., *et. al.*, "Helping the Police with their Enquiries" [1990] Crim.L.R. 22.
McWilliams, W. and Pease, K., "Probation Practice and an End to Punishment" (1990) 29
    Howard Jour. Crim. Just. 14.
Magistrates' Association: *Magistrates' Courts and the Probation Service* (1989).
Magistrates' Association: *Sentencing Guidelines* (1993).
Maguire, M., "Effects of the PACE Provisions" (1988) 28 Brit. J. Criminol. 19.
Maguire, M. and Corbett, C., *A Study of the Police Complaints System* (1991).
Maguire, M. and Norris, C., *The Conduct and Supervision of Criminal Investigations* (1992)
    (Royal Commission on Criminal Justice Research Study No. 5).
Maguire, M. and Vagg, J., *The Watchdog Roles of Boards of Visitors* (1984).
Maine, H., *Ancient Law* (1915).
Mair, G., *Probation Day Centres* (1988) (Home Office Research Study No. 100).
Mair, G. and Nee, C., *Electronic Monitoring* (1990) (Home Office Research Study No. 120).
Mainwaring-White, S., *The Policing Revolution* (1983).
Malleson, K., *A Review of the Appeal Process* (1993) (Royal Commission on Criminal Justice
    Research Series No. 17).
Manchester, A.H., *Modern Legal History* (1980).
Mark, R., *Minority Verdict* (1973).
Mark, R., *In the Office of Constable* (1979).
Marshall, G., *Police and Government* (1965).
Mathieson, T., *Prisons on Trial* (1990).
Maxfield, H., *Fear of Crime* (1984) (Home Office Research Study No. 78).
May, Lord Justice, *Report of the Inquiry into the United Kingdom Prison Services*, Cmnd. 7673
    (1979).
Mayhew, P., *Findings from the International Crime Survey* (1994) (Home Office Research and
    Statistics Department: Research Findings No. 8).
Mayhew, P., *et al.*, *The 1988 British Crime Survey* (1989) (Home Office Research Study No.
    111).
Mayhew, P., *et al.*, *The 1992 British Crime Survey* (1993) (Home Office Research Study No.
    132).
Mill, J.S., *On Liberty* (2nd ed.) (1859).
Milson, S.F.C., *Historical Foundations of the Common Law* (1981).
Milton, F., *The English Magistracy* (1967).
Mitchell, B., "Confessions and Police Interrogation of Suspects" [1983] Crim.L.R. 596.
Mitford, J., *The American Prison Business* (1973).
Moir, E., *The Justice of the Peace* (1969).

Moody, S. and Tombs, J., *Prosecution in the Public Interest* (1982).
Morgan, J. and Zedner, L., *Child Victims* (1992).
Morgan, N., "The Shaping of Parole in England and Wales" [1983] Crim.L.R. 137.
Morgan, N., "Binding Over: the Law Commission Working Paper" [1988] Crim.L.R. 355.
Morgan, P., *Pre-Trial Delay: The Implications of Time Limits* (1989) (Home Office Research Study 110).
Morgan, R. and Bowles, R., "Fines: Where does Sentencing End and Enforcement Begin?" [1983] Crim.L.R. 203.
Morgan, R., "Policing by Consent—Legitimating the Doctrine" in Morgan, R. and Smith, D., (eds.): *Coming to Terms with Policing* (1989).
Morgan, R. and Smith, D., (eds.) *Coming to Terms with Policing* (1989).
Morris, Lord, *Report of Interdepartmental Committee on Jury Service*, Cmnd. 2627 (1965).
Morris, A. and Gelsthorpe, A., "Not Paying for Crime: Issues in Fine Enforcement" [1990] Crim.L.R. 839.
Morris, A. and Giller, H., (eds.) *Providing Criminal Justice For Children* (1983).
Morris, P. and Heal, K., *Crime Control and the Police* (1981) (Home Office Research Study No. 67).
Moston, S. and Stephenson, G., *The Questioning and Interviewing of Suspects Outside the Police Station* (1993) (Royal Commission on Criminal Justice Research Study No. 22).
Mott, J., "Police Decisions for Dealing with Juvenile Offenders" (1983) 23 Brit. J. Criminol. 3.
Mountbatten, Lord, *Report of the Inquiry into Prison Escapes and Security* Cmnd. 3175 (1966).
Moxon, D., (ed.) *Managing Criminal Justice* (1985).
Moxon, D., *Sentencing Practice in the Crown Court* (1988) (Home Office Research Study No. 103).
Moxon, D. and Crisp, D., *Termination of Cases by the CPS* (Home Office Research Study—forthcoming).
Mullin, C., *Error of Judgement* (1989) (revised edition).
Murphy, P., *Evidence and Advocacy* (4th ed. 1994).
Murphy, P., (ed.) *Blackstones' Criminal Practice* (1991).
Musgrove, F., *Youth and the Social Order* (1964).

NACRO: Awaiting Trial (1993).
NACRO: Car Crime (Briefing No. 65) (1994).
NACRO: Electronic Monitoring of Offenders (Briefing No. 70) (1990).
NACRO: Fines and Fine Default (Briefing No. 72) (1990).
NACRO: Juveniles Remanded in Custody (Briefing No. 84) (1993).
NACRO: Remands in Custody (Briefing No. 32) (1993).
NACRO: Some Facts About Juvenile Crime (1992).
NACRO: Some Facts About Young Adult Crime (1993).
NACRO: Suicide in Prison (Briefing No. 103) (1990).
NACRO: The Cost of Penal Measures (Briefing No. 23) (1992).
NACRO: Youth Crime and Local Authority Action (1992).
NACRO: Young Offenders Committee: Diverting Young Offenders from Prosecution (Policy Paper No. 2).
NACRO: Work in Prisons (Briefing No. 21) (1990).
Newman, D.J., "Pleading Guilty for Considerations: A Study of Bargain Justice" (1956) 46. J.Crim.L., C. and P.S. 780.

O'Donovan, K., *Sexual Divisions in Law* (1985).
Osborne, P., "Judicial Review of Prosecutors' Discretion" (1992) 43 N.I.L.Q. 178.
Ottenberg, S., "Ibo Oracles and Intergroup Relations" (1958) 14 Southwest. Jour. Anth.

Packer, H., *The Limits of the Criminal Sanction* (1968).
Packer, H.L., "Two Models of the Criminal Process" (1964) 113 University of Pennsylvania Law Rev. 1.
Palley, C., *The United Kingdom and Human Rights* (1991).
Parole Board: Report 1993 (HCP 1993/94 450) (1994).
Pattenden, R., "The Submission of No Case to Answer" [1982] Crim.L.R. 558.
Pearson, G., *Hooligan* (1983).
Pennington, D. and Lloyd-Bostock, S., (eds.) *The Psychology of Sentencing* (1987).

Pigot Committee: *Report of the Advisory Group on Video-Recorded Evidence* (1989).

Piliavin, I. and Briar, S., "Police Encounters with Juveniles" (1964) 70 Am. Jour. Sociol. 206.

Ploscowe, M., "Development of Inquisitorial and Accusatorial Elements in French Procedure" (1932) 23 J.Crim.L., C. and P.S. 372.

Plotnikoff, J. and Woolfson, R., *Information and Advice for Prisoners about Grounds for Appeal and the Appeal Process* (Royal Commission on Criminal Justice Research Study No. 18) (1993).

Plucknett, T., *A Concise History of the Common Law* (1956).

Plucknett, T., *Edward I and the Criminal Law* (1960).

Police Reform, Cm. 2281 (1993).

Pollock and Maitland, *History of English Law* (1898).

Pratt, J., "Diversion from the juvenile court" (1986) 26 Brit. J. Criminol. 212.

Prior, P., *Report of the Committee on the Prison Disciplinary System*, Cmnd. 9641 (1985).

Prison Reform Trust: *Prison Overcrowding: A Crisis Waiting in the Wings* (1994).

Prison Reform Trust: *The Future of the Prison Education Service* (1993).

Prison Service: Annual Report 1991/92 Cm. 2087 (1992).

Prison Service: Annual Report 1992/93 Cm. 2385 (1993).

Punch, M., "The Secret Social Service" in Holdaway, S., (ed.), *The British Police* (1979).

Purves, R., "That Plea Bargaining Business: Some Conclusions from Research" [1971] Crim.L.R. 470.

Radzinowicz, Sir L. and Hood, R., *The Emergence of Penal Policy in Victorian and Edwardian England* (1986).

Raine, J. and Willson, M., "Reforming Magistrates' Courts: A Framework for Injustice?" (1993) 157 Justice of the Peace 661.

Registrar for Criminal Appeals, "A Guide to Proceedings in the Court of Appeal, Criminal Division" (1983) (reproduced in 77 Cr.App.R. 138).

Reiman, J., *The Rich Get Richer and the Poor Get Prison* (1984).

Reiner, R., *Chief Constables* (1991).

Reiner, R., *The Politics of the Police* (1992).

Reiner, R., "Police Accountability" in Reiner, R. and Spencer, S., (eds.) *Accountable Policing* (1993).

Reiner, R. and Spencer, S., (eds.) *Accountable Policing* (1993).

Richardson, G., *Law, Process and Custody: Prisoner and Patients* (1993).

Riley, D. and Vennard, J., *Triable Either Way Cases* (1988) (Home Office Research Study No. 98).

Roberts, C., "The Probation Officer's Dilemma: Preparing Social Inquiry Reports" in Pennington, D. and Lloyd-Bostock, S., (eds.): *The Psychology of Sentencing* (1987).

Rock, P. and MacIntosh, M., (eds.) *Deviance and Social Control* (1974).

Royal Commission on Police Powers and Procedures, Report, Cmd. 3297 (1929).

Royal Commission on the Police, Report, Cmnd. 1728 (1962).

Royal Commission on Legal Services, Report, Cmnd. 7648 (1979).

Royal Commission on Criminal Procedure, Report, Cmnd. 8092 (1981).

Royal Commission on Criminal Justice, Report, Cm. 2263 (1993).

Rusche, G. and Kircheimer, O., *Punishment and Social Structure* (1939).

Sanders, A., "Police Charging and the Prosecution of Offences Act" (1985) 149 J.P. 662.

Sanders, A., "Arrest, Charge and Prosecution" (1986) 6 L.S. 257.

Sanders, A., "Controlling the Discretion of the Individual Officer" in Reiner, R. and Spencer, S., (eds.): *Accountable Policing* (1993).

Sanders, A. and Bridges, L., "Access to Legal Advice" in Walker, C. and Sturner, K., (eds.): *Justice in Error* (1992).

Sanders, A., *et al.*, *Advice and Assistance at Police Stations* (1989).

Sanders, A. and Young, R., *Criminal Justice* (1994).

Saulsbury, W. and Bowling, B., *The Multi-Agency Approach in Practice—the North Plaistow Racial Harassment Project* (1991).

Scarman, Lord, *The Brixton Disorders 10–12 April, 1981*, Cmnd. 8427 (1981).

Scarman, Lord, *Report of Inquiry into the Red Lion Square Disorders*, Cmnd. 5919 (1974).
Schur, E.M., *The Politics of Deviance* (1980).
Scott, Lord, *Report of an Inquiry into the Matrix Churchill Affair* (1995) (forthcoming).
Sellin, T., "The Law and Some Aspects of Criminal Conduct" in Sellin, T., (ed.) *Aims and Methods of Legal Research* (1955).
Shapland, J., *Between Conviction and Sentence* (1981).
Shapland, J., *et al.*, *Victims in the Criminal Justice System* (1985).
Sheldon, D. and MacLeod, M., "From Normative to Positive Data: Expert Psychological Evidence Re-examined" [1991] Crim.L.R. 811.
Sheleff, L., "From Restitutive to Repressive Law" (1975) 16 Archiv. Europ. Sociol. 16.
Shubert, A., "Private Initiative in Law Enforcement" in Bailey, V., (ed.) *Policing and Punishment* (1981).
Simey, M., "Police Authorities and Accountability: The Merseyside Experience" in Cowell, D., *et al.*, (eds.): *Policing the Riots* (1982).
Simpson, A.W.B., *A History of Land Law* (1986).
Skogan, W., *The Police and Public in England and Wales* (Home Office Research Study No. 117) (1990).
Smith, A.T.H., *Offences Against Public Order* (1987).
Smith, A.T.H., "Judicial Lawmaking in the Criminal Law" (1984) 100 L.Q.R. 46.
Smith, D. and Gray, J., *Police and People in London* (1983).
Smith, J. and Hogan, B., *Criminal Law* (1992).
Softley, P., *Police Interrogation* (1980).
Spencer, J. and Flin, R., *The Evidence of Children* (1993).
Spencer, J., *Jackson's Machinery of Justice* (8th ed.) (1989).
Spencer, S., *Police Authorities During the Miners' Strike* (1986).
Spreutels, J., "Giving Reasons for Sentence in the Crown Courts" [1980] Crim.L.R. 486.
Stanley, C., "Making Statutory Guidelines Work" (1988) J.P. Oct 10, 1988.
Stephen, J.F., *A General View of the Criminal Law* (1890).
Stern, V., *Bricks of Shame* (1989).
Stevenson, R., *Winning the War on Drugs: To Legalise or Not?* (1994).
Storch, R., "A Plague of Blue Locusts" (1975) 20 International Review of Social History 61.
Storch, R., "The Policeman as Domestic Missionary" (1976) Journal of Social History 481.
Streatfield, Mr Justice, *Report of the Interdepartmental Committee on the Business of the Criminal Courts*, Cmnd. 1289 (1961).
Sutherland, D.W., *Quo Warranto Proceedings* (1963).

Tak, P.J., *The Legal Scope of Non-Prosecution in Europe* HEUNI Publications No. 8 (1986).
Tapper, C., (ed.) *Cross on Evidence* (7th ed.) (1990).
Tarling, R., *Sentencing Practice in Magistrates Courts* (1979).
Taylor, I., "Approved School: How Does It Feel?" (1969) 101 Anarchy 124.
Temkin, J., *Rape and the Legal Process* (1987).
Temkin, J., "Sexual History Evidence—the Ravishment of Section 2" [1993] Crim.L.R. 3.
The Adult Offender, Cmnd. 2852 (1965).
The Child, The Family and the Young Offender, Cmnd. 2742 (1965).
The Prison Disciplinary System, Cm. 9920 (1986).
Thomas, D.A., *The Principles of Sentencing* (2nd ed.) (1979).
Thompson, E.P., "The State versus its enemies" (1978) New Society.
Thompson, E.P., *Whigs and Hunters* (1975).
Thompson, E.P., *The Making of the English Working Class* (1968).
Thornton, P., *et al.*, *Justice on Trial: Report of the Independent Civil Liberty Panel on Criminal Justice* (1992).
Thornton, P., "Miscarriages of Justices: A Lost Opportunity" [1993] Crim.L.R. 926.
Thorpe, J., *Social Inquiry Reports* (1979).
Tombs, J. and Moody, S., "Alternatives to Prosecution: The Public Interest Redefined" [1993] Crim.L.R. 357.
Tomlinson, E.A., "Non-Adversarial Justice: The French Experience" (1983) 42 Maryland Law Rev. 131.
Troup, E., "Police Administration, Local and National" (1928) 1 Police Jour. 5.
Tuck, M. and Southgate, P., *Ethnic Minorities, Crime and Policing* (1981).
Tudor-Price, J., "Treasury Counsel at the Old Bailey ..." [1985] Crim.L.R. 471.

Uglow, S., "Independent Prosecutions" (1984) Jour. Law and Soc. 233.

Bibliography

Uglow, S., *Policing Liberal Society* (1988).
Uglow, S., *et al.*, "Cautioning Juveniles—Multi-Agency Impotence" [1992] Crim.L.R. 632.

Vennard, J., "The Outcome of Contested Trials" in Moxon D., (ed.) *Managing Criminal Justice* (1985).
Vinogradoff, P., *The Growth of the Manor* (1911).
Voakes, R. and Fowler, Q., *Sentencing, Races and Social Enquiry Reports* (1989).
von Hirsch, A., *Doing Justice* (1976).
von Hirsch, A., *Past or Future Crimes* (1986).
von Hirsch, A., "The Ethics of Community Sanctions" (1990) 36 Crime and Delinquency 162.
von Hirsch, A. and Ashworth, A., *Principled Sentencing* (1992).

Walker, C. and Sturner, K., (eds.) *Justice in Error* (1992).
Walker, N., Farrington, D. and Tucker, G., "Reconviction Rates of Adult Males after Different Sentences" (1981) 21 Brit. J. Criminol. 357.
Walmsley, R., *Managing Difficult Prisoners: The Parkhurst Special Unit* (1991).
Warren, W.L., *The Governance of Norman and Angevin England 1086–1272* (1987).
Wasik, M., "The Grant of an Absolute Discharge" (1985) 5 O.J.L.S. 211.
Wasik, M., "Rules of Evidence at the Sentencing Stage" (1985) Current Legal Problems 187.
Wasik, M., "The Arrangements for Early Release" [1992] Crim.L.R. 252.
Wasik, M. and Pease, K., "The Parole Veto and Party Politics" [1986] Crim.L.R. 379.
Wasik, M. and Munro, C., (eds.) *Sentencing, Judicial Discretion and Judicial Training* (1992).
Wasik, M. and Turner A., "Sentencing Guidelines for Magistrates' Courts" [1993] Crim.L.R. 345.
Weatheritt, M., *The Prosecution System: Survey of Prosecuting Solicitors' Departments* (1981).
Weatheritt, M., "Measuring Police Performance" in Reiner, R. and Spencer, S., (eds.) *Accountable Policing* (1993).
Wells, C., "Domestic Violence and Self Defence" (1990) New L.J. 127.
Whitaker, B., *The Police in Society* (1982).
White, R., *Administration of Justice* (1991).
Williams, G., "Evidence of Identification" [1976] Crim.L.R. 407.
Willis, C., *The Use, Effectiveness and Impact of Police Stop and Search Powers* (Home Office Research and Planning Unit Paper No. 15) (1983).
Windlesham, Lord, "Life Sentences: Law, Practice and Release Decisions 1989–93" [1993] Crim.L.R. 644.
Woffinden, B., *Miscarriages of Justice* (1989).
Woffinden, R., "The Case of the Winchester Three" (1990) 140 New L.J. 164.
Wolchover, D., "Keeping Witnesses Out of the Way" (1988) New L.J. 461.
Wolchover, D., "Should Judges Sum Up on Facts?" [1989] Crim.L.R. 781.
Wolfenden Report, *Report of the Committee on Homosexual Offences and Prostitution*, Cmnd. 257 (1957).
Woolf, Sir H., *Report of an Inquiry into Prison Disturbances, April 1990*, Cm. 1456 (1991).
Wootton, R., *Crime and the Criminal Law* (1963).

Zander, M., "Unrepresented Defendants in Magistrates' Courts" (1972) New L.J. 104.
Zander, M., "Access to a Solicitor in the Police Station" [1972] Crim.L.R. 342.
Zander, M., "The Investigation of Crime: a Study of Cases Tried at the Old Bailey" [1979] Crim.L.R. 203.
Zander, M., "What the Annual Statistics Tell Us about Pleas and Acquittals" [1991] Crim.L.R. 252.
Zander, M. and Henderson, P., *Crown Court Study* (1993).
Zellick, G., "The Role of Prosecuting Counsel in Sentencing" [1979] Crim.L.R. 493.
Zuckerman, A., *Principles of Criminal Evidence* (1989).
Zuckerman, A., "Trial By Unfair Means" [1989] Crim.L.R. 855.
Zuckerman, A., "Miscarriages of Justice and Judicial Responsibility" [1991] Crim.L.R. 492.
Zuckerman, A., "Miscarriages of Justice: A Root Treatment" [1992] Crim.L.R. 323.

Index